Cultural Entanglements

New World Studies
Marlene L. Daut, Editor

Cultural Entanglements

LANGSTON HUGHES AND THE RISE OF AFRICAN AND CARIBBEAN LITERATURE

Shane Graham

University of Virginia Press
Charlottesville and London

University of Virginia Press
© 2020 by the Rector and Visitors of the University of Virginia
All rights reserved

First published 2020

9 8 7 6 5 4 3 2 1

Library of Congress Cataloging-in-Publication Data

Names: Graham, Shane, 1970– author.
Title: Cultural entanglements : Langston Hughes and the rise of African and Caribbean literature / Shane Graham.
Description: Charlottesville : University of Virginia Press, 2020. | Series: New World studies | Includes bibliographical references and index.
Identifiers: LCCN 2019035410 (print) | LCCN 2019035411 (ebook) | ISBN 9780813944098 (hardcover) | ISBN 9780813944111 (paperback) | ISBN 9780813944104 (epub)
Subjects: LCSH: Hughes, Langston, 1902–1967—Criticism and interpretation. | Hughes, Langston, 1902–1967—Friends and associates. | Caribbean literature—20th century—History and criticism. | Caribbean literature—Black authors—History and criticism. | African literature—20th century—History and criticism. | African literature—Black authors—History and criticism. | Pan Africanism in literature. | Literature and transnationalism. | Hughes, Langston, 1902–1967—Influence.
Classification: LCC PS3515.U274 Z6435 2020 (print) | LCC PS3515.U274 (ebook) | DDC 818/.5209—dc23
LC record available at https://lccn.loc.gov/2019035410
LC ebook record available at https://lccn.loc.gov/2019035411

Cover art: Langston Hughes, 1924 (Photographs of Prominent African Americans, James Weldon Johnson Collection, Yale Collection of American Literature, Beinecke Rare Book and Manuscript Library); "The World: Colonial Possessions and Commercial Highways," *The Cambridge Modern History Atlas,* Cambridge University Press, London, 1912 (Perry-Castañeda Library Map Collection, University of Texas Libraries, The University of Texas at Austin)

Contents

	Preface	vii
	Introduction: Pan-African Entanglements and Cultural Exchange	1
1.	Vernacular Pan-African Entanglements: Langston Hughes and Claude McKay	35
	Scale Enlargement A: Langston Hughes and the Caribbean	59
2.	"Marks of a Rebellious Slave": Langston Hughes, Haiti, and Jacques Roumain	70
	Scale Enlargement B: Hughes, McKay, and Negritude	107
3.	"It Cancels the Slave Ship!": Aimé Césaire, the Haitian Revolution, and Langston Hughes	119
	Scale Enlargement C: Langston Hughes and Africa	153
4.	A "Song of Africa across Oceans and Centuries": Langston Hughes, Negritude, and South Africa	160
5.	Cultural Exchange in *Ask Your Mama*	189
	Coda: Paule Marshall and Langston Hughes	211
	Notes	227
	Bibliography	273
	Index	291

Preface

IN 2004, while still writing my first book during a postdoctoral fellowship at Wits University in Johannesburg, South Africa, I began to think ahead to a possible second book on African and Caribbean coming-of-age narratives. I even began to explore the archival resources that might inform such a project during a visit to the National English Literary Museum (NELM) in Grahamstown. But something I came across in the Richard Rive papers sent me in a very different direction: photocopies of letters that Rive had written to Langston Hughes between 1954 and 1966 piqued my interest in midcentury cultural exchange between South Africa and the United States. (I later learned that David Chioni Moore had been instrumental in arranging for NELM to obtain the photocopies.) Further investigation revealed that NELM also had copies of letters written to Hughes by Peter Abrahams, Es'kia Mphahlele, Bloke Modisane, and several other important writers from South Africa. Moreover, the originals, along with carbon copies of Hughes's side of the correspondence, were all archived at the Beinecke Rare Book and Manuscript Library at Yale University.

I was thus inspired to dive deeper into this web of connections, and in 2007 I spent two weeks in New Haven with the help of a New Faculty Research Grant from Utah State University. I brought back microfilms containing reproductions of Hughes's correspondence, not just with the South African writers but also with writers throughout Africa and the Caribbean, some of it going back to the early 1920s. I recruited a very smart and capable undergraduate student, John Walters, to help me edit the letters between Hughes and the South African writers. The resulting volume, entitled *Langston Hughes and the South African* Drum *Generation: The Correspondence,* was published by Palgrave Macmillan in 2010.

While I initially focused on Hughes's connections to South Africa, I never forgot that he also corresponded at least briefly with some of the major black twentieth-century writers in English, French, and Spanish from Africa and the Caribbean, among them Aimé Césaire, J. P. Clark, Léon-Gontran Damas,

Nicolás Guillén, George Lamming, Claude McKay, Regino Pedroso, Jacques Roumain, Léopold Senghor, and Wole Soyinka. The more I investigated these materials and the existing scholarship on Hughes, the more I realized that with a few exceptions, scholars have made little account of the relationships represented in these letters, of those relationships' influence on the rise of colonial and postcolonial literatures throughout the African world, or of their effect on Hughes's own literary output throughout his career.

I therefore plunged further into the rich archival troves that surround many of these writers when I was granted a sabbatical by USU in 2011–12. This year of raw data gathering laid the groundwork for what became *Cultural Entanglements*. I was aided in this project by a Scholars-in-Residence award from the Schomburg Center for Research in Black Culture at the New York Public Library and an Alfred A. and Blanche W. Knopf Fellowship from the Harry Ransom Center at the University of Texas. I am grateful for their financial support as well as the endlessly helpful assistance of their staffs. Naomi Bland, my research assistant at the Schomburg Center, deserves special thanks for turning up a gold mine of material. I am also thankful for the help provided by the staffs at the Beinecke, NELM, and the many other archives I investigated, including the Centre for African Literary Studies at the University of KwaZulu-Natal, the Huntington Library, the Bibliothèque Littéraire Jacques Doucet at the Sorbonne, the Bibliothèque Nationale de France, and the Archives Nationales in Pierrefitte-sur-Seine.

I particularly valued the community at the Schomburg Center as I conducted the preliminary research and began shaping the project. I am appreciative of all the scholars who participated in the weekly seminars during my time there: Giselle Anatol, Carolyn Brown, Lisa Collins, James De Jongh, Venus Green, Robin Hayes, Ryan Kernan, Esther Lezra, Kevin McGruder, Colin Palmer, Adrienne Petty, and Millery Polyne.

My gratitude and thanks go to everyone who provided advice, guidance, and/or helpful readings at various stages over the last fifteen years—a process so long I will surely make some important omissions. Nevertheless, I must thank the following people: Rita Barnard, Lawrence Culver, Ronit Frenkel, Alexander Gil Fuentes, Lisa Gabbert, Stephen Gray, Kathleen Gyssels, Barbara Harlow, Keri Holt, Jean Jonassaint, Doug Jones, Bernth Lindfors, Brian McCuskey, Kristine Miller, Ryan Moeller, Monica Popescu, Stéphane Robolin, Amrit Singh, Andrea Spain, Shaun Viljoen, John Walters, and David Watson.

I have taught many of the texts that I discuss in *Cultural Entanglements* in various courses over the years at USU. My students always humble me by showing me new ways of reading and thinking about the literature; my thanks to them for being rigorous respondents and sounding boards for so many ideas that ended up in the book. Thanks also to my colleagues in USU's remarkably collegial and supportive English Department.

A Creative Activities and Research Enhancement Award from USU's College of Humanities and Social Sciences allowed me to hire an editorial assistant, Jackson Bylund. His hard work and meticulous attention to detail through the final stages of manuscript preparation have been an incalculable boon.

I am grateful for the hard work and kind assistance of Eric Brandt and his staff and colleagues at what has always been my first choice of publisher for this book, the University of Virginia Press. Thanks also to the late J. Michael Dash for including *Cultural Entanglements* in the New World Studies series.

Pallavi Rastogi read every word of every chapter, many of them multiple times. When I foolishly disregarded her advice, it usually came back to haunt me. And when I despaired of ever finishing the book, she gave me a pep talk or a kick in the pants, as needed. Thanks, P.

To Christie Fox, who knows I always save the best for last: you've always been my sharpest interlocutor, my greatest support, and my safe harbor. My gratitude and disbelief that you've stuck with me all these years are boundless.

Sections of *Cultural Entanglements,* significantly revised here, have appeared in the following journal articles. I am grateful for the journals' permission to republish them: "'It Cancels the Slave Ship!': The Haitian Revolution in Langston Hughes' *Emperor of Haiti* and Aimé Césaire's *The Tragedy of King Christophe,*" *Modern Drama* 62, no. 4 (2019); "Cultural Exchange and the Black Atlantic Web: South African Literature, Langston Hughes, and Negritude," *Twentieth-Century Literature* 60, no. 4 (2014); "Black Atlantic Literature as Transnational Cultural Space," *Literature Compass* 10, no. 6 (2013).

Cultural Entanglements

Introduction

Pan-African Entanglements and Cultural Exchange

LANGSTON HUGHES has been read most frequently as an American (and most especially an African American) writer, one closely identified with a particular place, Harlem. To read his work through the lens of US traditions, themes, and concerns seems well justified by such iconic lines as "I, too, sing America"; by Hughes's professed debt to such quintessentially American poets as Walt Whitman, Carl Sandburg, and Paul Laurence Dunbar; and by his lifelong commitment to the cause of African American freedom and equality. Indeed, despite the long-established critical recognition that the "New Negro Movement" of the 1920s was an internationalist phenomenon centered in Paris as much as in New York, the very term by which it is now more commonly known, the "Harlem Renaissance," persistently links the artists associated with it, including Hughes, to a localized American identity.

Cultural Entanglements, however, emphasizes different sides of Langston Hughes, recognizing him as globetrotting cosmopolitan, travel writer, translator, anthologist, avid international networker, and maybe above all, pan-Africanist.[1] It thus contributes to a recent "transnational turn" in literary studies, and in the humanities more generally, with studies of Hughes's work being no exception.[2] Indeed, I will argue that Hughes's influence and self-assumed roles as editor, promoter, and facilitator of other people's art made him a crucial but undercelebrated figure in the mid-twentieth-century rise of postcolonial Caribbean and African literature in English, French, and Spanish. In other words—to anticipate the terminology I will be defining presently and using throughout this book—Hughes was a self-conscious advocate for and facilitator of cultural entanglement at a transnational scale; he invested heavily in but did not confine himself exclusively to entanglements with the pan-African world.[3] While any sense of transnational black community he helped form through cultural exchange and network building might have been fleeting and ephemeral, his increasingly deep and complex interactions with African and Caribbean writers changed the way Hughes thought and wrote about Africa and about blackness. It helped him develop an aesthetic of pan-African entanglement, complete with its own lexicon of tropes and its own performative repertoire, which he then helped set in motion within an emerging body of literature from across Africa and the Caribbean.

My study will try to separate out and highlight the strands connecting Hughes to just a few of the writers with whom he carried on a literary and epistolary exchange. Some of the threads linking and entangling these writers were figurative and transtemporal (involving ancestry, kinship, racial essences), but *Cultural Entanglements* will concentrate especially on mapping the *material* connections that relied on and extended technological developments (telegraphs and telephones, airmail and commercial air travel, radio and television networks) and institutional structures (publishing houses and journals, writers' guilds and cultural associations, conferences and festivals). To the extent that such connections can be traced, it is mostly through the vast archives that Hughes and many of the other writers left behind. Each of the first four chapters, then, singles out one or two of those relationships and presents diachronic snapshots of their rhizomatic, sometimes ephemeral, and multidirectional entanglements and cultural exchanges.

Among the writers from the West Indies, Claude McKay, Jamaican poet and novelist, corresponded at length with Hughes, and they expressed mutual admiration for one another's work. Jacques Roumain, Haitian novelist and poet, met Hughes in Port-au-Prince and Paris. Hughes translated his poetry and a novel into English, corresponded with Roumain a bit, and campaigned for the Haitian's release from prison when he was jailed by the US-backed dictatorship in the mid-1930s. Some years later, all the French-speaking Negritude writers acknowledged the Harlem Renaissance as important precursors to their own artistic projects, and many corresponded with Hughes and took every opportunity to link themselves to him and his legacy. Although this group included Léon-Gontran Damas from French Guiana and Léopold Sédar Senghor of Senegal, I will focus especially on the intertextual and personal entanglements between Hughes and Aimé Césaire of Martinique. Both of them celebrated not just ancestral links between the diaspora and Africa (which is what Senghor, for example, most emphasized in Hughes's verse) but also a contemporary web of exchanges and associations.

The reader might have noted that my quick sketch of Hughes's pan-African skein so far focuses mostly on writers and intellectuals from the Caribbean rather than Africa, even though a quasi-mythological idea of Africa was at the very center of Hughes's conception of black identity.[4] He had a lifelong interest in Africa and first traveled there at the age of twenty-one or twenty-two.[5] Yet it was not until the 1950s that he began really to develop a network of black writers, artists, and intellectuals from the

African continent. Roughly the last third of this book, then, will ask how the deeper entanglements to Africa that Hughes began to develop in the last twenty years of his life both expanded and complicated his efforts to realize a transnational black collectivity. In particular, the experiences of judging the annual short story competition for Johannesburg's *Drum* magazine in 1953–55 and of compiling the selections for two important anthologies of African literature published in the early 1960s put him in touch with what I have described as the *Drum* generation of black South African writers. My study will focus especially on Es'kia Mphahlele and Peter Abrahams, but Hughes also grew well acquainted with Richard Rive, Bloke Modisane, and others.[6] He met many of these writers in his travels to Europe and their trips to New York and in a flurry of trips he took to Africa in the 1960s, especially for conferences and festivals devoted to pan-African literatures and cultures. In those travels he also met many sub-Saharan African writers.[7] As his web of contacts expanded to include a new generation of writers on the African continent, his tendency to base pan-African unity on assumptions of cultural sameness also encountered new challenges. Implicitly accused of playing into South African apartheid's insistence on supposedly authentic, rural cultural traditions for black Africans, Hughes, in his poetry and in his role as cultural ambassador, had to devise new ways to negotiate and validate cultural difference.

In *Cultural Entanglements*, then, I will narrate a materialist history of pan-African interconnection, or at least a corner of it, by isolating and mapping one cluster of threads, interpreting their significance, and identifying the limitations of the resulting network and its accompanying aesthetic. I will outline Hughes's correspondence with the aforementioned writers, his translations of their works, and his other connections to them. I will ask what Hughes's transnational network of black writers made possible and set in motion and what alternatives it foreclosed. I will conclude with a brief coda devoted to Paule Marshall, the American writer of Caribbean descent whom Hughes befriended in the 1960s and invited to join him on a speaking tour in Europe. Nearly twenty years later, and many years after Hughes's death in 1967, Marshall wrote the novel *Praisesong for the Widow*, in which she clearly continued her mentor's project of gathering and nurturing the cultural strands that snarl the three points of the "Triangular Road" (the title of her 2009 memoir, referring to Africa, black America, and the black Caribbean) into a larger conceptual whole. The novel draws heavily on the aesthetic of pan-African entanglement developed in part by Hughes and his network of fellow artists.

Aside from their acquaintance with Langston Hughes, the writers considered in this study shared certain literary goals in common: first and most fundamentally, all of them aimed to distinguish themselves as black writers, though often with some misgivings about identifying themselves so singularly through their blackness. Second, they consciously wrote to advance a distinct black literary tradition that drew from an aesthetic of pan-African entanglement—that is, from a common pool of tropes, images, rhetorics, and performative devices, including memories of an imagined Africa; slavery and slave uprisings; and the persistence of African cultural forms in the modern world. Third, they aimed to contribute to the imagining of a collective memory that could enable solidarity across the African diaspora and give coherence to a transnational black identity. This memory of pan-African entanglement was forged out of "constructive engagements" of the sort Stéphane Robolin argues were fomented between US and South African writers throughout the twentieth century, conducting "an inquiry into the development of a common sense, understood here as a collective way of thinking about collectivity."[8]

The writers I am studying diverged and conflicted in their methods most frequently when it came to the aforementioned second and third goals: determining what relationship modern black identity should have to Africa. Some, like Jacques Roumain and the Negritude writers, invested heavily in notions of racial kinship among people of African descent and in ideas of an intrinsic African personality that borrowed from a romantic strain of modern primitivism. Like Hughes, too, the memory of pan-African entanglement that these writers helped imagine into existence often took the form of *vernacular* or *peasant memory* that located the persistence of African identity and racial memory in rural black cultures throughout the Americas. Likewise, the *aesthetic* of pan-African entanglement that McKay and Hughes helped to create and set in motion was deeply informed by the vernacular language and cultural practices of peasants, workers, and vagabonds.

For other writers in Hughes's circle, though—and especially those from South Africa in the 1950s, struggling against an apartheid system determined to force that country's urban population onto rural reserves—Hughes and the Negritude poets fell back too easily on rhetoric of intrinsic qualities associated with African ancestry. To the African writers reading his work, such rhetoric and imagery came across as romantic and unrealistic at best and an embrace of racialist impulses at worst. Thus, where Hughes might have hoped that drawing artists from Africa into his transnational skein of black writers and intellectuals would have revealed *sameness* and solidarity, instead it brought into stark relief the cultural *difference* between the various cultures comprising his network and forced the lexicon and repertoire of pan-African imagery to bend and adapt. Tropes and images drawn from the diasporic past—of the Middle Passage and fugitive slaves, for example—continued to circulate among this network of writers, but as they did so, they shifted and added new meanings, becoming mechanisms for weaving cultural difference into a larger transnational black collectivity.[9]

If Hughes's influence manifested itself in different forms among these various writers, his cultural exchange with an increasingly widespread network of black writers from the West Indies and Africa had a marked effect on his own work as well. This is especially clear later in his career when the curious, xenophilic temperament he had always possessed blossomed into a full-blown ethos and aesthetic of pan-African entanglement, grounded in a renewed interest in and respect for Africa. If his early poetry arguably depicted the continent two-dimensionally, as romantic lost motherland and source of primal creativity for the children of the diaspora, in his late long poem *Ask Your Mama,* Hughes had come to regard Africa as a great living continent, heterogeneous but united in struggle against its European rulers, and with much still to teach its far-flung descendants abroad. The ethos and the aesthetic of pan-African entanglement became part of Hughes's enduring legacy.[10] In the later works of Es'kia Mphahlele, Peter Abrahams, and Paule Marshall, we see the threads and arteries of pan-African entanglement continue to grow and find new connections, forging in the process an identifiably black contribution to modernity. Reading writers like these as part of a transnational black literary tradition rather than as peripheral figures within their national literatures helps us better appreciate both the commonalities and the cultural differences manifest in their works and to conceive new ways of canonizing, anthologizing, teaching, and thinking about black literature in the twentieth century and beyond.

Cultural Entanglement

The terminological system I have already begun to use requires some explanation. At the most general level, I mean *cultural entanglements* to refer to almost any kind of encounter or exchange with another person or group across a division of perceived difference. I do not claim that what I describe is a new phenomenon—indeed, cultural entanglements have formed throughout human history among nomads, traders, explorers, migrants, conquerors, and conquered. And Hughes and other writers in his circle perceived the web of historical entanglement as extending far back in time, connecting the black diaspora together through an imagined African past. But certainly the density of cross-cultural entanglements and the pace of new interconnections increased dramatically over the span of the twentieth century covered by this book.

Sarah Nuttall uses the term "entanglement" to highlight the ways in which the "story of post-apartheid" in South Africa, which has so often emphasized "the register of difference," also includes "intricate overlaps that mark the present and, at times, and in important ways, the past, as well."[11] Nuttall considers such entanglement primarily at the scale of cities within one country and therefore focuses on "sites and spaces in which what was once thought of as separate . . . come together or find points of intersection in unexpected ways."[12] And given South Africa's racially divided history, she focuses especially on entanglements across the lines of racial difference. *Cultural Entanglements* is, like Nuttall's book, similarly interested in points of unexpected intersection, contact, and recognition, but its theoretical frame does not necessarily derive from her conception of entanglement. Rather, my notion of transnational entanglement emphasizes the sense of solidarity, community, and identity that the circuits of cultural exchange provided to black people scattered over oceans and continents.

Human interconnection at a transnational scale manifests less frequently in physical sites and spaces than it does at the urban scale of Nuttall's analysis. I do, however, attempt in *Cultural Entanglements* to identify and map as closely as possible the exceptions—the (often transitory) spaces of cultural exchange such as festivals, conferences, and public readings. I intend the term cultural entanglements to be intentionally broad and flexible, to account for a wide variety of ways in which feelings of (in this case) pan-African interconnection were generated. But I will ground my analysis as much as possible in the *textual* and the *material*. Thus, for example, I look for mutual literary influence and intertextual conversations through dedications and epigraphs, references in essays and eulogies, direct or indirect allusions in literary texts, and the adoption and adaptation of elements of a shared pan-African past.

When I talk throughout this book about an aesthetic and a memory of pan-African entanglement, a large part of what I mean involves the artists engaging with this narrative of a shared black past, using it to foment a transnational sense of black community. My notion of a memory of pan-African entanglement borrows from Maurice Halbwachs's materialist "frameworks of collective memory"[13] but extends it to a transnational scale, where a group of writers set into motion a shared circuit of stories, tropes, and symbols in the hopes of establishing a collective memory of pan-African experience. I also pay special attention to tropes and symbols in the writers' works implying some form of entanglement or tying together: threads, rivers, webs, networks, matrices, cultural exchanges, and so on. I read these tropes and images as the authors attempting, consciously or otherwise, to conceptualize and learn to navigate a bewildering condition in which far-flung cultures are intermeshed in a vast global matrix of textual and material commodification and exchange.

My materialist approach to mapping Hughes's transnational entanglements also involves the time-consuming task of mapping his direct connections to the writers in his black literary network: telegrams and letters that survive in various archives; programs from and reports on various pan-African cultural conferences and festivals where the writers met in person; flight itineraries for lecture tours; packing slips for books, records, and other material items shipped across oceans; and so on. I will furthermore highlight the web of mutual support the writers established through translation, anthologization, introductions to publishers, and publicity. Rather than thinking of these entanglements across the pan-African world as inert threads, many of them might be better conceived as arteries or canals—channels through which infusions of cultural vitality and political solidarity could move, contributing to the midcentury rise of African and Caribbean literature, and helping create new outlets and new readers overseas for works by Hughes and other African American writers.

It might be helpful to distinguish at this point between two kinds of transnational entanglement. The first is a passive and generalized condition of human interconnection across borders and throughout time. The metaphor of entanglement might itself convey a certain passivity, and indeed, without constant recirculation and reanimation (which, I argue throughout the book, is partly the work of performance), these figurative and narrative links threaten to calcify into stereotypes, romantic essentialism, and inert, fixed formations. The ideal, then, is to organize the strands of cultural exchange into a second level of transnational entanglement, consisting of productive, orderly patterns of interwoven circuits. Such are the imperatives of what I am calling the "ethos of pan-African entanglement": to recognize and accept a generalized condition of interconnection; to cultivate and organize the circuits of cultural dissemination and exchange; and to exploit its motility and flexibility, all in such a way that entanglement ceases to be a passive condition of history and becomes the conductive fabric out of which black solidarity and identity might be sewn.

To help visualize this transnational skein, I refer to a chart of the world's principal international cables. The cables form a matrix of crisscrossing lines, clustered especially over the North Atlantic and the Mediterranean, but with no clear center to the network. They are operated by different countries and companies, many of them rivals and competitors, but together they form a dense network through which flowed a continual stream of communication. This map was published in 1924, the same year that Claude McKay wrote his earliest surviving letter to Langston Hughes.

It thus demonstrates the degree to which a condition of transnational entanglement already characterized the West, its colonies, and its trading partners at the time my narrative of pan-African cultural exchange really begins. The map is useful to understanding my model of transnational entanglements on two levels: first, the network of telegraph cables was one of the literal channels through which cultural exchange was conducted; and second, it serves as a metaphor for conceptualizing the desirable, productive, flexible state of entanglement that Hughes set out, more or less purposefully, to achieve. A map of Hughes's ongoing cultural exchanges with writers around the world would show clusters in different places but would reveal similarly complex skeins of interconnection. And like the telegraph cables, the "threads" of cultural exchange are not passive and inert but rather active conduits through which pass a continual stream of communication. In this regard, we might just as well substitute maps of shipping lanes, airline routes, fiber optic cables, or any other network through which people, commodities, and/or information flow.

Let me emphasize again the extent to which I see cultural entanglement as a material process, the speed and efficacy of which was greatly enabled by advances in communication and transportation technology throughout the twentieth century, leading to a steady intensification in cultural entanglements across ever greater distances. Eric Bulson argues that the scale of modernist networking would not have been possible without the little magazine, which "is to the modernist network what the wires are to the radio, telephone, and telegraph."[14] I concur but also see the radio, telephone, and telegraph themselves as constituting other channels of cultural exchange across still larger networks, as did airmail and other new developments.

Hughes was far from alone in his efforts to take advantage of such developments, but he approached the task with both pragmatism and singular energy and enthusiasm, and his transatlantic network became easier to construct and maintain as such technologies as radio and then television broadcasting, telephones, and air travel became widespread. Airmail came into existence during and after World War I and became commonplace by the 1930s; together with the older technology of the telegraph, it helped enable an international movement like the Harlem Renaissance, stretched as its participants actually were between New York, the US South, Paris, the Soviet Union, and elsewhere. These technological developments also made it possible for black writers from far-flung and often isolated locales to interact meaningfully and provide each other with artistic, financial, logistic, and moral support as well as intellectual stimulation. Moreover, the increasing affordability of air travel throughout the twentieth century

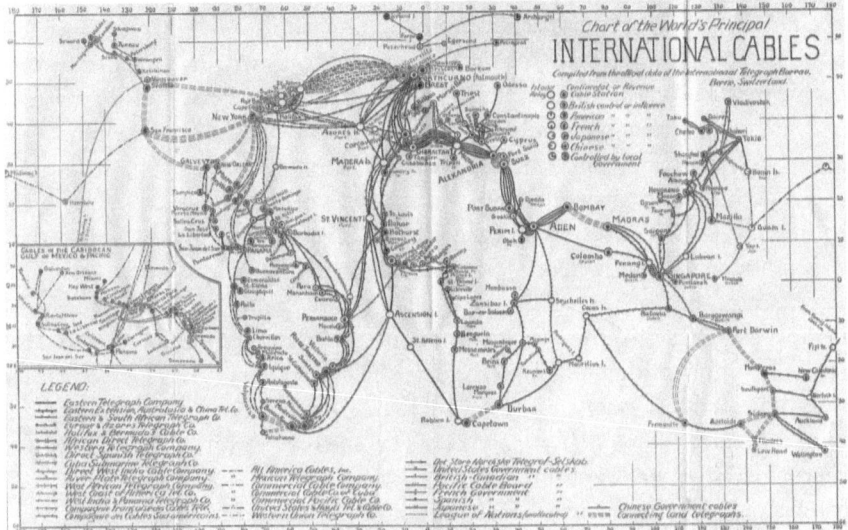

Chart of the world's principal international cables, from George A. Schreiner, *Cables and Wireless and Their Role in the Foreign Relations of the United States*, Boston: Stratford, 1924. (Reproduction courtesy Atlantic-Cable.com.)

enabled the rapid movement of people themselves, at least of a certain affluence or prominence. This is evident in Hughes's frantic travel itinerary in his last two decades and in the number of overseas visitors he regularly entertained at his Harlem brownstone.

Scales of Cultural Entanglement

The existence of concentric or overlapping *scales* and *planes* of analysis is crucial to my model of cultural entanglements, especially since Hughes focused his own efforts to highlight and cultivate such entanglements at different scales in different contexts and at different times in his life. The scale he prized most highly and consistently throughout his life was *pan-African entanglements* between and among inhabitants of the black diaspora and the African continent. But his loyalties to what he called "the Negro people" overlapped comfortably with a larger sense of connection to other cultures, at a scale I am calling *transnational entanglements*. It would be oversimplifying to describe the pan-African scale as a subset of the transnational, but the two overlap significantly in their spheres of concern and their disregard of the nation as the locus of primary identification. The transnational scale in turn contained other forms of connection and exchange that crossed borders, transcended nations, and overlapped with pan-African entanglements. For example, a concern for proletarian entanglements brought Hughes and some of the other writers in his network into contact, at least temporarily or sporadically, with the Soviet Union and other Marxist states that emphasized international worker solidarity.[15] At the same time, Hughes and many in his network also evinced a concern for the global dispossessed and the idle urban poor that I will characterize as vagabond entanglement.[16] My terms for these various scales are not interchangeable, but I will use them all at various times to account for how flexibly Hughes and the writers in his network moved between different scales of transnational entanglements.

Hughes's 1932 poem "Always the Same" exhibits that flexibility and motility in the space of two stanzas. The speaker begins, "It is the same everywhere for me," and proceeds to list sites of oppression of black and brown people: the docks of Sierra Leone, the cotton plantations of Alabama, the diamond mines of Kimberley, and places in Haiti, Central America, Harlem, Morocco, and Tripoli. The speaker bluntly spells out what they all have in common:

> Black:
> Exploited, beaten and robbed,
> Shot and killed.[17]

The "me" here does the same work as the "I" in "The Negro Speaks of Rivers," which links the modern Mississippi River to the ancient Congo, Nile, and Euphrates in a web of entanglement going back centuries. The common bond here linking black and brown people in Africa, the Caribbean, Central America, and the United States is a recently shared history of being "Exploited, beaten and robbed," of being treated like the raw materials (cotton, diamonds, coffee, bananas) whose extraction relied on black labor. The forceful assertion of that bond of labor and oppression, the speaker hopes, will be strong enough to override the linguistic, religious, and other cultural differences that always threaten to disrupt any real attempt to form true political alliances among the groups mentioned in the poem. At such moments, Hughes was both recognizing a condition of transnational entanglement along simultaneously racial and proletarian channels and attempting to unify the entangled groups under the label "Black."

The Ancestral Plane of Pan-African Entanglement

I refer throughout this book to different temporal planes across which Hughes and many of his contemporaries perceived pan-African entanglements. The most fundamental of these is the *ancestral plane* of interconnection. Writers such as Hughes, Roumain, Césaire, and Senghor spun myths and invented collective memories about Africa as healing motherland to the diaspora and about the survival of and resistance to slavery, with the aim of generating a sense of kinship and community across the pan-African world. We will see examples of this throughout *Cultural Entanglements*. The representations of ancestral Africa in particular are easily viewed as essentialist and racialist, and indeed many black intellectuals objected to it as such. But my argument is that, for the most part, these writers used this language purposively and strategically to cultivate a sense of ancestral entanglement among black people worldwide.

In its crudest forms, especially in the 1920s, Hughes's poetic evocations of ancestral pan-African entanglement did resemble sheer primitivism, albeit of a romantic and favorable bent. In "Danse Africaine" (1922) for example, the "slow beating of the tom-toms . . . stirs your blood,"[18] while "Nude Young Dancer" (1925) rhetorically asks the female "Midnight dancer" who stands in for all blackness: "What jungle tree have you slept under?"[19] Hughes claimed to have disavowed such primitivist themes after his break with his patron in 1930, and he even seemed to parody and critique white consumers of primitivist art in the 1934 short story "Slave on the Block." But as David Chinitz notes, even as Hughes increasingly tried to extricate himself and his writing from the primitivist movement, he attempted "to rescue elements of primitivism that he continued to find meaningful—especially those pertaining to African American jazz."[20] In other words, Hughes's efforts to cultivate pan-African solidarity by offering up a vision of ancestral entanglement waxed and waned in importance and emphasis throughout his career but never disappeared entirely. We will find the same productive tension—between romanticizing an imagined past Africa and making the case for black inclusion in the great skein of modern culture—permeating the works by many in Hughes's network.

In late works such as *Ask Your Mama,* Hughes began to integrate and braid together two visions of Africa, ancient and modern, allowing the continent to serve as imagined homeland for the diaspora while also drawing it into the circuits of contemporary transnational exchange. His successors such as Mphahlele and Marshall followed his lead and furthered his vision of pan-African entanglement. All of them either consciously recognized or unconsciously mirrored a condition of entanglement enmeshing black Americans, West Indians, and Africans across time, embedded in an ancestral past of shared (if fragmented and half-forgotten) African cultural practices.[21] In their writings, this condition of ancestral cultural entanglement manifested itself through a lexicon of images, tropes, and symbols they associated with Africa (e.g., tom-tom drums, jungles, rivers, palm trees, silver moons, black women's bodies) and a repertoire of putatively African performative devices (drumming, dances, rituals and rites of passage, foodways). In some ways this cluster of tropes and devices functions similarly to the "modern metaphors of black being that tend toward the secular" (especially the veil, the color line, and double consciousness) that Rebecka Rutledge Fisher sees as crucial to the creation of "black being,"[22] but Hughes's aesthetic of pan-African entanglement emphasized the vernacular to a greater degree and more consciously operated at the transnational scale. The lexicon and repertoire he helped develop highlighted the Americas' ancient links to Africa and tried to give a heritage and a usable past to the inhabitants of the black diaspora.

This ancestral tangle of connections was given further density within the American hemisphere with another set of tropes and performative devices involving the history of slavery (whips, lashes and scars, chains and coffles, work songs) and of resistance to slavery and oppression (runagates and underground railroads, revolts and revolutions). For Hughes and many other black writers, these tropes and performances resolved into a narrative of a transnational black community that was ripped from a precolonial African idyll and subjected to forced labor and horrific violence, but whose survivors ultimately fought back and recovered their humanity. In other words, they constructed a narrative to counter the assumption in Western discourse that the "humanity of Blacks had no history as such."[23]

A collective memory of pan-African entanglement would not be an effective counternarrative if it were purely a narrative of loss and victimhood. It needed tales of resistance and struggle to affirm the agency of the survivors and to make the stories about the past resonate with colonized and oppressed people in the twentieth century struggling for their own freedom. Roumain's descriptions of rural Haitian cane cutters in the 1930s, for example, were shot through with language and tropes evoking the island's history of enslavement. In text after text, Hughes and the authors in his network juxtaposed images of slavery with scenes of rebellion—most dramatically Dan Brown's, Nat Turner's, and the Haitian Revolution—and then linked them to twentieth-century revolts against colonial rule. The Haitian Revolution looms particularly large in black Atlantic literature as the only slave revolt to culminate in an independent nation and whose heroes became icons of black empowerment around the world. Haiti thus became a stage for dislodging or working through the psychic traumas of a slave ancestry—reversing the passivity and lack of agency that defines the victims of historical trauma.

Cosmopolitanism and the Twentieth-Century Plane of Entanglements

No matter how potent and inspiring the tales of slave resistance might have been, if the extent of pan-African entanglement remained on the plane of the past—of ancestry and kinship—it might have amounted to no more than primitivist nostalgia. But for Hughes and his network, this textual and figurative plane was enmeshed within another, ever-evolving skein of contemporary, material exchanges and circuits tying black America, the Caribbean, and Africa together into a "literary triangle trade."[24] Many scholars have devised useful theories and concepts to account for various facets of what I see as a condition of worldwide cultural entanglement. Cosmopolitanism, internationalism, the "transnational turn" in cultural studies, network aesthetics, Arjun Appadurai's scapes and cultural flows, Paul Gilroy's black Atlantic, Édouard Glissant's Poetics of Relation, Wilson Harris's the Womb of Space, Tsitsi Jaji's stereomodernism: these and other terms all offer useful insights and explore different tropes for conceptualizing what it means to live in a world where producers and consumers of art alike are inevitably linked to other producers and consumers around the world in a great skein of cultural memory, influence, commodification, and exchange.

That sense of inevitability, of being folded together with distant others, is what gives the metaphor of entanglement such explanatory power: people in the twentieth century found themselves already and increasingly enmeshed in a transnational knot of cultural threads and flows. As anyone who has ever tried to untangle a jumble of yarn or twine can attest, pulling against the knot only draws it tighter and makes it harder to untangle again. And if the threads of transnational interconnection are analogous to arteries, drawing the knot tighter threatens to choke them off and render them useless as channels for cultural sustenance. Hughes and many of the writers in his network recognized this inevitability and, rather than fighting it, worked to make the arteries of cultural exchange productive and flexible.

My thinking about the condition of transnational entanglement has taken shape within overlapping debates throughout the past two decades over cosmopolitanism and transnationalism. Kwame Anthony Appiah sees cosmopolitanism as arising organically from the process of simultaneous *conversation* and *contamination* that happens in cultural contact zones.[25] Appiah uses conversation as a metaphor for constructing cosmopolitan communities,[26] and he gives positive connotations to the term contamination, as a "counter-ideal" to notions of cultural purity.[27] Both tropes offer useful ways of conceiving of transnational entanglement: contamination hints at the irrevocability of allowing one's culture to become intertwined with another's, while conversation offers a useful metaphor for understanding one process by which a global fabric of cultural interconnection and exchange is woven.

I also find Appiah's model useful for his rejection of zero-sum competitions and insistence on the compatibility of nationalism and cosmopolitanism, as for instance when he envisions a "rooted cosmopolitanism, or, if you like, a cosmopolitan patriotism."[28] This seems to describe Langston Hughes's approach in his life and his writings, where he identified himself variously at the scales of neighborhood (Harlem), city, nation, race, and globe, seeing no contradiction between asserting his identity as an American author while also consciously linking himself to burgeoning black literary movements throughout Africa and the Caribbean.[29] Nor did he regard either scale as incompatible with an insistence on a common humanity across racial, national, and cultural divides. Hughes himself regarded African American culture, and his own writing, as existing within a particularly dense cluster of connections with Africa and the Caribbean. He tended moreover to focus his energies and his self-identifications most frequently at that scale of pan-African entanglements. Nevertheless, Hughes emphasized other scales and clusters of entanglement at various times and in various texts, and he never regarded one cluster of kinships and exchanges as precluding other connections, for instance to Latin America, Southern Europe, and Central Asia.

All of this suggests that Hughes perceived transnational entanglement as a state or condition, one that he pragmatically tried to navigate, cultivate, and turn to his benefit. And it suggests that although he prioritized race and blackness—or what he called "the Negro people"—as his principle mode of self-identification throughout most points in his life, his willingness to embrace different scales of human entanglement helped to mitigate some of the problematic aspects of accepting the oppressive designations of race and thus implicitly validating the concept. Achille Mbembe declares that the invocation of race "is born from a feeling of loss, from the idea that the community has suffered a separation . . . and that it must at all costs be rebuilt by reconstituting a thread of continuity beyond time, space, and dislocation."[30] Hughes certainly engaged in that task of "reconstituting a thread of continuity" but without letting himself or his people be wholly defined by their blackness, or their feeling of loss, and insisting that black culture was inextricably entangled in the great skein of global human culture.

The channels of transnational entanglement that Hughes saw himself as operating within sometimes resembled the conceptual model of a distributed network, which Wesley Beal claims was so central to the modernist project of "negotiating the social dialectic of centralization and dispersal and its aesthetic corollary, that of fragment and totality."[31] When, however, we expand the scale of our network analysis beyond the US context that is Beal's concern to the pan-African world, the ways in which this dialectic expresses itself changes. It takes on a particularly temporal dimension, for example: totality exists only in an imagined precolonial African past (and perhaps an envisioned postrevolutionary future), while the present and the recent past are characterized by the fragmentation and dispersal of slavery, colonialism, and diaspora. If we expand our analysis still further outward to the largest transnational scale, we arrive at Eric Bulson's "worldwide network" that results from the twentieth century's "burden of connectivity": "The network as a concept and literary networking as a process influenced how people imagined literary production and circulation on a global scale."[32] The network properly managed, then, can be a form of entanglement that permits the navigation of difference, disconnection, and fragmentation.

To work at this scale is to participate in a fairly recent "transnational turn" away from the national models that dominated the formation of canons and curriculums in previous eras.[33] To study literature through this transnational frame is also to practice "scale enlargement," which, as Wai Chee Dimock argues, "changes the perceptual field."[34] When we look at genre, for example, through the vast scale she calls "deep time," we see "a tangle of relations, one that counts as a 'system' precisely because its aberrations are systemwide, because pits and bumps come with many loops and layers of filiation."[35] In the case of twentieth-century black Atlantic literature, the "pits and bumps" and "layers of filiation" that resolve into kinship patterns manifest in the lexicon and repertoire of pan-African entanglements developed by Hughes and McKay and taken up by later generations of black writers.

Pan-African Entanglements, Diaspora, and the Black Atlantic

Such connections and exchanges as I have been describing were especially important within the configuration of transnational entanglements constituting the black diaspora. As Azade Seyhan observes, "Social ruptures caused by displacement, migrancy, and exile lead to impoverishment of communal life and shared cultural histories. This loss requires the restorative work of cultural memory to accord meaning, purpose, and integrity to the past."[36] For the descendants of African slaves in the Americas, the struggle against forgetting and cultural oblivion has been especially urgent, given slavery, the

Middle Passage, and societies that will always bear "the stamp of historical violence and rupture," as Stuart Hall observes.[37] Thus Seyhan's "restorative work of cultural memory" often took the form of recuperating or imagining memories and cultural traces of Africa.

Given such murky ancestry, roots have to be invented, and so in the early twentieth century we find "a group of diasporic Africans desperate to reach back across the Atlantic and history to reconnect to an ancestral 'homeland.'"[38] To name only two examples, Marcus Garvey led a back-to-Africa movement in the United States in the 1910s and 1920s; shortly thereafter the Harlem Renaissance and then the Negritude poets wrote lyrics romanticizing primitive Africa. Both might be read as attempts to imagine Africa as a lost ancestral homeland where the diaspora could embed its identity.[39] This symbolic return became part of a memory of pan-African entanglement that provided the requisite infrastructure for a diasporic identity and community to emerge across national borders, which in turn was entangled with an emerging body of international black literature.[40]

For Hughes and many of his black contemporaries, however, the imagining of a shared past for all the scattered descendants of Africa did not only fulfill a psychological need for roots and origins; it also aspired to generate feelings of kinship and common experience across the African world, as well as to grow a distinctly "black" aesthetic and artistic identity. To adopt the label that was created to oppress them ran a risk: "the Black Man is also the name of a wound,"[41] and an identity based on an ancestral Africa was an identity based on loss and rupture. But these writers accepted the trade-offs in pursuit of productive cultural entanglement within the pan-African world,[42] which in turn enabled a cognizance of what Gilroy has called the *black Atlantic*.

Though the term has many detractors, the concept has explanatory power and relevance for the scale of border-crossing networks that Hughes instigated. Paul Gilroy himself, in describing a "distinctive counterculture of modernity"[43] that emerged from black cultural expression in the United States and England in the nineteenth and twentieth centuries, used metaphors that suggest entangled threads connecting the various points along the triangle connecting Africa, Europe, and the Americas. Gilroy located the black Atlantic "in a webbed network, between the local and the global, [which] challenges the coherence of all narrow nationalist perspectives."[44] He therefore proposed that "cultural historians could take the Atlantic as one single, complex unit of analysis in their discussions of the modern world and use it to produce an explicitly transnational and intercultural perspective."[45] I see the category of "black Atlantic literature" as useful if we think of it as only one analytical scale, one cluster of entanglements in a larger skein of transnational black influence and exchange, rather than as a totalizing and final paradigm.[46]

Permutations and Implications of Entanglement

My project, then, is to study the writings of Hughes, McKay, Roumain, Césaire, Abrahams, Mphahlele, and Marshall and interpret the characteristics that come into focus when we consider them as all working within the knot of pan-African entanglement I will sometimes refer to under the name "black Atlantic literature." In making this case, I should emphasize again that to the extent these writers prioritized the pan-African connections, that devotion never precluded the cultivation of entanglements with cultural traditions far beyond the African sphere. Brent Edwards suggests reading Hughes's work at a very broad scale, as "a writerly engagement in the politics of capitalist globalization."[47] I will follow Edwards's lead, while also reading this engagement as an expression of Hughes's ethos of transnational entanglement.

As I argue in the first chapter, Hughes arrived at his recognition and embrace of pan-African entanglement in conversation (figurative and literal, at least through letters in the early days) with Claude McKay. McKay's first novel, *Home to Harlem* (1928), depicted the New York neighborhood as a space of pan-African entanglement, while its follow-up, *Banjo* (1929), similarly painted the Marseille Ditch as a microcosm of the African diaspora, complete with deep cultural differences and divides as well as threads of kinship and similarity: "The Negro-Negroid population of the town divides sharply into groups. The Martiniquans and Guadeloupeans . . . make a little aristocracy of themselves," with Malagasy somewhere below them and West Africans as the "savages" at the bottom of the hierarchy.[48]

McKay's description confirms Edwards's claim that often "black modern expression takes form not as a single thread, but through the often uneasy encounters of peoples of African descent with each other."[49] To be tangled up with strangers can be awkward and messy, after all, and an orderly and productive entanglement takes work, patience, and, not least, material resources. McKay's narrator puts this bluntly: a "magic thing" had "brought all shades and grades of Negroes together. Money."[50] This refers most directly to a Senegalese man who had earned enough money working in the United States to buy a tavern in Marseille that has become the social hub for black men in the port city. More generally, the novel acknowledges that capital, commerce, and commodity exchange were the primary channels through which any sort of larger pan-African community might be constituted (unless one opted instead to pursue cultural opportunities through the Soviet Union and its allied states, an option that McKay by the late 1920s had rejected and disavowed). McKay appears to have accepted that to entangle oneself in a transnational community of black people was also, of necessity, to be enmeshed in the great web of capitalism.

McKay and Hughes both formed important nodes in the black Atlantic literary network that took shape in the early and mid-twentieth century. I hasten to add that they were only two such nodes, two characters in a much larger story of pan-African literary entanglement in that period. Another book entirely might be written about (to name only one other example) Richard Wright's own connections to Africa and the black community in Paris.[51] Yet Wright, like James Baldwin after him, reacted rather pessimistically to visiting Africa in person. By contrast, Hughes's enthusiasm for the continent—often to the point of romanticizing it, speaking always favorably of it unless he was criticizing the European colonizers—made him a more willing and effective ambassador from the black diaspora to Africa and a more sympathetic interpreter of Africa for Americans. Even so, the larger conversation about the meaning of blackness and Africa also carried on independent of Hughes, within and beyond his circle of associates.

If entanglement were simply a matter of threads connecting one writer to another across national borders, the trope would have less explanatory power in relation to that transnational conversation. But in fact, the currents connecting any two writers quickly got crossed and tangled and intersected with other writers at multiple points. My chapter subtitles and "scale enlargement" titles are written to reflect this dynamic, multidirectional, and multinodal web of influences and exchanges: for instance, McKay's early poetry inspired the young Hughes, and both authors' works from the mid-1920s onward were written in conversation with one another's. Both writers, but especially Hughes, influenced Roumain, and the Negritude poets later read and responded to all three of them. Then in the second half of the twentieth century, African writers read the works of both the Harlem Renaissance and the Negritude writers; they often responded critically, even harshly, but even in their disagreement they continued to spin the web of interconnection and exchange across the pan-African world. Their various ethoses of entanglement impelled them to weave the connecting arteries carefully enough for them to continue serving as channels for cultural exchange. In this way the contamination effect from mutual entanglement could be nourishing and productive rather than toxic or constrictive.

I want to emphasize, finally, the crucial importance of these transnational entanglements to the writers scattered throughout the African world. The idea that one's ability to contribute to modern global culture was contingent on one's belonging to a national culture—an argument made quite forcefully by Frantz Fanon, among others[52]—was problematic for African American writers in the early twentieth century, often excluded as they were from the mainstream of the American literary establishment.[53] Furthermore, for writers in Europe's colonies in the Caribbean and Africa, national culture was only a distant hope they might aspire to.

In contrast to the foreclosed possibility of belonging to a national literary culture, Hughes's black literary network presented the writers drawn into it with immediate opportunity for publication, promotion, and a sense of belonging to a modern artistic movement. Sometimes these were the *only* channels through which isolated black artists from colonized territories or oppressed minorities could access cultural products from other places and disseminate their own works. Promotion by the likes of Langston Hughes validated their efforts as writers and gave them immediate international visibility and legitimacy. Pascale Casanova speaks of the "immense profit that writers from literarily impoverished spaces have obtained . . . from being published and recognized in the major centers."[54] Hughes gave writers from places with few outlets for disseminating their work some access to the "world republic of letters" that Casanova describes, especially to the American publishing market.

Hughes also collaborated with these writers to form a pan-African alternative to national cultures as the vehicles through which black writing could win international recognition and build a global readership. This entailed, among other things, establishing a pan-African network of communication, translation, publication, and mutual promotion. Hughes himself translated works by black writers in Spanish and French and edited anthologies of global black writing. He also did all he could to support magazines and journals that published work by black writers anywhere. The extent of his influence throughout the African world was clear from the twenty-five-page "Homage to Langston Hughes" that the journal *Présence africaine* published on the occasion of his death in May 1967: it featured touching eulogies from writers and artists from the West Indies (Nicolás Guillén and Andrew Salkey), Africa (Lamine Diakhaté and Eldred Jones), France (François Dodat, who had translated Hughes's poems into French), and the United States (Ted Joans).[55]

Throughout this period, too, Hughes did all he could to create an African American readership for international black literature, hoping to establish some of the strands of cultural entanglement more permanently.[56] As writers found outlets for their work through this burgeoning institutional network, many thereby discovered an artistic community in the black Atlantic and a larger tradition from which to draw themes, tropes, symbols, and allusions.

As it happens, this project also gave Hughes the perfect outlet to fulfill his temperamental and philosophical imperatives, which I am characterizing as his ethos of pan-African entanglement.

Ethos of Entanglement

Earlier I likened the condition of transnational entanglement to what many have labeled "cosmopolitanism," which Appiah says results from processes of conversation and contamination. But for Appiah and others, cosmopolitanism is not merely a condition resulting from countless centuries of human migration, conquest, and trade; it is also a worldview and an ethical attitude to the transnational movements of people, commodities, and capital. Those who adopt an ethos of entanglement do not fear "contamination" by other cultures, and they welcome the mutual benefits that transnational entanglement can engender. But for those who fetishize cultural or racial purity and adhere to what we might call an ethos of separation, the entanglements that arise from cross-cultural conversation are the source of fear and revulsion. Given a generalized condition of transnational entanglement, however, their only recourse is to violently sever the threads tying them to the contaminating Other, sometimes with literal acts of violence. The ethos of separation leads ultimately to Jim Crow, apartheid, and the Final Solution; it finds expression in what Mbembe calls "the work of race—the very negation of the idea of the common, or of common humanity."[57]

By contrast, an ethos of entanglement recognizes the inevitability of transnational interconnection and accepts the ethical obligations that result.[58] This is a project for which literary art is generally well suited, and at which Hughes was particularly adept.[59] His ethos of entanglement manifested itself on many fronts and at many scales. As I discuss in chapter 5, his second autobiography, *I Wonder as I Wander* (1956), was practically a manifesto of cosmopolitan tolerance and curiosity, beginning with the title and the epigraph from Romans, professing indebtedness "both to the Greeks and to the barbarians."[60] He writes about taking his phonograph player and a crate of records on his travels to Soviet Central Asia, where his room in the hostel became "a kind of social center. Everywhere, around the world, folks are attracted by American jazz. A good old Dixieland stomp can break down almost any language barriers."[61] In the last chapter, he says that through his travels, "my interests had broadened from Harlem and the American Negro to include an interest in all the colored peoples of the world—in fact, in *all the people* of the world, as I related to them and they to me."[62]

Hughes's network-building efforts, though, were always devoted most especially to establishing channels of cultural exchange between African

Americans and black people in Africa and elsewhere in the diaspora. On one level, this *ethos of pan-African entanglement* expressed itself as a compulsion to validate Africa, to hold up its so-called primitive cultures and values as antidotes to the cold taxonomical racism of Western discourse, and to demand inclusion and acknowledgment of black contributions to the skeins of world culture. He made such demands partly at the scale of American nationhood, calling for black inclusion in American public life. He wrote in 1926, for example, that someday America will see "how beautiful I am / And be ashamed";[63] later, in 1943, he wrote that the "plan and the pattern" of universal equality are "Woven from the beginning / Into the warp and woof of America."[64] The metaphor here makes clear that Hughes saw the inclusion of black people's stories into the larger American narrative as a process of weaving—a particularly ordered way of organizing a tangled skein.

Hughes did not limit his bid for recognition of black people's accomplishments to those in the United States, however, but made the same demands on a global scale. As early as "The Negro Speaks of Rivers," Hughes extolled black heritage and a black past of which all people descended from Africans and slaves could be proud. Some three decades later, the imperative to redeem black people from racist stereotypes that cast them as savages without history or heritage was even more boldly on display in "Prelude to Our Age." Written to be read aloud at a ceremony honoring the twenty-fifth anniversary of the Schomburg Collection of the New York Public Library in October 1950, and later published in *Crisis,* the poem is prosaic and sloganeering, but fascinating as an expression of an ethos of pan-African entanglement.

"Prelude" begins by sketching a transnational narrative of accomplishment by black scholars and writers throughout the ages, and thus highlighting entanglement on an ancestral plane. That narrative culminates in the American civil rights movement and the speaker's determination to "help to build democracy / For our nation."[65] But it begins with a broad view of the many strands of black history that have fed into that experience:

History's long page
Records the whole vast
Prelude to our age.

Across the chapters
Of recorded time
Shadows of so many hands
Have fallen,
Among them mine:
   Negro.[66]

Several aspects of these opening lines are worth noting. First, they introduce the first-person pronouns that run through the poem, establishing the "I"/"me" not as an individual but rather as a collective of "Negroes" throughout time. The public and historical figures named by the poet are entered into collective memory through cultural channels such as this poem and thus become synecdoches for black community across national borders.

Ron Eyerman identifies different approaches to the cultural memory of slavery—those of Zora Neale Hurston and Marcus Garvey among them—all of which provide "the basis for collective identity, by linking the individual to the collective through the concept of racial pride and the role of culture."[67] Hughes clearly recognized this unifying potential, but his vision extended beyond the nation to the creation of a transnational web of black kinship. Motifs of entanglement (in this case with chains) are established beginning in the ninth and tenth stanzas:

Meanwhile Jamestown links its chains
Between the Gold Coast and our land.
Jamestown, Virginia, 1619.

. . . .
As Sadi chronicles his great
    "Tarikh es Soudan,"
With Africa a link of chains connects our land.
Caught in those chains, my hand:
    Negro.[68']

The links of chain become strands in a great transatlantic net connecting West Africa to Jamestown and the American hemisphere more generally. The physical labor of the captive slave, moreover, is likened to the work done by a writer's hand—in this case the history of the Sudan written by North African scholar Abd al-Sadi—suggesting that both kinds of labor contributed to a pan-African past that black Americans could be proud of. That implication is later developed with allusions to the early modern black Spanish poet Juan Latino and to African American leaders such as Frederick Douglass, Sojourner Truth, and Harriet Tubman.

The speaker of "Prelude," then, expresses respect and admiration for the written word and for libraries and archives such as the Schomburg Center for their important role in preserving the written record of black accomplishments. But he is careful to acknowledge as well the unwritten legacies left by generations of illiterate slaves and their descendants, who "could not write" but "made songs" and kept the "spoken word" and "beaten drum" as traces and reminders of a lost African past and as tools of survival and resistance: "While we, who were not free and could not write a word, / Gave freedom a song the whole earth heard."[69] These oral and performative traditions function as alternative archives (e.g., a repertoire of songs, represented by the lyrics from black American spirituals scattered throughout the poem). Diana Taylor draws an important distinction between the *archive*, which documents written and recorded history, and the *repertoire*, which "enacts embodied memory: performances, gestures, orality, movement, dance, singing—in short, all those acts usually thought of as ephemeral, nonreproducible knowledge," but which nevertheless "participate in the production and transmission of knowledge."[70] The implication for "Prelude to Our Age" is that there is continuity between the "beaten drum / That carried instant history" in ancient eras[71] and African American gospels in the twentieth century. This is pan-African entanglement on the plane of ancestral memory of the sort I discussed earlier—the core around and through which grew all future channels of cultural exchange and thus a potential platform for building a transnational black community, or at least a fleeting but rejuvenating series of transitory interconnections.

"Prelude to Our Age" therefore exhibits the power of combining performative and archival knowledge, literacy, and print culture to facilitate transnational entanglement. As the narrative of black achievement in "Prelude to Our Age" builds to its climax, it catalogs black writers and intellectuals and the journals they founded and/or published in:

> Du Bois, Woodson, Johnson, Frazier,
> Robert S. Abbott, T. Thomas Fortune,
> "The Afro-American," "The Black Dispatch."
> All the time the written record grows—
> "The Crisis," "Phylon," "Opportunity."[72]

The metaphors of weaving and interlacing networks then become explicit in the next stanza—one that Hughes introduced only in the fourth draft (as the typescripts at the Schomburg Center reveal)[73] but that then survived virtually unchanged through several subsequent revisions:

> Surveys, novels, movies, plays
> That trace the maze of patterns
> Woven by democracy and me,
>   Now free.[74]

The tropes of webs and nets have become a metaphor of weaving, where the weaver is "democracy" working together with the first-person speaker, already established as speaking for black storytellers throughout the ages.[75] At the same time, when Hughes read the poem aloud at the Schomburg celebration, the "me" was also literally him, the poet, acknowledging the obligation he inherited in the speech act of inserting himself at the end of this catalog of black writers. Accepting the responsibility to "speak in the name of the black millions,"[76] as he writes in another poem, was another aspect of his ethos of pan-African entanglement.

To varying degrees and in different ways, the writers in Hughes's network likewise adopted and adapted Hughes's ethos of pan-African entanglement—sometimes following his lead, sometimes acting independently while responding to similar historical formations. This understanding is crucial to my readings of their books, plays, and poems, as it helps explain what might otherwise appear like ideological incoherence and self-contradiction on many of their parts. Claude McKay went through phases of avid attachment to Soviet communism, Afrocentric universalism, and Roman Catholicism; Jacques Roumain cycled through Indigenism, black nationalism, and communism; Peter Abrahams embraced communism in South Africa, retreated from politics in Europe, and turned to pan-Africanism in Jamaica. However much these serial conversions put many of them at odds with themselves and one another at various points, the attachments seem more cogent if understood as an ethos of entanglement (often more instinctive or temperamental than intellectual) continually in search of outlets for new or more productive cross-cultural links.

A *Vernacular* Ethos and Aesthetics of Entanglement

What distinguished Hughes and McKay from many of their black American and Caribbean contemporaries—but would prove influential on later generations of black writers—was their choice to ground their explorations of black culture in the vernacular cultures of peasants, workers, and the idle urban poor. Mbembe points to the emergence of two versions of cosmopolitanism in Africa in the late twentieth century: one a "practical cosmopolitanism, of a vernacular brand, carried by *petits migrants* (small migrants)," and the other an elite kind of cosmopolitanism "which strives to reconstruct an African identity and a public space following the universal rules of reason."[77] Hughes attempted to cultivate a third version from his position as an already famous but sometimes vagabond poet who traveled the world and assimilated cultural practices he encountered into a lexicon and repertoire of black entanglement. But this, too, amounted to a kind of elitism. What is more, in the service of valorizing their cultures, he and other writers risked reducing poor people to repositories of African cultural tradition on which cosmopolitan artists like themselves could draw for inspiration and cultural originality.

This uneven power dynamic was exacerbated by the fact that Hughes's literary network with its circuits of cultural exchange relied on English, French, and Spanish as global lingua franca, standardized to varying degrees. If that reliance necessarily involved a compromise and an alienation from a local vernacular (as it did for speakers of creoles in the West Indies or indigenous languages in Africa) and native traditions, then we must ask a number of uncomfortable questions: What is the cost of transnational entanglement, and how readily can its channels really be navigated by a non-elite population? To what extent did the existence of transnational channels of exchange depend on Hughes's privileged status as an American citizen (even one from a marginalized minority) and a well-known writer? Did Hughes exploit the poor black peasantry by relying on them as source material for his writing while building an international network inaccessible to the masses who spoke only their native languages? Even the benign notion of "cultural exchange" required some cultural tradition or originality to be preserved by the poor, while the cosmopolitans repackaged it in necessarily commodified forms. None of the writers in Hughes's network ever solved these ethical dilemmas entirely and for all time, but we will see most of them struggling with such questions. Indeed, both Hughes and Césaire wrote plays that push the question to its furthest implications: At what point does the self-designated authority to "speak in the name of the black millions" cross over into authoritarian rule over those millions?

I will, then, endeavor to keep in mind the troubling power dynamics and potential for exploitation in these relationships. I will nevertheless maintain that the appropriation of elements of peasant and working-class cultures was motivated by sincere respect, admiration, and affection and that it succeeded in helping generate transnational fellow feeling and cultural exchange, at least of a transient and tenuous kind, among black people at various crucial points in the twentieth century. It is worth emphasizing, moreover, that McKay, Hughes, Roumain, and some of their successors were notably positive in their attitudes toward the idle urban poor. This signifies a break from the Soviet Communist Party interpretation of Marxist orthodoxy to which those writers all expressed various degrees of commitment—a school of thought that was quite disparaging of the "lumpenproletariat."[78] The vernacular ethos and aesthetic of Hughes, McKay, and Roumain, though not without condescension, at least recognized a crucial role for the vagabonds of the black diaspora in keeping alive the spark of African cultural vitality that the writers prized so highly.

These poets' emphasis on the poorest black people as the true embodiments of pan-African cultures distinguished their vision of black solidarity from competing visions of black entanglement. The Pan-Africanist project of

Du Bois, for example, focused on cultivating connections among black elites around the world.[79] Alain Locke's attempts to give form to the "New Negro" movement through his work as an anthologist, columnist and essayist, and promoter and mentor of black artists were equally elitist but closer to Hughes in his emphasis on cultural production.[80] In some ways the poets' vernacular sensibilities put them closer to Fanon, who argued that "in colonial countries only the peasantry is revolutionary."[81] The stress these writers gave to blackness and the need for pan-African entanglement differed from Fanon's later ideas, however. In *Wretched of the Earth,* Fanon emphasized nationalism as the ultimate vehicle for overthrowing colonialism and enabling culture, treated the lumpenproletariat as a natural resource that must be harnessed to be made useful[82] and, most crucially, as Bhabha puts it, upheld the view that "the building of national consciousness demands cultural homogeneity and the disappearance or dissolution of differences."[83] This disavowal of difference would put Fanon's ideas at odds with Hughes's lifelong conception of a transnational network fed by circuits of *cultural exchange* across continents and oceans. The "cultural" part of this emphasis would likewise set Hughes's project apart from the Bandung Conference of 1955, which focused on anticolonial solidarity among political leaders in Africa and Asia.[84] Yet in terms of creating a sense of fellow feeling among black people worldwide, I would argue that Hughes's ethos of entanglement and his network-building efforts with African and Caribbean writers were at least as important to any sense of racial solidarity that might have been achieved in the mid-twentieth century as Bandung or the Pan-African Congresses, and it was conceivably more capable of creating a unified front against colonialism and racism than Fanon's revolutionary nationalism.

Such unity was hard to achieve, however, and harder to sustain. Hughes might have hoped that invoking and/or inventing a collective memory of pan-African entanglement would be enough in itself to engender a feeling of kinship among far-flung people of African descent. But his travels soon enough dispelled such ideas and exposed *differences* within the pan-African world that had to be navigated. He emphasizes those differences in his first autobiography, *The Big Sea* (1940), when describing his first voyage to Africa in 1923–24. He was excited to visit the "Motherland of the Negro peoples" but was soon disappointed to find his sense of kinship rejected by the Africans he did meet because of his lighter skin tone: "The Africans looked at me and would not believe I was a Negro."[85] Hughes would spend the rest of his political and literary life wrestling with this disappointment and the implications of the undeniable difference he discovered on that first trip between his African American community and the Africans with whom he came into contact. Later he went looking for vestigial traces of African culture in the West Indies, where he found not a feeling of racial unity but societies that were highly stratified along lines of class and skin color. "It was in Haiti," he wrote, "that I first realized how class lines may cut across color lines within a race, and how dark people of the same nationality may scorn those below them."[86] He was fascinated by locally specific, creolized practices such as Vodou, the rumba, and conga dances, which represented for Hughes an organic and delightful kind of cultural particularity—precisely the sort of cultural difference that made transnational exchange so invigorating. But he deplored class snobbery and color consciousness as artificial, destructive, divisive, and incompatible with his ideal of a unified pan-African culture. And of course, his efforts to facilitate the growth of such a culture had to overcome language barriers, as the writers in his own network included those working in French and Spanish.

Such cultural differences and internalized class stratifications were obstacles to Hughes's ethos of pan-African entanglement and the development of healthy strands of cultural exchange within the pan-African world. From the early 1930s on, therefore, he increasingly devoted himself to the pragmatic work of bridging differences and crossing borders. He translated poems and novels from French and Spanish into English, for instance, and edited anthologies that made the works of many Caribbean and African writers widely available to readers in the United States for the first time. He founded no journals after the ill-fated single issue of *Fire!!* that he coproduced with Wallace Thurman and five other writers in 1926. But he enthusiastically supported periodicals such as *Drum* magazine from South Africa, *Black Orpheus* from Nigeria, and *Présence africaine* from Paris, allowing his own work to be republished in their pages and promoting them in his newspaper column. Hughes also advanced the careers of many African and Caribbean writers in several anthologies he edited, and he put them in touch with agents and publishers. He worked closely, moreover, with organizations such as the Mbari Artists and Writers Club in Nigeria, the Congress for Cultural Freedom, and the Transcription Centre.

Complicating any attempt to read the aforementioned publications and institutions as evidence of true grassroots network building across the black Atlantic is the fact that so many of these institutions were secretly funded by the CIA as part of what Frances Stonor Saunders has aptly called the cultural cold war. The Congress for Cultural Freedom, in particular, was the centerpiece of a "secret program of cultural propaganda in western Europe."[87] Among its objectives were to be "a beachhead in western Europe from which the advance of Communist ideas could be halted" and to "act as an emissary for the achievements of American culture."[88] Scholars are still working through the implications of the cultural cold war for the rise of African and Caribbean literature, and that problem largely exceeds the scope of this current project. In the short term, at least, the funding and institutional support for the arts that these organizations provided turned into another accelerant for the process of transoceanic cultural exchange that Hughes regarded as fundamental to generating true pan-African interconnection. In short, even if he was aware that these organizations and publications were part of a cold war agenda,[89] Hughes tried to use them strategically in the service of building a material and institutional infrastructure for an emerging black Atlantic literary skein. And just as the web of pan-African cultural exchange was inextricably bound up with the larger networks of capitalist commodity exchange, so was it entangled in the political machinations of the cultural cold war.

Cultural Exchange and the Aesthetics of Pan-African Entanglement

I have already had frequent occasion to use the term *cultural exchange* to describe one of the most important types of connection in a tangled pan-African network. This notion became increasingly important in Hughes's thinking about the relationship between black people of different nationalities, languages, skin tones, and religions throughout his life. He said in a speech at the opening of the US library in Accra, Ghana, in 1962: "Today, when America comes to Africa, as through these library shelves, to offer an *exchange* of knowledge (not merely to *give* in the old patronizing sense), America is bolstering her *own* basic dreams, and finding here in Africa a new strengthening of the old concept of freedom in your liberated lands."[90] It is significant, too, that the first section of Hughes's long poem *Ask Your Mama* (1961) is entitled "Cultural Exchange." In both the poem and the speech, Hughes no longer regarded Africa as a purely mythical land of talking drums and ancestral rivers, though the ancestral plane still persisted as the symbolic "Mama" in his otherwise irony-drenched title. Hughes now saw Africa more complexly as a vast, modern, living place whose occupants had much to teach the world and whose struggles both paralleled and intersected with the civil rights struggle in his own country in potentially illuminating ways. No longer, moreover, was cultural influence flowing one way out of a timeless African motherland; the emphasis now was on a newly intensified "*exchange* of knowledge" between black America and black Africa. And Hughes put his rhetoric into action, carrying on a prodigious stream of correspondence with writers throughout Africa and the Caribbean and visiting the African continent several times in his last decade.[91]

Hughes's extended contact with this pan-African network combined with his ethical devotion to cultivating pan-African interrelation and exchange. The result was a border-crossing "aesthetic of pan-African entanglement" that both shaped and took shape within his poetry, and then was set into motion in the works of other black writers. It is on display in his first adult poem, "The Negro Speaks of Rivers," which remains probably his best-known single poem. It conceives of black American identity, embodied in the "muddy bosom" of the Mississippi River, as intertwined on an ancestral level with the "Ancient, dusky rivers" of the Euphrates, the Congo, and the Nile.[92] Later iterations of this pan-African aesthetic made cultural exchange and transnational entanglement a dominant source of motifs—as the speaker of Hughes's *Ask Your Mama* quips, "CULTURE ... IS A TWO-WAY STREET."[93] This aesthetic engaged closely (sometimes approvingly, sometimes critically) with the lexicon and repertoire of pan-African cultural expression that Hughes and McKay cultivated between them. It also valued creoles and hybrid styles and forms over adherence to cultural purity or authenticity. The notes for musical accompaniment that appear alongside the main text of *Ask Your Mama,* for example, call on everything from African and Vodou drumming to jazz and blues to German *lieder.* Even the form of the poem, fragmented into twelve interconnected "moods," illustrates the "network aesthetics" described by Beal in his discussion of the modern short story cycle.[94] Elements of this aesthetics of transnational entanglement were present in Hughes's earliest work, but it found its purest expression in *Ask Your Mama,* and it took on new forms in the work of his successors.

Methodology and Organization

Because Hughes's status as a sort of godfather of African and Caribbean literature in European languages has been, to my mind, underappreciated, one of my intentions in writing this book is to serve as literary historian and detective. Having spent over a decade investigating Hughes's archival and published legacies, I aim to document with some care the massive paper trail he left behind in his correspondence and professional and personal relationships with writers throughout the West Indies and Africa, especially South Africa. Hughes was a packrat, keeping virtually every letter ever sent to him, and from the late 1940s onward keeping carbon copies of his own outgoing correspondence.[95] My methodology for making sense of this vast assemblage of material consists of toggling between macroscopic overviews of Hughes's black Atlantic literary networks and microscopic studies of a few particular entanglements. My goal is to balance attention to nuance and granular texture in individual literary texts with an aerial view of the circuits of black Atlantic exchange that informed and shaped the texts.

The greater part of this book is made up of five chapters, together telling a narrative in roughly chronological order, each focusing primarily on some period in Hughes's lifelong network-building project. But the story *Cultural Entanglements* tells grows increasingly knotty and self-referential as the later writers respond to the contributions of Hughes and McKay and then Roumain and then the Negritude writers in an ever-expanding tangle of influences and conversations and reactions to what came before. The major chapters are interspersed with three "scale enlargements," a term I borrow from Dimock, and which has an explanatory precision that I hope compensates for its clunkiness. These shorter sections zoom out to give larger "bird's-eye views" of the networks Hughes helped build and their literary expressions. These scale enlargements serve as a preliminary mapping of areas for potential future scholarship; I attempt through them to document Hughes's connections to African and Caribbean writers whom space precludes me from exploring in depth. By way of conclusion, a final coda will explore how the aesthetic of pan-African entanglement that these writers developed was later given new expression in the hands of Paule Marshall, one of the last of the young writers to benefit from Hughes's mentorship, who brought his legacy well into the twenty-first century.

Chapter 1, "Vernacular Pan-African Entanglements: Langston Hughes and Claude McKay," focuses on the curiously understudied relationship between two of the principal poets of the Harlem Renaissance. Through an epistolary relationship beginning in the mid-1920s, and through each author's careful readings of the other's work, McKay and Hughes negotiated a vision of vernacular black entanglement based partly in a primitivist romanticization of African, American, and Caribbean peasant cultures in rural areas, and partly in the figure of the deracinated *vagabond* in urban areas. Yet as Hughes traveled in the West Indies himself, his own social network of sustained contact was inevitably dominated by the educated and literate elite, especially other writers. I briefly sketch his connections to those writers from the Caribbean in scale enlargement A: "Langston Hughes and the Caribbean."

The figures of noble peasants and nomadic workers that emerge from Hughes's and McKay's writings also dominate the work, especially the novels, of Jacques Roumain. The friendship between Hughes and Roumain, and Hughes's more general fascination with Haiti and its history, are the subjects of chapter 2, "'Marks of a Rebellious Slave': Langston Hughes, Haiti, and Jacques Roumain." Hughes in particular was fascinated by the

Haitian Revolution, which he saw as both a model and a cautionary tale for black autonomy and self-empowerment. Particularly in his play *Emperor of Haiti* (1936) and its adaptation into the libretto for the opera *Troubled Island* (1949), Hughes attempted to reanimate the history of Dessalines's authoritarian rule and eventual assassination in ways that highlighted the relevance of that history for the twentieth century's own struggles against racial discrimination and colonialism. Hughes also made clear the urgency of Haiti's contemporary struggle against despotism and/or foreign occupation by translating into English Jacques Roumain's work, including several poems and (with Mercer Cook) the major novel, *Masters of the Dew*. In all this work, and even the children's book he wrote with Arna Bontemps, *Popo and Fifina* (1932), Hughes helped enshrine Haiti as the ultimate repository of African cultural traditions in the Americas and began to assimilate elements of Haiti's history—from African roots and the experience of slavery to revolt and the successful creation of a black republic—into his lexicon of pan-African tropes.

Scale enlargement B, "Hughes, McKay, and Negritude," does not zoom out quite as far as the first or third scale enlargements but rather focuses on Hughes's and McKay's entanglements with the Negritude poets from the French Empire. Léopold Sédar Senghor from Senegal and Léon-Gontran Damas in particular drew heavily on Hughes's primitivist poetry and McKay's raucous celebrations of black embodiment in *Banjo* to affirm the plane of ancestral entanglement among people throughout the black diaspora. Hughes had less sustained contact with the third and arguably the greatest of the Negritude writers, Aimé Césaire of Martinique. Yet in chapter 3, "'It Cancels the Slave Ship!': Aimé Césaire, the Haitian Revolution, and Langston Hughes," I find significant points of resonance between their two bodies of work, especially when we read Césaire's play *The Tragedy of King Christophe* (1963) in light of Hughes's earlier depiction of the Haitian Revolution's aftermath. As in Hughes's play, Césaire's hero makes a tragic mistake in turning his back on the symbols and traditions of his African ancestors and accepting the mental subjugation of the European former colonizers. Césaire furthermore built on the foundations Hughes had laid of a memory and an aesthetic of pan-African entanglement, which in Césaire's case he labeled Negritude. Césaire's vision included, for example, images of an imagined precolonial Africa and narratives from the history of slavery and revolt. He used these primitivist tropes pragmatically and strategically, even if he had some misgivings about doing so. Moreover, the conception of an African-rooted, border-crossing community of black people, which Césaire borrowed and adapted from Hughes and McKay, among others, provided a cohesive platform for carrying on his sustained debate with his former student Frantz Fanon, who dismissed blackness as a unifying category and insisted that only the nation can give a culture "credibility, validity, dynamism, and creativity."[96]

Hughes attempted early on to expand his transatlantic network of black writers beyond the Caribbean, but notwithstanding his occasional correspondence and encounters with Senghor, his efforts to cultivate connections to African intellectuals were often frustrated. It was not until the 1950s that this began to change. By then, Africans whom Hughes knew through Lincoln University (Nnamdi Azikiwe of Nigeria, Kwame Nkrumah of Gold Coast / Ghana) and others he had corresponded with (e.g., Senghor) were gaining prominence first as anticolonial leaders, then as heads of state of newly independent countries. A series of invitations to attend conferences and festivals and to judge contests in Africa and his compiling of multiple anthologies of African writing further entangled him with a rising generation of writers from the continent, as I describe in scale enlargement C, "Langston Hughes and Africa."

The most sustained and important of these connections were to the *Drum* generation of black and mixed-race writers from South Africa. John Walters and I have edited a collection of letters between those writers and Hughes,[97] and I wrote recently about Hughes's connections to and influence on Richard Rive.[98] Chapter 4, "A 'Song of Africa across Oceans and Centuries': Langston Hughes, Negritude, and South Africa," singles out two others of those writers—Peter Abrahams and Es'kia Mphahlele—and studies their different strategies for coping with exile in the larger African diaspora. Both writers—the "coloured" or mixed-race Abrahams, and the black African Mphahlele—began with a skeptical posture toward Negritude, with its tendency to accept, and even embrace, essentialist views of racial similarity. Yet, writing from exile, both South Africans began to adopt the lexicon and repertoire of pan-African entanglement, including those associated with Negritude, especially those tropes derived from the history of slavery. They would, however, end up in different places: Abrahams eventually succumbed to a fatalistic call for defensive self-segregation on the part of black people. Mphahlele, by contrast, developed his philosophy of "African Humanism," which I argue is a more explicitly articulated version of the concentrically organized ethos of entanglement that I am ascribing to Hughes: embedded in African cultural practices and values, but intertwined and in conversation with other cultures, and of universal human relevance and interest.

Hughes delivered his own fullest expression of his ethos and aesthetic of pan-African entanglement in two late works that I study in chapter 5, "Cultural Exchange in *Ask Your Mama*." The first was his autobiography

I Wonder as I Wander (1956), in which he described having found both the primal earthiness and the revolutionary spirit he craved among the gypsies in war-torn Spain and among the peasants in Soviet Central Asia, as well as in Haiti and Cuba. The second was the long poem I have already referred to, *Ask Your Mama: Twelve Moods for Jazz* (1961). In it we see how Hughes's ideas about Africa had evolved since the relatively straightforward primitivism of his poetry from the 1920s. He still evoked images of ancestral Africa through images of drums and bare feet dancing, but these were now shot through with references to anticolonial and postcolonial leaders and writers throughout contemporary Africa. In both texts, and in other nonfiction writings from the same era, Hughes made explicit the need for genuine cultural exchange between the Americas and Africa and simultaneously laid claim to being both an American and a "Negro" in a profoundly transnational sense.

I conclude *Cultural Entanglements* with a coda devoted to Paule Marshall, the only woman writer to feature significantly in my narrative.[99] The American novelist of Barbadian parentage practiced something very similar to Hughes's flexibly concentric ethos and aesthetic of pan-African entanglement. For context, I will look briefly at Marshall's memoir *Triangular Road* (2009), which begins with a chapter on her friendship with and intellectual indebtedness to Langston Hughes. Then I will turn to her novel *Praisesong for the Widow* (1983), which interweaves ancestral kinship, articulated through collectively imagined cultural memory, with the negotiation of contemporary cultural difference, in ways similar to Hughes's writing. But unlike Hughes, *Praisesong* puts the repertoire of women's performances at the center of the exchange and multidirectional understanding. My inclusion of Marshall at the end is intended not as a token gesture of gender inclusion but as a foil to critique Hughes's masculinist model of pan-African entanglement, the weaving of which would only have been enriched by having women artists play more active and dynamic roles in earlier periods.

Nevertheless, Marshall's example allows us to see the profound and enduring influence of Hughes and his efforts at building transnational entanglements among black writers. Just as Hughes devoted himself to documenting the genealogy of great accomplishments by black historical figures, Marshall takes on a similar project and apotheosizes Hughes into the pantheon. In her memoir she continued to hail him as "a kind of West African griot, a tribal elder passing down black American culture and history in an endless wreath of cigarette smoke."[100] In the same memoir, Marshall went on to document her travels in the Caribbean and ended with an account of the Second World Festival of Black and African Arts in Lagos, Nigeria, in 1977. This gathering of writers and artists from across the African continent and the diaspora was precisely the sort of activity Langston Hughes threw himself into in the last ten years of his life. And so the currents of pan-African interconnection that Hughes began to set in motion almost a century before continued to flow outward and find new points of intersection and exchange, opening up spaces for writers from oppressed minorities and colonized territories around the world to write and find audiences for their work.

1 Vernacular Pan-African Entanglements
Langston Hughes and Claude McKay

HUGHES'S FRIENDSHIP with Jamaican poet Claude McKay, and the intertextual relationship between their works, is a surprisingly understudied aspect of both writers' corpora. In fact, I've been able to find almost no criticism that explicitly links the two men and puts their works into conversation with each other's, beyond the general association both writers share with the Harlem Renaissance. This apparent oversight in the scholarship exists despite McKay's significant influence on Hughes's literary practice (McKay was the older writer by twelve and a half years), despite their extensive correspondence with one another, and despite a very similar aesthetic operating in both their writings. This aesthetic of vernacular pan-African entanglement sought to find commonality and to enable identification through the cultural practices of ordinary working and poor black people across Africa and the diaspora.[1] If, as Bruce Robbins claims, Gilroy's *The Black Atlantic* attempted to "salvage the concept of [cosmopolitanism] from its associations with class and Western privilege by demonstrating the existence of a sort of popular, non-Western or nonelite cosmopolitanism,"[2] Hughes and McKay were (at least unconsciously) participating in a similar ethos of xenophilia and curiosity, and in conversation with one another.

My argument in this chapter is that Hughes's relationship with McKay, including his engagement with his novels and poems, was among the earliest and most significant of the multidirectional intellectual entanglements Hughes would cultivate with the black world outside of the United States. McKay too often served as a negative example—never quite resolving the conflicts between universalism and black particularism that bogged down his thinking on race, and prone to sabotaging himself socially with a quick and contrarian temper. Hughes nevertheless learned from the Jamaican writer how, and how not, to reconcile and navigate tensions and contradictions in his cultivation of a black Atlantic literary skein. The ongoing conversations (literal and figurative) between the two writers fed directly into a conception that emerged in their work of global black solidarity grounded simultaneously in peasant cultural practices and in denationalized, gritty urban locales, in the hopes for kinship and in the embrace of difference. The ties linking Hughes and McKay to one another, to Africa, and to the larger black diaspora perfectly exemplify the kind of fruitful and dynamic entanglement that Hughes would later spend the rest of his life cultivating.

Early Entanglements between Hughes and McKay

The paucity of scholarship on the interconnections between Hughes and McKay is surprising, as there is a strong case to be made for reading their works in conversation with each other's, based on a number of parallels between the two: both writers were infamous political radicals early in their careers and made trips to the Soviet Union, where each was treated, in McKay's words, as a "black ikon in the flesh."[3] Both authors later renounced Soviet communism but continued to be haunted throughout their lives by their younger selves' radical writings and associations. McKay and Hughes were also the two anglophone writers who had the most pronounced influence on black internationalism and the Negritude movement in the francophone world, as I will discuss in scale enlargement B and in chapter 3. Finally, parallels might be drawn on the basis of their sexuality: McKay was more or less openly gay, notwithstanding an early marriage in Jamaica to a woman who gave birth to his daughter. Hughes meanwhile never married, and his homosexuality has been asserted or taken for granted by his biographer Faith Berry and many critics.

Such overlaps in their attitudes and life experiences were only strengthened by the mutual influence and extensive direct contact each man had with the other. Arnold Rampersad describes McKay as "the principal influence among blacks on Langston as a young writer."[4] Indeed, in the early 1930s, Hughes called McKay "the greatest living Negro writer in creative literature today"[5] and said that McKay's contributions to the *Liberator* in the late 1910s taught the young Hughes "the revolutionary attitude toward Negroes" and "started me on this track" of writing radical poetry.[6] The two men began corresponding at least as early as 1924, with the earliest surviving contact between them a postcard from McKay dated from September of that year, containing references to some earlier correspondence. Faith Berry notes that during much of the time Hughes spent in Paris in the mid-1920s, his correspondence with McKay was his only "literary" contact in Europe.[7] The correspondence also suggests that Hughes introduced McKay by letter to Charlotte Osgood Mason, their New York patron in common for a time, who instructed the artists on her payroll to call her Godmother. Despite a few failed attempts to meet in Europe, the two did not meet in person until

McKay returned to the United States in the mid-1930s—in fact, McKay lamented in a letter from April 1934, "People I meet here mention you all the time and are very surprised when I tell them that we have never met! I hope we shall soon."[8] McKay, Hughes, and Countee Cullen collaborated years later in the planned editing of a collection of African American poetry, though as Rampersad explains it, the volume was intended mostly as a fund-raiser to benefit McKay after a debilitating stroke in 1943.[9]

The mutual admiration between Hughes and McKay is well documented in their archives. After reading an advance copy of McKay's first novel, *Home to Harlem,* in March 1928, Hughes wrote to him privately: "I was mighty pleased to have your letter and right on the heels of it came your book—which is the most exciting thing in years. Undoubtedly, it is the finest thing 'we've' done yet. And I don't mean limited by the 'we.' It's a very fine novel.... Lord, I love the whole thing. It's so damned real!"[10] McKay in return offered praise, support, and advice for the younger poet; in his earliest surviving letter to Hughes from September 1924, for example, he wrote: "I want to talk to you about your writings. Your stuff seems the most sincere and earnest to me of any that young Afro-America is doing."[11] Hughes sent the senior poet a typed copy of his poem "Broadcast to the West Indies" around 1943, inscribed "For Claude—Sincerely—Langston."[12] After McKay's death, Hughes wrote a list of his "Twelve Favorite Negro Poems" for the Indian magazine *United Asia,* which included McKay's "If We Must Die."[13] When the posthumous *Selected Poems of Claude McKay* was being planned, Hughes wrote an endorsement to Carl Cowl, the administrator of the estate: McKay's lyric poetry, he wrote, "is as gentle and as warm as this famous sonnet ["If We Must Die"] is powerful and angry. Every poem of Claude McKay's is filled with emotion, clear, moving, and beautiful in color and in rhythm."[14]

Hughes and McKay's friendship began through letters; those that survive mostly reside in the Beinecke Library at Yale University, which holds most of both men's papers, but there are large gaps in the archival record. Nevertheless, the conversation is intact enough to see clearly how both writers felt themselves allied in a shared project of giving voice to the voiceless masses of the peasantry, poor workers, and the idle urban poor—especially the black poor. As McKay reports in *A Long Way from Home,* his own earliest patron and mentor, Walter Jekyll, praised his youthful poems because "they sounded like *the articulate consciousness of the peasants.*"[15] McKay used similar language in a letter to praise Hughes's second collection, *Fine Clothes to the Jew,* in 1927: "I seem to find a definite plan of weaving verses out of the common everyday words of the American Negro of today and the *ensemble* is a complete and worthy achievement."[16] Hughes reciprocated this emphasis on the voices of ordinary people in the endorsement for *Home to Harlem* that he sent to McKay's publisher and copied to McKay himself: McKay, he wrote, "makes alive and singing, alive and terrible, the movements of the lower classes at work and at play and at love. Beautiful because it is true and fascinating because it is so vividly alive, this book is, to my mind, the first real flower of the Negro Renaissance."[17] McKay responded, "I am glad you like *Home to Harlem*. My characters are the people you sing about, the people I really love and . . . they were the people I sang about when I was your age!"[18]

McKay is virtually a textbook example of a transnational literary figure whose biography and writings are difficult to slot into national categories and canons. His earliest poems take their themes from his native Jamaica, and many of them are written in Jamaican vernacular dialect, making him an important figure in the history of Caribbean literature. But he left Jamaica for the United States in 1912 at the age of twenty-two and would never again live in the West Indies or write poetry in the Jamaican patois. Partly by virtue of his association with the Harlem Renaissance and the inclusion of his writing in such important anthologies as Alain Locke's *The New Negro*, Langston Hughes and Arna Bontemps's *The Poetry of the Negro*, and David Levering Lewis's *Harlem Renaissance Reader*, McKay is often counted as an honorary African American. But he spent most of the crucial years of the Harlem Renaissance (roughly 1917–29) living not in Harlem but in England, Russia, southern Europe, and northern Africa.

The most profound precedent that McKay set for the younger Hughes, I maintain, was an aesthetic deeply planted both in politics and in the soil of ordinary people's cultural life. Hughes drew vernacular influences from Whitman, Sandburg, and Dunbar as well, but McKay's brand of proletarian art had a demanding political urgency to it that appealed to Hughes the radical sloganeer who would emerge in the 1930s. The defiant political stance McKay took or implied in his writings might well have emerged from his admiration for Russian literature and his engagement with Soviet society, which, as Kate Baldwin notes, "produced theories about using culture not only as a tool of internationalism but also interracialism."[19] Wayne Cooper, in one of his section introductions in *The Passion of Claude McKay*, argues that McKay had a vision of black identity very different from the elitism of Du Bois's belief in the "talented tenth": "McKay pushed forward in his novels and stories the ignorant black folk of farm and city as the potential directors of their own fate. He tried to show that they were the living basis upon which any valid black identity had to be constructed. For McKay, the true exemplars of the race were uprooted but self-sufficient urban drifters."[20] McKay's characters such as Jake, Ray, and Banjo might be seen, then, as direct predecessors and inspirations for Langston Hughes's own uprooted urban drifters such as Jimboy from *Not without Laughter* and the iconic and popular Jesse B. Semple, aka "Simple."

Vernacular Entanglements and Transnational Wanderings

For both writers, using such language and creating such characters was a matter of both artistic authenticity and political urgency. We see this in McKay's remarks to James Weldon Johnson in 1928: "I consider the book [*Home to Harlem*] a real proletarian novel, but I don't expect the nice radicals to see that it is, because they know very little about proletarian life and what they want of proletarian art is not proletarian life, truthfully, realistically, and artistically portrayed."[21] McKay's insistence on depicting the disreputable aspects of proletarian life, then, became a crucial part of his vernacular aesthetic. In that same letter to Johnson, McKay went on to remark, "With the Negro intelligentsia it is a different matter, but between the devil of Cracker prejudice and the deep sea of respectable white condescension I can certainly sympathise, though I cannot agree, with their dislike of the artistic exploitation of low-class Negro life."

McKay and Hughes bonded in their letters over the disapproving responses that their gritty depictions of black urban working-class life (especially in McKay's novels and Hughes's blues poems) received among black intellectuals, coming across as gleeful and resentful in equal measure. Hughes predicted correctly in March 1928 after reading an advance copy of *Home to Harlem*: "It's going to be amusing reading what the colored papers will say about it. They will want to tear you to pieces, I'm sure, but since they used up all their bad words on [Carl Van Vechten's] *Nigger Heaven,* and the rest on me—I don't know what vocabulary they have left for you."[22] On cue, the novel was savaged in print by none other than W. E. B. Du Bois.[23] McKay wrote to Hughes, "I see Du Bois has given me hell in the *Crisis*. If he had praised me, it would have been a greater surprise."[24] Hughes, generally more circumspect than the hotheaded McKay, stayed on somewhat better terms with Du Bois, but he too rejected the professor's elitist brand of Pan-Africanism. Instead, both Hughes and McKay sought to celebrate and facilitate productive cultural entanglement stretching across the African diaspora, not led by groomed elites but arising organically from the lives and practices of the poor and dispossessed. If we think of the great skein of pan-African culture as a kind of organism consisting of veins and arteries, nerves, tendons, tissues, and other intricately entangled parts, then the nomadic vagabonds that both men celebrated through their writings served as figurative arteries, carrying the "blood" of cultural invigoration throughout this global body.

The black intelligentsia in the United States was troubled by how McKay and Hughes set their novels and poems in bars, shacks, and houses of ill repute, as well as by their embrace of vernacular language. Their critics felt that black writers should present black characters in the most flattering light possible, including giving them standard or "proper" English.[25] By contrast, both Hughes and McKay delighted in the disreputable haunts of poor and working-class blacks and in the rhythms and resourcefulness of black dialects. In *My Green Hills of Jamaica,* McKay recalls the period when he was writing poems in the Jamaican patois while working as a constable in Spanish Town: "My association with my comrades seemed to help inspire the writing. . . . Also my comrades and sometimes the peasants going to market, to whom I would read some of them, liked them. They used to exclaim, 'Why they're just like that, they're so natural.' Then I felt that I was fully rewarded for my efforts."[26]

These remarks make clear that McKay saw his experiments with vernacular poetry as a vehicle for maintaining artistic integrity as well as building solidarity with black peasants and workers. This helps explain the criticism he privately leveled against Hughes for so often breaking the unity of a vernacular poem by inserting a more formal line: "That blues thing for instance I thought remarkably good but you should have made the whole of it more colloquial. You bring in some literary words which appear strange in such an atmosphere."[27] At any rate, through the exchange of letters we can see the elder writer consciously inculcating a grassroots, working-class aesthetic in the younger writer from their first exchanges, though of course the willful Hughes often had his own ideas about the forms that proletarian art should take.

It is important to note, though, that their correspondence and mutual reading had a multidirectional and self-reinforcing effect on their vernacular aesthetic of entanglement. McKay's first two novels were written in the latter third of the 1920s, well after Hughes had begun his experiments in blues poetry using vernacular African American dialects and some fifteen years after McKay dropped the Jamaican patois from his poetry and reverted to more orthodox verse forms. His characters' thick vernacular dialects in *Home to Harlem* (1928) and *Banjo* (1929), then, might be seen as a reversion to the vernacular forms he explored in his youthful poetry. If calling Hughes an influence on the elder writer might be overstating the case, McKay certainly wrote those novels aware that Hughes had helped establish certain literary precedents and possibilities when it came to using such registers of African American speech and also certainly aware that he and Hughes would be categorized together as the bad boys of the Harlem Renaissance.

With both writers, it is difficult to extricate their shared vision of an art for the uprooted proletariat from their own restless temperaments and nomadic impulses. In fact, their shared preference for visiting poor and working-class areas in their travels was another point of early bonding, as when McKay wrote to Hughes in 1928 wishing that the latter would visit Marseille: "[Alain] Locke told me when he came to Toulon that you had some of my taste for low-down places, so I think we could knock around without getting on each other's nerves."[28] McKay even began his autobiography by describing a "lust to wander and wonder. The spirit of the vagabond, the daemon of some poets, had got hold of me."[29] The title of Hughes's second autobiography, *I Wonder as I Wander,* exploited the same homophonic pun (with both of them probably borrowing from the title of John Jacob Niles's popular Christian folk hymn from 1933), and Hughes's title likewise implied the sort of purposeless migration that Glissant describes as "errantry" or "circular nomadism."[30] It is through their separate wanderings that the writers began to imagine or "wonder" into existence a shared vision of a collective black transnational identity, rooted in the black poor, laboring, and unemployed classes—a phenomenon that Edwards, in the context of McKay's *Banjo,* calls "vagabond internationalism" but might be productively recast as vagabond entanglements.[31] This burgeoning identity provided flexibility and cultural mobility at a time when technology and bureaucratic state apparatuses made it more difficult than in earlier periods to lead a nomadic life in the interstices of the nation.

McKay's peripatetic life, indeed, was driven in large part by a fundamentally internationalist outlook and cosmopolitan temperament—in other words, an ethos of transnational entanglement—which he saw as standing in explicit opposition to national loyalties. McKay expressed this opposition through, for example, his fictional alter ego Ray in the novel *Banjo:* "The sentiment of patriotism was not one of Ray's possessions, perhaps because he was a child of deracinated ancestry. To him it was a poisonous seed. . . . It seemed a most unnatural thing to him for a man to love a nation."[32] McKay in his own voice laid claim to similar feelings in *A Long Way from Home* when he recounted a conversation with a native messenger from the British consulate in Marseille, who asked if McKay was American: "I said I was born in the West Indies and lived in the United States and that I was an American, even though I was a British subject, but I preferred to think of myself as an internationalist. The *chaoush* said he didn't understand what was an internationalist. I laughed and said that an internationalist was a bad nationalist."[33] In a 1929 letter to his French agent, McKay expressed a similar reluctance to be identified with any particular nation's literature: "I don't want to be a one hundred percent American, nor a patriotic British subject, not, (worst fate of all) un ami de France—in literature I want to be myself."[34]

Banjo reveals a number of reasons why a "wandering black without patriotic or family ties"[35] might resent being tied to a national identity, intertwined as such an identity was with a growingly complex and restrictive state bureaucracy. The narrator describes black and brown people being denied entry to the United Kingdom "so that white men should have their jobs."[36] The novel dramatizes how modern bureaucratic methods begin to control human migration through passports, visas, and such designations as "Nationality Doubtful." Far from making possible a great utopian grassroots cosmopolitanism, then, the era between the wars as McKay depicts it saw an encroachment of forced national identities on a nomadic class of people that in previous eras had been allowed to lead, "in the great careless tradition,"[37] more truly cosmopolitan lives emphasizing routes and journeys rather than roots and places.[38] Even as twentieth century technologies began to accelerate processes of global cultural exchange and contamination, they also limited the ability of people lacking wealth and privilege to live nomadic lives free of bureaucratic ties to modern national identity.

Spaces of Transnational Entanglement

Driven by his view of the nation as a confining force for social control rather than as a locus of political mobilization or staging ground for a literary career, McKay found himself drawn all the more powerfully to spaces of transnational entanglement. This helps confirm Mbembe's claim that "the processes of identity formation were shaped by the same logic that governed the institution of borders and the social struggles linked to their constitution. It was a logic of networks that operated according to the principle of entanglement."[39] Mbembe's remark helps explain McKay's admiration for New York, especially Harlem, made up as it was of black people from throughout the African diaspora:

> Harlem is the queen of black belts, drawing Aframericans together into a vast humming hive. They have swarmed in from the different states, from the islands of the Caribbean and from Africa. . . . Harlem is more than the Negro capital of the nation. It is the Negro capital of the world. And as New York is the most glorious experiment on earth of different races and diverse groups of humanity struggling and scrambling to live together, so Harlem is the most interesting sample of black humanity marching along with white humanity.[40]

In such places, the vernacular languages and traditions of the American South, the West Indies, and Africa are all uprooted and set afloat in the international cultural space of the black Atlantic, where they serve as testament to black people's inclusion in modernity.

We find an echo of McKay's proud recognition of Harlem's pluralistic and transnational character in Langston Hughes's 1951 poem "Good Morning," whose speaker describes the growth of Harlem's black population, as they poured out of

> planes from Puerto Rico,
> and holds of boats, chico,
> up from Cuba Haiti Jamaica,
> in buses marked New York
> from Georgia Florida Louisiana.[41]

In the imagery of black West Indians rushing onto the docks, we find yet another incarnation of Gilroy's chronotope of the ship, updated to include airplanes and motor buses as other vehicles for mobility and cultural exchange. But if the ship is the channel through which transnational circuits are routed, Harlem (that "dusky sash across Manhattan")[42] is a uniquely powerful crucible for forging a border-crossing black identity where none existed in the isolated locales from which each group migrated.

Yet McKay depicted his own Caribbean as similarly cosmopolitan and polyglot: despite having found Jamaica "too small for high achievement,"[43] later in life he recalled the island from his childhood not as a melting pot but as a garden of wildflowers: "Chinese, or East Indians, mulattoes and Negroes who had arisen to the position where they could take part in the management of the island's affairs. In spite of its poverty, *my island of Jamaica was like a beautiful garden in human relationships*. . . . We all grew up together like wild flowers."[44] McKay similarly valued the Kingston of his childhood for embodying transnational entanglement:

> Besides the big buildings, there were the fishermen's boats and the foreign ships in the harbour. The ships were of all kinds, the native sailing boats which were used to catch the fish around the coast, besides the steamships which came in from foreign ports with their flags swaying in the wind. There were ships from the United States, Panama, Cuba, Canada, South America, Germany and Britain. Kingston, Jamaica, was an important port of call in the West Indies, so ships from all over were attracted there. As I thought of the places from which those ships came, I wondered if I would ever have a chance to visit them.[45]

This ship's inevitable associations with slavery and the Middle Passage have slipped far into the background; as remembered through his eyes as a child, McKay instead associated the ships with mobility and liberation from national and provincial boundaries. The same association runs through Hughes's *The Big Sea,* where he described himself as a young man attempting to jettison the past by setting off to sea and throwing overboard his books, which "seemed too much like everything I had known in the past."[46] For a while in the mid-1920s Hughes lived a denationalized existence, working on boats and scrounging on the shores and in the cities of Europe. He lived, in short, the life of vagabond internationalism that he and McKay wrote about.

McKay's fascination with docks and similar spaces of transnational entanglement is strikingly evident in his depictions of mongrel, polyglot Marseille. In a 1927 letter to Hughes, he wrote: "Marseille I really love more than any place in France. It is the most vivid port I ever touched. Wonderful, dirty, unbeautiful, rolling in slime and color and hourly interest. *There all the scum of the sea seems to drift on to natural soil.* I love it more than any of the English American or German ports."[47] The phrasing here associates Marseille's transnational black community—the "scum of the sea," a phrase that emphasizes the humble and ordinary people at its foundation—with the globe-spanning seas and oceans, an association he would return to in *A Long Way from Home:* "It was a relief to get to Marseille, to live in among a great gang of black and brown humanity. Negroids from the United States, the West Indies, North Africa and West Africa, all herded together in a warm group."[48] Some were dockworkers or sailors, while "others were waiting for ships—all wedged in between the old port and the breakwater, among beachcombers, guides, procurers, prostitutes of both sexes and *bistro* bandits—all of motley-making Marseille, swarming, scrambling and scraping sustenance from the bodies of ships and crews."[49] Like Marseille itself, McKay's alliteration—the recurring use of *B, M,* and *S* sounds in this sentence—creates unity out of chaotic and "motley" pluralism and helps braid these disparate groups together in the reader's mind. It is important that McKay finds a community with a strong group identity in this most denationalized of places, where belonging is determined by racial identification rather than by citizenship or place of birth. Such a community is inevitably transient, but that transience works to its advantage, as it inhibits the privileging of racial similarity from becoming entrenched and discriminatory, as it might in a racial nationalist state, for example.

Hughes, like McKay, was fascinated by docks, ports, and beaches. He devoted several chapters of his autobiographies to scenes set on docks and beaches: "Haunted Ship," "Beachcomber," and parts of the Africa chapters in *The Big Sea,* for example, and "Official Delegation" in *I Wonder,* wherein he recounts his meeting with Jacques Roumain while aboard a ship waiting to leave the dock. For McKay and Hughes alike, ports and beaches figure significantly as liminal spaces where nationality and immigration status fade into background and also as vectors for international encounter where African Americans, West Indians, West Africans, and North Africans all blend together into a new black collectivity. The docks are thus a corollary to Gilroy's trope of ships, which he claims "immediately focus attention on the middle passage, on the various projects for redemptive return to an African homeland, on the circulation of ideas and activists as well as the movement of key cultural and political artefacts: tracts, books, gramophone records, and choirs."[50] The docks, then, are the points of intersection between this nomadic and oceanic "space" of the ship and the seemingly more fixed spaces of city and nation; they are the narrows through which multiple channels must pass, becoming entangled in the process.

Nationalism, Modernism, Primitivism

My premise throughout this book is that the ethos of concentric entanglement that Hughes helped cultivate and that guided his career considered national loyalties or identification to be compatible with other scales of fellow feeling, including the familial, the racial, and the universal. Nevertheless, the first half of the twentieth century tested this view. It saw the encroachment of technologies and bureaucratic apparatuses that increasingly tried to fix individuals within a national identity, a fixity that continually threatened to impinge on the freedom associated with the docks and beaches. Indeed, both writers regarded the institutions of national sovereignty with ambivalence at best, and at worst as de facto prisons for black people denied full citizenship to those nations.

This negative perception of modern urban life was part of a larger movement, which we might call "modern primitivism" and to which McKay subscribed.[51] In the realm of visual and plastic arts, it included Picasso's African period and the vogue for the works of Paul Gauguin in the early twentieth century and arguably reached its pinnacle in the English-speaking world with the translation of Paul Guillaume's *Primitive Negro Sculpture* in 1926. In the anglophone literary world, perhaps its most influential practitioner was D. H. Lawrence, whom both Hughes and McKay admired, and whose fiction frequently put in rhetorical opposition a wild and atavistic life force versus a cold, oppressive modernity.[52] To cast this in my terminology of cultural entanglements, modern primitivism marked an important shift in Western discourse. At that moment, arguably for the first time, art and culture from Africa and other putatively primitive places were taken seriously as contributions to the skein of modern world culture. European and American primitivism could be condescending and appropriative,[53] but it at least acknowledged that the margins of global power had cultural practices worth appropriating.

One thing that some black artists and intellectuals found liberating or illuminating in modern primitivism was the challenge it posed to Western civilization's claims to embody universal humanity and principles of freedom. Accordingly, the speaker of McKay's "In Bondage," originally published in 1920, locates freedom in a distant past and associates life in the West with the "bondage" of the title: he spends the first three quatrains of the sonnet longing nostalgically for "distant fields / Where man, and bird, and beast, lives leisurely."[54] Such evocations of a lost paradise run through McKay's poetry of the early 1920s, with references for example to the "dead past" in "Heritage"[55] and the turn at the end of "Africa" in which he calls the apostrophized continent "the harlot, now thy time is done, / Of all the mighty nations of the sun."[56] Like the speaker of Hughes's "Lament for Dark Peoples," who complains that "They drove me out of the forest,"[57] the speaker of McKay's "In Bondage" turns in the closing couplet from fantasies of a land "Where life is fairer, lighter, less demanding," to the contemporary plight of black people in the Americas: "But I am bound with you in your mean graves, / O black men, simple slaves of ruthless slaves."[58]

The words "simple" and "mean," connoting average or mundane, reveal McKay's eager alliance with the poorest and humblest of his race, where he most easily discovered sparks of the primitive that he found so rejuvenating. Take for example the moment in *Banjo* when the narrator lingers romantically on the black sailors, soldiers, pimps, prostitutes, and beachcombers who populate the *Vieux Port* area of Marseille: "Black youth close to the bush and the roots of jungle trees, trying to live the precarious life of the poisonous orchids of civilization."[59] Such examples make me question the extent to which the patronage of the English expatriate Walter Jekyll *forced* McKay in his earliest vernacular poetry, as Heather Hathaway claims, "to perform the primitive if he wanted to be taken seriously as a poet by the friend and critic he most admired."[60] In his novels and later poems, McKay continued to find both gratification and utility in the idea that the residents of the modern black diaspora—the "despised, oppressed, / Enslaved and lynched"[61]—were entangled with ancient Africa and "bound with" their "simple slave" ancestors through a shared essence and common history.

The same opposition between the warm African past and the cold, harsh Western present runs through Hughes's poetry of the 1920s. See for example the speakers of "Poem [1]," who is "afraid of this civilization";[62] of "Lament for Dark Peoples," who feels "caged . . . In the circus of civilization";[63] and of "Afraid," who says, "We cry among the skyscrapers."[64] Knowing furthermore that Hughes read many of the poems from McKay's *Harlem Shadows* when they were first published in *The Liberator* between 1920 to 1922, it makes sense to see them as precedent and inspiration for Hughes's own evocations of ancient Africa, as in "Danse Africaine," where the "slow beating of the tom-toms . . . / Stirs your blood,"[65] and "Poem [1]," which includes the epigraph "For the portrait of an African boy after the manner of Gauguin," and which likewise evokes tom-toms and jungle moons.[66] In short, Hughes's early poems, like McKay's writings from the same era, consistently imagine Africa as both spiritual homeland and as antidote to the harsh alienation of living as a black man under Western civilization.

Many critics have regarded Hughes's primitivism of the late 1920s as solely a response to Godmother's shaping and censoring of his writing. Charlotte Osgood Mason had an "obsession with primitive purity" and urged the recipients of her patronage to "slough off white culture" and instead to listen to the "harmony flowing toward you from the Souls of the Slaves from Africa."[67] She considered Hughes her "most precious child,"[68] and for three years he was able to work within her primitivist constraints and prescriptions to advance his own burgeoning ethos of pan-African entanglement. But the relationship collapsed over Godmother's disapproval of the more topical and overtly antiracist content of his novel *Not without Laughter.*

The importance of this break to Hughes's sense of self and his career as a writer is reflected in the fact that he ended *The Big Sea* by narrating his estrangement from his godmother and began his second autobiography, *I Wonder as I Wander,* at the same point. By way of explaining the end of her patronage, he wrote in *The Big Sea:* "She wanted me to be primitive and know and feel the intuitions of the primitive. But, unfortunately, I did not feel the rhythms of the primitive surging through me, and so I could not live and write as though I did. I was only an American Negro—who had loved the surface of Africa and the rhythms of Africa—but I was not Africa. I was Chicago and Kansas City and Broadway and Harlem. And I was not what she wanted me to be."[69] The "unfortunately" in the second sentence is not wholly ironic—a tinge of genuine sadness and rue pervaded Hughes's recognition of his basically urban character, here and elsewhere. Having been "contaminated" by modernity and civilization, he demanded that he and other African Americans be recognized as belonging to that modernity, and he rejected any reduction to the "intuitions of the primitive." Even so, he lamented feeling cut off from an African origin he could find only traces of in the fragments of African cultural life surviving among the descendants of slaves in the rural United States, Cuba, and Haiti, as well as among the refugees from the Great Migration out of the South to Harlem and other northern cities. Ironically, he mitigated his sense of existential uprootedness by nevertheless representing—and to some extent commodifying—the cultural practices of poor black people. That is, he presumed to speak for people whose situation he did not share and whose instincts he did not feel but who often lacked the literacy to represent themselves in Western discourses.

After losing Godmother's patronage, Hughes's relationship with modern primitivism was fraught. He caustically satirized it in the story "Slave on the Block" (1933) through the Carraways, a white couple who "went in for Negroes. . . . But not in the social-service, philanthropic sort of way, no. . . . Leave them unspoiled and just enjoy them, Michael and Anne felt. So they went in for the Art of Negroes—the dancing that had such jungle life about it, the songs that were so simple and fervent, the poetry that was so direct, so real."[70] Critics have often assumed, then, that Hughes abandoned and rejected primitivist themes and rhetoric after 1930.[71] I agree with Chinitz,[72] however, that Hughes continued throughout his life to feel drawn on some level to the notion of a primitivist essence of blackness and never fully gave up the tropes and imagery associated with that notion. Consider for example the speaker of "The Negro Mother" (ca. 1932), who claims, "I am the child they stole from the sand / Three hundred years ago in Africa's land."[73] The rhetorical effect of asserting continuity among blacks throughout history—an assertion we will see later in the works of Senghor and Césaire, for example—is further enabled by the poetic conceit of using first-person pronouns to speak for blacks throughout time. Hughes used this device regularly from "The Negro Speaks of Rivers" onward, and though we will see its use grow more complex and layered in his later poetry, the use of "we" or "I" as the disembodied voice of pan-African entanglement persists throughout his career.

Ancestral Pan-African Entanglements

Such assertions of continuity and kinship with the poet's African ancestors were necessary precisely because the cultures of those uprooted ancestors were in fact lost in the mists of time. One function of the black poet's work, as Hughes and McKay conceived it in common, was to help imagine into existence a skein of ancestral entanglement between black people in the diaspora and those in Africa, thus forming the foundation for future entanglements and growth within the pan-African community. But neither proffered illusions about any restoration of past unity. When he first visited Africa in 1923–24, rather than an idyll of palm trees and tom-toms, Hughes found a continent enslaved by colonialism, and he realized that his ship was there "to carry away the treasures of Africa."⁷⁴ More important than his disappointment at the squalor and desperation he encountered, though, Hughes found his feelings of kinship rejected by the Africans he did meet because of his lighter skin tone: "But there was one thing that hurt me a lot when I talked with the people. The Africans looked at me and would not believe I was a Negro."⁷⁵ Later he asks a Kru companion to take him to see a Ju-Ju ceremony, but the Kru man refuses because "white man never go see Ju-Ju."⁷⁶

Hughes's partial disillusionment with or estrangement from Africa is reflected in his poetry from the late 1920s, such as "Afro-American Fragment" (1930):

> So long,
> So far away
> Is Africa.
> Not even memories alive.⁷⁷

Even in protest poems like "Johannesburg Mines" (1925), the African people who were subject to exploitation by European colonialism appear as faceless statistics whose reality his poetry is powerless to convey, much less change: after declaring the existence of 240,000 people laboring in the mines, the speaker asks:

> What kind of poem
> Would you
> Make out of that?⁷⁸

Hughes's direct encounter with Africa as a young man, in short, restrained but did not dispel a romantic belief in kinship among all people of African descent.⁷⁹ Such images would continue to appear in his writings throughout his life, even as he worked with increasing purpose to navigate and accommodate difference.

McKay, too, wrestled with ambivalence and inconsistency over his understanding of race, blackness, and primitive instinct. There were times when he seemed to reject racial categorizations outright, as when he took the Marxist line on the primacy of class over race in a 1921 article: "I see no other way of upward struggle for colored peoples, but the way of the working-class movement, ugly and harsh though some of its phases may be. . . . The yearning of the American Negro especially, can only find expression and realization in the class struggle. Therein lies his hope."⁸⁰ A few years later, he wrote to Langston Hughes that he was rewriting the novel that became *Home to Harlem*: "It was bad as a novel—no form to it and I didn't want to publish a novel by 'a Negro poet.' I wanted to publish a novel."⁸¹

Such reluctance to be thought of purely in terms of his blackness persisted throughout McKay's life. But this existed alongside "the fierce, unswerving loyalty he demonstrated toward the 'common people' of his race, a loyalty that amounted at times to an incipient black nationalism that seemed to contradict other aspects of his thought."[82] In *A Long Way from Home* McKay acknowledged: "Color-consciousness was the fundamental of my restlessness. . . . For all their knowledge and sophistication, [the white expatriates] couldn't understand *the instinctive and animal and purely physical pride of a black person* resolute in being himself and yet living a simple civilized life like themselves."[83] When the narrator of *Banjo* declares a link between black youth and "the bush and the roots of jungle trees,"[84] he seems to go even further in buying into pure racial essentialism. We might say the same of the scene in *Home to Harlem* when two women fight naked in a Harlem courtyard: "An old custom, *perhaps a survival of African tribalism*, had been imported from some remote West Indian hillside into a New York back yard."[85] Yet the word "survival" could also imply that similarities among black people across the African diaspora might be a product of history and cultural persistence rather than intrinsic qualities attributable to the essence of blackness.

Adding to the difficulty of pinning down McKay's views on race, such nuanced ideas did emerge from his nonfiction writings. In *A Long Way from Home,* for example, he developed a seemingly very modern conception of race and blackness as choices rather than as inborn traits: "To me a [fair-skinned] type like Walter White is Negroid simply because he closely identifies himself with the Negro group—just as a Teuton becomes a Moslem if he embraces Islam."[86] Hughes, too, offered an ironic commentary on race through such short stories as "Passing" (1934) and "Who's Passing for Who?" (1952), making it clear that racial identification was a matter of self-identification and performance rather than any intrinsic and essential properties of one's ancestry. These views seem to be in tension with their claims elsewhere to an ancestral plane of pan-African connection, but such tensions often result when a tangle of similarities and negotiated differences becomes a hopeless knot. And if Hughes sometimes got himself knotted up in paradoxes of kinship and difference, McKay was even more prone to tying himself in rhetorical knots.

Both men, when pushed on the question of racial determinism outside the poetic license afforded by their literary writings, often came down on the side of blackness as a cultural and historical construct rather than a biological essence. The resulting conception of racial identity as something pliable and subject to choice and revision also facilitated linkages with people of other races and ethnic groupings, confirming the nonexclusive nature of pan-African entanglement. McKay wrote to Nancy Cunard from Morocco in 1931, "I feel close to the Moors and have a profound sympathy for certain features of their social life." He likewise said of the people of Spain that they have "big moments of spontaneous joy that I've never noticed among any other people excepting Negroes."[87] The same impulse to highlight similarity and assert analogies drove McKay's criticism of Langston Hughes's articles "published in the Negro press" about the Spanish Civil War, which he otherwise declared "excellent": "In none of those articles did I discover any significant reference to the native problem of North Africa and its relation to the Spanish Civil War. How many Americans are aware that the native North African problem is similar in some aspects to the Afro-American problem in the South?"[88]

Indeed, McKay's thinking about group identity, driven by an incipient ethos of transnational entanglement, was most fruitful not when it sought to define blackness through exclusion or opposition to other groups but rather did so through similarity and comparison to the plight of other peoples in analogous circumstances, as in the above passages. Incidentally, this is a rhetorical move Langston Hughes made with increasing frequency in his later writings, especially in *I Wonder as I Wander,* where he continually drew parallels between blacks in the United States and people he encountered on his travels to Spain, Central Asia, Japan, and elsewhere. McKay's similar impulse to find kinship and similarity in his travels and encounters with others helps explain his "frustrations with divisions and limitations that are imposed by categorical assumptions based on race, ethnicity, nationality, or political conviction."[89]

Notwithstanding those frustrations, McKay himself often made categorical assumptions about African ancestry that sometimes bordered on the mystical and easily resorted to the essentializing language of roots and blood. In *Banjo,* we see such language in the description of a dance from Martinique that the narrator notes is identical to dances in the United States, Jamaica, and Senegal: "'Beguin,' 'jelly-roll,' 'burru,' 'bombé,' no matter what the name may be, Negroes are never so beautiful and magical as when they do that gorgeous sublimation of the primitive African sex feeling. In its thousand varied patterns, depending so much on individual rhythm, so little on formal movement, this dance is key to the African rhythm of life."[90] Here, it seems, what links people across Africa and its diaspora is not the persistence of cultural practice and collective memory but something much more instinctual and felt—the "primitive African sex feeling" and the "African rhythm of life" seem to be at the root of whatever transnational black collectivity might be formed through music and dance.

Indeed, *roots* were the operative trope shaping McKay's views of the African past and the black American present, just as Hughes regarded black spirituals as being *rooted* in African songs, as the extended metaphor in one 1927 poem suggests: "The branches rise / From the firm roots of trees."[91] Similarly, McKay's fictional alter ego Ray in *Banjo* posits the need for black group identity growing out of "native roots": "Getting down to our native roots and building up from our own people . . . is not savagery. It is culture."[92] He continues: "You're a lost crowd, you educated Negroes, and you will only find yourself in the roots of your own people."[93] In *A Long Way*, McKay suggests that the sinking of cultural roots should be the basis of any poet's literary practice, when he writes that with all the poets he admires, "in their poetry I could feel their race, their class, their roots in the soil, growing into plants, spreading and forming the backgrounds against which they were silhouetted."[94]

McKay's Ethos of Transnational Entanglements

In trying to understand how this preoccupation with finding one's racial roots could exist side by side in McKay's writing with the more rationalist and scientific understanding of race noted earlier, I am tempted to invoke what Gayatri Spivak calls a "*strategic* use of positivist essentialism in a scrupulously visible political interest."[95] Yet strategic essentialism more closely describes the self-aware approaches of Aimé Césaire and the older Langston Hughes, as I will argue in later chapters. The passages above from *A Long Way from Home* and *Banjo*, by contrast, suggest a close link in McKay's mind between poetry/music/art and racial personality or instinct: he seemed to *feel* a sense of racial belonging. Such a belief in a bodily connection through blood and ancestry would seem to be in conflict with the idea that racial identity can be chosen. But ultimately both beliefs were manifestations of his attempts to establish racial kinship on an ancestral plane—that is, to spin a narrative of a shared black heritage and history.

This worldview that appreciated and embraced intercultural connections drove him in the 1920s to embrace the cause of international communism—first getting involved in "the nest of extreme radicalism in London"[96] around Sylvia Pankhurst and the *Workers' Dreadnought* and then paying an extended visit to postrevolutionary Russia—before eventually becoming a vocal critic of Soviet dogmatism and authoritarianism.[97] At the end of his life he converted to Catholicism, another institution with global scope and aspirations, as "a bulwark against the menace of Communism."[98] Here too some might think these conversions are contradictory and symptoms of intellectual incoherence, but I see them rather as expressions of an instinctive ethos of transnational entanglement.

The contortions that McKay put himself through in trying to reconcile the universal and the racial scales of entanglement (without quite realizing that was what he was doing) were perhaps most clearly visible in his ever-changing, often contradictory views of Marcus Garvey. In *Workers' Dreadnought* in 1920, McKay wrote with cautious approval about the Jamaican orator and labor leader turned businessman and icon of black self-empowerment and the organization he founded, the Universal Negro Improvement Association: "Although an international Socialist, I am supporting [Garvey's] movement, for I believe that, for subject peoples, at least, Nationalism is the open door to Communism."[99] Two years later his take was rather more jaundiced when he wryly titled an article in the *Liberator* "Garvey as a Negro Moses": Garvey's "spirit is revolutionary, but his intellect does not understand the significance of modern revolutionary developments. Maybe he chose not to understand; he may have realized that a resolute facing of facts would make puerile his beautiful schemes for the redemption of the continent of Africa."[100] By the time McKay published *A Long Way from Home* in 1937, he was bemused by Garvey's influence: "A West Indian charlatan came to this country, full of antiquated social ideas; yet within a decade he aroused the social consciousness of the Negro masses more than any leader ever did. When Negroes really desire a new group orientation they will create it."[101] Finally, in his 1940 book on Harlem, McKay discussed Garvey as the "peacock-parading Negro of the New World"[102] but nevertheless expressed grudging admiration for the way that Garvey stirred "Negroes of all classes . . . to a finer feeling of racial consciousness."[103] Given his own battles with the black literati in the United States, it is unsurprising that McKay also sympathized with Garvey for the "intellectual Negro's hostility to and criticism of Garvey."[104]

Langston Hughes, by contrast, had surprisingly little to say on the subject of Garvey. One of the few comments he committed to print appeared in his chapter in *The Big Sea* on Africa, and it is especially telling that it appears just before his complaint about not being received as a "Negro" among the Africans he encountered: "At that time, 1923, the name of Marcus Garvey was known the length and breadth of the West African Coast of Africa. And the Africans did not laugh at Marcus Garvey, as so many people laughed in New York. They hoped what they had heard about him was true—that he really would unify the black world, and free and exalt Africa."[105] For Hughes, then, as for Claude McKay, Garvey's value lay in his efforts to bring about black unity; Garvey seemed to follow his own ethos of pan-African entanglement. Those efforts consisted not just in elevating the racial consciousness of black people but also in building institutions, publications, and organizations for achieving both material uplift and cultural enrichment for black people throughout the diaspora.

If McKay and Hughes admired any part of Garvey's legacy, then, it was likely to be his efforts to cultivate such institutions of black empowerment and interconnection. Unlike Garvey's emphasis on black-owned businesses, however, or Du Bois's efforts to establish a Pan-African community of political leaders and intellectuals, Hughes and McKay focused their efforts on building cultural institutions and networks that could contribute to a black Atlantic literary counterestablishment, which could serve in turn as incubator and outlet for a transnational black aesthetic. I have already discussed Hughes's lifelong efforts to promote the work of black writers, as editor, anthologist, columnist, and translator, among other capacities. McKay likewise served as editor, first of the *Liberator* in New York and then of the *Workers' Dreadnought* in London. And he participated in an incipient group called the Negro Writers' Guild in the late 1930s, a "democratic association of Negro writers" that he thought "would be beneficial to all our writers and especially to those younger and potential ones who may look to the older for inspiration."[106] He launched these latter efforts soon after he publicly denounced the League of American Writers, affiliated with the American Communist Party. As McKay turned more decisively away from international communism as a means toward a transnational black community, it seems, he turned his attention instead to creating or nurturing institutions such as writers' guilds that could in theory provide similar opportunities for fostering creative art.

McKay often effectively sabotaged his efforts by being moody, contrarian, and individualist. But his commitment to such unifying cultural work is unquestionable. He wrote to James Weldon Johnson in 1934, "I am certain that Negroes will have to realize themselves as an organized group to get anything. Wherever I travelled I observed that the people who were getting anywhere and anything were those who could realize the strength of their cultural group, their political demands were considered and determined by the force of their cultural grouping."[107] Skeptical of what he saw as the cautious conservatism of the NAACP, McKay lamented the absence of any kind of group consciousness among black people. Three years later his autobiography would echo this argument: "When you have your own group, your own voting strength, you can make demands on the whites.... Every other racial group in America is organized as a group, except Negroes."[108] That same year, McKay published an article in the *Jewish Frontier* lauding various ethnic groups within the American "melting pot," especially "the Jewish group," for "building up themselves fraternally, culturally, politically and economically as groups [while] contributing their special part to the greatness of the American nation as a whole."[109] This is as close as McKay ever came to reconciling national identity formations (which he had previously distrusted so strenuously) with the imperative to cultivate entanglement and fellow feeling with distant cultures, including the culture of one's ancestors. In positing a place for a cohesive black identity group within the larger United States, McKay thus began to conceive of identity in terms of concentric circles rather than zero-sum oppositions, a model that would become centrally important to Hughes's vision of pan-African entanglement in later years.

We can see McKay thinking about the possibilities of a productive pan-African web of interconnections in *A Long Way from Home*. He dwelt, for example, on education policy and curriculum and forcefully argued that lessons for black children should include such major black figures as the Arabic poet Antar: "The Negro child, born into an inferior position in the overwhelming white world . . . should know something of the Antar who was born a slave, who fought for his liberation, who loved so profoundly, passionately and chastely that his love inspired and uplifted him to be one of the poets of the Arabian pleiades."[110] The creation of a transatlantic black history that McKay proposes is akin to Hughes's didactic project in poems like "Prelude to Our Age" (which I discussed in my introduction) and "Ballad of Negro History," where he took great pains to document the accomplishments of black writers throughout the ages.

I thus depart on one small point with Edwards, who reads a conscious critique of black internationalism into, for example, *Banjo*'s "stark performance of linguistic difference."[111] Edwards is right that McKay's novel shows us "the ways that black internationalism is necessarily haunted by difference," and he is correct furthermore in claiming that *Banjo*'s musical passages "are the closest the book comes to espousing any form of black internationalism," through the trope of the jazz orchestra.[112] I would argue, though, that McKay did deeply desire a transnational black collectivity and see it as necessary to the survival of black people everywhere, even as he glumly recognized the obstacles to achieving it.[113] Moreover, I believe we have to emphasize Hughes and McKay's shared belief in the power of music to translate difference and facilitate cultural exchange. Furthermore, McKay regularly insisted throughout his career on the necessity of group identity for black people, and his efforts in that regard were tireless, if sometimes self-defeating.

That project required Hughes and McKay to engage in a dialectical shuttling between similarity and difference and between particularity and universality. Those dialectics increasingly shaped McKay's subject matter and his aesthetic, manifesting as a strategy of hybridity and creolization.

Consider for example his essay "A Negro Writer to His Critics," published in 1932: "I am as conscious of my new-world birthright as of my African origin, being aware of the one and its significance in my development as much as I feel the other emotionally. . . . The Aframerican may gain spiritual benefits by returning in *spirit* to this African origin, but as an artist he will remain a unique product of Western Civilization, with something of himself to give that will be very different from anything that may come out of a purely African community."[114] McKay here discussed both African and Western cultures as founts of raw material for cultural production and exchange. The implication is that blacks in the Americas were not endowed with any pure essence of African originality but were instead hybrid and mixed. This notion made it possible to recognize and valorize cultural differences within the pan-African world while still asserting a deeper entanglement linking it all together. We see this dialectic at work in a letter McKay wrote to his agent in 1927, describing the real-world inspiration for the Marseille bar owned by the Senegalese man that was the setting for many scenes in *Banjo*: "The Negroes around dance there every night. It is very amusing to remark the difference between the Senegalese, the Martinquan, and the American negroes."[115] McKay's instinctive ethos of pan-African entanglement impelled him both to appreciate and to bridge such differences, which profoundly shaped the form and content of his literature, especially his novels.

Commodification of Cultural Exchange

While the aestheticization of cultural particularities within the larger pan-African world was intended to valorize and celebrate them, it also had the effect of *commodifying* the very cultures for which they were trying to earn recognition. McKay confirms Gilroy's argument that cultural exchange was inseparable from commercial or commodity exchange, which in turn was inseparable from the sea. McKay wrote in his autobiography that his decision to leave Jamaica in 1912 was motivated by "the dominant desire to find a bigger audience. . . . There, one was isolated, cut off from *the great currents of life.*"[116] The ocean currents metaphor for the international circulation of cultural commodities suggests that what McKay longed for as a young man was what Bruce Robbins calls "feeling global," or Freud's "feeling as of something limitless, unbounded—as it were, 'oceanic.'"[117] Ironically for a one-time communist, McKay came closest to fulfilling his need for this feeling when he witnessed the great capitalist exchange of raw materials and commodity goods. Life on the Marseille docks as he described it centered on the coming and going of trade goods: "The eternal harvest of the world on the docks. African hard wood, African rubber, African ivory, African skins. Asia's gifts of crisp fragrant leaves and the fabled old spices with grain and oil and iron. All floated through the oceans into the warm Western harbor where, waiting to be floated back again, were the Occident's gifts."[118]

Cultural exchange across the world's oceans, such as we see happening within the blended community of vagabonds, dockworkers, and sailors in Marseille, was part of "this great commerce of all the continents"[119] that McKay described with such surprisingly warm and positive tropes ("harvest," "gifts") and also found a metaphor for itself in the exchange of goods. As Paul Jay observes, "One of the central points of globalization studies in the humanities is that cultural forms (literary narrative, cinema, television, live performance, etc.) are commodities.... We can no longer make a clear distinction between exchanges that are purely material and take place in an economy of commodities and exchanges that are purely symbolic and take place in a cultural economy."[120] This will be an important point to keep in mind in relation to Hughes's notion of *cultural exchange:* whether he acknowledged it or not, the cultural forms he was so intent to trade across the black Atlantic *were* commodities, subject to exploitation and abuse as well as being potentially beneficial to both parties in the exchange.

The example of *Banjo,* furthermore, drives home the point that the movement of commodities coincided with a movement of people and thus contributed to an ever-accelerating process of cultural conversation and contamination (in the positive sense that Appiah proposes), which from McKay's perspective was an unqualified good. We find a perfect example of Appiah's xenophile cosmopolitanism in the character of Ray, for whom "the most precious thing about human life is difference. Like flowers in a garden, different kinds for different people to love. I am not against miscegenation."[121] Though he does "hate to think of a future in which the identity of the black race in the Western World should be lost in miscegenation,"[122] Ray clearly rejects all notions of cultural purity and is unafraid of the contamination or cross-pollination that came with international commerce, as his use of the "beautiful garden" wildflower metaphor reveals. McKay seconded the rejection of cultural purity in his own voice in "A Negro Writer to His Critics" in 1932: "The time when a writer will stick only to the safe old ground of his own class of people is undoubtedly passing. Especially in America, where all the peoples of the world are scrambling side by side and modern machines and the ramifications of international commerce are steadily breaking down the ethnological barriers that separate the peoples of the world."[123] These are the words of a writer who has come to recognize the extent of his entanglement in a great global web of cultural forces, flows, and exchanges and has decided to accept and embrace its potential good for black people everywhere.

Curiously, though, for someone who once fervently proclaimed his radical views, McKay seemed untroubled in the above description of the Marseille docks by the regimes of exploitation and coercion that produced the "eternal harvest of the world." Nor did he seem particularly troubled by his own appropriation or perpetuation of essentialist rhetoric about blackness, exoticism, and "the primitive." He presented a microcosm of this process in his autobiography when he described being caught up in a police raid on vagrants in the railroad yard but then being released by a judge who became more sympathetic to him when he heard his Jamaican accent. "As he handed me the slip, he smiled and said: 'You see, I could place you by your accent.' I flashed back a smile of thanks at him and resolved henceforth to cultivate more my native accent."[124] Later McKay was able to use his "exotic" origins and appearance to similar effect in the Soviet Union. He wrote: "I had *mobilized my African features* and won the masses of the people. The Bolshevik leaders, to satisfy the desires of the people, were using me for entertainment."[125] Given that he tolerated this treatment and recounted it here wryly but without complaint, it seems McKay was willing to use his racial difference, as with the Jamaican accent, to his advantage when he could, even when it verged on caricature.

As we have seen, one of the most important parallels between Hughes and McKay is that they both chose (and presumed) to speak for the peasants, the working classes, and the vagabonds throughout the black Atlantic. They also tried to make these people's cultures the foundation of a kind of pan-African community. It must be acknowledged that the collectivity they envisioned, through cultural encounters and exchanges in such spaces as the Marseille Ditch and the jazz clubs of Harlem, was fleeting, ephemeral, and fraught with contradictions. I would argue that it nevertheless filled a need and offered a locus of identification for black writers excluded from the usual structures of national belonging and literary establishments. As I will argue in my chapter on his late poem *Ask Your Mama,* Hughes in the long run would prove more nimble than McKay at negotiating the tensions between the modern and the primitive; Africa and the West; and nationalism, universalism, and racial particularism. But McKay's life and writings provided a crucial precedent (and in some ways a cautionary tale) for Hughes's own ethos and aesthetic of pan-African entanglement, which continued to develop for another two decades after McKay's death in 1948.

Scale Enlargement A
Langston Hughes and the Caribbean

WAI CHEE DIMOCK speaks of "scale enlargement" as a way of enlarging "our sense of shared kinship." Threads such as religion and language, she says, can "knit together kinships" that "owe their legibility to the deep field of time: its scope, its tangled antecedents, and its ability to record far-flung and mediated ties."[1] One of my premises in this book is that studying the connections between Hughes and the black writers through Dimock's notion of "deep time" helps us see how those writers imagined, disseminated, adapted, and repurposed a skein of ancestral pan-African memory. And one means of achieving this larger view of Hughes's web of transnational connections is through these short subchapters I am calling "scale enlargements," where I provide a more superficial mapping of a larger cluster of interconnections. In this first scale enlargement, I zoom out to the macroscopic view in order to take stock of Hughes's entanglements with the Caribbean throughout his lifespan.

Those entanglements began to form early. Hughes was on a first-name basis with Eric Walrond, the Guyanese-born fiction writer and journalist, at least as early as 1924.[2] Around that same time he began corresponding with Claude McKay, and in July of that year he wrote to Countee Cullen from Paris that he had just met René Maran,[3] the French Guianese writer whose novel *Batouala* had been published in 1921 to great excitement in black Paris.[4] Early poems such as "Brothers," first published in *Crisis* in 1924 and later reprinted in *Montage of a Dream Deferred* (1951), lay emphatic claim to blood relation between African Americans and West Indians: "We're related—you and I, / You from the West Indies, / I from Kentucky." The second stanza likewise declares Africans and Americans "Kinsmen," and the short poem closes with the assertion that they are "Brothers—you and I."[5] Even an ostensibly lyrical ode to the beauty of the islands such as "Caribbean Sunset" (1926) revealed his interest in the Caribbean as a locus for the history of the black diaspora, with references to God "having a hemorrhage" that stained the "dark sea red,"[6] hinting at the bloody history of the Middle Passage.

Hughes made his first trip to the Caribbean when he went to Havana in 1927 as a mess boy aboard the *Nardo;* he returned briefly in 1930 and then for a more extended stay in Haiti and Cuba in 1931. Not coincidentally, he also evoked the Caribbean more frequently in his poetry of the 1930s, and in a more politically charged way. Indeed, his writings from the 1930s in general were strident and angry. His outrage at the unfettered capitalist practices that led to the Great Depression was compounded by his fury at ongoing violence and discrimination aimed at African Americans, especially the unjust imprisonment on concocted rape charges of the young black Scottsboro Nine in Alabama.[7] This led him to write the openly socialist agitprop play *Scottsboro, Limited* (1931), which ended with a call to "Rise, workers, and fight!"[8] It was in this decade that he visited Russia and Central Asia as a guest of the Soviet government and covered the Spanish Civil War as a journalist from a perspective clearly sympathetic to the socialist government.

The 1930s were also a decade when Hughes grew highly indignant against US and European military and economic domination of the Caribbean islands. Having seen firsthand the treatment of black people under the US-backed regimes in Haiti and Cuba, Hughes increasingly came to treat them as examples of modern oppression and exploitation, listing them among the catalogs of downtrodden peoples that became his hallmark from this period. Consider the 1930 poem "Merry Christmas": after gifting China with "Ten-inch shells," Africa with "murder" and "rape," and India with Christmas bells for "Gandhi in his cell," the poet turns his acid pen to Haiti and Cuba:

> Ring Merry Christmas, Haiti!
> (And drown the voodoo drums—
> We'll rob you to the Christian hymns
> Until the next Christ comes.)
>
> Ring Merry Christmas, Cuba!
> (While Yankee domination
> Keeps a nice fat president
> In a little half-starved nation.)[9]

Haiti is evoked briefly through the "voodoo drums" that link the Haitian peasantry to ancestral Africa, a collective memory fragment that is repressed and "drowned" out by "Christian hymns." But the speaker quickly shifts to the violence and domination inflicted on workers in both Haiti and Cuba—not a century or two before, during the days of slavery, but in the contemporary dictatorships installed in both places by the United States. As we will see in coming chapters, however, Hughes and many of the writers in his sphere of influence eagerly highlighted parallels between the crimes of history and twentieth-century oppression, purposefully exploiting their multidirectional symbolic potential. Thus the Caribbean's history of slavery, oppression, and resistance became not just the foundation for an imagined pan-African community but also an allegorical vehicle for critiquing and commenting on contemporary situations.

In the 1930s Hughes also resorted less frequently to the rhetoric of kinship and blood that he deployed in "Brothers" and instead sought internationalist solidarity in similar and interconnected histories of oppression. So whereas "Always the Same" (1932), like "Brothers," links the West Indies and black Americans, now the tissue that connects them is labor: the "coffee hills of Haiti" are cataloged alongside the "docks at Sierra Leone," the "cotton fields of Alabama," and the "diamond mines of Kimberley." The poem culminates in a call for solidarity and revolution, with blood imagery used literally instead of as a trope for ancestry: "Better that my blood makes one with the blood / Of all the struggling workers in the world."[10] Likewise, in "Ballad of the Seven Songs" (1949), Cudjoe, the runagate slave who led the rebel maroons in a decades-long guerilla war against the British and Spanish in Jamaica, is listed among the "Seven names" of black people who led the way to freedom, including Sojourner Truth, Harriet Tubman, Frederick Douglass, Booker T. Washington, George Washington Carver, and Jackie Robinson.[11] Even as late as 1957, in "Memo to Non-White Peoples," Hughes insisted that things are

> The same from Cairo to Chicago,
> Cape Town to the Carib Hilton,
> Exactly the same.[12]

But this sameness resulted not from race but from racism—that is, not from any intrinsic genealogical determinism but from similar conditions of oppression.

In short, Hughes found the earliest outlet for expressing his ethos of pan-African entanglement in the Caribbean, and he seized every opportunity to cement the idea in his readers' minds that black Americans were deeply intertwined with their "brothers" in the West Indies. One particularly clear example came in the middle of World War II, when ideas about transnational alliances had never seemed more urgent, with "Broadcast to the West Indies" (1943). In highly didactic and prosaic verse, the speaker maintains that African Americans and blacks in the Caribbean "share so much in common."[13] The fifth stanza repeats the refrain "like me" at the end of several lines:

> You are dark like me,
> Colored with many bloods like me,
> Verging from the sunrise to the
>   dusk like me,
> From day to night, from black to
>   white like me.[14]

Hughes here was establishing a kinship with the West Indies that he would later try to extend to South Africa in the late poem "Questions and Answers" (1966), which explicitly pairs Durban with Birmingham, Cape Town with Atlanta, and Johannesburg with Watts. As Robolin argues, "By pairing symbolic sites from two seemingly independent movements almost halfway around the world from one another, Hughes de-individualizes insurgent black self-assertion, transnationalizes it, and thus frames local instances of opposition to racial subjugation as part of a larger, interconnected phenomenon."[15] Moreover, while we find Hughes in this poem still asserting similarity based on "black blood" and shared skin tone, we also see him beginning to acknowledge the existence of "many bloods" and many shades from "sunrise to the dusk" throughout the hemisphere. In other words, he is allowing for difference within the black Atlantic world, even as he tries to find and generate a sense of community there. The vision that begins to be articulated in this poem, then, is one of a negotiated, concentrically organized, borderless black collectivity—a transnational entanglement that resembles Paul Gilroy's model of the black Atlantic as a unit of analysis that breaks "the dogmatic focus on discrete *national* dynamics which has characterised so much modern Euro-American cultural thought."[16]

The figure that Hughes used to give form to this incipient transnational collectivity was, once again, the first-person pronoun. In this case, the "I" of "Broadcast to the West Indies" speaks for Harlem:

> I, Harlem,
> Island within an island, but not
>   alone.
>
> I, Harlem,
> Dark-face, great, enormous
>   Negro city
> On Manhattan Island, New York,
>   U.S.A.[17]

These lines do not suggest that Hughes had abandoned the demand for acceptance as an American. Rather, the speaker of "Broadcast to the West Indies" positions himself, like Appiah's "rooted cosmopolitan,"[18] within a series of concentric circles: Harlem is a "Negro city" and a figurative island of blackness within the larger literal island of Manhattan, which in turn remains part of New York and of the United States. Moreover, the declarations that the West Indians to whom the poem is addressed are in so many ways "like me" expands the concentric identifications to the hemisphere as a whole. And the poem's epigraph, which names the "wave length" through which this message is being broadcast "The Human Heart," casts the final circle of identification in terms of a shared humanity. If, as Beal argues, the medium of radio in the early twentieth century "prompted a general distributed understanding of the United States,"[19] Hughes used the figure of radio to effect a distributed understanding of blackness and the pan-African world and to give black people a sense of their own coentanglement.

More broadly, the ethos of pan-African entanglement to which Hughes gave expression in "Broadcast" enabled two things: first, it helped Hughes establish a broader pan-African collective that could supplement or, if necessary, replace nationalist identification for blacks whose belonging to their respective nations might be tenuous and unreliable. Second, it gave Hughes a larger perspective from which to criticize the hypocrisy of American race relations. Thus in the middle of the poem we find a stanza that begins, "They say—the Axis—/ That the U.S.A. is bad,"[20] and then goes on to catalog lynching, discrimination, and disenfranchisement of black Americans. The multiple drafts of this poem that survive in the Langston Hughes Papers at Yale's Beinecke Library show him struggling with the line that follows this litany: from "To an extent, that's true," to a blunt "That's true," to a more tempered "That's almost true, too!," before finally settling on the phrasing that appeared in the published version, "Those things are partly true."[21] Presumably Hughes wanted to maintain the poem's iambic rhythm, but more importantly, he probably also wanted to avoid accusations of sympathizing with the enemy. Having been hounded by right-wing protesters and red-baiting since he wrote his radical verse of the 1930s (a persecution that would later come to a boil during the McCarthy hearings), Hughes was by 1943 treading a more cautious path—one that would soon have him looking more to Africa than to the Soviet Union for inspiration and moral models in the struggle for civil rights and black consciousness. Even in this earlier poem he was appealing to the broader black diaspora to find a moral framework for criticizing the hypocrisy of America's treatment of its black citizens.

That moral framework required the longer perspective afforded by deep time. In one case, for example—the short poem "To the Little Fort of San Lazaro on the Ocean Front, Havana," published in the radical journal *New Masses* in 1931—Hughes showed how modern capitalism was linked to the history of slavery and piracy. The "Little Fort" in the title was part of the fortification system for old Havana. It was, the speaker says, "Watch tower once for pirates"; he mentions Drake and the slave trader known as "EL GRILLO" by name, in all capital letters. The poem continues:

> Against such as these
> Years and years ago
> You served quite well—
> When time and ships were slow.
>   But now,
> Against a pirate called
> THE NATIONAL CITY BANK
> What can you do alone?[22]

Several aspects of these lines warrant attention. First, the appearance in all capital letters of the First National City Bank of New York—one of the largest investors in Cuba's sugar industry—links it to the pirates and slave traders mentioned in the previous stanza, while also implying that the twentieth-century scoundrels are more dangerous than their sixteenth- and seventeenth-century forebears. Yet these lines imply that the fort's inefficacy results as well from an acceleration of human migration and commerce in the modern age: where once the fort offered protection when "time and ships were slow," in the speaker's own age capital has begun to flow across national borders with a speed and assiduity that circumvent the place-bound protections of stone. Thus the poem ends by emphasizing the futility of the fort's efforts at protecting the island: Would it not be better, the speaker asks, if the fort "tumbled down, / Stone by helpless stone?"[23]

The "Little Fort," I would suggest, exemplifies Pierre Nora's concept of *lieux de mémoire,* or sites of memory, which exist "because there are no longer *milieux de mémoire,* real environments of memory. . . . If we were able to live within memory, we would not have needed to consecrate *lieux de mémoire* in its name."[24] One of Nora's principle examples of a situation that generates *lieux de mémoire* is "the Jews of the diaspora, bound in daily devotion to the rituals of tradition, who as 'peoples of memory' found little use for historians until their forced exposure to the modern world."[25] What Nora says of Jews holds equally for the African diaspora: West Africans living in their traditional family structures and practicing their oral traditions would have had no use for written history, archives, or stone monuments. It was only after the profound rupture in the continuity of memory caused by captivity, Middle Passage, and slavery in the Americas that their descendants would need to engage in the kind of documentary endeavors to which Hughes devoted many of his lifelong energies. Yet in "To the Little Fort of San Lazaro" Hughes seems to recognize that the memorial to the past represented by the ruins of the old fort succumbs to the pitfall identified by Maurice Halbwachs: "It is of the nature of remembrances, when they cannot be renewed by resuming contact with the realities from which they arose, to become impoverished and congealed."[26] Any efforts of Hughes's own to revive the spirit of survival once symbolized by the fort, moreover, would not be a revivification of a real social memory but rather the creation of what Nora calls "history, which is how our hopelessly forgetful modern societies, propelled by change, organize the past."[27]

We have already discussed how important a collective memory was to the establishment of productive webs of pan-African entanglement. Yet "To the Little Fort" and other works show us how easily attempts to memorialize the past can congeal into inert placeholders. Thus Hughes's ethos of pan-African entanglement drove him to try to resolve these paradoxes of memory and remembrance and to reanimate and "organize the past" in such a way as to guarantee black people a place in modern culture. In the next chapter we will see this in operation, in Hughes's depiction of the Haitian Revolution in the play *Emperor of Haiti*. On the one hand, Hughes clearly wanted to find towering heroes in the leaders of the revolution. On the other hand, it must have seemed absurd in the early 1930s to paint the revolution as a shining example of self-governance by black people, since Haiti had subsequently fallen into a cycle of corruption, authoritarianism, foreign military occupation, and political instability and violence that had already lasted more than a century. Hughes attempted to resolve this tension by writing *Emperor of Haiti* as a cautionary tale for a nation newly released from the restraints of foreign occupation, as Haiti was in both the 1800s and the 1930s. The urgency introduced by the analogy to the present made the history of the revolution more relevant and helped to register the founding of Haiti, the world's first black republic, as a momentous event in world history.

Even as his writings worked to weave the Caribbean and the African American pasts into a shared memory of pan-African entanglement, Hughes also worked behind the scenes to develop a network of black writers in the Caribbean, thus establishing skeins of black entanglement on both the ancestral and the contemporary planes. Because his earliest travels were to Cuba and Haiti, his deepest connections were to writers from those countries, especially to Jacques Roumain (which I discuss further in the next chapter) and Nicolás Guillén. His connections to Guillén ran particularly deep, as Vera Kutzinski and Ryan Kernan, among others, have fruitfully explored. The correspondence between them preserved at the Beinecke is extensive and covers more than three decades. During that time Hughes (with Bontemps) included several poems by Guillén in the anthology *Poetry of the Negro,* and later Hughes and Benjamin Carruthers published a translation of Guillén's poetry collection *Cuba Libre.* In October 1948 Hughes used his weekly "Here to Yonder" column in the *Chicago Defender* to promote the translated collection, hailing Guillén as "the great Cuban Negro poet."[28]

Hughes and Guillén had the opportunity to meet and socialize together not just in Havana but also in Paris, Spain, and presumably New York during some of Guillén's trips to the city in the late 1940s and early 1950s. We also have some glimpses of the relationship between the two men from the Cuban's perspective: in recounting his first meeting with Hughes to interview him, Guillén explains he was told to look out for a tall man in his forties who was almost white and with an English mustache. Instead, "When Mr. Hughes appeared, we encountered a twenty-seven-year-old boy, short and thin, of a brownish color, and who does not wear a mustache in the English or the fashion of any other nation. He looked just like a Cuban mulatto."[29] Like Hughes, it seems, Guillén was receptive to signs of kinship and similarity with another mixed-race artist—and indeed, it is often noted that Guillén did not begin to write about racial themes in his poetry until he met Langston Hughes.

Most of Hughes's translations of Guillén's poetry, as well as those of fellow Cuban poet Regino Pedroso, did not see publication until 1948 and 1949, but he actually began working on them much earlier, as he wrote to Claude McKay in September 1930:

> I've been translating some lovely Cuban poetry lately. There's a Chinese-Negro poet in Havana named Regino Pedroso who works in an iron foundry and writes grand radical poems and Chinese revolutionary stuff and mystical sonnets, and there's another boy named Nicolas Guillen who has recently created a small sensation down there with his poems in Cuban Negro dialect with the rhythms of the native music, sort of like my blues here—the first time that has been done in Latin-America. I've translated some of the revolutionary poems, and some of Guillen's straight Spanish, because neither the sonnets nor the dialect could I do over very well into English.[30]

In this letter Hughes both acknowledged unbridgeable differences (i.e., the untranslatable sonnets and dialects) and simultaneously asserted similarity by comparing Guillén's *son* poems to his own blues verse. The revolutionary poems likewise formed another easy bridge between North American and Cuban cultures.

By the late 1940s, Hughes's status as the best-known black American writer in the Hispanic world had been established.[31] His connections to the

West Indies had likewise solidified, culminating in 1949 with the publication of *Poetry of the Negro* and *Cuba Libre* and the premiere of Hughes's opera (composed by William Grant Still), *Troubled Island,* about the Haitian Revolution. It helped, also, that he took a trip in September 1947 to Jamaica, where he gave a lecture at the University College of the West Indies and was a guest of honor at a luncheon of the Poetry League of Jamaica.[32] During that visit he met Louise Bennett,[33] Roger Mais (with whom he had briefly corresponded in 1944), Victor Reid, and other local writers,[34] along with Wycliffe Bennett of Jamaica's PEN Club, who helped assemble the Caribbean section of Hughes and Bontemps's 1949 anthology *The Poetry of the Negro*.[35] Following Hughes's return to New York, there was a flurry of exchanges between him and both Mais and Reid in 1948 and 1949 (the former partly in connection with Mais's inclusion in the anthology).

The extent to which Hughes constituted a direct influence on the writings of any of these writers in his network is difficult to declare with certainty. But it is not hard to imagine Hughes's blues poems, or his rendering of black American speech patterns in his fiction and plays, as conscious precedent for (among others) Una Marson's and Louise Bennett's use of the Jamaican patois and folklore in their poems and plays. Were there a clearer documentary or intertextual trail linking Hughes to these women, I would probably have devoted a chapter to them. But since the longer chapters are devoted to fine-grained materialist readings of Hughes's web of transnational connections, I will limit myself to a quick and speculative take on a couple of examples.

It would be interesting, for example, to read Marson's "Quashie Comes to London" (1937), about a homesick working-class Jamaican immigrant in England, within the framework of Hughes's ethos and aesthetic of black entanglement, which emphasized the vernacular, the nomadic, and the marginal. (Quashie's similarities to Hughes's later character Simple might also prove illuminating.) Both women's brands of Jamaican feminism could also serve as a counterbalance to the masculinity of Hughes's Caribbean network, even as they extended his tactics of entanglement. Bennett's "Jamaica Oman" (1966), for example, celebrated a history of black resistance and rebellion and linked historical figures to the present through juxtaposition in ways very similar to how Hughes linked figures through catalogs and analogies:

From Maroon Nanny teck her body
Bounce bullet back pon man,
To when nowadays gal-pickney tun
Spellin-Bee champion.[36]

The key difference, of course, is that Bennett's examples are of black *women* becoming the active embodiments of black empowerment, especially the figure of Nanny, queen of a group of maroons who legendarily had the power to repel bullets. Bennett's poem, then, could quite profitably be read as both an adoption of Hughes's aesthetic of pan-African entanglement, grounding the present in the past, and a rebuke by contrast with the narrowness of Hughes's expression of that aesthetic. But the evidentiary trail is currently too thin to sustain an extended analysis of this intertextual conversation.

As for Hughes's larger network, his decision to include a section on "The Caribbean" in *The Poetry of the Negro* proved important in building out his network of black writers throughout the American hemisphere: Hughes and Bontemps included selections by some forty writers throughout the West Indies. Of those, Hughes's papers at the Beinecke show brief exchanges around 1948–49 with Raymond Barrow, Roussan Camille, George Campbell, Frank Collymore, Una Marson, Stephanie Ormsby, Regino Pedroso, Walter Adolphe Roberts, Emile Roumer, A. J. Seymour, Louis Simpson, Harold Telemaque, H. A. Vaughan, Duracine Vaval, and Vivian Virtue—all featured in the anthology, and a few of them sustaining the correspondence after the anthology was published. Hughes also had a few exchanges with Jamaican novelist Andrew Salkey, whom he later had the chance to meet when Salkey was in New York for a Guggenheim Fellowship in 1961. And he corresponded briefly with Haitian poet Jean Brière and translated a few of his poems, along with a poem by another Haitian, Anthony Lespes.[37]

The 1950s saw another burst of network building on Hughes's part. He corresponded briefly, for example, with Wilson Harris and George Lamming, the novelists from Guyana and Barbados, respectively. At the end of that decade, in 1959, Hughes visited Trinidad for a lecture tour, during which he met future prime minister Eric Williams, historian C. L. R. James, and poet Derek Walcott along the way.[38] Finally, keeping in mind that Hughes's network of black artists was by no means confined to literary writers, it is worth noting that Hughes knew Trinidadian dancer and choreographer Beryl McBurnie from her days dancing in New York,[39] and that he corresponded repeatedly between 1960 and 1967 with Harry Belafonte, the New York–born Calypso singer and actor of Caribbean parentage, and collaborated with Belafonte on a television project in 1965.[40]

My particular focus in this book is on mapping Hughes's role as both catalyst and hub for the network of black Atlantic writers that helped usher in the era of postcolonial literature, but it is worth pausing to stress that many connections arose independently alongside Hughes's efforts. Guillén and Roumain, for example, knew each other going back at least to the Writers Congress in Paris in 1937. At the end of 1940, Roumain, in exile from

Haiti, accepted Guillén's invitation to conduct anthropological research in Cuba for several months. Later Roumain worked on a book of translations of Guillén's poetry into French. When Roumain died, Guillén wrote a poem entitled "Elegía a Jacques Roumain,"[41] and years later in 1961 he wrote a piece in commemoration of his departed friend, "Sobre Jacques Roumain."[42] In short, while Hughes might have sat at the center of the web between black writers in the United States and the Caribbean, it was nevertheless still a web, with connections extending always in multiple directions simultaneously.

2 "Marks of a Rebellious Slave"
Langston Hughes, Haiti, and Jacques Roumain

IN CHAPTER 1 I discussed Hughes's defiant and explicit rejection, at the end of the 1920s, of the primitivist mold his patron, Mrs. Mason, wanted for him. He begins his second autobiography by complaining, "She wanted me to be more African than Harlem—primitive in the simple, intuitive and noble sense of the word. I couldn't be, having grown up in Kansas City, Chicago and Cleveland."[1] Hughes chafed at the racialism in his patron's assumption that black skin intrinsically brought with it the intuitions of the primitive, which she associated with an exotic African paradise. He chafed even more at her imperative to confine the black artist to themes of tribal Africa. Yet there is a certain rue to Hughes's recognition of his modern, urbanized character. As we have seen, Hughes in his twenties, feeling caged by modernity and civilization, sought remedy in primitivism and romantic evocations of ancestral Africa. Chinitz is right to argue that Hughes's "rejection of primitivism was never a complete repudiation, for even as he left the primitivist movement behind Hughes strove to conserve what had attracted him to it and to distinguish that from what he was rejecting."[2]

After his break with his white "Godmother" in 1930, however, and after his ambivalent early encounters with Africa, Hughes shifted the geographic focus of his search for transnational black kinship and similarity. In the 1930s, he became intensely interested in the cultural practices of poor black people, especially peasants and sharecroppers, in the American hemisphere, especially in the Caribbean islands: in Havana, among the "the Negro musicians at Marianao, those fabulous drum beaters who use their bare hands to beat out rhythm, those clave knockers and maraca shakers who somehow have saved—out of all the centuries of slavery and all the miles and miles from Guinea—the heartbeat and songbeat of Africa"; and in Haiti, among the "black Haitians of the soil [who] seem to remember Africa in their souls and far-off ancestral tribes."[3] In Haiti he responded as though he had found embers kept alive from an ancient African fire, the source of the warmth and vivacity he always attributed to black people.

Michael Largey provides some context about the era of the US occupation of Haiti (1915–34), when "African American intellectuals turned to Haiti as an alternative repository of African-based folk culture. Haiti appealed to African Americans not only as a storehouse for those cultural qualities that were believed to be an 'authentic' foundation for an African-based national culture but also as a politically-independent black nation."[4] Clare Corbould adds that black Americans in the 1930s and 1940s "regarded Haitian culture as evidence of the syncretism and adaptability that characterized black life throughout the diaspora, and which formed the basis of black political struggle." Haiti, she clarifies, "became something of an anvil on which to forge a diverse and vibrant African American identity. This identity took in an affinity to people around the black diaspora, based on shared histories of enslavement and experiences of racism . . . rather than a biological racial connection."[5] Hughes too was by this point emphasizing those shared histories over any racial essence, even as he continued to use the most romantic of primitivist rhetoric to describe the rural peasantry in Haiti: "People strong, midnight black. Proud women whose heads bear burdens, whose backs are very straight. Children naked as nature. Nights full of stars, throbbing with Congo drums."[6] Hughes condensed his narrative of a pan-African past into that brief description: the midnight blackness and "Congo drums" evoke ancient Africa; the phrase "bears burdens" hints at a long history of slavery and hard labor, whereas the women's proudness and straight backs remind us of the fortitude of their ancestors who defeated three empires to form a black republic. These narrative strands are interwoven to become the foundation of a transnational black community—the ancestral plane of pan-African entanglement.

At the same time, on the contemporary plane, Hughes found in his travels in Haiti an intellectual elite who had worked out a complex and sophisticated understanding of their relationship to Haiti's African heritage: "Haitians did not need to return to the land of Africa if, in their minds, the idea of Africa already existed within the confines of their nation-state. As the self-proclaimed representatives of African culture in the Americas, Haitians were well situated to encourage a vision of an authentic, black, African based culture" among black people elsewhere in the hemisphere.[7] Hughes in particular came to see the spark of Africa still alive in Haitian culture through what Diana Taylor calls the "repertoire" of performative knowledge: music, dance, foodways, tales, religious rites, etc.[8] Part of my argument in this chapter, in fact, is that he attempted to reanimate Haiti's past by performing these repertoires himself in his writings, especially the play and opera he wrote about the revolution.

In short, then, Hughes treated Haiti, with its history of slavery, revolution, authoritarianism, foreign occupation, and resistance, as a microcosm of the African diaspora; he used it as a model for thinking through questions of racial kinship as well as cultural difference; and he used it to further develop his ethos and aesthetics of vernacular black entanglement. Especially in the 1936 play *Emperor of Haiti,* he incorporated images and figures from the Haitian Revolution into his growing lexicon of black Atlantic images, tropes, and symbols. Most importantly, Hughes apotheosized the trinity of revolutionary generals, Toussaint Louverture, Jean Jacques Dessalines, and Henri Christophe, and elevated the great Citadelle Laferrière that Christophe built near Cap Haïtien into a symbol of black power and grandeur. Through these figures, Hughes began to envision a transatlantic and transcaribbean black collectivity based not solely in the passive longing for a lost homeland but in active resistance to ongoing oppression. Sites of memory such as the citadel served in his writing as both inspiration and cautionary tale, and narratives of the Haitian Revolution became "multidirectional memories" (in Michael Rothberg's phrase)[9] for the situation of blacks in the United States as well as in his contemporary Haiti.

Hughes's thinking on these subjects took shape in the context of his friendship with Jacques Roumain of Haiti. This chapter, then, will focus especially on that friendship and his English translations of Roumain's poetry and fiction, which functioned as counterpoint to Hughes's own treatment of Africa, blackness, and primitivism. We can see that he regarded Roumain as a kindred spirit from an editorial he wrote in 1934, when Roumain was imprisoned by the Haitian authorities on charges of distributing subversive materials: Roumain, he wrote, "is one of the very few upper-class Haitians who understands and sympathizes with the plight of the oppressed peasants of his island home."[10] Crucially, too, this identification with the Haitian peasantry was also grounded in an appreciation for the African origins of that peasant culture. By translating into English several of Roumain's poems, but most especially his novel *Masters of the Dew,* Hughes was attempting likewise to register the stories and "primitive" cultural practices of the Haitian peasantry in a larger black Atlantic consciousness and to use poor black people as microcosms for a universal humanity. In Roumain's late work, Hughes discovered a universalist outlook inflected by both Africanism and Communism that he found appealing and resonant with his own ethos and aesthetic of pan-African entanglement.

Langston Hughes and the Haitian Revolution

The Haitian Revolution began with a coordinated uprising of slaves on several plantations on the northern plain of Saint-Domingue (as the territory was then called by its French masters) in 1791; for more than a decade the revolutionaries, under the leadership of Toussaint Louverture with his generals Henri Christophe and Jean-Jacques Dessalines, held off French, Spanish, and English forces who attempted to take control of the island and led the French National Convention to abolish slavery throughout the French Caribbean in 1793. After allowing French forces to resume control in early 1802, Toussaint was captured by Napoleon's forces at a meeting, just weeks after the French passed a law reinstituting slavery in the colonies they had recently recovered from Great Britain. The forces of the revolution, now under Dessalines's command, again revolted. In January 1804, Dessalines declared Haiti an independent nation, of which he declared himself emperor some months later. After two years of increasingly tyrannical rule, Dessalines was assassinated in 1806, at which point Christophe became the king of Haiti.

Faith Berry explains the importance of Haiti to the imagination of the young Langston Hughes: "Since childhood, he had wanted to see the world's first black republic, whose legendary history he had learned from his grandmother. She had told him how the slaves in the early 1790s had revolted against the French for twelve years and finally, after defeating Napoleon Bonaparte's expedition, won their independence. The black Haitian generals, Toussaint L'Ouverture, Jean Jacques Dessalines, and Henri Christophe remained Hughes's heroes even as an adult."[11] Hughes was hardly alone in the esteem in which he held the leaders of the Haitian Revolution. As Maurice Jackson and Jacqueline Bacon note, "The Haitian Revolution has been for African Americans of different eras a vehicle through which collective memory and identity has been created and transformed and an event that has inspired and influenced black nationalism, abolitionism, black socialist and revolutionary thought, and Pan Africanism."[12] Yet Philip Kaisary notes that even among black writers and intellectuals, responses to the revolution and its aftermath have varied greatly, with more conservative representations emphasizing the despotism and violence that the revolution ultimately spawned. Kaisary puts Hughes, by contrast, firmly into the "radical camp" among twentieth-century writers, together with such Caribbean writers as Aimé Césaire, C. L. R. James, and René Depestre—writers for whom "the Haitian Revolution is retrieved as a decisive and transformational historical moment" and whose recuperation and representation "offered the opportunity to articulate a narrative of emancipation in which black agency and universal intent were central."[13] Still, few would contest Mbembe's assertion that the Haitian Revolution was "a turning point in the modern history of human emancipation";[14] nor would many quibble with James's assessment that "the only successful slave revolt in history" culminated in "one of the great epics of revolutionary struggle and achievement."[15]

In Haiti itself, this admiration for the revolution found sympathetic reception among the writers associated with *Indigenisme*, a militant movement that J. Michael Dash explains took as its aim "to make admissible in art a [Haitian] reality whose worthiness was once questioned" and was "increasingly preoccupied with the culture of the peasants in Haiti."[16] From the opening article in the first issue of *La revue indigene* in 1927, Jacques Roumain and his cofounders looked to the Haitian Revolution as "a crucial moment in the universal and transnational project of liberation," in Valerie Kaussen's summary.[17] Roumain and other figures in the Indigenist movement were deeply influenced by Haitian intellectual Jean Price-Mars, who wrote in his 1928 book *Thus Spake Our Uncle*, "Our only chance to be ourselves is to repudiate no part of the ancestral heritage. Well, for eight-tenths of us this heritage is the gift of Africa."[18] This call for acknowledgment and celebration of Haiti's African patrimony informed the work of an entire generation of Haitian writers and resonated well with Hughes's interest in finding a primitivist African spirit in the peasants of Haiti.

Though the aim of Indigenism was to cultivate a locally particular culture, Kaussen emphasizes the broad and syncretic international influences that fed into its aesthetic: "Indigenist writers demonstrated allegiance to the Harlem Renaissance, Latin American literary traditions, surrealism, Nietzsche and Marx, forms of ultra-nationalist thought and Eastern mysticism."[19] That Roumain, at least, was highly aware of this cosmopolitan mélange of influences is clear from an interview he gave in 1927: "In the twentieth century, one is a citizen of the world. More and more national literatures tend to escape the limitations of borders to influence one another reciprocally."[20] The simultaneous move inward to the local and outward to the international resonated powerfully with Hughes's own project of facilitating cultural entanglement across the black Atlantic. Likewise, the conditions that gave rise to Indigenism in Haiti—urbanization and the emigration of Haitian workers to the Dominican Republic, Cuba, the United States, and beyond—also presented parallels to the situation in the United States, where the Great Migration of blacks to northern cities was at a peak in the early 1930s. Kaussen argues that the "deterritorialization" of Haitian migrants ironically made it possible for them to create "subaltern forms of pan-Americanism and *antilleanité* that concretized in new ways the ideal of a transnational Haitian nation that was open and syncretic, anti-colonial and resistant to all forms of enslavement."²¹ This assessment explains some of the fascination Haiti held for Hughes, who likewise attempted to simultaneously ground an aesthetic of black entanglement in invented traditions and vernacular practices, while giving it purchase and motility within a global system of cultural exchange.

Indigenism found particular inspiration and utility in the black American identity that Hughes and the other writers in the "New Negro Movement" had articulated in the 1920s. Price-Mars, for example, wrote a series of articles in the literary journal *La relève* on the Harlem Renaissance, recognizing "in writers such as Claude McKay, Langston Hughes and Countee Cullen a new thrust and an unfettered imagination in their expression of thematic content."²² Roumain himself frequently looked toward the Harlem Renaissance as a model for the "Haitianization" of his country's literature, telling one interviewer in 1927: "We have frankly ignored the fact that there is in the United States, four days removed from us, a flourishing Negro poetry. And an original one. Countee Cullen, for example."²³ Hughes, his peers associated with the Harlem Renaissance, and Roumain would all prove influences, moreover, on a slightly later generation of Haitian writers associated with the journal *Les griots*, founded in 1938, whose writers "demanded a greater incorporation of folk practices, especially vodou, in national life. It is from the peasantry, the Griots argued, that Haitian culture derives."²⁴ Like his interest in Africa, a deep investment in peasant life and culture would continue to characterize Roumain's work even after his political loyalties shifted from nationalism to communism. It also, of course, resonated strongly with Hughes's own views that peasants and sharecroppers in the West Indies and the US South constituted the truest repositories of the traces and fragments of African culture in the Americas.

Hughes's first visit to Haiti in 1931, as Edward Mullen puts it, "seems to have intensified his outrage at the treatment of blacks" worldwide.²⁵ That same year, Hughes wrote numerous reportorial articles about Haiti and its people for *New Masses* and *Crisis* (most famously the polemic "People without Shoes"),²⁶ some of them contrasting Haiti's glorious revolutionary history with its sordid present of occupation and despotism. Later he would devote four chapters in *I Wonder as I Wander* to the Haiti visit, one of which rewrote "People without Shoes." He also mentioned Haiti and Haitian themes in his poetry with increasing frequency thereafter. In "Scottsboro" (1931), for example, the speaker intones the name of Dessalines among a catalog of historical leaders that includes Christ, John Brown, Moses, Joan of Arc, Nat Turner, Lenin, and Gandhi.²⁷ This genealogy of revolution functions much like the omniscient first-person speaker who uses the expansive pronoun "I" in so many of Hughes's poems: it establishes continuity between ancient tales of oppression and liberation, the fight against slavery in the Americas in the nineteenth century, and modern struggles against imperialism and feudalism. Its inclusiveness suggests that the pan-African entanglement that Hughes perceived and worked to develop was not defined restrictively by skin color or lineage but rather worked through accretion, analogy, and openness to alliances wherever in the world they could be forged.

"Scottsboro" was a passing attempt to rank rebel slaves like Dessalines and Nat Turner among the pantheon of what the poem calls "Fighters for the free." Elsewhere, Hughes more emphatically apotheosized Dessalines and other leaders of the Haitian Revolution and in a more sustained and thoughtful way cast Haiti as a symbol of both the dream of liberation and that dream's failure. That he did this deliberately and consciously becomes clear from an essay he published in *Crisis* in 1941, lamenting the paucity of histories by black scholars of the Haitian Revolution and pointing out the "need for heroes" in the black community: "But where, in all these books, is that compelling frame of spirit and passion that makes a man say, 'I, too, am a hero, because my race has produced heroes like that!'?"[28] Here again Hughes saw Haiti through his presumption of kinship or bonding rooted in African ancestry—a presumption that, as we will see in chapter 4, both facilitated and frustrated his attempts to expand his network of black artists to Africa. It also allowed him, in his own mind at least, to appropriate the Haitian Revolution and its images of black resistance and self-governance into his lexicon of pan-African entanglement, with little apparent self-reflection on the ethics of this appropriative act.

Hughes, then, from the 1930s on, engaged in a kind of excavation project to unearth the buried history of black heroes in Haiti. At times the excavation metaphor became nearly literal, as when he drew our attention to the way the history of the revolution was inscribed in Haiti's landscape. Kaussen claims that the Haitian countryside is "a palimpsest of Haiti's revolutionary history."[29] In that palimpsest we can see an operation that Anne McClintock has labeled "imperial ghosting," which "takes the form of a doubleness, whereby administered forgettings and guarded secrets leave a kind of counter-evidence: material and spectral traces, shadowy aftereffects, and temporal disturbances."[30] Hughes contested the "administered forgettings" of Haiti's revolutionary history; he highlighted and made visible the palimpsestic, partially erased traces of the past to apotheosize that history into mythology. Such spectral traces recall the African past, in the form of drums, music, dancing, and foodways, as well as the past of slavery and subjugation, as they did in his own African American context.

Commemorating Resistance

Haiti, though, also offered Hughes the promise of something too often lacking in US history: a heroic counternarrative of a past in which black slaves joined with free people of mixed race to fight for freedom and the end of white domination. He finds one such half-erased trace in a forgotten battlefield near St. Marc: "When we went down to the sea to bathe, I discovered, buried among the bright flowers, the barrels of old cannon and here and there heavy, round iron shot left over, no doubt, from some battle that had taken place on this coast in the distant days when Napoleon's troops had attempted to crush the slave revolt that freed the people and gave them their own rulers."[31] The parenthetical phrase "no doubt" is curious: Hughes's supposition is entirely plausible, yet in fact he does not know without doubt that these are relics of the Haitian Revolution, as no marker or plaque tells the story of this site. The confidence with which he asserts this speculation as fact is a product of his ethos of pan-African entanglement, which in this instance drives him to solidify the narrative of a "slave revolt that freed the people and gave them their own rulers" with material evidence.

The same imperative led Hughes to enshrine the figure of the citadel as a symbol of that glorious history. He described it thus, for example, in a 1931 letter to the editor of *New Masses:* "The citadel, twenty miles away on a mountain top, is a splendid lovely monument to the genius of a black king—Christophe. Stronger, vaster, and more beautiful than you could possibly imagine.... [It] stands in futile ruin now, the iron cannon rusting, the bronze one turning green ... while the planes of the United States Marines hum daily overhead."[32] This passage encapsulates the ambivalence of the citadel for Hughes: simultaneously a symbol of Haiti's historical greatness and a rueful reminder of the potential that had been lost by Hughes's own day. The same ambivalence runs through his descriptions of the citadel in *I Wonder as I Wander,* published more than two decades after his first visit to Haiti. He calls it the "storied Citadel" and "one of the great feats in the history of human energy and determination."[33] And he relays the wonder felt by Blair Niles and John Vandercook, authors of two classic accounts of the Haitian Revolution, at "this great relic of Negro pride."[34] Yet that word "relic," like the word "ruins" that he also uses repeatedly, hints at Hughes's sense of regret and disappointment regarding Haiti's subsequent degeneration, perfectly symbolized by the rusting iron cannon. Here and elsewhere, Hughes oscillated between treating the citadel as an archive and monument of the Haitian Revolution and acknowledging the need to resist its congealment into an inert museum.

In Hughes's imagination, the citadel built by Christophe at Cap Haitien embodied a revolutionary brand of anticolonialism he saw as highly pertinent to the twentieth century. Yet the actual location was remote and required an arduous journey to reach, and the fortress was long since a disintegrating ruin by the 1930s. Even should the citadel somehow be restored and made into a memorial to the revolution, it would threaten to calcify into a "lieu de memoire" or site of memory in the sense explained by Pierre Nora—an archive or memorial "where memory crystallizes and secretes itself."[35] But I concur with Diana Taylor in rejecting Nora's memory/history binary of a "temporal before and after, a rift between past . . . and present."[36] Instead, Taylor proposes a differentiation between, on one hand, "archival memory"—documents, letters, newspapers, videos, "items supposedly resistant to change"—and on the other hand, the "repertoire," which "enacts embodied memory: performances, . . . orality, . . . dance, singing—. . . all those acts usually thought of as ephemeral, nonreproducible knowledge."[37] Seen in this light, it is not an accident that when Hughes told stories about Haiti, he used the media of theater, opera, children's books, and poems such as *Ask Your Mama* that lent themselves to active performance: such performances reanimated Haiti's revolutionary past and brought it into the repertoire of living, embodied memory.

Hughes made the contrast between Haiti's glorious past and its dismal contemporary condition more explicit still in the thumbnail history of the island he presented in his 1932 essay for *Crisis:* "But after Christophe's death in 1820, misfortune set in. Revolution after revolution kept the country in turmoil. Politicians and grafters gained control. The Citadel, the palaces, the schools, the roads were left to rack and ruin. The mulattoes and the few blacks with money set themselves apart as an aristocracy, exploited the peasantry, did little to improve the land, and held their heads high in a proud and snobbish manner, not unlike the French masters of old."[38] Hughes recoiled at the manufactured divisions and differences among people of African descent and frequently railed against the snobbishness he found equally distasteful among middle-class black people in, for instance, Washington, DC. A similar critique of class stratifications among black and mixed-race people in Haiti runs through the 1936 play *Emperor of Haiti* and through its adaptation as an opera libretto called *Troubled Island* (1949; also the original title he gave to *Emperor of Haiti*).

In those texts, though, Hughes offered a more specific and more fundamental explanation for Haiti's dysfunction, rooted in decisions Dessalines and Christophe made soon after establishing Haiti as an independent republic. A primary source of Haiti's political and spiritual malaise, Hughes implied, is its leaders' abandonment of their African heritage—that is, their disavowal of the foundational plane of pan-African entanglement. It is worth recalling that *Emperor of Haiti* was written some six years after Godmother cut off her patronage to Hughes and only four years before he explained in *The Big Sea* that he earned her disapproval by refusing to "live and write as though" he felt "the rhythms of the primitive surging through me."[39] Despite these protestations, however, Hughes continued in this play to evoke a symbolic Africa tinged with wistful romance and primitivist nostalgia.

Haiti's relationship to Africa is established in the first five minutes of dialogue, when Josef and Martel, two former slaves who are now members of Dessalines's inner circle, discuss Josef's mother, who came to the island "in a slave ship. She still remembers Africa."[40] This prompts Martel to exclaim, "Africa! So long, so far away!,"[41] echoing the opening lines of Hughes's poem from 1930 "Afro-American Fragment," with its "song of atavistic land":

> So long,
> So far away
> Is Africa.
> Not even memories alive
> Save those that history books create.[42]

The implication that the kind of memory contained in "history books" is inert and artificial calls to mind Nora's opposition between memory and history of a particular sort: "At the heart of history," Nora says, "is a critical discourse that is antithetical to spontaneous memory. History is perpetually suspicious of memory, and its true mission is to suppress and destroy it."[43] This tension is also evident in the aria that Martel sings early in the opera *Troubled Island*, "Rememb'ring Africa": the apostrophe in the title is consonant with the vernacular register of language used by Hughes's slave characters but also denotes an absence at the very heart of the remembrance.

That these implied tensions or paradoxes are introduced into both play and libretto in their opening moments prepares us to read a site such as the citadel as a *lieu de mémoire* in Nora's sense: at best, an attempt to preserve the memory of the revolution against the "acceleration of memory," at worst, an attempt to "suppress and destroy" a true "environment of memory."[44] Taylor acknowledges that her own categories of the archive and the repertoire track closely with what Nora calls history and memory, but she insists that these categories are not binary opposites but "usually work in tandem and they work alongside other systems of transmission," including digital.[45] She argues further that knowledge can pass fluidly from repertoire to archive and back again. This fluidity helps account for Hughes's depictions of the Haitian Revolution in *Emperor of Haiti* and elsewhere: by performing parts of the repertoire of pan-African entanglement, he attempted to reanimate the forgotten history of a glorious revolution led by black men. The tropes and images generated by this newly reactivated memory then became the potential raw material for a collective memory recorded in archivable forms; that is, Hughes tried to inscribe these tropes and images into a written lexicon of pan-African entanglement. Both the archive and the repertoire proved crucial to his project of reanimating and setting into motion a usable past for the black diaspora.

Emperor of Haiti

At the symbolic heart of Hughes's lexicon were the evocations of ancient Africa I've already discussed. The fact that Josef's mother arrives in the West Indies on a *ship* introduces a second, related symbol, here associated with slavery and the Middle Passage's traumatic uprooting. A third trope, equally bound up in Haiti's African heritage—that of the *drum*—is introduced almost immediately after Martel expresses his longing for "our sweet motherland" of Africa, and Josef says he waits "for the beat of the drums to tell me when to lift this knife."[46] Martel replies that when "the slave Boukman lays his fingers on the great drums hidden in the cane-brake tonight, he'll beat out a signal that'll roll from hill to hill, slave hut to slave hut, across the cane-fields, across the mountains, across the bays from island to island, until every drum in Haiti throbs with the call to rise and seek freedom. Then the moon will smile, son."[47]

The drum for Hughes is the most significant cultural totem linking the diaspora back to its African heritage—a link reinforced by the closing reference to the moon, which Hughes also frequently uses in association with Africa.[48] Later lines in the play associate drums, especially the drums of Vodou, with both Haiti and ancestral Africa, as when Celeste says, "Drums is for Legba and Dambala, Nannan and M'bo," and Congo replies, "African gods been knowin' drums a long time."[49] Yet the drums represent more than Africa in *Emperor of Haiti*; they take on the added association of revolt, just as they do in Roumain's calls to revolution in the *Ebony Wood* poems. Furthermore, after Martel and Josef prime us to expect the drums and tell us their significance, the performance of the drums in later scenes has the effect of calling both actors and audience "to rise and seek freedom."

Dessalines's tragic error, as Hughes's play depicts it, is in forgetting the drums' triple meanings—African heritage, slavery, and the fight for liberation—and thus disavowing his entanglements with his own ancestral and personal pasts. Before the revolution, Dessalines observes the beliefs of his

African ancestors when he orders his rebel army to retreat to the hills, where "on the mountain top we'll sacrifice a goat to Legba. We'll dance Obeah. We'll make powder and bullets."[50] The juxtaposition of these sentences implies that paying tribute to the old African gods and ancestors is as important an aspect of preparing for war as making ammunition. By contrast, in act 2, after the revolution has succeeded and Dessalines has declared himself emperor, he basks in the radiance of his own power and increasingly disregards the advice of Martel—who often serves as the play's moral center, and of whom Dessalines in the opening scene of the operatic adaptation *Troubled Island* says, "Martel! Wise art thou! / Old art thou! Africa art thou!"[51]—just as he increasingly turns his back on the African gods of Vodou and abandons his black wife from his days as a slave. Instead he marries the mixed-race Claire, who persuades him to ban drums from the court: "I hate these ignorant people and their drums. I can't stand those drums every night, beating, beating, back there in the hills."[52]

By the end of act 2 of *Emperor*, just before his downfall, Dessalines has succumbed to his wife's baleful influence. He worries that an outsider would "think we were all savages," and declares, "We ought to be done with voodoo drums—all of us!"[53] After commanding the assembled guests to "Drink to your Emperor!" Dessalines orders "music and dancing—violins, not drums!"[54] The orchestral minuet that follows marks the triumph of European cultural traditions over those of Africa in the court of Dessalines, even as the play implies the futility of disavowing one's African heritage through the stage directions for the distant offstage Vodou drum, whose "monotonous beat continues, as if calling for one knows not what,"[55] which is heard "ever louder in the darkness"[56]; at the end of act 2, "The far-off beating of a voodoo drum fills the silence."[57] Yet Dessalines refuses to follow the "calling" of the drum and is ultimately betrayed by the wealthy mixed-race men who rose to power during the revolution. The lesson is clear: the revolution succeeds when its leaders invest in an Africanist identity. When they disavow the African-derived elements of their heritage, even the so-called primitive, they disavow any kind of pan-African unity, generate unproductive difference, and create a class hierarchy closely correlated with lightness of skin.

The alternative that *Emperor of Haiti* suggests to Dessalines's Eurocentric denial of African cultural practices and values, however, is not an equally reductive and exclusionary Afrocentrism but rather a pluralistic and creolized blending of traditions. Tellingly, Hughes reveals this alternative via a conversation among a group of market women on the quay of a coastal fishing village at the beginning of act 3. This scene would appear to be drawn from Hughes's own experiences spending several idle weeks at Cap Haitien, which he describes in *I Wonder as I Wander*: "I sat down with the market women and the fishermen and listened to their chatter, of which I understood not a word for many days. But I began at once to like 'au Cap' as the Haitians call that city where the slaves, years ago, planned the revolt that shook the foundations of human bondage in the Western world."[58] This juxtaposition within a single sentence of the modern-day peasants and fishermen and the area's history as the birthplace of the revolution effectively positions those peasants as the keepers of the revolution's legacy of freedom. It also shows Hughes working to navigate and bridge the differences between himself, a light-skinned African American, and these black Antillean peasants; as Kaisary notes, Hughes's Haitian writings revealed "a desire to dissolve linguistic and cultural barriers, to speak of Haitians as brothers and sisters, and to substantiate a radical racial and political solidarity with Haiti's black peasantry."[59]

On one level, Hughes's assumptions of kinship and presumptions to speak for black people everywhere replicated the essentialist rhetoric of colonialism itself. Compounding this problem, Hughes's repeated use of Haitian *women* to embody African tradition threatened to make the same move that anticolonial nationalists in nineteenth-century India made in response to the "women's question," which they situated, as Partha Chatterjee explains, "in an inner domain of sovereignty, far removed from the arena of political contest with the colonial state. This inner domain of national culture was constituted in the light of the discovery of 'tradition.'"[60] Especially given the underrepresentation of women in Hughes's network of black writers outside the United States, his tendency to locate the living fragments of African repertoire in the practices of poor Haitian women similarly threatened to relegate those women to receptacles for tradition.

In limited defense of Hughes's appropriative representational practice, though, let me interject that Hughes did sometimes use poor West Indian women characters to articulate views that were more syncretic than traditionalist and allowed them to play an active part in bringing African cultural practice into an increasingly globalizing modernity. In *Emperor of Haiti*, for example, it is one of the women selling coconuts in the market who best articulates Hughes's own easygoing ethos of pan-African entanglement. When asked how she can join the Catholic Church when she also attends Vodou dances, she replies: "Oh, I believes in voodoo, too. . . . Might as well believe in all kinds of gods, then if one fails you, you got another one to kinder help out."[61] For her, the various cultural strands that make up Haitian identity are not exclusive but accretive, hybrid, and endlessly flexible.

Insofar as the market woman embodies Hughes's ideal of a diasporic subject who embraces the full panoply of her ancestry, then, she serves as foil to her king, who comes to disavow the African and slave aspects of his heritage. This contrast would have had strong resonances for an audience in Port-au-Prince in 1936, had it been performed there.[62] The US Marines had withdrawn from Haiti in August 1934, inaugurating what Matthew J. Smith calls "modern Haiti's greatest moment of political promise": "At its outset, black consciousness and an intense cross-class nationalism produced a rare opportunity for lasting political change. These years witnessed the establishment of a popular labor movement; the rise of political parties; a bitter and vibrant ideological struggle; and a shift toward an assertive brand of Haitian black nationalism, *noirisme,* that not only defined the future of Haitian politics, but also prefigured similar developments elsewhere in the Caribbean region."[63] Yet the postoccupation period was also a moment at which the government of President Sténio Vincent grew increasingly dictatorial: "Once in power Vincent, fearing that the spread of radical ideas posed a potential challenge to his regime's nationalist allure, commented in private that when the 'Americans have gone the government will . . . have to rely on force to maintain itself in power.'"[64] Vincent made this a self-fulfilling prophecy after the withdrawal of US Marines when he declared periods of martial law, deported many foreign nationals, and imprisoned many radicals, including Jacques Roumain, whose trial and conviction Hughes strenuously protested, and who was granted a pardon in the summer of 1936, only two months before the premier performance of *Emperor of Haiti.*

It seems clear, then, that Hughes meant his representation of the Haitian Revolution in *Emperor of Haiti* to be interpreted on multiple levels. It hardly bothered to veil its "critique of racial and class prejudice within black society,"[65] especially its critique of contemporary Haitian politics. In Hughes's version of events, for example, the mixed-race aristocrat who gives the order to assassinate Dessalines is named Stenio, a name certain in the 1930s to evoke Haiti's authoritarian president. On another level the play aspired to an act of performed memorialization, functioning to register the stories and iconic images from the Haitian Revolution—narratives of resistance and black empowerment—into a larger black imaginary. Or as Kaisary puts it, Hughes's play and his opera attempt "to communicate the heritage of the Haitian Revolution to African Americans, and in telling the story of the Haitian Revolution, to make it stand as a metonym for black agency in the context of a black Atlantic modernity."[66] I would only add that Hughes's desired audience for his dual message of resistance and commemoration transcended African Americans to include blacks in the West Indies and beyond.

In the latter regard, it is worth pausing to dwell on one last symbol that circulates throughout the play: the scars on Dessalines's back left by his master when he was caught returning to the plantation after leaving it without permission overnight. At the end of act 1, when he is rallying the crowd of slaves to begin the revolt, "He rips his shirt wide open, exposing his back covered with great red welts."[67] While drums are beaten and shots are heard offstage, "Dessalines stands with his arms uplifted, his back bare. In the lantern light, great red scars gleam like welts of terror across his shoulders."[68] The scars, which his treacherous mixed-race wife Claire is secretly revolted by and calls the "marks of a rebellious slave!"[69] are transformed in the audience's view from marks of punishment and degradation to marks of rebellion and self-determination. At the end of the play, when Dessalines's dead body lies on stage, "the old welts of his slave days stand out like cords across his shoulders," and the stage directions tell us that Claire "shudders with a memory she can never lose."[70] This is McClintock's imperial ghosting[71] at work—the scars are the spectral traces of a violent past that will not stay interred, just as the drumbeats from the lost African past are never fully silenced.

The scars, then, are multivalent and open to plays of meaning: the traces of a violent past that will not stay interred, they are also reminders of resistance and agency. Hughes saw the usefulness of this malleable symbolism extending far beyond Haiti for all of the African diaspora: he implied that disavowing one's slave ancestry was not the same as losing or escaping it, and the phantoms of the unsettled past would always return to haunt survivors and their descendants and urge them to rebellion. In dramatizing this truth as he saw it, Hughes reinvented the history of slavery and resistance in ways meant not to exorcise them but to make them generative and useful in his own twentieth century. More specifically, he attempted to weave the symbols and chronotopes from his memory of pan-African entanglement into the foundation of a transnational black community and identity he spent his life cultivating.

To recap, then: in Hughes's writings from the 1930s, Haiti carried a complicated mélange of associations, containing possibly the purest embodiments of African cultural life in the American hemisphere through its music and its Vodou, possessing one of the cruelest histories of slavery and racial domination, and symbolizing the fight for freedom and resistance to oppression. But it also symbolized loss, and lost opportunity. This latter theme might be seen as a prescient caution to anticolonial struggles such as Haile Selassie's fight to expel Italian forces from Ethiopia, still in progress when Hughes wrote this play. Finally, I would like to suggest that Hughes, especially in *Emperor of Haiti,* used the platform of nineteenth-century post-revolutionary Haiti to work through some of the dilemmas that threatened perpetually to splinter the pan-African unity he hoped to bring about. The most pressing of those dilemmas grow out of the tension between Hughes's attachment to primitivist tropes and the dangers in primitivism's essentialist assumptions—that they might both appear to endorse racialist ideologies and lead to an emphasis on racial purity that might exclude people of mixed race such as himself.

In this context, cultural differences among black people around the world were simultaneously a source of attraction for a xenophile such as Hughes and a threat to his psychological, political, and artistic impulsion toward black unity. Predictably enough, given Hughes's preoccupation with skin color, the most obvious cultural difference he dramatized in the play was the fault line between dark-skinned Haitians of African descent and lighter-skinned people of mixed race, or "mulattoes." The character Congo, whose very name associates him with the heavily mythologized heart of Africa, and who says he was a boy when he was abducted from Africa, resents and mistrusts the mulattoes. Moreover, the sympathetic character of Dessalines's first wife, Azelia—another dark-skinned woman character whom Hughes makes the keeper of simple African values—complains that they "look down on us for being black."[72] Dessalines defends his mixed-race coconspirators on the grounds that "they're smart. They've been to school and got an education. We need their heads."[73]

Congo's mistrust proves justified in act 2, when we learn that the mulattoes, including Dessalines's new wife, Claire Heureuse, have only contempt for their "emperor" and are plotting his downfall in part by exploiting his dependence on their literacy and education. Thus emerges another difference that splinters any possibility of pan-African solidarity: the division of Haitians into those with literacy and those, like Hughes's romanticized black peasants, still living a purely oral tradition—which overlaps closely with the division between black and mixed-race Haitians and the division between the poor and the affluent. The same fault line underlies the earlier split between characters who feel and want to maintain a connection to the traditions of Africa and those who, like Dessalines at the end, disavow the drums of their African heritage and turn instead to the violins of Europe.

That Dessalines possesses such an obvious Aristotelian flaw, and that his assassination is the climax of the play's action, makes it clear that Hughes is working firmly in the tragic mode with *Emperor of Haiti*. The mode in effect continues the themes of lamentation and loss that Hughes had articulated in 1930 in "Afro-American Fragment," where "Subdued and time-lost / Are the drums."[74] Yet the tragic mode, with its sense of inevitable doom and resignation, sits uncomfortably with the call to action implied by the play's allegorical critique of its own contemporary political situation in Haiti. Perhaps it resulted from Hughes's recognition that any geographical or temporal web of cultural exchange was inevitably intertwined with the rhetoric and structures of capitalism and of colonialism, with their patriarchal hierarchies and prioritizing of Western poetic and narrative traditions. Regardless, the generic constraints of tragedy worked against his own project of integrating the Haitian Revolution into his black Atlantic repertoire as figures of resistance and agency.

In other projects, however, Hughes was arguably more effective at balancing representations of Haiti as a source of heritage and African essence, with Haiti as an active protagonist in the modern world. For instance, he translated several of Roumain's early proto-Negritude poems, and later cotranslated Roumain's novel *Gouverneurs de la rosée*, which operated in the very different and more politically optimistic mode of heroic romance. These modes, I will argue in the next two sections, helped Hughes to assimilate both Haiti's tragic history and its degraded present into a vision of diasporic community and interconnectedness in the future.

Langston Hughes and Jacques Roumain

During that crucial summer of 1931, as we have seen, Hughes was intent on establishing a connection to the "people without shoes," the peasants he regarded as both repositories of African cultural practices and the inheritors of the legacy of the revolution. And so he put off visiting Jacques Roumain, to whom he had a letter of introduction from a mutual friend, until his last day in the country. In *I Wonder as I Wander*, Hughes remembers that if Roumain and his wife, Nicole, "were typical representatives of the Haitian elite, then I regretted not having met more of them."[75] Roumain was distressed not to be able to celebrate his American guest's visit more formally, and after Hughes went back to his ship to await departure, Roumain organized a delegation of writers and government officials to give him a send-off. Not expecting their visit, Hughes and his traveling companion Zell had stripped down to their trousers and were eating greasy sausage on the deck of their ship when they were discovered by the "long line of elegantly dressed gentlemen, some in tail coats and gloves." Hughes later remembered, "To receive these gentlemen, I had hardly time even to wipe my mouth, let alone put on a shirt or coat. I was caught greasy-handed, half-naked—and soxless—by an official delegation of leading Haitians."[76]

Jacques Roumain was five years younger than Hughes, born in 1907 to an elite Haitian mixed-race family. As Naomi Garrett summarizes, "Roumain was haunted by a vision of a united Haitian people, a vision which dominated his actions and obsessed his mind; he knew that this could be achieved only by securing a better life for the oppressed masses. As a result, he turned his back upon a life of luxury to become a social menace to his class and a spokesman for the inarticulate masses."[77] At the time the above comical scene took place, he was already well known in Haiti as a poet and nationalist and worked for the Department of the Interior. Notably, even his brand of nationalism was marked by an openness to models from far abroad, as he made clear in a series of articles from that period expressing admiration for Gandhi's nationalist movement in India, which worked "for a strong union" by appealing to "the aspirations common to all Indians."[78]

Roumain's nationalist activities put him at odds with the US occupation, and he was imprisoned for several months in 1928–29, but when Eugène Roy became, briefly, president with the backing of a nationalist coalition in 1930, he appointed Roumain to oversee the Department of the Interior. As Carolyn Fowler explains, Roumain quickly grew disenchanted with the emancipatory potential of nationalism, realizing that it would not change the social and economic conditions of workers and the poor, and he "began to turn to Communism as an alternative."[79] This might be regarded, however, as part of a more general emphasis, intensifying throughout Roumain's career, on internationalism and border-crossing solidarity or, as Martha Cobb puts it, a shift "from Haitianization to a collective black experience which his thought and writing needed to express."[80] In other words, he was increasingly motivated by an ethos of pan-African entanglement, developed in conversation with Langston Hughes.

Long interested in the writers of the Harlem Renaissance, Roumain's connection to that movement deepened when he met Hughes in person and resulted in a deeper commitment to fostering black solidarity around the world.[81] In a letter to Tristan Rèmy the following year, Roumain wrote, "I am of the opinion that our literature should be *Negro* and largely proletarian. I am working equally for the coming together of Negro writers of all countries. It is to this end that I am preparing, under the title *Afro-American Poems*, a small volume of translations of poems by American Negroes, Langston Hughes, etc."[82] Likewise, on a trip to New York and Washington, DC, in early 1932, Roumain seized the opportunity to meet Alain Locke and other influential African Americans, expanding his transnational web of contacts.[83]

This manifest interest in disseminating the work of other black writers was either instigated or reciprocated when Hughes translated two of Roumain's poems into English in 1931: "When the Tom-Tom Beats" and "Guinea" were two of four poems Roumain published in 1931 (the other two were "Langston Hughes" and "Créole"). Cobb notes that these poems marked a break from Roumain's earlier verse, with its "dependency on French ways of expression," and toward "a sensitivity which responded to Haitian experience."[84] Fowler argues, however, that these poems were closer in theme to Negritude than to Indigenism, in that they "reflect not the local but the universal black experience."[85] Hughes's translations of the poems have appeared in no fewer than four anthologies.[86] Indeed, until the 1995 publication of Fungaroli and Sauer's translations of Roumain's collected poems in *When the Tom-Tom Beats,* Hughes's translations of "Tom-Tom" and "Guinea," and later of the novel *Masters of the Dew,* were the vehicles through which Roumain's writings were most readily available in the English-speaking world. In his first letter to Hughes in 1931, Roumain thanked the American for the "splendid translation" of his poems.[87]

Even if Roumain hadn't titled one of his 1931 poems after Langston Hughes, the influence of the American on Roumain's other poems of this period would be evident. As we have already seen, Hughes's earliest verse treated Africa as a timeless and almost mythical source of primal life force, pulsing with rivers and drumbeats. Roumain likewise drew on images of an imagined African motherland in, for example, "Guinea," which plays on the belief held by many Haitians that a person's spirit migrates across the Atlantic Ocean after death to rejoin the ancestors in Africa. Significantly, the poem locates this imagined afterlife

> around the eye of the river. . . .
> There, there awaits you beside the water a quiet village
> and the hut of your fathers, and the hard ancestral stone where your head
>   will rest at last.[88]

Roumain deploys very similar tropes in "When the Tom-Tom Beats," echoing Hughes and anticipating the Negritude poets with exotic images of a "tom-tom panting like the breast of a young black girl"[89] and a river that "Carries you toward the ancestral landscape."[90] As in Hughes's primitivist poems from the 1920s, Roumain uses the tom-tom drum as a symbol of Africa; the fact that tom-toms actually originate in South Asia only confirms Dimock's recognition of a "complex tangle of relations" that serves as "connective tissues binding America [and, implicitly, Haiti and Africa] to the rest of the world."[91] Fowler furthermore links the water images in these poems to Hughes's own frequent use of river and sea imagery; in both writers' hands, she says, "Water, the river, represents the flow of life from past to present, linking one generation to another."[92] The same interconnectivity also bridges geographic space and crosses national borders, tying the black Atlantic together into a skein of cultural exchange that is simultaneously a part of and distinct from modern world culture.

Perhaps, though, this continuity was more aspirational than actually existing, as these images of Africa were also associated with mourning and heartache. As Roumain put it in his 1943 essay on the Vodou ritual of the

Sacrifice of the Drum Assoto, at the end of the ritual the "divinity has been sent back forever to Africa, to that ancestral Guinea which covered with mythological mists, still lives on with extraordinary tenacity in the faithful memory of the descendants of slaves."[93] The longed-for homeland in this vision can only be accessed through a nostalgic and melancholy veil—what Hughes translates in "Tom-Tom" as "the sweet sorcery of the past," or in Fungaroli and Sauer's version, "the sweet sorcery of memory."[94] This is the memory of pan-African entanglement on a remote ancestral plane.

We find the same tone of longing and lamentation in Roumain's poem "Langston Hughes," but here the plane of entanglement in the past is linked to the present through contemporary exchange and restless wandering. This short lyric describes the American poet in Lagos, where he "knew those melancholy girls"; in France, where the "Seine appeared less beautiful than the Congo"; and in Venice, where a girl "wept and claimed her twenty lira from you." Then in a final bit of apostrophe the speaker says:

> Your nomad heart wandered
> like a Baedecker from Harlem to Dakar
> The sea bestowed a sweet, rasping rhythm to your songs, and
> its bitter flowers opened in the salt spray.
> Now in this cabaret at sunrise you murmur:
> Play the blues for me
> O play the blues for me
> Do you dream of palm trees and negro paddlers singing down the dusk?[95]

I have made a couple of changes here to Fungaroli's and Sauer's translation, including changing their rendering of "ses fleurs d'amertume" from "its biting flowers" to "its bitter flowers." In conjunction with the "sweet, rasping rhythm" in the previous line, this conveys the speaker's bittersweet sentiments toward the blues, which are wrapped up in a history of slavery and trauma and thus serve as a prolific source of multidirectional memories.

In "Langston Hughes," then, Roumain linked the poem's namesake to a nomadic restlessness and diasporic longing. The sea represents the travels that Hughes would later recount in *The Big Sea* (also evoked in the reference to Baedecker Guides), but more generally it represents the interconnectedness of people across oceans and national borders, from Lagos and Dakar to Paris, Venice, and Harlem. Not only does the poem not situate Hughes as an American poet; it emphasizes Hughes's own *refusal* to pander for the privilege of claiming such a title: "You saw France without pronouncing historical words: / *Lafayette, we are here.*"[96] The allusion is to US Army colonel Charles Stanton, who during World War I visited the grave of the Marquis de Lafayette and spoke the italicized words to honor the

Frenchman's role in the US Revolutionary War. That Hughes would have visited France without speaking such words suggests that he arrived in Paris not as an ambassador of US letters and culture but as a representative of the African diaspora, a black transnational collectivity. This suggests further that while Roumain in 1931 had not yet shifted his allegiance to communism, he was already disenchanted with nationalism and feeling the pull of a broader ethos of transnational entanglement and coalition building.

This radical internationalist turn led Roumain to cofound the Haitian Communist Party in 1934, and later that year he was arrested by the government of Sténio Vincent. Tried for possessing communist literature (Hughes would erroneously report in *Dynamo* that Roumain was imprisoned for circulating the newspaper *Le cri des nègres*),[97] Roumain served nearly three years in prison before being released in 1936. During that time, Hughes was active in protesting what he saw as Roumain's unjust imprisonment.[98] Following his release from prison in 1936, Roumain went into exile and lived several years in Europe, where the Spanish Civil War and the rise of fascism and Nazism led his writing to take on even more strongly "an international, even global, quality. Survival [for him was] no longer merely that of a nation, but of mankind."[99]

While working for the Musée de l'homme in Paris, Roumain was reunited with Langston Hughes on multiple occasions, including at the Second International Writers Congress in Paris in July 1937, which Nicolás Guillén also attended. Hughes gave a speech to the gathering in which he inveighed against fascism and racial oppression and invoked global solidarity in opposition: "We are tired of a world where, when we raise our voices against oppression, we are immediately jailed, intimidated, beaten, sometimes lynched. Nicolás Guillén has been in prison in Cuba, Jacques Roumain in Haiti, Angelo Herndon in the United States. Today a letter comes from the great Indian writer, Raj Anand, saying that he cannot be with us here in Paris because the British police in England have taken his passport."[100] This tribute led Jacques Roumain in the audience to whisper admiringly to Nancy Cunard, "He never forgets his comrades."[101] On the eve of World War II, Roumain left Europe for New York, where he was honored by a reception whose attendees included Hughes, Alain Locke, Richard Wright, and Jessie Fauset.[102] He later went to Cuba in 1940 or early 1941 at the invitation of Nicolás Guillén before returning to Haiti in late 1941 following the election of Elie Lescot as Haiti's president.

During the last year that he spent back home in Haiti, Roumain continued his lifelong project of archiving Haitian culture and disseminating and translating black literature. For example, he founded the Bureau d'Ethnologie, devoted to documenting Haitian folk culture, and he worked on a book of translations of Nicolás Guillén's poetry into French. This, again, made him and Hughes allies in the project of documenting and valorizing the accomplishments of black people, as well as making black writing and oral culture available through collection, translation, and anthologization. Roumain's final move was in 1942, when he was assigned to a post at the Haitian embassy in Mexico City. That same year, he completed his final collection of poetry, *Bois d'ébène* (*Ebony Wood*), and later wrote the novel *Gouverneurs de la rosée* just before his death in 1944.

Ebony Wood

What Roumain arrived at in his mature poetry and fiction, and what Hughes found valuable in that work, was something like universalism, but read through the lens of both Africanism and Communism. Fowler claims that the four poems published in 1931 were "the sole expression of Negritude (uncontaminated with proletarianism) in the poetry of Jacques Roumain."[103] Indeed, the poetry written after his turn to communism and his three-year prison sentence was shaded much more heavily by class concerns and the global oppression of peasants and workers. In the title poem of his posthumously published collection *Ebony Wood,* he wrote:

> I only want to be of your race
> workers peasants of all countries
> that which separates us
> climate distance space
> the oceans
> a bit of foam sailboats in a bucket of indigo.[104]

That he called workers and peasants a "race" suggests that—unlike Hughes, who always saw the world through the primary lens of race—Roumain had internalized a certain Marxist orthodoxy that race was a construct of capitalism and therefore secondary to the class struggle. In my terminology, although he continued to work within an ethos of entanglement, he had chosen for that moment to privilege the scale of workers worldwide rather than the scale of pan-African interconnection. As he put it in "Filthy Negroes" from the same collection, after the revolution "even the tom-toms will have learned the language / of the *Internationale.*"[105]

The global scope of his call for solidarity, which Ellen Conroy Kennedy calls "the broader expression of the brotherhood of all exploited peoples,"[106] is made clear in "Ebony Wood" when the speaker emphasizes his similarity with "workers peasants *of all countries.*" Roumain articulated this prioritization of class over race more explicitly in a collection of articles collectively titled *L'homme de couleur,* or *The Man of Color,* published in Paris in 1939: as Fowler summarizes it, he argued that the "notion of race is therefore unscientific, and the notion of a French race, of a German race, and so on is a metaphor."[107] At the same time, there is little doubt that he also wanted the word "race" to convey a sense of African identity, which continued to remain central to Roumain's worldview. He partially reconciled the tensions between the essentializing tendencies of Negritude and Marxism's nonracialism by making the black peasant the archetypal hero in a romantic narrative of revolution. As Fowler characterizes his late work, "The past sufferings of the black man provide the springboard for the revolution which will release all oppressed men everywhere from bondage. The black collectivity becomes the epic hero who will lead mankind beyond his present state."[108] At any rate, both senses of "race" enable the speaker's solidarities to transcend "climate distance space" and to shrink the ocean to a "bucket of indigo." Thus Roumain again uses oceanic and water imagery to emphasize not separation, but interconnection.

In "Ebony Wood," furthermore, the speaker makes explicit the ambivalence and paradox inherent in his treatment of the New World's African past:

> Africa I kept your memory Africa
> You are in me
> Like a splinter in the wound
> Like a guardian fetish in the village center
> make of me your catapult stone
> of my mouth the lips of your wound
> of my knees the broken columns of your abasement.[109]

A wound with a splinter still lodged in it might heal poorly and fester. One interpretation of these lines, then, is as a warning against the dangers of traumatic memories being repressed but remaining lodged in the unconscious. The next simile, however, implies that this memory of Africa can also be the basis for a feeling of group identity and belonging, just as a guardian fetish provides the metaphysical foundation for an African clan. The subsequent series of metaphors shifts meanings again, implying that this memory of Africa can be a weapon, like a catapult, or can equally well serve as a kind of megaphone or amplifier, giving voice to the grief and affirming the reality of diasporic history. The line about the "broken columns of your abasement" implies that the edifice of African identity is in ruins and must be reimagined and rebuilt, in part through the poet's apostrophes and invocations. The newly reanimated African past in the poet's hands is flexible, mutable, paradoxical, but ultimately empowering and useful.

As the above examples reveal, apostrophe is a dominant mode in Roumain's poetry, and by directly addressing that which is absent—in this case, Africa as abstract ancestral memory—the speaker draws attention to its loss. Yet apostrophe can serve another purpose as well, as when Roumain uses it in "Ebony Wood" to conjure an archetype of the "Negro peddler of rebellion," of whom the poet says, "you know all the routes of the world / since you were sold in Guinea."[110] Here he directly confronts Africa's association with human bondage in the diasporic imaginary. But the poem also implies that slavery is the precondition for the "nomadic heart" of the diasporic black man, who knows "all the routes of the world." Thus the iconic image of the rebellious slave, the "Negro peddler of rebellion," stands in for and becomes a multidirectional memory of Haiti's own famous slave revolution (which is at the heart of the country's national self-conception) and of the maroons in Jamaica and of Nat Turner in Virginia and countless other acts of revolt by captive Africans. The poem then quickly expands the web of associated memories to include the plight of Jews in ancient Egypt prior to Exodus: "Each word reminds you of the weight of Egyptian stones," the speaker says.[111] And then the chain of association leading from Africa to New World slavery doubles back again to include forced labor in the Congo in Roumain's own day:

> Mandingo Arada Bambara Ibo
> wailing a song strangled by iron collars
> (and when we reached the coast
>
> . . . .
> there remained of us
> Bambara Ibo
> only a fistful of scattered grains
> in the hand of the sower of death)
>
> . . . .
> But I also know a silence
> a silence of twenty-five thousand negro corpses
> twenty-five thousand railroad ties of Ebony Wood
> Under the iron rails of the Congo-Océan.[112]

The image of workers' bodies lying underneath the Congo-Océan Railroad is multidirectional and variegated, containing not just its own horrors but also traces of collective memories of the Middle Passage, in which hundreds of thousands of slaves died crossing the Atlantic Ocean and were thrown overboard. The train is also of course a quintessential symbol of modernity, and of movement and migration, as well as a space of cultural mixing. In this case, the poem makes clear how the histories of black people are woven violently into the larger history of modernity.

Roumain used similarly multidirectional imagery in the poem "Filthy Negroes." The speaker evokes the specter of slave auctions when he describes pimps and prostitutes at a nightclub as

> no more than a commodity
> to be bought and sold
> on the pleasure market
> no more than a negro
> a nigger
> a filthy negro.[113]

According to Rothberg, multidirectional memories enable "a remapping of memory in which links between memories are formed and then redistributed between the conscious and the unconscious."[114] Roumain's poem effects this remapping by overlaying contemporary Haiti's political and economic struggles, in which ordinary people are reduced to commodities, with the much older history of slavery and revolt and the still older narratives of biblical Exodus and diaspora evoked in other lines. This interpolation of historical layers accomplished several things for Roumain: it commemorated and valorized the historical struggle of African peoples in the Americas and in Africa under colonialism. It historicized and helped explain the present conditions of black people worldwide. And it began the project that Rothberg sees Aimé Césaire engaged in some decades later in *Discourse on Colonialism*: "attempting to further a multidirectional vision of cosmopolitanism,"[115] one that insisted on the humanity of African victims of slavery and colonialism by interweaving their narratives with those of Abrahamic universalism (represented by the Holocaust for Césaire, writing some five years after it ended, and by biblical Egyptian slavery for Roumain, writing in the prewar years).

This process of forging links, redistributing memories, and making conscious collectively repressed memories is especially important in the case of a traumatic event of both the scale and temporal remoteness of the mass enslavement of Africans in the Americas. Unlike the Holocaust—with its overwhelming evidentiary trail of bureaucratic records, photographic documentation, and survivor testimony—slavery in the United States and the Caribbean is far murkier, with no survivors left to tell their stories and only a meager few autobiographies of slaves, many of them mediated by white editors and amanuenses. Partly as a result of this, slavery is a partial lacunae in the self-conception of the West, with even the descendants of slaves ignorant of their own history and heritage. One challenge facing writers such as

Hughes and Roumain, then, in their efforts to develop a pan-African black collectivity, was to dredge to the surface repressed memories of slavery and in doing so, make history visible to its descendants. But these writers also attempted to work through the traumatic legacy of slavery more indirectly, by finding analogous scenarios elsewhere in the world to serve as multidirectional memories.

The conception of slavery and diaspora that served as backdrop to Roumain's representations in these late poems was not, I want to emphasize again, one of lament and passive victimization but rather of black agency, struggle, and resistance. The speaker of "New Negro Sermon," for example, looks forward to a time when "No more will we sing the sad despairing spirituals" but will march under "red banners / Stained with the blood of our just."[116] Hughes had used similar language just a few years earlier, as when he wrote, "Put one more s in the U.S.A. / To make it Soviet."[117] Just as Roumain and Hughes both used water imagery and multidirectional tropes to link instances of oppression and revolt throughout time, Roumain borrowed another technique from Hughes's poetry of the 1930s—the list of peoples around the world—to help the reader envision the kind of border-crossing worker solidarity on which the revolution would depend. Hughes particularly used this technique in 1931–32, as in "Chant for Tom Mooney," which links the plight of the wrongfully imprisoned labor leader in San Francisco to that of workers around the world:

> And the sound vibrates in waves
> >   From Africa to China,
> >   India to Germany,
> >   Russia to the Argentine,
> >   Shaking the bars,
> >   Shaking the walls,
> >   Shaking the earth,
> Until the whole world falls into the hands of
> >   The workers.[118]

On one level this is boilerplate communist rhetoric—"Workers of the world unite!" Hughes might have come to regret publishing such lyrics, as he was increasingly subjected to protests and red-baiting attacks in the press and the US Congress.[119] Yet as we will see in later chapters and scale enlargements, Hughes's fondness for cataloging the names of places and people in his poetry continued long after he stopped publishing revolutionary agitprop, indicating a deeper interest in forging an international community of the poor and dispossessed. His attachment to Soviet communism, I maintain, was a relatively fleeting manifestation of a larger ethos of transnational entanglement; at other times he focused instead on connections within the pan-African world but continued to use the technique of asserting commonality through juxtaposition.

In the poems in *Ebony Wood*, likewise, Roumain used lists of oppressive situations to help envision an international revolution. Earlier I noted, per Fowler, that in Roumain's romantic and patriarchal vision, it is the black man who leads the revolution. This is sustained in the climax of "Filthy Negroes," which commences with images that evoke ancient Africa:

> Too late
> deep into the heart of infernal jungles
> will throb the terrible telegraphic beating
> of the tom-toms tirelessly beating beating
> beating
>
> . . . .
> too late
> for we will have risen
> from the thieves' dens from the gold mines in the Congo
> and South Africa
> too late it will be too late
> on the cotton plantations of Louisiana
> in the sugar cane fields of the Antilles
> to halt the harvest of vengeance of the negroes.[120]

The tom-toms here are no nostalgic fragment of a ruined African past but rather (as in Hughes's *Emperor of Haiti*) the sound of war drums uniting the African diaspora. Colonialism in Africa and the Caribbean is linked to the cotton fields of the American South, and the uprising of workers in all these situations is described with the metaphor of a "harvest of vengeance," an agricultural trope that would no doubt resonate with the experience of the worldwide peasantry in which Roumain invested his political loyalties and his artistic sensibility.

Before turning from Roumain's late poetry to his final novel, let me pause to highlight several aspects of the literary relationship between Hughes and Roumain that have already risen into view. First, as with Hughes's translations of the poetry of Cuban writers Nicolás Guillén and Regino Pedroso, we see Hughes from the early 1930s onward consciously and pragmatically bridging the divide created by linguistic difference among peoples of African descent throughout the American hemisphere. His correspondence reveals how hard he worked to try to get these translations published and read, despite the difficulties almost all writers encountered selling any books to publishers during the Great Depression, especially translations of Latin American writers.[121] By making it possible for anglophone readers to encounter the works of francophone and hispanophone writers, Hughes laid the groundwork for and gave substance to a black Atlantic literary network and an aesthetic of pan-African entanglement. As Vera Kutzinski puts it, "It is through actual and represented acts of translation that Hughes connects all these different sites into a global geography that extends well beyond early-twentieth-century pan-Africanism and even beyond more recent critical conceptualizations of the African diaspora."[122] It is worth emphasizing, as Kutzinski does in relation to Hughes's translations of Hispanic poets, that this was a reciprocal, multidirectional effort: Roumain and other Haitian writers translated Hughes's and Guillén's verse into French, and many Latin American writers rendered Hughes's poetry into Spanish.[123] In doing so, as Anita Patterson argues, they plunged Hughes into a "dense, surprising matrix of transatlantic and hemispheric convergences" that contributes to "the subsequent growth of Caribbean modernisms" and "would foster the cultivation of modernism and Négritude in the Francophone Caribbean."[124]

The cultural exchange between Langston Hughes and Jacques Roumain furthermore reveals both continuities and distinct differences in how both men approached the key concerns raised by pan-African entanglement: the meaning of Africa and blackness, the role of black people in the modern world, the memorialization of slavery and resistance, and the forging of transnational alliances based not on European bourgeois standards but on a universalism rooted in the cultures of peasant and workers. As in Hughes's early poetry, there is a strong element of romanticism both in Roumain's poetic treatment of Haiti's African and slave heritage and in his use of the figure of the black man returned from abroad as a heroic archetype in *Masters of the Dew*. But whereas the primitivism of Hughes's 1920s poems about Africa resisted political mobilization and historical particularity, Roumain's work fully exploited the political potential that Yogita Goyal identifies in romance: for the writers she studies, romance "suggests a movement outside of the linearity of time and history into the cyclic nature of myth and prophecy."[125] Romance, Goyal says, "fits the elasticity and semantic openness required for such activities of cultural reconstruction and remembrance, but also for its ability to signal the freedom of possibilities beyond the degraded reality of the present."[126] My argument is that his study and translation of Roumain's work helped Hughes transform his own literary renderings of diasporic memory from politically passive elegy and lament for the past into the usable foundation for black subjectivity and resistance in an imagined future. The fullest expression of this transformative potential can be found in Roumain's final novel, *Masters of the Dew,* the subject of the next section.

Masters of the Dew

Roumain finished *Gouverneurs de la rosée* in 1944, but before it could be published he began suffering mysterious health problems and died on 18 August 1944, of causes that remain undetermined.[127] The novel was published posthumously in 1944, with an English translation by Langston Hughes and Mercer Cook published as *Masters of the Dew* in 1947. In a letter from March 1946, Roumain's widow, Nicole, on receiving word that Hughes had agreed to undertake the cotranslation, wrote to him: "You cannot imagine with what emotion and what pride that I learn this news: the dream Jacques had in Mexico while finishing the novel, of seeing it translated into English and presented to the public by Langston, is to become reality."[128]

As we saw in the last chapter, the ethos of vernacular black entanglement that arose in conversation between Langston Hughes and Claude McKay expressed appreciation for the culture of the peasantry but in practice focused most intensively on the proletarian cultures (and those of the people that Marxist orthodoxy would dismiss as the lumpenproletariat) of the cities they lived in and wrote about—New York, Kingston, Paris, Marseille. Roumain likewise wrote about urban life in Port-au-Prince, in *Les fantoches* (*The Puppets,* 1931) and *Le champ de potier* (*Potter's Field,* not published until 2007). But the works for which he is best known—*La montagne ensorcelée* (*The Enchanted Mountain,* 1931) and *Gouverneurs de la rosée*—are set in rural villages and concern themselves with the African-derived culture of Haiti's peasantry. As Michael Dash puts it, Roumain, influenced by Price-Mars, refused "to see peasant culture as hopeless and confining" and instead "conceived the peasant experience as a metaphor for a larger ideological and moral vision of man faced with his destiny."[129] Certainly Roumain saw in the peasantry a basis for international, even global, solidarity and folded-togetherness, articulated in *Masters of the Dew* by the protagonist Manuel Jean-Joseph's vision of "one family of peasants united in friendship." He declares, "All peasants are equals. . . . They're all one single family. . . . One needs the other."[130]

This theme is established in the first chapter, when Manuel's father, Bien-aimé Jean-Joseph, nostalgically recollects the *coumbites* or agricultural collectives that used to harvest cane to the rhythms of drums and chanting. I have been suggesting that one productive way of thinking about the channels of exchange that constitute the global skein of cultural entanglements is to trope them as veins and nerves in a living organism. Roumain's narrator uses precisely such a metaphor: "There sprang up a rhythmic circulation between the beating heart of the drum and the movements of the men. The rhythm became a powerful flux penetrating deep into their arteries and nourishing their muscles with a new vigor."[131] The primitivism that ran through Langston Hughes's early poems manifests itself here in Roumain's novel as well, with the drums (always associated, in both writers' works, simultaneously with Africa, with slavery, and with rebellion) providing a kind of nourishment and energy—an antidote to sterile modernity—while also embedding itself in the ancestral plane of pan-African entanglement.

Like Hughes and McKay before him, Roumain often grounded his conception of that ancestral kinship in nostalgic evocations of Africa. Early in the novel, the narrator compares Manuel's homecoming to the peasants' belief that the souls of dead Africans return across the sea to their ancestral soil: "Far back into the past he looked. . . . The dead, they say, come back to Guinea, and even death is only another name for life."[132] This foreshadows Manuel's funeral at the novel's end, when his mother, Délira, exclaims, "My boy is dead. He's going away. He's going across the sea. He's going to Guinea."[133] The mother's beliefs grow out of the animism of Vodou, whose "associations with insurgency" and transgressive threat to the US occupation were emphasized in earlier short stories by Roumain.[134]

But Roumain's romanticization of Haiti's African heritage was also tempered by the scientific rationalism of his Marxist philosophy. In contrast to his mother's devotion, Manuel is deeply critical of religious teachings (be they Vodou or Roman Catholicism) that induce fatalism and resignation in their followers. He indulges his mother in a ceremony to thank the *loas* for his return, but he later complains to Anna that such practices have taken the place of action to improve the peasants' plight: "But all that's just so much silly monkeyshines. That doesn't count! It's useless, and it's wasting time."[135] While he appreciates the link that Vodou ceremonies and beliefs provide to Haiti's African past, his appreciation is wholly secular, if viscerally experienced: "When the drums beat, I feel it in the pit of my stomach. I feel an itch in my loins and an electric current in my legs, and I've got to join the dance. But that's all there is to it for me."[136]

The ambivalence that Manuel feels toward Vodou is reinforced by the narrator's own commentary on the sacrifice to Legba: "Nevertheless, the fête went on. The peasants forgot their troubles. Dancing and drinking anesthetized them—swept away their shipwrecked souls to drown in those regions of unreality and danger where the fierce forces of the African gods lay in wait."[137] The African-derived religious rites here function as opium for the peasant masses. The same ambivalence runs through Roumain's nuanced prescriptions for how scientific socialism should approach Vodou in the series of articles that were republished under the title *On Superstitions:* "Naturally, we must relieve the Haitian masses of their mystical impediments. But we will not win over these beliefs by violence or by the threat of Hell. It was not the executioner's axe, the flames of the stake, the auto-da-fés which destroyed sorcery [in Europe]. It was the progress of science, the continued development of human culture, an understanding of the structure of the universe."[138] In this view Vodou is "a stage in religious development characteristic of all peoples,"[139] but it is now time for Haitians to graduate and leave it behind.

This skeptical view of Vodou as part of a "mentalité archaïque"[140] set Roumain apart from Hughes, whose anthropological fascination with the religion outweighed whatever secularist concerns he might have shared with Roumain about religion's "anesthetizing" effects, and who saw in Vodou a rich source of images and tropes to draw on in imagining an aesthetic of pan-African entanglement. To some extent, and in spite of his scientific rationalist views, Roumain clearly saw some of the same potential in Vodou and more generally in Haiti's African-derived heritage. In this regard Manuel serves a similar function to Dessalines in Hughes's *Emperor of Haiti,* refracting the present of the African diaspora through the revolutionary past. As Kaussen puts it, "*Gouverneurs de la rosée*'s image of a socialist pastoral paradise can be viewed as the ghost of the missed revolutionary dream of the St. Domingue slaves,"[141] and on an allegorical level, "Manuel's memories of Cuba perform a demystifying function, reviving the historical memory of slave uprising that lies" in the Haitian countryside.[142] I would add that this overlaying of the past over the present, and the historically particular over the global, allowed Roumain to balance and navigate the different scales and planes of cultural entanglement—reconciling his racial loyalties and his more general universalism of the proletariat, for example. Cobb says that the novel describes "a universally human predicament in terms of the dilemmas and aspirations of a unique people,"[143] and indeed, it situates the African diaspora as one cluster of transnational entanglement within an imagined larger community of the dispossessed and oppressed.

Lest the reader overlook these sympathies for the poor, the narrator openly and defiantly declares them early in the novel: "The high-class people in the city derisively called these peasants 'barefoot Negroes, barefooted vagabonds, big-toed Negroes.' (They are too poor to buy shoes.) But never mind and to hell with them! Some day *we* will take our big feet out of the soil and plant them on their behinds."[144] The critique of class snobbery and the emphasis on the peasants' barefootedness echo Hughes's essay "People without Shoes," which Roumain had likely encountered when it was published in *New Masses* in 1931. Roumain himself came from the mixed-race aristocracy of "high-class people in the city" (les bourgeois de la ville),[145] yet his narrator's use of "we" and "them" in this passage suggests a conscious alliance with the peasantry and, as with Hughes, a refusal of the privileges afforded him by his lighter complexion. This refusal is actually more emphatic and vulgar in Roumain's French: what Hughes and Cook render as "never mind and to hell with them" appears in the original as "tant pis et la merde pour eux" (too bad and shit for them); and "on vous les foutra un dans le cul, salauds"[146] (we will fuck them one in the ass, the bastards) is bowdlerized to "plant [our big feet] on their behinds." In the original even more than in Hughes and Cook's English version, then, this odd editorial intrusion by the narrator early in the novel establishes a deliberately crude vernacular register seemingly designed to offend the sensibilities of the bourgeoisie and a political outlook highly sympathetic to the people Roumain had once called "ye wretched of the earth."[147]

The phrase "barefooted vagabonds" from the above-quoted passage is curious because it does not appear in Roumain's original, which instead repeats the noun "nègres" for a third time ("nègres pieds-à-terre, nègres va-nu-pieds, nègres-orteils"). Recall that the concept of vagabondage figured prominently in the works of Claude McKay, especially *Banjo*. While we cannot say with certainty that "barefooted vagabonds" was Hughes's phrasing rather than his cotranslator Mercer Cook's, its use so early in the novel does effectively bring *Masters of the Dew* into the circuits of vagabond internationalism that I discussed in the last chapter and at the same time implies that the lumpenproletariat is likewise part of the novel's community of the shoeless and dispossessed.

The word "vagabond" is likewise interesting because it *does* appear in the French original a few pages later, where it describes not a person but the hidden spring that Manuel Jean-Joseph makes it his mission to find to bring water to his drought-stricken village. The narrator, recounting Manuel's mood and thinking, says: "Water sometimes changes its course like a dog changes masters. Who knew where the vagabond was flowing now?"[148] (Qui sait où elle coulait à l'heure qu'il est, la vagabonde).[149] We have already seen the importance of water imagery in both Roumain's and Hughes's poetry, as an emblem of continuity through time and coentanglement over distance. Dash furthermore characterizes the spring that Manuel does eventually discover in *Masters* as one of the "universal poetic symbols" that

Roumain uses, in this case to represent "potential and rebirth."[150] In this early passage, Roumain's choice of the phrase "la vagabonde" to describe the elusive stream also links it with the "linguistic migrancy and cultural homelessness" that Kutzinski identifies in the life and writing of Langston Hughes[151]—that is, it links the water to the "nomad heart" that Roumain attributed to Hughes in the poem named after him[152] and that Hughes himself expressed even in the title of his second autobiography, *I Wonder as I Wander*.

Given his emphasis on vagabondage and nomadism, it seems fitting that Roumain chose as his protagonist and hero a *viejo*, a migrant cane cutter who has traveled beyond Haiti and gained a broader international perspective. Manuel Jean-Joseph spent years working on the cane plantations in Cuba, which had made him feel "like an uprooted tree in the current of a river. I drifted to foreign lands."[153] But it also gave him firsthand lessons on the need for unity and organization among workers and showed him that "what counts . . . is rebellion, and the knowledge that man is the baker of life."[154] As Manuel relates to his fiancée, Annaise, "At first, in Cuba, we had no defense and no way of resistance. One person thought himself white, another was a Negro, and there were plenty of misunderstandings between us. We were scattered like grains of sand, and the bosses walked on that sand. But when we realized that we were all alike, when we got together for the *huelga* [strike]"; and he shows her his fist as a demonstration of how strong the individual fingers become when they come together.[155] If we keep in mind the etymology of *diaspora* as a scattering, as of seeds or in this case "grains of sand," this passage implies that the African diaspora was weakened by its dispersal and by the bosses' ethos of separation; the alternative metaphor of a fist then counters that dispersal with a figure of unity.

Kaussen points out that the figure of "border-crossing *viejos*" as "ineluctable products of the operations of capital in the Caribbean" was a recurring one in twentieth-century Haitian literature and that the labor rebellions these characters instigate effectively reenact the eighteenth-century slave revolt: "Roumain's and [Jacques-Stephen] Alexis's depictions of the *viejo* suggest that the transnational and global reach of slave revolt finds its ultimate condition of possibility in the twentieth century when global networks of migration and contact had begun to vastly multiply."[156] Kaussen usefully reads this figure as navigating the interplay that Glissant identifies between relation and diversity. Read in this light, Manuel is not just a universal heroic archetype, as Fowler regards him, but also the embodiment of Roumain's Marxist-inflected ethos of pan-African entanglement. This view has the advantage of circumventing problematic notions of purity and racial essence that seem to emerge elsewhere in Roumain's writing, by basing itself on similarity of historical circumstance rather than on race. And it both prefigured and influenced the aesthetics of entanglement that Hughes himself would later put forward most convincingly in *Ask Your Mama*.

Assessing Hughes's and Roumain's Vernacular Pan-African Entanglement

If the empowering potential of this aesthetic and vision were revealed in Roumain's novel, we can also see some of its limitations. For example, Hughes's attempts to tie Haiti, its revolution, and its African-derived culture into the collective memory of pan-African entanglement faced the danger of appropriation and commodification. Kaisary recounts the fate of *Troubled Island* after Hughes had a falling out with his collaborator, composer William Grant Still: the composer produced it at the New York City Opera on his own, without Hughes's firsthand knowledge of Haiti and Vodou, leading to "a tension that does not exist in the play [*Emperor of Haiti*], due to a collision of form and content."[157] This shows the danger of trying to take up a cultural practice like Haitian Vodou into the lexicon and repertoire of pan-African entanglement: once captured in fixed forms, those representations can be commodified, flattened, manipulated, distorted, or downright garbled. The delicate balancing act between, on one side, racialist essentializing, and on the other, romantic celebrating of an imagined African past—the balancing act that had presented such difficulties to Hughes in his primitivist poetry of the 1920s—would continue in subsequent decades to present challenges in his writings about Haiti, and Africa.

Another limitation of Hughes's and Roumain's visions of a pan-African community was their very unsatisfying range of roles for black women. Just as *Emperor of Haiti* makes them into repositories of folk culture or symbols of grief, loss, and suffering, so does *Masters of the Dew* deny the two central women characters, Délira Délivrance and Annaise, any interiority beyond their love for and devotion to Manuel. Likewise, they and other women often seem more symbols than actual characters. One peasant woman whose husband has crossed the border into the Dominican Republic to look for work is described by Simidor as having cried so much that "soon there won't be a single drop of water left in her body"[158]—a comment that links her body to the drought-stricken Haitian landscape. Délira is likewise represented as the embodiment of Haiti's grief and sorrowful history: her singing "knew no language other than this sorrowful plaint. . . . Life has taught black women to sing as though they are choking back a sob, and it's a song that ends always with a beginning because it's in the image of misery. And does the circle of misery ever end?"[159] As in so much anticolonial nationalist rhetoric and literature, the figures of these grieving women become tropes embodying the grieving nation.

Anna's significance is more positive: the narrator describes her in one scene bent over the wash, looking like "some queen of Guinea with her curved hips, her naked breasts, hard and pointed, her skin so black and smooth."[160] Elsewhere in the novel, when Manuel shows her the fig grove at the mouth of the spring, he compares her to Eve: "Because at the beginning of beginnings, there were a woman and a man like you and me. The first spring flowed at their feet, and the woman and the man entered the spring and bathed in life."[161] These two passages taken together position Anna as the embodiment and keeper of an African Eden but also as the symbol of future hope and fertility, as we learn in the novel's last paragraph that she is carrying the murdered Manuel's child in "her belly where the new life was stirring."[162] Anna thus becomes central to fulfilling the generic expectations of the heroic romance, with its emphasis on liberation and rebirth. But it also reduces her, and by extension all Haitian women, to the role of receptacles for men's legacies, with no active role in advancing the international community of workers Roumain envisions.

By the same token, the fact that Hughes's outreach to black writers in Africa and the Caribbean was so heavily targeted at men means that his black Atlantic network similarly excluded women from the emerging canon of black postcolonial literature of the twentieth century. In pointing this out I do not mean to judge these two writers by the retroactive standards of the twenty-first century, especially given their remarkably forward-looking positions on race and class. Rather, I simply want to point to both writers' blind spots toward black women's interiority and potential for artistic and/or political agency as one possible cause of the difficulties they encountered as they tried to formulate and sustain an ethos and aesthetics of pan-African entanglement and a corollary black Atlantic literary network.

The conversation between Anna and Délira that concludes *Masters of the Dew* contains one passage that, while still positioning men as the active agents of change, nevertheless accords women the crucial role of the keepers of communal memory: Délira explains to her daughter-in-law that she sews compulsively because "it keeps me occupied, daughter. I sew, I sew—and I stitch the old days and the new. If only we could mend life, Anna, and catch up the broken threads!" This leads Anna to recount something Manuel once told her: "Life is a thread that doesn't break, that is never lost, and do you know why? Because every man ties a knot in it during his lifetime with the work he has done. That's what keeps life going through the centuries—man's work on this earth."[163]

I suspect that this passage resonated deeply with Hughes when he read it and when he and Cook translated it. It emphasizes human labor, especially of those who work directly "on this earth." It suggests that present achievement builds on the accomplishments of the past—a sentiment Hughes later extolled in "Prelude to Our Age" and elsewhere. Perhaps most significantly, despite deeming it "man's work on this earth," the passage presents sewing (an activity usually gendered as female) as a metaphor for stitching together "the old days and the new" (je raccorde l'ancien temps avec ces jour-ci).[164] The metaphor is one of quilting, rather than the weaving metaphor that will become important to understanding Hughes's later vision of a diasporic community. But Roumain's quilting trope is nevertheless rich in its potential for integrating the past into the fabric of the present and for joining people across time and space.

Hughes tried to articulate this project that he and Roumain shared in common when he wrote "A Poem for Jacques Roumain" in honor of Roumain's life and death. The poem, which actor Canada Lee read at a memorial for Roumain in New York in May 1945,[165] does not appear in *The Collected Poems of Langston Hughes* but does survive in Hughes's papers as well as in the collection of Nancy Cunard, the French writer and anthologist with whom Hughes corresponded occasionally and who was friends with Roumain. The poem emphasizes Roumain as a "citizen of the world" in its opening stanza: "When did you / Find out about the world, / Jacques?"[166] Later it links Roumain's urban identity with his allegiance to peasant life:

> You've gone—
> But you are still here
> From the point of my pen in New York
> To the toes of the blackest peasant
> In the *morne*.[167]

"Morne" is the word in Antillean French Creole for a small mountain—a locally specific usage that casts the poem's subject as a Haitian as well as a well-traveled citizen of the world. The speaker concludes the poem by reinforcing this connection between the global and the local, casting Roumain in the role of black man as romantic hero that Roumain himself had explored so heavily in his writings:

> Always you will be
> Frontiersman,
> Pathfinder,
> Breaker down of

> Barriers,
> Hand that links
> Erzulie to the Pope,
> Damballa to Lenin,
> Haiti to the universe. . . .
>
> Strange
> About eternity
> Eternal
> To the free.[168]

Hughes's praise poem, then, positions Jacques Roumain as the "Hand that links" the Yoruba divinities at the heart of Haitian Vodou to the "universe," or at least to transnational institutions with the scope and ambition of the Roman Catholic Church and Soviet communism. In other words, Roumain had helped render Haiti's African-derived past usable and relevant to a modern world in which the processes we now identify with globalization were already beginning to accelerate. In this regard, we should see Roumain as both a key contributor to Hughes's lifelong project of building transnational black cultural institutions and an inspiration to continue his efforts to advance the simultaneous causes of black entanglement and a larger humanism.

Scale Enlargement B
Hughes, McKay, and Negritude

WHILE THE other two scale enlargements zoom out to the continental view, surveying Langston Hughes's engagements over a long period with the Caribbean and Africa, respectively, this one settles on a different analytical scale: Hughes's (and McKay's) engagements with mid-century black writers in French, especially the Negritude poets. Since the next long chapter will focus on Aimé Césaire, here I will take stock quickly of Hughes's and McKay's connections to the other two major Negritude writers—Léopold Sédar Senghor from Senegal and Léon-Gontran Damas from French Guiana—and establish Hughes's relationship with Negritude as a concept.

Scholars have thoroughly established the importance of the Harlem Renaissance as precedent and influence for francophone black writers living in Paris in the 1920s and 1930s.[1] Writers and intellectuals including Countee Cullen, Jean Toomer, Alain Locke, Jessie Fauset, and others spent significant time in France in the 1920s, and most of them passed through the Paris salons run by René Maran and later by the Nardal sisters.[2] But special esteem was felt for McKay, who lived for many years in France, and whose novels and poems were translated into French early on, and for Hughes, who spent several months in Paris in the mid-1920s. Hughes had two poems appear in 1924 in the French periodical *Les continents,* which Edwards notes for its self-conscious efforts "to articulate itself as part of a broader multilingual diasporic dialogue about the shape and direction of black modern culture."[3] Hughes and McKay both had poems appear in translation and in English in 1931 in the influential Paris publication *La revue du monde noir,* where they found a comfortable fit among the journal's "ambitious pan-Africanism."[4]

Both writers were also celebrated in 1932 in the sole issue ever to be published of the journal *Légitime défense,* produced by a group of Martinican students in Paris. The issue included an excerpted chapter from McKay's *Banjo,* the one in which Ray lectures a Martinican student on the need to "find yourself in the roots of your own people."[5] As Edwards points out, the excerpt "seems to serve a clear didactic purpose, preaching respect for black folk, [and] praising the beauty of 'native African dialects.'"[6] That issue of *Légitime défense* also included an essay by Étienne Léro that singled out McKay and Hughes as "two revolutionary black poets . . . [who offered] the African love of life, the African joy of love, the African dream of death."[7] Lilyan Kesteloot's conclusion about the journal is telling in its comparison to the Harlem Renaissance: "With *Légitime Défense* the New Negro movement in French letters was officially inaugurated."[8]

Both *Revue du monde noir* and *Légitime défense* were avidly and closely read by a group of black students in Paris who would later publish two issues of their own journal, *L'etudiant noir,* and founded what would in time become an internationally famous black artistic movement of their own, known as Negritude. Césaire and Senghor both wrote pieces for the journal; Damas did not, but claimed it to have been "a result of the initiative of Césaire, Senghor, and myself."[9] According to Kesteloot, the *L'etudiant noir* group "used contemporary Western values with discrimination, choosing from them only what was likely to promote the dignity of black peoples."[10] Already, we can see the strategic syncretism that characterized Hughes's ethos of transnational entanglement also driving the thinking of the Negritude writers. Indeed, their reclamation of a frequently derogatory French word was driven by the imperative to reclaim and valorize blackness, just as the Harlem Renaissance authors had done: "For them, the noun 'Nègre' no longer referred to an experience of emptiness that had to be filled. Through the creative work of Black poets it became what Aimé Césaire called a 'miraculous weapon.'"[11]

What the Negritude poets admired in the Harlem Renaissance writers, then, was their dedication to rehabilitating the image and perception of black people (including their own self-perception). Senghor confirmed this in an essay he wrote for *L'etudiant noir* in 1934 but never published, which held up McKay and Hughes as exemplars of black self-assertion, just as the authors of *Légitime défense* had done. He quoted the same chapter from *Banjo,* featuring Ray's declarations of black identity to make the case that "assimilating" European culture and values—much emphasized in French colonial rhetoric—was compatible with embracing one's African-derived identity: "We assimilate the French, Latin and Greek cultures. Let us learn also to discover ourselves and to express ourselves. Humanism, for us, can have no other meaning. 'Getting down to our native roots,' writes McKay, 'and building up from our own people . . . is not savagery. It is culture.'"[12] Senghor concluded that this racial self-identification was "far from falling into racism." Rather, studying and writing about black people "can only work to enrich the French patrimony, the human patrimony. It is our contribution to the work of civilization"; he ended the piece by quoting two lines from Langston Hughes's "I Too": "I, too, sing . . ." / "I am the darker brother."[13]

Senghor's rhetoric here and elsewhere fits well with the model I have been developing, of pan-African entanglement existing concentrically within a larger web of transnational genealogies and flows. He insisted, for example, on the need for black writers around the world to "enrich . . . the human patrimony" by creating distinctively black art, nurturing an aesthetic and values proudly derived from putatively African cultural practices rather than mimicking European forms. Ironically, though, in the early decades of the twentieth century, proud assertions of black heritage were for the most part not emanating directly from Africa itself but rather were refracted through the black diaspora in the United States, the Caribbean, and Brazil, including the Harlem Renaissance writers but also figures such as Du Bois and Marcus Garvey. In a 1950 essay on black American poetry, Senghor credited African American literature, especially of the Harlem Renaissance generation, as offering the most forceful and inspiring early examples of art that valorized black heritage—that is, it made the existence of an ancestral plane of pan-African entanglement the basis for black people's claims to a stake in the larger skein of modern culture: "The black personality is affirmed in the past; the experience of slavery did nothing but enrich him in depth," Senghor wrote as prelude to quoting Hughes's manifesto "The Negro Artist and the Racial Mountain."[14]

Later in the same essay Senghor would quote one of Hughes's quintessentially primitivist poems about Africa, "Danse Africaine," with its "slow beating of the tom-toms," as an example of poetry that channels "the African songs, where a musical ear soon discovers underneath the apparent simplicity and monotony a quite uncommon richness and subtlety."[15] Senghor concluded the essay by noting that in recent years black American poetry had "tried to go beyond the theme of the *Race*, by union with God—or with the *Proletariat*. Claude McKay and Langston Hughes are the best representations of this new tendency."[16] Senghor was the Negritude writer whose poetic practice has been most frequently accused of reducing black cultures to a fixed and static African essence or personality, but such essays show Senghor's thinking about race to be as strategic and critical as it was romantic. They likewise reveal his development of Negritude as a unifying concept to have been a vehicle for navigating cultural differences across the black diaspora—and ultimately for achieving a greater universality, whether conceived in religious or Marxist terms.[17]

Léon Damas, too, insisted that "Negritude, in our interplanetary era, is a means and not an end."[18] Accordingly, his definition of Negritude emphasized both its Afrocentricity and its fundamentally protean and transnational nature. Negritude, he wrote in 1974, was not "conceived by Africans in the Motherland" but instead was an outgrowth of a great diasporic web—"those influenced by the spirituals, blues, and jazz of the United States of America; the sound and dance of Cubans; the *batucada, samba, frevo,* and *capoeira* of Brazil; the *meringue* and *petro* of Haiti; the *meringué* of the Dominicans and Puerto-Ricans; the *calypso* of Trinidad and Jamaica . . . all of which originated from Africa."[19] Reiland Rabaka tells us, "It was Damas who first systematically studied and then introduced Cesaire and Senghor to the aesthetics, poetics, and politics of the New Negro Movement and Harlem Renaissance," and argues that Damas "synthesized elements from African American, Latin American, Caribbean, and continental African intellectual and political traditions."[20]

It is clear, in fact, that Damas conceived of Negritude in self-consciously transnational terms, and not just on an ancestral plane of heritage and genealogy but on a contemporary plane of communication and exchange. He points out, for example, that when Alioune Diop was leading the African Society of Culture, "he was always able to call upon Langston Hughes, Jean Price-Mars, Aimé Césaire, others and myself to spread the word from one continent to the other, from one country to the other, from one town to the other."[21] It is clear, furthermore, that Damas regarded the Harlem Renaissance, especially the works of McKay and Hughes, as the primary twentieth-century catalysts sparking cultural exchange and interconnection among these various diasporic nodes. Like Senghor, Damas quoted Hughes's "Negro Artist and the Racial Mountain" in one essay where he sketched a genealogy of black literary influence emanating out from the Harlem Renaissance to the black colonies of France: "Starting from this immersion, which McKay's *Banjo* was for us, and after *Home to Harlem, Banana Bottom,* not even mentioning his poems, the writings of Langston Hughes, Sterling Brown, Walter White, led us to one revelation after another discovering other lands than ours."[22]

Despite this fervid admiration of the Negritude poets for his work, Hughes was surprisingly slow to embrace the francophone writers in turn, especially in contrast to his eagerness to correspond with and promote the South African writers he would begin to acquaint himself with in the 1950s. Linguistic differences might have played a role, as each writer typically wrote in his own language. Yet Hughes had previously formed relatively close connections with Jacques Roumain. Moreover, the language barrier would not have prevented Hughes from discussing Negritude in his prolific essays and columns, but the word did not appear in his weekly column in the *Chicago Defender* until 1965, long after debates over Negritude had become common in black cultural discourse in the anglophone world—and even then he mentioned the word only in the context of a passing jab at Senghor for having married a white woman.[23] Ryan Kernan attributes Hughes's failure to comment on Negritude during the postwar period partly to his long-developing skepticism of racial essentialism and partly to his fear of being associated with another left-leaning movement when his radical writings of the 1930s were already coming back to haunt him, culminating in the McCarthy hearings of 1953.[24]

Whatever the cause, despite the survival of occasional correspondence spanning a couple of decades, Hughes did not write to Damas and Senghor in the 1940s with the kind of warmth and exuberance he would show a few years later to Peter Abrahams, Bloke Modisane, and Richard Rive from South Africa; nor for that matter did he seem to reciprocate the eagerness to cultivate relationships that Senghor and Damas conveyed in their letters. Hughes may have met Damas as early as 1938,[25] but seemed not to remember the encounter some years later. In the spring of 1946 Damas sent Hughes a handwritten note in English that took an amusingly familiar tone: "Dear, very Dear Lang, A good friend of yours, Mr. Damas, Léon Damas, is to be in New York a week. I shall be pleased much pleased to see you my old, very old brother. Damas." As if to reject the presumption of kinship, Hughes typed an explanatory note on the back for his records: "French-Guiana Negro writer living in Paris" and then wrote by hand, "en route to West Indies / May, 1946 / L.H."[26]

Hughes and Damas apparently did not meet on that trip, as Damas's next letter was from Cayenne that August, expressing his regrets that he had been unable to see Hughes before leaving New York and asking permission to translate a number of Hughes's poems and prose pieces into French. Hughes's reply came a month later and was congenial but businesslike, granting his permissions where he was contractually free to do so. There was another round of correspondence in 1948, when Hughes was collecting permissions for his *Poetry of the Negro* anthology, which included selections from Damas (translated by Hughes himself) and Césaire but not from Senghor or any other African poet except Aquah Laluah. And then a third burst of exchanges happened in 1953 when Damas wrote again for permission to translate Hughes's poems for an anthology that Damas planned to produce for the French publisher Éditions Seghers. As Kernan explains, though, Seghers removed Damas from the project and gave it instead to François Dodat, who produced *Poèmes* (1955), "an anthology devoid of any content stemming from politics, radicalism, or contemporary events that did not speak directly to the 'race problem' in the U.S."[27] If the perception of Hughes in the francophone world was already one based heavily on his vernacular blues poetry and his idealized representations of Africa, Dodat's anthology only reaffirmed that perception.

In the meantime, Hughes had also carried on an intermittent correspondence with Senghor. The earliest surviving letter is a handwritten note from Senghor to Hughes on French National Assembly letterhead in January 1945, basically thanking Hughes for his work toward "the emancipation and affirmation of your people."[28] From 1950 to 1967, most of their correspondence took the form of letters thanking each other for having sent copies of their books; parcel post and airmail both proved to be crucial channels through which cultural exchange happened and transnational entanglements were formed. Likewise, commercial air travel increasingly facilitated such entanglements. Rampersad's biography of Hughes narrates his first meeting with Senghor in 1961, when the by-then president of Senegal visited the Kennedy White House for a dinner in Senghor's honor and had Langston Hughes added to the guest list. In what was for Hughes "the social highlight of the year—perhaps of Langston's life," Senghor gave a toast in which he specifically mentioned Hughes as "a major early source of inspiration."[29]

The African writer and head of state paid a similar honor in April 1963 in a letter written in English, asking Hughes not only to participate in the festival being planned for Dakar, Senegal, but also to serve on the American Committee of Friends of the World Festival of Negro Arts (commonly known by its French acronym FESMAN), to which Hughes agreed. Senghor declared a primary aim of the festival to be illustrating "the unique creative contributions of the Negro race to universal channels of thought and art" and praised Hughes as "a writer whose work is known and loved by millions, and . . . an outstanding literary spokesman for Negro-Americans [who has] enriched the legacy of everyone."[30] This language was strategically composed to appeal to Hughes's ethos of pan-African entanglement, including his lifelong dedication to having black cultural products recognized as contributions to the world's heritage. Senghor's praise continued after the American poet died, as when he borrowed the title of a Hughes poem for the subtitle of a 1975 speech he gave at the annual dinner of the PEN Club of American Writers ("Negritude and Americanism, or 'Let America Be America'") and called Hughes "the most Negro and at the same time the most American of the Black American poets, and the most universal"; he concluded the speech by quoting from "I, Too."[31]

Perhaps all these plaudits coming from the Negritude poets helped Langston Hughes warm toward them; certainly, by the early 1960s he was more openly expressing admiration for their works and acknowledging similarities in their artistic visions. In his remarks on the panel "What Is

African Literature?" at the Mbari conference in Uganda in 1962, for example, Hughes compared Negritude to his own "New Negro" movement: "In the writing of that period there was a very conscious attempt to appreciate and celebrate and spread about through writing the good qualities, the interesting qualities, the amusing qualities of the black people . . . to lift up the beauty of Negro-ness. . . . Perhaps you'd call it negritude, but we have no phrase for it."[32]

Hughes echoed this sentiment in 1966 when he wrote about what he and his fellow writers were trying to accomplish in the 1920s: "To us, *négritude* was an unknown word, but certainly pride of heritage and consciousness of race was ingrained in us."[33] He repeated it also that April, just over a year before his death, at a FESMAN colloquium. Hughes argued that Negritude was the equivalent to the African-American notion of "soul," which he defined as "a synthesis of the essence of Negro folk art redistilled—particularly the old music and its flavor, the ancient basic beat out of Africa, the folk rhymes and Ashanti stories—expressed in contemporary ways so definitely and emotionally colored with the old, that it gives a distinctly 'Negro' flavor to today's music, painting or writing. . . . Soul is contemporary Harlem's *négritude*."[34] Any argument that Hughes after the 1930s was a fully recovered primitivist who renounced the very concept of a racial essence must reconcile itself with statements like these made toward the end of his life, positing seemingly intrinsic "qualities of the black people," an "essence of Negro folk art," and "a distinctly 'Negro' flavor." I do not entirely agree with Tsitsi Jaji's reading of this speech as an implicit critique of Senghor's anachronistic views, then, as this speech still shows him strategically deploying the rhetoric of racial essentialism. But I do concur with Jaji that Hughes called for a "renewal" of Senghor's ideas—their reanimation, that is, within contemporary, vernacular folk cultures.[35]

Hughes's efforts to cultivate transnational black solidarity with the Negritude poets also included his anthologization and translation work. In Hughes and Bontemps's *The Poetry of the Negro,* Césaire and Damas were the only francophone writers represented who were not from Haiti. Tellingly, the excerpts from Césaire's *Notebook of a Return to the Native Land* include an extract that envisions Toussaint Louverture in his prison cell in France. It is no surprise that Hughes would have chosen passages that reinforced his own lexicon and repertoire of pan-African entanglement, in which the Haitian Revolution figured largely. Of the three short poems by Damas, translated by Hughes himself, none are overtly racial or political in theme, though the middle poem, "Trite without Doubt," does faintly evoke the primitivist imagery so common in Hughes's early poems and many other works of Negritude:

before giving over
entirely beautiful and black

. . . .

to the mountains
where a bamboo flute
cries in the night.[36]

The imagery is not far, for example, from Hughes's "Nude Young Dancer," whose speaker asks, "What jungle tree have you slept under, / Night-dark girl of the swaying hips?"[37] It seems, then, that Hughes (in collaboration with Bontemps) was choosing Caribbean poems for the anthology that selectively carried on the parts of his own literary legacy—his aesthetics of pan-African entanglement—that he wanted to preserve.

In the 1950s and 1960s, as Hughes's interests turned more decisively back to Africa, he likewise included Senghor in his anthologization efforts and continued to emphasize the Negritude writer's works that best embodied his own ethos and aesthetics. *An African Treasury* (1960) included the single poem "To the American Troops"; the translation is unattributed and may belong to Hughes himself. The poem narrates a feeling of racial kinship between African and black American soldiers: "I had only to touch the warmth of your dark hand—my name is *Africa!* / And I discovered lost laughter again, and heard old voices, and the roaring rapids of the Congo."[38] Two years later, when Hughes worked with Christiane Reygnault to produce the *Anthologie africaine et malgache* for Éditions Seghers, it included many of the selections from *An African Treasury* translated into French but had a substantially larger francophone component, including six poems ("To the American Troops" not among them) and three essays by Senghor. The new selections included "Congo," with its opening that sounds that name "On rivers, on every memory," and its concluding image of a pirogue "reborn in the water lilies of spume,"[39] imagery we will encounter again in Césaire's work in the next chapter. The selections furthermore included Senghor's most overt lyrical tribute to Hughes and the Harlem Renaissance, "To New York," which I discuss briefly below. In 1963, when Hughes included five poems by Senghor in his *Poems from Black Africa,* "To New York" was the only poem repeated from either of the two previous anthologies.

It is worth noting that the anthologization and translation work also ran in the other direction, as we have already seen with Damas's intentions to translate Hughes's poetry into French. Furthermore, the journal *Présence africaine,* effectively the mouthpiece for Negritude from its founding in 1947, published French translations of one of Hughes's Simple stories in

1951, of the poem "The South" (1926) in 1955, and of another poem, "Let America Be America Again" (1936), in 1966. As with Dodat's anthology, the selections of Hughes's work focused intensively on the American race situation, but *Présence africaine* also presented the more radical and revolutionary Hughes of the 1930s; both, along with the periodic eruptions of primitivist imagery and rhetoric in Hughes's work, would be (selectively and to varying degrees) influential on the Negritude poets.

The Negritude writer who most earnestly mimicked Hughes's romantic evocations of a precolonial African paradise was Senghor—ironically so, since he was the only one of the three leading figures in the movement to come from Africa. Perhaps it was his many decades of living in France that led him to express such longing and nostalgia for an imagined African motherland, figured in explicitly gendered terms. One of his earliest poems, "Night in Sine," begins with images of black womanhood: "Woman, place your soothing hands upon my brow, / Your hands softer than fur." This comforting maternal figure with her lullaby containing the "beat of our dark blood" is presented as the antidote to the alienation experienced by those "Exiled like us."[40] The same 1945 collection, *Shadow Songs,* also contained "Black Woman," which likewise flattens the woman to whom the poem is an ode into a symbolic repository of African virtues: "Ripe fruit with firm flesh, dark raptures of black wine, / Mouth that gives music to my mouth." Making love to the black woman is compared to the "sculptured tom-tom, stretched drumskin / Moaning under the hand of the conqueror."[41] In still another poem, the "African night" is personified as a black woman who "dissolves all my contradictions, every contradiction / In the primal unity of your negritude."[42] These lines bring together the idealization of African values and aesthetics with the Marxist/Hegelian language of "melting contradictions." If to live in the African diaspora is to be fragmented, Senghor offers a vision of Negritude as the "primal unity" that can restore wholeness. Dixon's observation seems largely true, then: "The most powerful African elements in Senghor's poetry are in fact images from the past rather than verbal constructions of a present reality"[43]—and, crucially, they are problematically gendered images, ones that relegate black women to passive receptacles for Africa's cultural heritage.[44]

Nevertheless, we should also note the ways in which Senghor's lyrical treatments of race and Negritude were frequently more nuanced, pragmatic, and rooted in history and culture than he is often given credit for. Consider for example his commentary on the intuitive and emotional "Negro-African knowledge," which he insisted was potentially compatible rather than necessarily at odds with Western rationalism: "We must maintain the Negro-African method of knowledge, but integrate into it the methods Europe has used throughout her history—classical logic, Marxian dialectics, and that of the twentieth century."[45] I would argue that, here and elsewhere, Senghor adopted the concentrically ordered vernacular ethos of black entanglement earlier expressed in the works of McKay, Hughes, Roumain, the Haitian Indigenists, and others. To name only one example, in "To the Music of *Koras* and *Balaphon*" (1945), Senghor engaged in the first-person claiming of a group identity so common in Hughes's poetry:

> I would choose the poetry of the rivers, the winds, the forests. . . .
> I choose my toiling black people, my peasant people,
> And the entire race of peasants throughout the world.[46]

As in Hughes's work, rivers and seas recall the interconnectedness of peoples scattered around the world, and as in Hughes's writings, the group loyalties the speaker expresses in these lines side first with black workers and peasants and then "the entire race of peasants" (toute la race paysanne)[47] everywhere.

Perhaps Senghor's poem that most overtly laid claim to the legacy of Hughes and other African American poets was the one that Hughes included in two of his anthologies, the ode to Harlem entitled "To New York." I will quote Ulli Beier's translation that Hughes included in *Poems from Black Africa*:

> You must but listen to the trombones of God, let your heart beat in the rhythm of blood, your blood.
> I saw in Harlem humming with noise with stately colours and flamboyant smells.
> . . . .
> At the feet of police horses roll the mangoes of love from low houses.
> And I saw along the sidewalks streams of white rum streams of black milk in the blue fog of cigars. . . .
> Listen to the distant beating of your nocturnal heart, rhythm and blood of the tom-tom, tom-tom blood and tom-tom.[48]

The reference to "God's trombones" evokes James Weldon Johnson's book of poems with that title and by extension the entire "New Negro Renaissance" for whom Johnson was an elder and a pioneer. It also reminds us of the centrality of jazz music (where trombones feature prominently) to Senghor's "formulation of the essential characteristics of *l'âme noire*, the black soul," in Jaji's summation.[49] Subsequent lines associate Harlem with the larger African diaspora through images of Caribbean mangoes, rum, and cigars, before linking it all together with the pervasive beating of the tom-tom, thus evoking Hughes and Roumain. In Senghor's version the tom-tom is like a "nocturnal heart" pumping black blood through New York and the American hemisphere. For Senghor, this black blood, or Negritude, or what he called the "spirit of Negro-African civilization," which animated work by "the best Negro artists and writers today, whether from Africa or America,"[50] imbued their art with the rhythms and values of Africa.

As for Damas, his thematic and stylistic palette as a poet was broader than Senghor's, less singularly preoccupied with race and Africa, but at times Damas's verse too showed itself to be clearly in conversation with McKay's and Hughes's conceptions of ancestral pan-African entanglement and kinship. Damas's first collection of poems, entitled *Pigments* (1937), opened with an epigraph from McKay's poem "To the White Fiends," including the lines "am I not Afric's son, / Black of that black land where black deeds are done?"[51] Having thus identified himself with McKay's proud and defiant assertion of black heritage, Damas then began the collection with a poem called "They Came That Night" ("Ils sont venus ce soir"). Dedicated "For Léopold Sedar Senghor," it echoes the rhetoric of primal African rhythm that Langston Hughes had effectively enshrined in the lexicon of pan-African entanglement:

> They came that night as the
>   tom
>   tom
>   rolled
>   from
>   rhythm
>   to rhythm
>   the frenzy
> of eyes
> the frenzy of hands
> the frenzy
> of statue feet.[52]

The "frenzy / of statue feet" recalls Hughes's romanticizing depictions of Haitian peasants and their barefoot dancing, just as the images of tom-toms stoking dancers into a frenzy evokes many of Hughes's early poems. By quoting the Jamaican McKay in the epigraph, dedicating the first poem to the African Senghor, and borrowing the symbology of the American Langston Hughes, Damas announced himself to the world in his first collection by triangulating his aesthetic and his conception of West Indian poetry in relation to other Caribbean authors, to African writers, and to black poets from the United States, all simultaneously.

The third major figure in the Negritude movement, Aimé Césaire, performed a similar triangulation, and like Senghor and Damas, he regularly borrowed themes, images, and tropes from Hughes, McKay, and Roumain. Yet Césaire drew the least direct influence from those writers on a stylistic level. This fact, and Césaire's many nuanced and careful declarations that black community should be founded on cultural and historical commonality rather than biological essence, have together convinced many scholars that his thinking about race and blackness was therefore less embedded in the essentialist rhetoric of McKay's and Hughes's modern primitivism than was, for example, Senghor's writing. In the next chapter, I will complicate this perception as I argue that, whether or not he ultimately believed in a racial essence, Césaire in fact deployed the lexicon of primitivism quite readily, as for example in my primary case study, his dramatic masterpiece *The Tragedy of King Christophe*. At the same time, he also exposed the contradictions and limitations of that primitivist tropology in a way that suggests his use of its essentialist premises was strategic and self-aware.

3 "It Cancels the Slave Ship!"
Aimé Césaire, the Haitian Revolution, and Langston Hughes

COMPARED TO the other writers I have chosen to focus on in this book—compared even to Damas and Senghor, the other two leading poets in the Negritude movement—Aimé Césaire's connections to Langston Hughes were relatively superficial. The only surviving correspondence consists of four brief, businesslike letters, two in each direction, dated 1948, mostly concerning Césaire's inclusion in Hughes and Bontemps's *Poetry of the Negro* anthology. They met on two occasions that I have been able to document, both late in Hughes's life: once in Berlin in 1964 and once in Dakar in 1966, both meetings in the context of festivals where Césaire's play *The Tragedy of King Christophe* was being performed.

If direct contact between the two men was infrequent and fleeting, the precedent Hughes set and his influence on Césaire's early writings were nevertheless profound, a fact to which the Martinican often and readily attested, along with the influence of McKay and other writers of the Harlem Renaissance.[1] In an interview a few years after Hughes's 1967 death, Césaire noted that he and Senghor had encountered the work of African American poets in the pages of *La revue du monde noir*: "Before the war, in 1938, 1939, Senghor and I frequented the works of Langston Hughes, Countee Cullen, Claude McKay, especially the novel *Banjo*. . . . They formed a part, if I may say so, of our personal luggage."[2] Rabaka argues that "what is most important is not so much who or what influenced Cesaire, but what he innovatively did with his varied influences."[3] What Césaire did with the influence of Hughes, I maintain, was to channel it in the service of his own political and cultural vision of transnational blackness. On the other side, the similarities between their visions did not go unnoticed by Hughes. If for André Breton in the early 1940s, as Bulson explains, Césaire had been "the voice of the exile . . . [who] was capable of describing it through a style of writing that was both *surréaliste* and *étranger*," for Hughes, Césaire represented a natural outgrowth of his ethos and aesthetics of pan-African entanglement.[4]

Indeed, we will see in this chapter that Césaire not only read the American poets avidly; he also quite readily adopted their quasi-essentialist rhetoric, imagery, and philosophy—their collective black Atlantic memory, to which Haitian writers such as Roumain had also contributed. Like Hughes, Césaire would over time grow more wary of the essentializing tendencies of primitivism and more nuanced in his pronouncements about race, blackness, and Africa. Yet, like Hughes, he continually looked to Haiti as a repository of fragmented African cultural traditions and sometimes as a proxy for Africa in the black imagination. He found himself unable to avoid treating African-derived practices and values romantically, as an antidote or inoculation against the alienating qualities of Western civilization. In fact, some degree of essentialist rhetoric, even if it was a strategic essentialism (to use Spivak's term),[5] was always at the core of Césaire's formulation of a transnational Negritude. My argument in this chapter assumes that he, like Hughes, was wary of racial essentialism but willing to incorporate its tropes and symbols into a narrative of pan-African entanglement through ancestry and shared history.[6] Césaire hoped, in turn, that this narrative might generate a sense of racial kinship in the present and advance his political and artistic quest to achieve transnational black solidarity and, ultimately, a broader humanistic vision.

I argued in scale enlargement B that the "adherence to an essentialist view of racial identity"[7] that is often attributed to Senghor has been overstated. Here I will argue that the extent to which Césaire fully disassociated himself from such views in favor of "a dynamic, historically rooted locus of cultural interaction"[8] between Africa and Europe has likewise been overstated by critics eager to distinguish Césaire's work from Senghor's exoticism. In fact, by the 1960s—particularly by the time *The Tragedy of King Christophe* was given its first staged reading in 1963—the primitivist tendencies and global ambitions of previous generations of black literature had become important buttresses for Césaire's position in his ongoing dispute with his former student Frantz Fanon, a debate Césaire continued to engage even after Fanon's death in 1961. It might be characterized as a conflict between transnational Negritude and Fanon's national consciousness. Césaire's implicit dramatization of this debate in *Christophe,* I will argue, at times made the case for a powerful rhetoric of black kinship and solidarity and at times undermined that case and exposed certain limitations in Césaire's (and, by association, Hughes's) conception of a black Atlantic cultural collectivity. Yet I will also propose that the flexibility and concentricity of Hughes's conception of pan-African entanglement, and even its ephemerality, helped Césaire to justify in his own mind his strategic use of a similar essentialist or primitivist symbology.

Césaire and the Lure of the Primitive

Many critics have emphasized the importance of surrealism, especially the work of André Breton, on Césaire's writing. There is ample justification for this, as surrealism's emphasis on irrationality and the unconscious (in contrast to Western positivism and rationalism) did prove highly productive to the Martinican's poetic output.[9] Jean Jonassaint argues, however, that critics' attention to Césaire's European influences has sometimes overshadowed any discussion of his indebtedness to a previous generation of Haitian and other West Indian poets, including the Indigenist poets Carl Brouard and Philippe Thoby-Marcelin, as well as Roumain and Damas. Jonassaint identifies important points of intertextual conversation with these writers and regards Césaire's *Christophe* as "inscribed within a double Caribbean tradition: that of the patriotic Haitian theater . . . and that of the writers of the Caribbean with its confusion of languages to draw from on the history of Haiti."[10] A. James Arnold notes further that as early as *Cahier d'un retour au pays natal* (*Notebook of a Return to the Native Land*, 1939), Césaire was developing "blackness as a positive value against the cold, lifeless, and deadly whiteness of European civilization,"[11] a primitivist conceit that had no doubt resonated strongly for him when he encountered it in his early readings of his Caribbean predecessors.

The significance of blackness to his thinking was only reinforced when Césaire later studied Haitian history and folklore more intently. Part of what fascinated him about Haiti was its living tradition of Vodou, as an embodiment of African-derived folk art. He confirmed this in an interview when he referenced an idea from Léo Frobenius: "A culture is born, not when man *seizes*, but when man *is seized*," which happens "exactly as in Vodou. There are rites of possession. . . . One dances, one dances, and suddenly, 'the guy' is possessed; he turns into something else. He is no longer Mister or Miss So-and-So; he is Shango, he is Ogun, he is Erzulie."[12] In chapter 2 I noted that Hughes's romanticization of Vodou stood in contrast to Roumain, who had impatiently dismissed Vodou as a superstitious distraction from the class struggle. Césaire's admiration in the above passage was closer to Hughes's representation, but the simile comparing the birth of black culture to a Vodou ritual is ambivalent: to give birth to black culture was, for Césaire, to be possessed by the old African gods, but refracted through the American hemisphere's history of slavery, oppression, and resistance. Crucially, their memory persisted through the performative medium of dance, along with a larger repertoire of pan-African entanglement, including drumming, music, song, acting, foodways, and ritual.

In the same interview, Césaire lamented Martinique's paucity of such overt manifestations of African cultural practices, though he felt it did preserve phantasmal traces of Africa. Vodou did not exist in Martinique, he said,

> as a *constituted religion*, but it exists, to my mind, as a tendency, as aftermath.... There is a whole emotional attitude which has nothing to do with Europe and which appears during carnival, during elections ... which resembles what we see in Vodou. But it is not a true Vodou. The Blacks were too heavily influenced by the Whites.... By contrast, in Haiti, they [black people] were transported in large numbers, especially in the last ten years preceding 1789. They represented, over there, nine-tenths of the population in all the provinces. That is how the African customs have been able to be preserved.[13]

Note his emphasis here is on the preservation of African customs and an "emotional attitude" rather than any intrinsic qualities of blackness. Elsewhere Césaire, echoing his language from the *Notebook,* declared that "Haiti represented for me the heroic Antilles, *the African Antilles*.... Haiti is the country where Negro people stood up for the first time, affirming their determination to shape a new world, a free world."[14] For Césaire as for Hughes, then, Haiti's vernacular culture and its history of defiance and rebellion served as proxy for Africa in the Americas, fulfilling a need for proud assertions of blackness to resist the pressures of assimilation to French cultural hegemony in Martinique and of white supremacy in the United States. Furthermore, and similar to what we've already seen in Hughes, McKay, and Roumain, Césaire's rhetoric also relegated the black masses to passive keepers of "African customs."

That Césaire deployed rhetoric about Africa and Haiti so similar to that of his predecessors, and exhibited the same blind spots toward his potential exploitation of the peasantry and proletariat, is no accident but a product of his purposively taking up the threads of pan-African entanglement that the earlier generation had spun and woven. Even more than in Haitian Indigenism and Damas's earliest poetry, the Harlem Renaissance authors he read in the 1920s and 1930s helped Césaire articulate a vision of blackness that was proudly embedded in African practices and beliefs. In 1967 he described his "three main influences" as a young writer: French literature; his study of Africa; and "the Negro Renaissance Movement in the United States, which did not influence me directly but still created an atmosphere which allowed me to become conscious of the solidarity of the black world."[15] Many years later, he recalled that the "black Americans were a revelation to us.... What counted the most for us was encountering another modern civilization, the Blacks and their pride, their awareness of belonging to a culture."[16]

Though he characterized black American art as part of "modern civilization," often it was the primitivist facets of that art that Césaire most emphasized in his commentary, reflecting his efforts to establish pan-African connection on both an ancestral plane and in his present. In the journal *Tropiques* that he cofounded in Fort-de-France in the early 1940s, for example, Césaire introduced a selection of poems by Claude McKay, James Weldon Johnson, and Jean Toomer with a brief essay declaring that everything in African American culture "has more rhythm, but of a primitive sort, as in jazz or tom-toms, which is to say that it pushes man's resistance to the deepest humanity."[17] In his "Presentation" to the same issue, he evoked the diverse and troubled genealogy of the Caribbean: "Europe. Africa. Asia. I hear screaming steel, the tom-toms in the bush, the temple prayer among the banyans."[18] The reference to "screaming steel" evokes European industrialization and the modern world (and indirectly, the history of slavery with its associations with steel chains), in contrast to the iconic images of primitive Africa evoked through the tom-toms, which are then linked to the banyan trees, indigenous to Asia but also found in the modern Caribbean. Such passages read like primitivism, but without primitivism's assumption that some atavistic quality is inherent to one's heritage. To the contrary, in fact, this passage insists on hybridity and mixture as the dominant feature of Caribbean identity. If Césaire was willing to indulge in the rhetoric of primitivism (even at the cost of accepting its racialist premises, as he surely did in his introduction to the Harlem Renaissance poets), he nevertheless consistently kept in view the modern and the primitive, the African and the global, all at once, in his efforts to imagine a transnational Negritude embedded in both past and present.

The glimpses of a transnational black culture that Césaire imagines for us through his contributions to *Tropiques* are of a complex, hybrid, and protean phenomenon rather than a fixed and inert essence. "It is by man's cry that we recognize him," he declares. "By the oldest cry in life, or rather life itself, which . . . is embodied in the immediacy of the voice. And here is the cry of the Negro poet."[19] This passage embodies the paradox of Césaire's conception of Negritude: on the one hand, the cry's age, "the oldest," suggests that the New Negro poets were giving expression to some ancestral and atavistic entanglement. But on the other hand, the poet's speech act, his cry of self-proclamation, symbolizes birth and *newness*, suggesting that blackness for Césaire was something performative, ongoing, and self-defining.

Those lines in Césaire's introduction are followed by two unattributed quotations from Langston Hughes, whose selection tells us much about how Césaire perceived, borrowed, wrestled with, and adapted Hughes's larger narrative of pan-African continuity with the past. The first consists of five lines from "Afraid" in French translation, the original of which begins,

> We cry among the skyscrapers
> As our ancestors
> Cried among the palms in Africa.[20]

These lines embody one of the central tenets of primitivism, the idea that modern civilization and urban life are utterly alienating and dehumanizing, hence the speaker's crying "among the skyscrapers." Interestingly, in this case the ancestral motherland that the next lines evoke is presented not as the healing opposite of Western life but as its analog. Nevertheless, these lines do posit historical continuity between blacks living alienated in American cities and their ancestors in ancient Africa.

In "Afraid," Hughes used a characteristic device, the first-person pronoun (in this case a plural "We") that makes the black poet a synecdoche for people of African descent everywhere. In the other Hughes poem that Césaire quotes in his introduction, "A New Song" (1933), the speaker makes this presumption explicit with the Whitmanesque declaration, "I speak in the name of the black millions."[21] Césaire reproduces this first line of the poem in English, thus confirming what Gregson Davis calls Césaire's own "explicit desire to play the role of major spokesman for the black world."[22] And it reveals Césaire's awareness of a precedent for his own use of the expansive "I" in the *Notebook*, first published two years before *Tropiques*, as when the speaker declares "that I demand of myself to be a digger for this unique race."[23]

Yet Césaire's choice of "A New Song" itself is revealing: first published in 1933 at a time when Hughes was writing some of his most politically radical work, the poem is emphatically future oriented and declares that the day of bowing "beneath the slaver's whip ... is past." "A New Song" almost reads as a refutation of Hughes's own tendency to base a black identity on twin pillars from the past—slavery and Africa. Looking ahead to a revolutionary future, the speaker ends the poem:

> The past is done!
>
> > A new dream flames
> > Against the
> > Sun![24]

In contrast to his most openly primitivist poems from the 1920s, Hughes here sounds closer to the exasperated Fanon, who wrote two decades later, "I will not make myself the man of any past. I do not want to sing the past to the detriment of my present and my future."[25] The context of Césaire's encounter with Hughes's poetry is also significant: "A New Song" gave its title to the first book to translate a significant number of Hughes's poems into French, *Un chant nouveau* by René Piquion, published in Haiti in 1940, which Ryan Kernan characterizes as framing Hughes as "a revolutionary poet."[26] We can say with certainty, then, that at least as early as the second issue of *Tropiques* in 1941, Césaire was aware of Langston Hughes as a modernist and a radical committed to future justice, not just as a bard of ancient African cultural values.

One might wonder, then, why Césaire quoted only the first line of "A New Song" and omitted the following line that completes the sentence—"I speak in the name of the black millions / Awakening to action"—never mind the more openly agitprop calls to revolution that follow. Perhaps Césaire wanted to signal to the knowing reader that the "cry of the Negro poet" was also a cry of rebellion, while hoping to avoid the ire of the Vichy regime's censors (who would nevertheless shut down *Tropiques* less than two years later). But it seems to me that omitting the lines in the poem about the past being "done" also allowed Césaire to keep in play both versions of Langston Hughes and both senses of the term "radical": Hughes as radical in that he endorsed the overthrow of the status quo and Hughes as "radical" in the etymological sense of wanting to *root* himself in a supposedly primitive past of ancestral Africa and of practices forged in slavery. Césaire would need both Langstons—both understandings of black people's relationships to the past and the future—when he grappled with Haiti's post-revolutionary legacy in *The Tragedy of King Christophe*. In effect, Césaire recognized these aspects of the work as personae Hughes had assumed at various times—masks that others could put on and voices that others could adopt. Césaire would prove willing to adopt these personae himself, selectively, in a pragmatic pursuit of black collectivity and of solidarity among the global oppressed.

Césaire and his coeditors of *Tropiques* likewise presented both the revolutionary and the romantic view of Hughes and McKay in their response to the Vichy censor, who, in announcing a ban on the journal in 1943, accused its authors of being "racists," "sectarians," "revolutionaries," and "ingrates and traitors to the Fatherland." The editors responded by boasting that they were ingrates "like Zola," revolutionaries "like Hugo," and racists like the "racism of Toussaint Louverture, of Claude MacKay[27] and of Langston Hughes—against that of Drumont and Hitler."[28] This merits attention on multiple levels; to start with, it conflated the black American writers with the general of the Haitian Revolution and accorded them legitimacy and stature comparable to Zola and Hugo as well as Racine and

Rimbaud, mentioned elsewhere in the same document. The response to the censor also seemed to confirm Jean-Paul Sartre's claim that Negritude was in effect an "antiracist racism,"[29] since the Césaires and their colleagues admitted to the racialism inherent in embracing a black identity but contrasted it favorably with the toxic racism and anti-Semitism of, in this case, Hitler and protofascist French journalist Édouard Drumont. The very positioning of black American writers against fascism again deploys both versions of Langston Hughes, the revolutionary iconoclast interlinked with the nostalgic primitivist. If Hughes and McKay were "racists" for assuming the existence of an African essence, the *Tropiques* editors' response turned that racialism into an effective weapon against the more malignant racism of colonialism and fascism.

Césaire, in short, tried to keep open all possibilities for cultivating pan-African community and solidarity, highlighting black entanglement in the past and facilitating new entanglements in the present. Abiola Irele insists that Negritude was not essentialist in its emphasis but was rather "a *social and cultural* movement closely related to African nationalism."[30] Mireille Rosello notes that as early as the *Notebook*, "a political construct of Blackness replaces the biological definition of a race" in Césaire's writing.[31] Parry is more precise: "Négritude [in Césaire's poetry] is not a recovery of a preexistent state, but a textually invented history, an identity effected through figurative operations, and a tropological construction of blackness as a sign of the colonized condition and its refusal."[32] I largely concur with these judgments and see Césaire's conception of Negritude as characterized more by fluidity, multiplicity, and flexibility than by the fixities of ancestry or rootedness. At the same time, we must also acknowledge that African nationalism, for black people outside of Africa, necessarily denoted a *transnational* identity rooted in the past and in a sense of kinship across the diaspora. The two phenomena are interconnected: in turning to Hughes's ready-made lexicon and repertoire of pan-African entanglement, Césaire found the primitivist elements of that narrative woven in too deeply to consistently avoid.[33]

Various interviews from the 1960s and 1970s show Césaire attempting to rhetorically reconcile his loyalties to Caribbean identity, African heritage, and universal humanism. What might seem like contradictions are in fact signs of his shifting between different but concentric scales of cultural entanglement. "I have always striven to create a new language," Césaire said in 1967, "one capable of *communicating the African heritage*. . . . In other words, for me French was a tool that I wanted to use in developing a new means of expression. I wanted to create *an Antillean French,* a black French that, while still being French, had a black character."[34] Notice how Césaire threaded the needle here: he wanted a language and poetry specifically Antillean, but part of what it meant for that language to have a "black character" was for it to communicate the "African heritage" of the Antillean people. He thus simultaneously assumed a black personality rooted in one's past or heritage and insisted on flexible, modern, transnational conceptions of both blackness and "Antilleanity" that allowed "a new means of expression." A few years later, Césaire would characterize the ethos of Negritude as the "affirmation of a solidarity" across time and across the world and as "a sort of black ecumenism."[35]

In his mid-1970s interview with Jacqueline Leiner, Césaire refused to be pinned down on the question of whether there was in his writing "primitive belief, African belief" (la croyance primitive, la croyance africaine). Césaire initially responded impatiently, "That's it, *primitive*, period, not necessarily *African!*"[36] He claimed to find elements of the primitive in Greek poetry and drama, not just in African art. This allowed him to associate the primitive qualities he admired in African culture with something more broadly universal. The interviewer then shifted the terms of her questioning and brought up contradictions in Césaire's past statements about biology versus culture, leading him to reply, "I couldn't say that I don't believe at all in the importance of [biological] race. I think that, in effect, one is born white, one is born black, etc. But that gets confused, for me, *very quickly*, with culture. When I lay claim to Africa, that means that I am laying claim to *African cultural values*."[37] For Césaire, then, race and ancestry were deeply entangled with culture and history, and the different scales of the national, the regional, and the racial were folded into one another in compatible layers of self-identification. This African-centered, concentrically organized, thoroughly transnational vision of black culture resonated powerfully with and built upon Hughes's ethos of pan-African entanglement. By the 1960s, as I elaborate below, this model of a border-crossing, solidarity-enabling Negritude also served as Césaire's implicit rebuttal to Fanon's insistence on national consciousness as the only path to a true culture.

Another point in Césaire's thinking that resonated powerfully with Hughes's ideas about "Negro" identity was the pedestal on which he placed black peasants, workers, and other ordinary people throughout the diaspora, as the hereditary keepers of the African cultural values he prized so highly. Michel Fabre sees this as a lesson that all the Negritude writers took from McKay's *Banjo*, which "spelled the first step toward negritude: no enduring cultural renaissance could occur unless it went back to the folk."[38] It is worth noting that Césaire's interest in working-class cultures was not confined to people of African descent, as we see in the 1955 version of his manifesto *Discourse on Colonialism*, which concluded with overtly Marxist rhetoric: "The salvation of Europe is not a matter of a revolution in methods. It is a matter of the Revolution—the one which, until such time as there is a classless society, will substitute for the narrow tyranny of a dehumanized bourgeoisie the preponderance of the only class that still has a universal mission, because it suffers in its flesh from all the wrongs of history, from all the universal wrongs: the proletariat."[39] If Césaire saw potential for solidarity with working people in Europe and around the world (i.e., at the scale of proletarian entanglement) his literary writings expressed a special kinship, bordering on a mystical connection, with poor black people. His literary works depicted them as incarnations of Negritude and relied on a symbolic economy of shacks, pirogues, and other vernacular elements of humble black lives. Haitian peasants in particular—victimized and degraded by slavery, colonialism, and poverty and yet valorized by their noble history of rebellion and self-assertion—were raised to the status of icons and exemplars of African cultural values persisting in the Americas. Indeed, in due course I will discuss Césaire's *Tragedy of King Christophe* as an implicit critique of the king's betrayal of the African cultural values embodied in the Haitian peasantry. But first I want to quickly turn to Césaire's most celebrated poem, the *Notebook of a Return to the Native Land,* to note how it anticipates these same themes.

The *Notebook* and the Birth of Negritude

In the original 1939 version of the *Notebook,* the narrative begins with a stroll through "this inert town" of Fort-de-France, which the speaker sees inhabited by "cette étrange foule" ("this strange crowd" in one translation, "this strange throng" in another).[40] The narrative lens then zooms out to the larger island, "this most essential land,"[41] before zooming in again on the speaker's childhood home, which Arnold calls "a synecdoche of colonial society":[42] "At the end of first light, another little house very bad-smelling in a very narrow street . . . and my temperamental father gnawed by one persistent ache . . . and my mother whose legs pedal, pedal [a sewing machine], day and night, for our tireless hunger. . . . And the bed of boards from which my race arose, my whole entire race from this bed of boards . . . that bed, and its kidskin, and its dry banana leaves, and its rags, yearning for a mattress, my grandmother's bed."[43] The grandmother recalled here was probably inspired by Césaire's paternal grandmother Eugénie Macri, whom Césaire remembered as "visibly African in origin."[44] For her to be evoked through the metonymy of her bed, and for that bed to then be described as the source "from which my race arose," elevates the figure of the poor old black woman to an emblem of transcendent pan-African identity—"my whole entire race." At the same time, it also elevates the speaker himself to that race's embodiment and spokesman, like the speaker of Hughes's "A New Song."

In this sense, the grandmother's bed symbolizes the same force of black self-assertion and self-(re)generation as the island of Hispaniola. Significantly, Haiti is first mentioned in the context of a strophe devoted to a view of the entire world as seen from the Caribbean Sea:

> its flanks secreting for Europe the sweet liquor of the Gulf Stream, and one of the two slopes of incandescence between which the Equator funambulates to Africa. And my non-enclosure island, its clear boldness standing at the back of this Polynesia, before it, Guadeloupe split in two along its backbone and sharing our misery, Haiti where negritude stood up for the first time and said it believed in its humanity and the comic little tail of Florida where the strangulation of a nigger is about to be completed and Africa gigantically caterpillaring as far as the Hispanic foot of Europe, its nakedness where Death swings its scythe widely.[45]

This is the first known use of the term "Negritude" in print, and it is significant that the speaker describes Negritude as "standing up" (se mit debout), an image and trope we will encounter frequently in Césaire's *King Christophe*.[46]

Yet in the *Notebook*, the defiant gesture of declaring that the black world "believed in its humanity" had yet to spread far or for long, as blacks continued to be lynched in the US South, and fascist troops in the Spanish Civil War, only recently concluded, had "scythe[d] widely" through, among others, the Moorish troops from North Africa that had so interested Hughes in his reporting from Spain. That Africa is described as "caterpillaring" (chenillant)[47] suggests that, far from being fixed and immutable, the continent is awaiting a great metamorphosis. Note also the use of metaphors from peasant life: "Guadeloupe split in two along its backbone" (fendue en deux de sa raie dorsale) evokes filleting a fish, while the scythe imagery (la Mort fauche à larges andains) is drawn from agricultural labor and connotes Soviet communism. Thus from its earliest usage, the concept of Negritude was transnational in scope and vested, at least rhetorically, in the lives of ordinary black people around the world.

Césaire reinforced this rhetorical homage to ordinary black lives in his introduction to African American poetry in *Tropiques*: "The black courtyard of miracles is standing up. All the suffering humanity in the Harlem slums, in the corn fields of Maryland, in the Carolina cotton plantations. . . . And that of the chain-gang, and of the embittered, the optimists, the resourceful, the fools, those from Mississippi, those from New Orleans and Atlanta; the musicians playing syncopated rhythms, the picanninies without shoes, the prostitutes with the chocolate complexion illuminated with red, the epileptic Trombone players, the jazz players who launch their sticks at the moon."[48] In its identification with workers, sharecroppers, and the lumpenproletariat, the inclusive vision of a "black courtyard of miracles" that we see here resonated with and built on the ethos of vernacular pan-African entanglement pioneered by McKay, Hughes, and Roumain, among other black poets in the Caribbean and the United States. Indeed, this passage echoes many of Hughes's favorite poetic devices, among them the list of places that creates a sense of unity through juxtaposition, the celebration of blues and jazz music, and his nonfictional homages to the Haitian "people without shoes." It recalls also McKay's raucous descriptions of black nightlife in *Home to Harlem* and *Banjo*. And it repeats one of Césaire's central themes: of black people *standing up* in an act of defiant self-assertion and self-definition.

For black people in the West Indies, of course, to ground a poetic practice in a vernacular aesthetic meant of necessity to engage with the islands' African heritage and its history of slavery.[49] After asserting his humble origins—"No, we've never been Amazons of the king of Dahomey, nor princes of Ghana"—the speaker of the *Notebook* sees visions of the Middle Passage and cracking whips and then visions of ancient Africa.[50] One passage is remarkably evocative of Hughes's "The Negro Speaks of Rivers," whose speaker's soul "has grown deep like the rivers" and who "built my hut near the Congo and it lulled me to sleep":

> I have looked and looked at trees and so I have become a tree and this long
>   tree's feet have dug great venom sacs and tall cities of bones in the ground.
> I have thought and thought of the Congo and so, I have become a Congo
>   rustling with forests and rivers
> where the whip cracks like a great banner.[51]

The "I" in the poem is by now declaring itself boldly and confidently, speaking for the African diaspora just as the first-person pronoun serves in Hughes's poetry as synecdoche for a shared African heritage. We see the same presumptuous posture in the speaker's vow to the people of Martinique that "my mouth will be the mouth of those griefs which have no mouth, my voice, the freedom of those that collapse in the dungeon of despair."[52] This is the "messianic discourse" through which Awendela Grantham believes Césaire "advances Negritude" in the *Notebook* and beyond, and it effectively claims for the poet the controlling hand in weaving and conducting cultural exchange within the pan-African skein.[53]

If imagined scenes from a preslavery Africa constituted one act in the ur-narrative of pan-African memory that Césaire told in the *Notebook* and scenes of slavery and oppression comprised the second act, the crucial third act consisted of scenes of resistance and self-assertion, albeit still of a humble nature. The slave ship that earlier loomed so large now "cracks from one end to the other. . . . The ghastly tapeworm of its cargo gnaws the fetid guts of the strange suckling of the sea!"[54] In place of the slave ship, and in contrast to its grim vastness, the poet offers us the image of a modest dugout canoe: "give me on this diverse ocean / the obstinacy of the proud pirogue / and its marine vigour."[55] The history of slavery and the prehistory of Africa remain central to this humble symbol of Negritude, as they do to the poem's closing invocation to the ancestral dances:

> Come to me my dances
> my bad nigger dances
> come to me my dances
> the breaking-the-yoke dance
> the jump-jail dance
> the it-is-beautiful-and-good-and-legitimate-to-be-a-nigger dance.[56]

These African-derived folk and ritual dances recall the bare dancing feet Hughes romanticized in the Haitian peasantry and prefigure such later literary representations as the Big Drum ritual in Marshall's *Praisesong for the Widow*. The apostrophic form implies that the speaker is invoking African muses and a black aesthetic kept alive through centuries of slavery and its cultural aftermath. That this is a gesture of defiance and resistance is made clear from the metaphors implied in the names of the dances, tropes of breaking eggs and escaping jails.

The above-quoted line about Haiti being the place where Negritude first "stood up" marks the turning point in the *Notebook* from dwelling on the degradations of colonialism and the squalors of poverty to asserting "a heroic opposition to the diminished sense of self inculcated by colonialism."[57] This turn, away from the past and its aftermath and toward visions of a revolutionary future, is foreshadowed earlier in the poem by repeated images of navels, umbilical cords, and pregnant women, implying both a link to one's ancestors and the birth of something new. We get a glimpse of a ghostly "woman [who] seems to be floating in the Capot river (her luminously dark body obediently organises itself at her navel's command) but she is only a bundle of resounding water."[58] This image is not far removed from Hughes's idealized black woman in "Fascination" (1926), who has lips like "dark ripe plums" and hair in a "midnight mass, a dusky aurora."⁵⁹ It also prefigures any number of Senghor's poems, such as "Black Woman," where the naked African woman's body is described as "Ripe fruit with firm flesh, dark raptures of black wine."⁶⁰ But Césaire's emphasis on the woman's *navel* also associates her specifically with reproduction, birth, and ancestry. These themes are confirmed a few strophes later when we see a flash of "the umbilical cord restored to its ephemeral splendor."⁶¹

Just as the navel and umbilical imagery simultaneously evoke the past (one's own birth) and the future (the birth of the next generation), other tropes in the *Notebook* likewise call on origins and ancestry in ways that open out toward the future. Consider strophes 59 and 60 in the original 1939 text:

> Tepid first light of ancestral heat and fear
> I now tremble with the collective trembling
> That our blood sings in the madrepore.
>
> And these tadpoles hatched in me by my prodigious ancestry!⁶²

The last line beautifully encapsulates the paradox at the heart of Césaire's conception of Negritude: it is the "prodigious ancestry" doing the hatching, implying a kind of genetic destiny, perhaps even an "essence" associated with "our blood" and with "ancestral heat." Yet that ancestry is generating "tadpoles," symbols (like the earlier reference to Africa's "caterpillaring") of future potential and metamorphosis. The poet embeds a similar paradox in the image of the madrepore, a genus of spiny coral whose skeletons form the bulk of giant tropical reefs on which living coral build. This image, then, could serve as a metaphor for Hughes and Césaire's shared conception of pan-African entanglement, where the ancestral plane of interconnection forms the core over and through which new links and arteries can cohere in the present.

The madrepore trope is also evocative of volcanoes, as coral reefs most frequently form around volcanic submarine mountains that slowly subside.⁶³ Volcanoes, in fact, are one of the most frequently recurring images and tropes in Césaire's writing. The speaker of "Lost Body" (1950), for example, opens the poem by turning the name of a famous volcano into a verb, an assertion of existence and identity so forceful that it warps grammar: "I who Krakatoa" (Moi qui Krakatoa).⁶⁴ Later the speaker uses the same "verbifying" device with a navel reference: "I omphale" (J'omphale), alluding to a figure from Greek myth but also evoking the Greek word *omphalos* and the concept of the navel of the world. Describing Césaire's poetry as "language that is blatantly making itself up" in a "poetics of cultural *invention*," James Clifford declares that it forces readers "to *construct* readings from a debris of historical and future possibilities."[65] This aptly describes the ending of "Lost Body," with its paradoxical vision of destructive violence and creative regeneration wrought by "the revolutionary strength of the volcano"[66]: "I will raise a cry so violent / that I will spatter the sky utterly. / . . . I shall command the islands to exist."[67] The speaker's forceful and repeated "I" deploys one of Hughes's favorite devices, the first-person pronoun that unifies the race. Furthermore, his cry evokes the "cry of the Negro poet" that Césaire had praised in *Tropiques* some nine years earlier. Thus Césaire's admiration for proud assertions of black identity by the Harlem Renaissance writers was intermeshed with his belief in the "operation of poetry as a liberation of the unconscious,"[68] and this liberating power manifested itself to him as a volcano, a force of nature with the ability to reshape reality.

Césaire himself, describing his method of writing in intense bursts after long quiet periods, declared his poetry "a Pelean poetry,"[69] referring to Mount Pelée, an active volcano on Martinique that erupted in 1902, killing thirty thousand people and wiping out the cultural capital of Saint-Pierre. A volcano, with its pattern of dormancy followed by sudden eruption, is also a fitting metaphor for Césaire's conception of Negritude: a sudden, violent disruption of racist European structures of thought. This accounts for a strophe in the *Notebook* in which the speaker prophesies that "the volcanoes will break out and the naked water will sweep away the ripe stains of the sun."[70] Soon after, the poem describes the people's pent-up frustration at oppression and poverty as "fumaroles of anguish" and the "repressed fire of the morne"[71] ("morne" being the word in Antillean French for a small mountain), and their slave ancestors as "chained volcanoes."[72] Like the navel imagery, the trope of the volcano is multidirectional, pointing to both past (the Lesser Antilles were mostly formed from volcanic eruptions and deposits millennia ago) and future (some of the islands, including Martinique, are home to smoldering volcanoes that could at any time erupt and radically reshape the island's geography). Having already established the radical power of the volcano to remake the future, the poet then makes clear the island's amnesiac history, while also suggesting the people's obliviousness to their own explosive potential: "the morne, forgotten, forgetful of blowing up."[73]

My analysis of the *Notebook* has revealed a conception of Negritude that closely resembles the ethos of pan-African entanglement I have been ascribing to Hughes. Césaire's conception of a transnational black collectivity was similarly inclusive and concentric, existing in fact within a larger circle of concern for humanity, as when the speaker prays not to become

> that man of hatred for whom I feel only hatred
> for sheltered as I am in this unique race
> you still know my catholic love
> you know that it is not from hatred of other races
> that I demand of myself to be a digger for this unique race
> that what I want
> is for universal hunger
> for universal thirst
> to summon it free at last
>
> to generate from its intimate closeness
> the succulence of fruit.[74]

These lines are from the original 1939 version of the *Notebook*. Arnold points out that Césaire later struck the word "catholic" from later editions of the poem, then changed the phrase to "tyrannical love" in 1956. Arnold attributes this to Césaire the veteran politician of the 1950s playing down the poem's drama of spiritual transformation and personal sacrifice in favor of a "sociopolitical" agenda "that calls for decolonization and the democratization of economic institutions."[75] I would note, however, that the lowercase rendering of "catholique" is ambiguous in French, referring either to the Roman Catholic Church or to the etymologically older sense deriving from the Greek word for "universal." An emphasis on the second sense is strongly suggested by the subsequent references to "universal hunger" and "universal thirst," which lead presumably to a universal search to "summon it free." As early as his first published poem, then, Césaire articulated a vision of Negritude that nested inside a larger humanistic worldview.

Further evidence that Césaire's black transnationalism did not compete with or exclude a larger devotion to universal humanism—so long as it were seated at least in large part in African cultural values rather than solely in the European enlightenment—emerged in *Discourse on Colonialism* (1955): "At the very time when it most often mouths the word, the West has never been further from being able to live a true humanism—a humanism made to the measure of the world."[76] This sentiment strikes me as not so dissimilar to what Christopher Lee calls Fanon's "revolutionary humanism." The primary difference was in their means: Césaire aimed to root his humanism in recuperated African values and practices,[77] whereas Fanon located his in the struggle to develop national consciousness. In the next section, then, I will briefly survey Fanon's critique of Césairean Negritude before reading

The Tragedy of King Christophe as Césaire's defense of Negritude as a pan-African cultural force.

Césaire and Fanon

Not all critics are convinced that Césaire's and Fanon's ideas are so mutually antagonistic as I (following the lead of many previous commentators) will argue here. Parry, for example, regards both writers "as authors of liberation theories which today could stand accused of an essentialist politics" and argues that in both of their works "nativism remain[ed] audible despite the strenuous endorsement of a post-European, transnational humanism as the ultimate goal."[78] More positively, Lee sees Fanon's ultimate aim as "a new, more inclusive humanism unburdened by preceding hierarchies of racial, cultural, economic, and political discrimination."[79] Fanon himself offered evidence for Lee's view in *Wretched of the Earth:* "Let us endeavor to invent a man in full, something which Europe has been incapable of achieving."[80] And in the abstract, indeed, one might expect this call for an alternative universal humanism that is explicitly *not* Eurocentric in its foundation to sit well with Césaire, who likewise blamed Europe for failing to imagine "a humanism made to the measure of the world."[81]

Yet the ongoing dialogue between Césaire and Fanon through the 1950s and 1960s did not take place in the abstract but in the context of a relationship between two men who had known each other since Fanon was a student in Césaire's class at Lycée Victor Schoelcher in Fort-de-France in the early 1940s. Fanon had some early associations with the Negritude movement (publishing in *Présence africaine,* for example), and he quoted Césaire extensively in 1952's *Black Skin, White Masks* and wrote that "we would like a lot of black intellectuals to get their inspiration from him."[82] Yet already in that book we can see signs of the differences that would arise between Fanon and Césaire (and in Césaire's camp, by extension, Langston Hughes). One crucial emerging difference between Fanon and Césaire concerned their respective attitudes toward representing, recuperating, or excavating the past, which for a black person meant Africa and slavery. Jay Garcia argues that "Fanon takes on a dissenting, even combative, position in relation to cultural representation in general";[83] certainly he took such a position with regard to representations of black heritage. In his last chapter of *Black Skin,* Fanon complained, "The black man, however sincere, is a slave to the past. . . . Confronted with the white man, the black man has to set a high value on his own past, to take his revenge."[84] His summary of his position two pages later could serve as an implicit indictment of Negritude: "Haven't I got better things to do on this earth than avenge the Blacks of the seventeenth century?"[85] A decade later in *The Wretched of the Earth,* Fanon leveled a similar critique against other black intellectuals' fixation on the past: "This passionate quest for a national culture prior to the colonial era can be justified by the colonized intellectuals' shared interest in stepping back and taking a hard look at the Western culture in which they risk becoming ensnared. Fully aware they are in the process of losing themselves, and consequently of being lost to their people, these men work away with raging heart and furious mind to renew contact with their people's oldest, inner essence, the farthest removed from colonial times."[86] Fanon's attitude toward the quest to uncover ancient civilizations that could give the lie to colonialism's racist bias appears as a mixture of sympathy (noting that the impulse is "justified") and pity, bordering on condescension. Hughes and Césaire were both exemplars of that quest.

In *Wretched,* Fanon also made his disagreements with the tenets of Negritude more explicit. One of these was the critique that the Negritude writers basically accepted the racial frameworks of European colonial discourse: "In Africa, colonized literature over the last twenty years has not been a national literature but a 'Negro' literature. The concept of negritude for example was the affective if not logical antithesis of that insult which the white man had leveled at the rest of humanity."[87] Wrapped up in this critique, also, was his disparagement of Negritude for looking outside the confines of national culture for its sources of identity and succor: "The bards of negritude did not hesitate to reach beyond the borders of the continent,"[88] he wrote, but in doing so they encountered the "first limitation" of Negritude:

> "Negro" or "Negro-African" culture broke up because the men who set out to embody it realized that every culture is first and foremost national, and that the problems for which Richard Wright or Langston Hughes had to be on the alert were fundamentally different from those faced by Léopold Senghor or Jomo Kenyatta.... Colonialism's insistence that "niggers" have no culture, and Arabs are by nature barbaric, inevitably leads to a glorification of cultural phenomena that become continental instead of national, and singularly racialized. In Africa, the reasoning of the intellectual is Black-African or Arab-Islamic. It is not specifically national. Culture is increasingly cut off from reality.[89]

Indeed, as I will discuss in chapter 5, Fanon was correct in thinking that Hughes had been forced to reckon with cultural difference (and not just between national cultures), particularly in his later years when he came into increasingly close contact with African writers and intellectuals.

Fanon's critique makes clear how emphatically he insisted that the *nation* (or, more precisely, the struggle to found the nation) was the only mechanism able to achieve global emancipation. It thus complicates Parry's and Lee's assertions that Fanon aspired ultimately to a transnational humanism[90] and corroborates Anthony Alessandrini's reading of his "complex and agonized engagement with humanism."[91] Fanon wrote that the struggle for national sovereignty, "which aims at a fundamental redistribution of relations between men, cannot leave intact either the form or substance of the people's culture."[92] He allowed that this "new humanity, for itself and others, inevitably defines a new humanism."[93] But he ended the essay by reiterating that this new humanism can only be achieved via national consciousness: "If culture is the expression of the national consciousness, I shall have no hesitation in saying, in the case in point, that national consciousness is the highest form of culture."[94]

Fanon's insistence on national consciousness as the crucible for pan-African liberation is not necessarily incompatible with Parry's attribution to him of a "transnational politics."[95] Lee, for example, explains that "through a twofold process, national consciousness could instigate a concurrent international consciousness, as aspired to by pan-Africanism, yet one attuned to ongoing varieties of colonialism that rendered the postcolonial nation-state 'fragile and in permanent danger.'"[96] Certainly, though, his insistence that the path toward such a transnational humanism must proceed through national consciousness put Fanon at odds with Césaire, who founded his political career on a rejection of Martinique's nationalist aspirations. In 1958, less than three years before Fanon published *Wretched*, Césaire had cofounded the Martinican Progressive Party, which advocated for Martinique becoming an autonomous overseas department with representation in the French National Assembly.[97] Césaire's decision to come out against full independence for Martinique put him squarely at cross-purposes with Fanon's insistence on national consciousness as the only route for cultivating a true culture among a colonized people. Indeed, it put him frequently at odds with the leading journal of pan-African studies of the era, *Présence africaine*, in whose pages, according to Belinda Jack, "nationalism was to provide the focus for much that was discussed."[98]

Because of these various political pulls, even quite late in life, Césaire continued to vest Martinican identity not in Fanon's "building of the nation" but in the recuperation of an ancestral Africa through "an Antillean self, a deep self, coated in all sorts of more-or-less-superficial layers, and it is this deep self that I would like to find. . . . For me, Martinican, to find the deep self was to strip myself of all the Western and French castoffs and recover Africa."[99] This interview was conducted in 2002, and even then Césaire continued to use the essentialist rhetoric of a "deep self" and a "recovered" Africa—precisely the sort of language and thinking Fanon had criticized him for in the early 1960s. My argument in the next section is that in *The Tragedy of King Christophe*, Césaire was using similar rhetoric, borrowed in part from Hughes, McKay, Roumain, and other black Atlantic writers, to implicitly defend and shore up his conception of a matrix of pan-African entanglement.

Negritude and *The Tragedy of King Christophe*

To recap: Fanon's critique of Césaire and Negritude amounted to their divergent answers to two key questions: First, to what degree should one's attempts to bring about nonracial, postcolonial humanism and culture be oriented toward the past—in the case of the black diaspora, the twin pasts of Africa and slavery? And second, should the path toward a universal humanism—whether Fanon's "new humanism" or Césaire's "humanism made to the measure of the world"—proceed through national consciousness or instead via a transnational conception of black solidarity? Given the context of this debate, it seems unlikely to be coincidence that Césaire's *The Tragedy of King Christophe*—act 1 of which was published the same year Fanon published *The Wretched of the Earth* (shortly before his death)—concerns the first black nation in modern history and is set at the very point in its history where questions of national identity and culture, and questions about the obligations that the present owes to the past, rose to the forefront. The most stirring testimonials within the play to Christophe's ultimate aims, if not his means of achieving them, come from characters who praise the king's efforts to achieve global black liberation.

This is the sense in which Césaire's vision of black identity and culture most resembled Hughes's ethos and aesthetic of pan-African entanglement. Indeed, I read *Christophe* in dialogue with the American poet's earlier play about the Haitian Revolution, which Césaire may or may not have been familiar with.[100] Certainly his affinity for Hughes's broader literary oeuvre informed the proud black transatlantic aesthetic and ethos that the Martinican poet deployed in *Christophe*. But if he thus extended Hughes's skein of pan-African entanglement on both the ancestral and contemporary planes, he also interrogated it and highlighted its contradictions and paradoxes. In the process, Césaire's play brought him into closer agreement with Fanon's postcolonial humanism than either man might have wanted to admit.[101]

My discussion of the *Notebook* has already established Césaire's early interest in Haiti and its revolution. This interest was profoundly reinforced in 1944, when he went there for a lecture tour and stayed for seven months. Davis calls this Césaire's turning point "in his quest to recuperate an African cultural legacy";[102] Arnold notes that after the visit, "Haiti did take on a kind of exemplary value for him," representing "the possibility of cultural autonomy for blacks in the Caribbean."[103] In the 1950s, Césaire dug deeply into the historical archives documenting the Haitian Revolution. The first fruit of this research was his historical monograph *Toussaint Louverture: The French Revolution and the Colonial Problem* (1960). In an interview many years later, Césaire would remember this book with "a special fondness. . . . I needed to understand the history of the French Revolution in the Caribbean, for I was lost in a jumble of events and contradictory realities. This book helped me to see my way through clearly. After that all was settled in my mind."[104] One of the crucial questions he wrestled to resolve was why Toussaint went to meet the French commander despite suspecting it was a trap: "This role of martyr Toussaint accepted, better yet, preempted, because he regarded it as in effect indispensable. . . . I see in it something more than a mystical gesture: [I see it as] a political gesture."[105] For Césaire, Toussaint's struggle was "the struggle for the *recognition* of man, and that is why it both inscribes itself and inscribes [il s'inscrit et inscrit] the revolt of the black slaves of Saint Domingue in the history of world civilization."[106]

The narrative of a black leader sacrificing himself for his people and the recognition of their humanity reappears in *The Tragedy of King Christophe,* published serially in the three years after *Toussaint Louverture* was published. But the play is set some years after Toussaint's death, and its protagonist is more ambiguous in his heroism. Haiti has suffered Dessalines's tyrannical rule and, now, his assassination. The play opens in 1806 with the country teetering on the brink of civil war. The senate has offered Christophe the presidency of the republic, but on the condition that a new constitution be adopted that would limit the powers accompanying the presidency. When the senate's representative Pétion offers these terms in act 1, scene 1, Christophe angrily rejects them as "an act of defiance against me, against my person; these are measures to which my dignity will never submit."[107] He therefore claims the northern province of the country as his own state, setting off a civil war that gradually settles into a stalemate and the partitioning of the republic. Christophe's rule soon slides into tyranny as he declares himself king and imposes a semifeudal agricultural system on the peasants in order to increase the country's productivity. He proves his own worst antagonist, and his cruelty and obsession with building his massive citadel eventually drive his subjects to revolt. At the end of the play, paralyzed by a stroke and abandoned by everyone except his loyal secretary Vastey, the king takes his own life.

Despite Christophe's increasingly cruel and despotic behavior, Césaire gives him a certain nobility of character and purpose. After all, as Césaire declared in an interview in 1964 about his character Christophe: "He incarnates Negritude.... He assumes responsibility for it according to his ideal. From the mythological perspective he represents the Thunder God, the will to power, at once destructive and benevolent."[108] Certainly in act 1 Christophe presents himself as the champion of black people in Haiti and, by implication, around the world. In the middle of an act that should be, according to the stage directions, in "a clownish and parodic style,"[109] and in an absurd scene in which a ridiculous "Master of Ceremonies" sent by Napoleon gives lessons in French ballroom dance to the assembled court, Christophe suddenly grows serious and reflective as he explains why he has created a whole mock nobility:

> These names, these noble titles, this coronation!
> Long ago, someone stole our names!
> Our pride!
> Our nobility, someone—oh, yes, *someone*—stole them from us!
> Pierre, Paul, Jacques, Toussaint! Someone branded us with these marks of humiliation, *someone* destroyed our true names.
> Even mine.
> I, your king.
> Do you feel the grief of a man who does not know what his name is? Or what his name means? Alas, none but Mother Africa knows. Well, claimed or unclaimed, we have to decide. And I say, "claimed." It's ourselves that we claim in our names![110]

This soliloquy links the lament for life in "Mother Africa," the humiliation of life under slavery, and the profound act of resistance involved in claiming new names—even, apparently, if said names and titles are borrowed from Europe. This narrative progression—from paradise lost through captivity survived and ultimately to revolution—is at the very core of Césaire's conception of Negritude. Christophe's soliloquy, then, reveals Negritude to be in part a performative reinvention of Africa, of slavery, and of the struggle to be free.

The revolutionary phase in this narrative becomes, in Césaire's repertoire, the act of standing up that I noted already in the *Notebook*. And the ultimate symbol in *Christophe* of standing up is the mighty citadel that he has his people build, as the king makes clear to the engineer tasked with its design: "To each people its monuments! For this people forced to its knees, a monument that will set it upright!"[111] As a hallucinated vision of the mountaintop fortress appears to him at the end of act 1, he exclaims, "Its lights blaze at nightfall! It cancels the slave ship!" (Annulation du négrier!)[112] The play continues to develop the associations between Christophe, his citadel, and the pervasive image of standing or putting upright. The trope becomes bitterly ironic after Christophe is paralyzed by a stroke yet continues to insist "that my soul / stands upright, inviolate, sound, just like our Citadel."[113] Being confined to his bed is a particularly cruel and ironic fate for a king who prided himself on standing up for the downtrodden black people of Haiti and the world. This gives added poignancy to his defiant cry to the gods,

> I demand for this people
> its rights!
> Its share of good fortune![114]

And it explains Vastey's instructions to the porters charged with entombing Christophe's body in the final scene:

> Stand him upright.
> In the ready mortar. Turned to the south.
> That's good. Not lying down, but standing.[115]

In his final tribute to the king, Vastey says, "You are once more the king who stands" (te revoilá roi debout).[116]

The "putting upright" of Negritude and thereby "canceling" the humiliation and suffering of the past has by this point in the play ceased to be mere abstraction and become synonymous with the construction of a physical edifice, a memorial to the revolution. But here again we find the paradox of memorialization: fixing the past in static form to create "a bulwark against obsolescence and disappearance" only inhibits the flexibility and mutability necessary for the past to be useful and relevant in the present and in fact destabilizes "any secure sense of the past itself."[117] Indeed, the fact that writers such as Hughes and Césaire continually revisited and reanimated the history of the Haitian Revolution suggests that avoiding the paradox of "musealization," as Andreas Huyssen calls it, requires continual reperformance, reinvention, and renewal.[118] This is confirmed by the fact that they and so many other writers reinvented this history through the medium of drama (and opera, too, for Hughes), where the narrative is reperformed and thus brought to life anew every night.

If, as Césaire claimed, Christophe "incarnates Negritude," he does so most obviously at the beginning of the play. At the end of the play, at least until he commits suicide, he attempts once again to "stand up" in performative affirmation of the dignity of black people in Haiti and worldwide. In between, however, he betrays Negritude's Afrocentric orientation and resorts to outright despotism to build his new nation. The violence of his reign is so over the top that it is not even clear we should regard Christophe as the hero of the play, unless it as a *fallen* hero in the tradition of Shakespeare's Macbeth.[119] It falls on other characters, especially his secretary and loyal aide Vastey, to remind the audience, and the Haitian people, of the vision of Negritude that Christophe once stood for. In act 2 we see Vastey defending Christophe from a lady of the court's complaints that the king's rule "looks horribly like the same old thing that you, to your honor, once fought against." Vastey declares in response that his own God "is the greatness of the state and the liberty of black people."[120] It is telling that he alludes to Christophe's nation-building ambitions in the same breath in which he mentions the more global aim of freeing black people, suggesting that the nation-state is not incompatible in his view with a broader circle of concern and allegiance. Later the internationalist scope of Vastey's vision for the king's rule becomes more overt still. When one of the women sings a sad song of a little black girl growing up in France who is rejected because of the darkness of her skin, Vastey replies passionately: "Do you know why [Christophe] is working day and night? . . . It's so that never again, *anywhere in the world,* shall there be a young black woman ashamed of the color of her skin, who finds her color an obstacle to realizing the wishes of her heart."[121]

If Vastey is therefore the chief spokesman of the play's vision of pan-African entanglement, he is also, ironically, one of the strongest influences pushing the king away from his African heritage and into the arms of European culture. Vastey clearly shares some of the blame, for example, for Christophe's forcing Haitians to assimilate to French culture and prove themselves by European standards.[122] When we first see Vastey in the second scene of the play, he is exhorting the crowd to rally around Christophe: "The whole world is watching us, citizens, and its multitudes think that black men lack dignity. A king, a court, a kingdom—*that,* if we want respect, is what we must show them. A leader at the head of our nation!"[123] Vastey's intentions are clearly noble, but his rhetoric about the need to prove black people's equality to Europeans (this speech is motivated by concern that "the French . . . hold us in scant esteem")[124] leads to absurdities such as the lessons in ballroom dance on the brink of civil war. Vastey's rhetoric also anticipates Christophe's increasingly tyrannical edicts, such as forcing peasants to marry one another at random and sending his personal guard to break up Vodou rituals.

It is clear in *Christophe* that we are meant to disapprove of the king's attempts to suppress or distance himself from African-derived cultural practices of all sorts. Among his many grotesque abuses of power, Christophe has a count demoted and banished from court for dancing the *bamboula,* an African-derived dance performed to the accompaniment of drums at many celebrations and ceremonies.[125] We find parallels, then, with Hughes's Dessalines, who bans drumming from his court. Yet as in Hughes's play, the drums refuse to be silenced in *Christophe*: late in act 1, for example, the king exclaims, "Listen! Somewhere in the night, the tam-tam beats" (le tam-tam bat).[126] Here Césaire appears to riff on one of Jacques Roumain's most famous poems, "Quand bat le tam-tam," or "When the Tom-Tom Beats," which evokes black ancestry figured in the most crudely gendered terms: "that tom-tom panting like a young black girl's breasts."[127] This allusion suggests that the ancestral plane of pan-African entanglement persists and intrudes itself into the present despite the king's efforts to disavow and eradicate it.

We also see the king grow increasingly alienated from the culture of the peasants in whose name he presumes to rule. This becomes clear when Christophe orders his people to take their farming tools and use them to fill in the "raque," the crevasses alongside the river. One wise peasant grumbles, "The *raque* is a trap. You better off taking the river—leave all the muck to the left and right, cut through by the river. Nuncle, *you'd have to know the rivers*" (Faudrait, n'oncle, savoir les fleuves).[128] The echo here of Hughes's career-defining line "I've known rivers" lifts the peasant's critique from a simple reproach for Christophe's forgetting of his own people's folk wisdom to a broader indictment of how the king has lost sight of African-derived traditions and values like those famously celebrated by Hughes.

And indeed, throughout the play the peasants give voice to an ethos of vernacular pan-African entanglement strongly reminiscent of Hughes's own. Such expressions appear in scenes and "interludes" in which farmers, fishermen, market women, and other ordinary characters play a far more prominent role than would be necessary if their only function were to provide comic relief along the lines of Shakespeare's servants and clowns. Indeed, while they serve that function as well, their primary role is closer to that of a Greek chorus, serving as the voice of community wisdom and collective memory.[129] The play is framed by a prologue in which a group of black people in "Blue peasant's clothing" is gathered around a cockfight between two cocks named Christophe and Pétion, respectively; the stage directions describe the people's cries as *"the voice of Haiti."*[130] Between the three acts are two interludes featuring raft keepers and peasant farmers. The first begins with a "Commentator" who waxes lyrical about the Artibonite River, the "father-river of Haiti."[131] This segues to a raft keeper and his apprentice, who work and earn their living on the river. They introduce a vernacular register into the play with their informal speech patterns and their folk songs, and they bring in a distinctively African thread with a reference to the West African and Caribbean aquatic spirits known as "Mama Water."[132]

Christophe's distancing himself from African traditions is inseparable from his growing contempt for the Haitian peasantry. In act 1, that contempt is still mixed with pity and affection, and at his coronation he solemnly pledges to "never permit on any pretext whatsoever the return of slavery or any measure contrary to the freedom and full exercise of civil and political rights by the people of Haiti."[133] Yet his growing alienation from both Africa and the Haitian poor is evident in this soliloquy:

> Poor Africa! Or rather, poor Haiti! It's the same thing anyway. Back there, the tribes, the languages, rivers, castes, forests, town against town, village against village.
>
> Here, blacks, mulattoes, quadroons, obeah-men, God-knows-what, clan, caste, color, distrust and rivalry, cockfights, dogfights over a bone, louse-fights![134]

Far from celebrating the unifying power of blackness, this speech laments the countless differences and divisions splintering black communities on both sides of the Atlantic. Clearly, then, the Césaire of the 1960s recognized that a transatlantic Negritude could not rely on an innate feeling of kinship among black people worldwide but would have to negotiate these divisions and cultivate channels of cultural exchange.

Perhaps Christophe's dismay at the people's failure to transcend their cultural differences explains why he betrays his promises to them. Despite his oath to prevent the return of slavery, he issues an edict requiring workers to be treated as soldiers, subject to command, and forces them to work on his citadel: "Liberty cannot exist without labor," he declares,[135] in a chilling echo of the Nazi concentration camp slogan "arbeit macht frei," or "work sets you free." Christophe increasingly speaks of the peasants with disdain, calling them "that rabble" (cette canaille),[136] and exclaims in one megalomaniacal rage that before he took power, "There was shit, do you hear me, and nothing but shit!"[137]

Some of Césaire's less charitable critics have read Christophe's contempt for the poor and his growing despotism as simply the theatrical manifestation of an elitist and authoritarian streak in Césaire's own political temperament, but I find such readings hard to reconcile with the voices critical of Christophe's rule that the playwright weaves into the text.[138] One peasant complains, "What I love is the earth. I believe in the earth that I work with my own arms, but the fat king won't put it in our arms to keep."[139] Whereas Christophe is obsessed with stone and with building something permanent and solid, the peasants are simply interested in soft soil that they own for themselves and can use to sustain themselves in perpetuity. The contrast highlights the gap between what his people want and what he is convinced they need, and his obsession with building a solid legacy is by no means a pure virtue. Indeed, I read it as Césaire's self-reflexive critique of his own project of excavating and preserving a pan-African past—a reminder that too much fixity renders history inert and unusable, in contrast to the ephemerality but fecundity of living memory, symbolized by soil in the peasants' dialog.

Furthering the play's self-reflective criticism of Christophe's rule, Césaire also includes a speech by Metellus, the captured chief of the rebel army, who expresses pride in having

> kept watch
> on this black soil we stand on, reddening it
> with our peasants' blood.[140]

Like the peasants, Metellus values the ephemeral fertility of the soil over the enduring fixity of Christophe's great monument to himself. Moreover, his words recall Césaire's own from the *Notebook:*

> my negritude is not a stone, its deafness hurled against the clamour of the day
> . . . .
> My negritude is neither tower nor cathedral,
> it takes root in the red flesh of the soil.[141]

Taken together, these passages pose a caution against investing too much cultural capital and human labor in such putatively permanent embodiments of collective memory as towers, cathedrals, and citadels.

Furthermore, in contrast to his memory of the revolution's glittering ideals in the early days, Metellus finds only disappointment in Christophe's Haiti:

> We were going to found a country
>   that was shared among all of us,
> not just the landholders list on this island!
> Open to all of the islands,
> to all of the blacks! All of the blacks of the world!
> But then came the procurators,
> dividing the house,
> laying their hands on our mother. . . .
> Christophe! Pétion!
> I turn my back on this double tyranny.[142]

Significantly, Metellus's vision of what the revolution stood for is pitched first in pan-Caribbean terms and then in terms of global blackness: "all of the islands" and "all of the blacks in the world!" It is hard to imagine why Césaire would have written Metellus into the play to give this single speech and then be immediately executed if he did not intend it as a kind of indictment of King Christophe for moving away from this vision of a concentric universality rooted in blackness, in Africa, and in a shared history of enslavement and resistance.[143]

If characters such as Metellus and the peasants articulate Césaire's vision of Negritude, they also reveal the blind spots in the author's ethos of vernacular pan-African entanglement. In its romanticization of the peasantry, Césaire's Negritude fell into some of the same pitfalls as McKay, Hughes, and Roumain before him, of reducing poor black people to raw materials for the poet's appropriation and consumption. In this regard Raphaël Confiant has a point when he criticizes Césaire for his supposed messiah complex, posing as "Christ, as savior not only of the Martinican people, but of the entire black race."[144] And Christophe's tyranny in the play in many ways merely takes this exploitative attitude toward its logical extreme.

Césaire's Negritude also shared with his predecessors unfortunate shortcomings in his representation of women and his use of gendered tropes, such as Metellus's implied rape metaphor about the "procurators . . . laying their hands on our mother." Such gendering is also evident in a peasant's complaint: "When we beat the whites back into the sea, that was to have this land for ourselves, not to toil on the land of others, even if they are black, but *to have it for ourselves like a wife,* no?"[145] Césaire here duplicates the move for which Ella Shohat criticized *Discourse on Colonialism,* of "using gendered discourse to articulate oppositional struggle. [He] writes about 'that collection of adventurers who slashed and violated and spat on Africa to make the stripping of her easier.'"[146] This move reduces black women, however romanticized, to tropes and to the passivity of the soil and the rivers. It seems to conceive of Negritude as an international brotherhood and to preclude black women from playing active roles therein.

The treatment of black women as passive repositories of cultural knowledge and values is compounded by the fact that the only significant female character in the play is the king's wife, and she is developed more fully as a symbol than as a character. A hand-corrected typescript of act 3 shows that many of Madame Christophe's lines were introduced after the first draft (perhaps after the first production of the play), and those lines primarily consist of her reciting invocations to the gods of Vodou and reminding Christophe of his humble slave past.[147] The inability or unwillingness to acknowledge female agency inhibited the universal reach the author aspired to and weakened the potency of the play's vision of Negritude as a political and artistic force by neglecting the role of black women as active agents in Caribbean history.

If Césaire appeared blithe to the implications of his gendered rhetoric of rape and possession, he was at least self-aware and reflexive when it came to enshrining Christophe and his citadel as beacons of and memorials to black achievement and self-empowerment. Indeed, the play implicitly reproaches the king for his vanity—reminiscent of the Egyptian pharaohs[148] but also of Shelley's Ozymandias—in building a gigantic monument to his own greatness. This is the Hegelian side of Christophe that Paul Breslin describes: "Christophe is a builder, an architect, a shaper of raw material. He must force Haiti to enter modernity by building the visible and invisible structures of a modern nation-state."[149] This impulse is revealed not just through his determination to build the citadel but through the dozens of tropes involving construction, stones, and buildings that characterize his speech. He begins the play with noble intentions, envisioning

> A shaking with power to speak,
> To do, to construct, to build,
> To be, to name, to bind, to remake.[150]

This speech is revealing, as Christophe quickly shifts from the realm of the discursive and performative—speaking and doing—to the concrete and material acts of building, binding, and remaking, which soon become parts of a tyrannical obsession. When he looks at Haiti, he sees "No stone, only dust! Only shit and dust. . . . The human material needs recasting."[151] As a counterbalance to the fixed and unyielding monolith that Christophe aspires to build, the peasants' emphasis on soil and earth makes visible Césaire's conception of Negritude as something flexible, fertile, and malleable: the king's "shit and dust" are the peasants' fertile soil and their key to self-sufficiency.

If King Christophe is at times too fixated on building a material legacy of the revolution, at other times he recognizes the need for fluidity in conceptualizing black identity, a recognition most strongly implied in the many references to seas and rivers that run through his speeches. Rivers in his rhetoric are associated with fertility, malleability, and future potential—thus linking them with the gendered images of nation and soil. The Artibonite River becomes especially symbolic; Christophe declares that it "could be transformed to the Nile of Haiti,"[152] thus linking the river with the grandeur of ancient Egypt and replicating the move Hughes makes in "The Negro Speaks of Rivers" of superimposing a major river in the American hemisphere onto the Nile.[153] The commentator in the interlude to act 1 of *The Tragedy of King Christophe* similarly claims that the Artibonite "carries and carries away, transports, pours and divulges all."[154] There are traces in this imagery not only of Hughes's "ancient, dusky rivers" but also of the spring that Manuel makes it his mission to discover in Roumain's

Masters of the Dew, which he compares to the "first spring" that flowed through Eden.[155] In short, Césaire offers the river as an alternative metaphor for continuity between a diasporic community and its imagined past—that is, a metaphor for what I am calling ancestral pan-African entanglement. A major river carves itself into the land and will flow long after even the greatest human feats of construction, including the citadel, have crumbled; yet the river constantly changes and finds new paths and generates new life along its course.

Seas and oceans similarly become tropes for transnational entanglement in the play. Vastey, for example, exclaims: "Look where God has placed us! Our backs pushed against the Pacific, in front of us Europe and Africa; at our sides, either way, the Americas! At the confluence of all the tides of the world, at the node of all the ebb and flood, there is—at all points of this vista, the enormous spectacle—there is this extraordinary amalgam of the Atlantic!" (il y a cette pas banale concrétion atlantique!), to which Magny replies, "Haiti is itself a great ship."[156] The rich marine metaphors in this exchange paint the "extraordinary amalgam of the Atlantic" as a fluid, amorphous sea of interconnection. Moreover, as with the similar passage I quoted earlier from the *Notebook,* the position of the West Indies within this world ocean is a defensive one, with "our back pushed against the Pacific" and the Americas closing in from either side. Magny here implies that the nation of Haiti can become a transnational emblem of black freedom, a "great ship," and provide a core or hub through which an aspiring pan-African community can anchor its strands of memory and identity.

As I have noted, in his monomaniacal push to memorialize the revolution through the citadel, the king frequently loses sight of the very different kind of continuity with the past symbolized by soil and dust, rivers and seas. But at the end of the play, humbled by the betrayals of both his paralyzed body and his rebellious body politic, Christophe tries once more to recuperate attachments to rivers and soil, to the African-derived traditions of his ancestors, and to a history of enslavement and resistance. In the process he recovers some of the Christophe whom Breslin describes as "intuitive or even mystical in his divination of Haiti's destiny."[157]

This Christophe, avatar of Negritude, delivers an extraordinary final monologue to Vastey, who has stayed by his side as the rest of his subjects revolt. Through this speech the king simultaneously defines blackness in a flexible, inclusive, modern way and anchors it in the twin ancestral pasts of an imagined precolonial Africa and slavery:

> Little mulatto, you're not black, you're mulatto. But just as the earth preserves in its foldings the trace of its past upheavals, you have known, . . . no, . . . you have

lived in the red of your hair burning like fire, the infernal breath of the lightning; no? On your shoulders, there, between your two shoulders, I'm sure of it, the invisible collar, unbreakable; on the path through the sands, the caravan's sudden arrival: these are pains and horrors come from as far away as the underground caves; from these nauseous origins, yes? Ah! As deep as the rivers and our laughter also, that bursts forth like a red bull in the storm of the furious pastures of driven clouds! Therefore, you are black. In the name of disaster, in the name of my heart that raises my life into my throat with a belch of disgust, I baptize you; I name you; I anoint you black.[158]

In the line "As deep as the rivers" (profondes comme les fleuves),[159] we find another echo of "The Negro Speaks of Rivers," and the speech as a whole resonates with the mixed-race Hughes's decision to proudly identify himself with the darkest people of his race. Like Vastey, Hughes chose to reject whatever privileges lighter skin might have afforded him and allied himself with black people. Blackness emerges in the king's vision as an identity that is both biologically inherited and capable of being affirmatively chosen or bestowed. Through the allusion to the Hughes poem, Césaire links Negritude to Hughes's idea of African ancestry as a source of cohesion; through the references to the "invisible collar" of slavery's legacy, he manages at the same time to vest Negritude in a history of "pains and horrors."

Christophe's speech further expresses the fluid and plastic nature of a productive pan-African web of entanglement through the volcano imagery, which serves much the same multidirectional function that it did in the *Notebook*: gesturing at once back toward past history and ahead toward future potential. Christophe describes the past as a palimpsest akin to the volcanic geological prehistory of the Antilles, in which "the earth preserves in its foldings the trace of its past upheavals." Yet like the speaker of "Lost Body" commanding the islands to exist, Christophe claims for his speech act bestowing blackness on Vastey the transformative force of a volcanic eruption—it "bursts forth like a red bull in the storm." The implication is, first, that Negritude is like magma, something more amorphous and plastic than a fixed or ossified essence and capable of hardening into new formations, and, second, that however much King Christophe tried to suppress the primal, animalistic force of Negritude, it had simply lain dormant as a protean, subterranean force of nature and finally erupts in this inclusive gesture of reclamation and transformation. The volcanic eruption thus connects the ancestral and contemporary planes of pan-African entanglement and injects the past as an animate force into the present and future.

We have already been prepared for Christophe's speech above by earlier moments in the play when traces of African-derived beliefs erupt despite the king's ambivalence. This takes the form of a literal haunting, for example, when Christophe sees a ghost and concludes that he has been cursed by an evil spirit from Vodou, "Bakulu Baka."[160] Ancestral entanglements manifest themselves again in his last scene when he calls on the *loa:*

> Gods of Africa!
> > *Lwa!*
> Strong rope of the blood
> Father, fastener of blood
> Abobo
> Africa, my place of power.[161]

The ambivalent phrase "rope of the blood" implies a nearly tangible continuity across generations of the African diaspora, linked through the suffering conveyed in the connotations of a lynching noose. These lines offer a variant of the weaving trope that I will argue in chapter 5 becomes increasingly important to understanding the late work of Langston Hughes. And it anticipates similar imagery I will note in my analysis of Paule Marshall's *Praisesong for the Widow* in my coda: strings, cords, and ropes that connect present-day African Americans and Afro-Caribbeans to their slave ancestors and to their foreparents in Africa before that.

As much as the symbolic economy of the play requires Christophe to recommit to an ethos of vernacular, pan-African entanglement, the move comes quite late. For most of acts 1 and 2, he seems to serve as an embodiment not of Negritude but of nationalism gone wrong. As Thomas Hale and Kora Véron remark, Césaire's plays from the 1960s "warned his readers and audiences, especially in Africa, of both the internal and external pitfalls on their path to independence."[162] And this is the level at which the play seems to most directly engage with Fanon's avowal that the only path toward true revolution and postcolonial culture went through "national consciousness" (conscience nationale). That phrase would have been closely associated with Fanon by the time of *Christophe's* writing in the early 1960s, and so Fanon comes to mind when the soon to be king appears before the crowd that Vastey has worked up and exclaims, "What is this people, which has, for a national consciousness, only a pudding-stone of assorted gossip? Haitian people: Haiti has less to fear from the French than from herself!"[163] One might read Christophe's disdain for his subjects as confirming Fanon's diagnosis of anticolonial nationalist movements whose urban elites have failed to establish "practical ties between them and the masses," particularly the rural peasantry. Without those connections underpinning national consciousness, Fanon concedes that nationalism becomes "nothing but a crude, empty, fragile shell. The cracks in it explain how easy it is for young independent countries to switch back from nation to ethnic group and from state to tribe."[164]

There is little indication, however, in the play or elsewhere, that Césaire particularly valued the nation even when it *was* grounded in the culture and labor of the proletariat and the peasantry. Whereas his implied criticism of Christophe for abandoning his African heritage rings out loud and clear in the text, there is little indication of any disapproval of the Haitian king for insufficient nation-building efforts. Indeed, when Hugonin sings a song that ends with the line *"This nation not so good,"* Christophe himself replies: "My poor Hugonin, nations are never good. And that's why kings shouldn't be too nice either."[165] Christophe's skepticism of nationalism as political policy echoes the playwright's skeptical assertion in a debate with René Depestre in the mid-1950s that, as Jack summarizes it, "defining the 'national' in poetry was an extremely precarious task."[166] My argument, then, is that the king's cynical view of the nation as a necessary evil constitutes a riposte to Fanon's criticism of Negritude and insistence on the nation as the ideal and only vehicle for achieving liberation.[167] Indeed, given both Césaire's long association with Negritude as an expression of border-crossing blackness and his complicated position on the question of Martinican independence, it should not surprise us that he placed much higher value on the transnational pan-Africanism of Hughes and McKay than on the nationalism that had by 1963 turned so toxic in Haiti under François "Papa Doc" Duvalier (of whom Césaire would later say, "Papa Doc shocks me, shocks me deeply")[168] and was already beginning to reveal its limitations in newly liberated African and Caribbean countries.[169] In contrast to the immutability of the nation, then, the vernacular channels of continuity with the past that Hughes had cultivated offered Césaire a flexible and inclusive basis for cultural identity whose ephemerality he deemed more desirable than the sort of fixities that Christophe demands.

Hughes, Césaire, and Negritude as Pan-African Entanglement

Hughes in turn came to recognize the Negritude movement as the inheritors of his own lifelong campaign to cultivate a sense of ancestral pan-African entanglement. Rampersad quotes a piece from Hughes's unpublished papers, dated December 1964, declaring that Césaire "takes all that we have, Senghor, Guillén and Hughes, and flings it at the moon, to make of it a space-ship of the dreams of all the dreamers in the world."[170] Note the similarity of this image to the one in Césaire's "Introduction à la poésie nègre américaine," where jazz players launch their drumsticks at the moon. The similarity is probably coincidental but reveals how close the two writers were in their thinking about the power of an affirmative vision of blackness. Hughes had earlier asserted such a similarity at the Mbari conference in Uganda in 1962: "Césaire had done exactly what the writers of the Harlem Renaissance had done before [him], back in the nineteen-twenties; only the Harlemites had not given it a name."[171]

Clearly, then, Langston Hughes and Aimé Césaire recognized each other as jointly engaged in a project of international black empowerment. That their only meetings in person were at festivals where *Christophe* was being performed hints at how important Haiti was to the memory of ancestral pan-African entanglement they constructed in common: of Africa lost, slavery endured, and freedom won. At the same time, we have seen how attempts to fix this narrative of a pan-African past in stone, literally or figuratively, can inhibit its motility and relevance in the present. Césaire also warns us through *Christophe* that building monuments to the past can become part of a larger need to fix in place the world more generally, a compulsion that too quickly begins to mimic and perpetuate the conditions and power dynamics of slavery. Perhaps, the play implies, we need both the permanence of the archive and the embodied immediacy of the repertoire, both the stone memorial and the river. The citadel helps enshrine the memory of the Haitian Revolution, but the performance of *Christophe,* like that of Hughes's *Emperor,* brings that memory into modern discourse through the fluidity and dynamism of nightly performance and makes it part of a larger tale of pan-African survival and resistance.

While Hughes and Césaire were busy affirming their mutual vision of transatlantic blackness, however, the emergence of Negritude into the anglophone world had set off a heated debate among black intellectuals in Europe and the Americas. Its reception was especially skeptical among African commentators, as I discuss in scale enlargement C. Most famously, at the same conference where Hughes spoke in Kampala, Wole Soyinka had quipped, "A tiger does not proclaim his tigritude, he pounces."[172] Similarly, as I will discuss in chapter 4, many South African writers were skeptical of Negritude's sweeping assertions of pan-African kinship and used Negritude as a proxy for working through their disagreements with Langston Hughes, however influential the American writer had been on their own development. Ironically, then, Hughes's success at finally expanding his black Atlantic network to include African writers created the greatest challenge to his ethos and aesthetic of pan-African entanglement.

Scale Enlargement C
Langston Hughes and Africa

I HAVE already mentioned numerous examples of Hughes's lifelong fascination with Africa. I can thus be brief in this section in which I zoom out to the scale of his connections to and sympathies for the continent. These operated on both ancestral and contemporary planes, but the contemporary entanglements began to form somewhat later. His earliest poems had romanticized Africa as a spiritual homeland, as the source of original black personality, and as antidote to the coldness, sterility, and alienation of life in American cities. These primitivist ideas are reflected, for example, in poems like "Our Land" (1923), whose speaker longs for a "land of trees" filled with "chattering parrots.... / And not this land where birds are grey."[1] Such lines do hint at threads of connection entangling black Americans with Africa, but primarily along ancestral vectors; the early poems rarely posit Africa as a source for contemporary cultural exchange.

The young Hughes did try, however, to establish links with modern Africa. In his first autobiography, *The Big Sea* (1940), he described his excitement as a young man in his early twenties, after dropping out of Columbia and joining the crew of a steamship headed for the west coast of Africa, when he first encountered Africa in person in 1923: "My Africa, Motherland of the Negro peoples! And me a Negro! Africa! The real thing, to be touched and seen, not merely read about in a book.... And farther down the coast [from Dakar] it was more like the Africa I had dreamed about—wild and lovely, the people dark and beautiful, the palm trees tall, the sun bright, and the rivers deep. The great Africa of my dreams!"[2] This description is missing only a reference to drums to complete the catalog of tropes that Hughes used throughout his poetry of the 1920s to imagine his ancestral Africa. For example: the "rivers deep" echo Hughes's first published poem, "The Negro Speaks of Rivers."[3] And the "sun bright" evokes the "land of sun" wished for by the speaker of "Our Land."[4]

Yet in Hughes's autobiography he quickly proceeded to dispel any illusions his readers might have shared with his youthful self about twentieth-century

West Africa as idyll or paradise. One scene he witnessed encapsulated "today's Africa, real, beyond humor—the raised club, the commanding white man, and the frightened native."[5] His earliest published account of traveling to Africa, a series of impressionistic fragments that appeared in *Crisis* in December 1923, hinted at the desperate poverty and exploitation of the people, especially in the Niger delta: "The young boy from the customs, brown with the dreams in his eyes . . . 'America, is it a wonderful place?' . . . The policeman whose salary is four pounds a month. . . . The dirtiest, saddest lot of Negro workers seen in Africa . . . Black soldiers with bayoneted guns pacing the docks."[6] Moreover, as I noted before, an even greater disappointment for Hughes was the refusal of the Africans he encountered on that first trip to "believe I was a Negro."[7]

His younger self's enthusiastic desire for shared African ancestry to exert a unifying effect in his encounters with other black people faced an early crisis at this moment, one that Hughes would continue to struggle with in his poetry and elsewhere in years to come. His poetry continued to feature representations of Africa where a "great golden moon" really does rise "behind palm groves," and "tom-toms do beat / In village squares under the mango trees."[8] But he increasingly sought out fragments or residues of African cultural practice in his own hemisphere, among the peasants and sharecroppers, urban workers, and the idle poor. At the same time, Africa increasingly came to represent for Hughes a land of colonial exploitation and injustice on the one hand and resistance and revolution on the other. In the 1930s, when Hughes wrote *Emperor of Haiti*, Africa was almost entirely colonized by Europe, and memories of African agency and resistance from the preslavery era had been forgotten or suppressed, so the Haitian Revolution became a proxy for African humanity in the black American imagination. By the 1960s, however, Africa offered Hughes many examples of revolution and self-governance, which transformed the way he wrote about Africa.

We can see the beginnings of that transformation in his poetry over a twenty-year period. The early tendrils of an ethos of pan-African entanglement were always there, emerging for instance in 1925 in "Johannesburg Mines," though the "240,000 / Native Africans" working in the mines are shown only as faceless victims of an oppressive system.[9] In the early 1930s, Africa most frequently appeared among a catalog of places where oppressed workers should rise up, as in "Good Morning Revolution" or "Chant for Tom Mooney." But in the late 1930s, events in the Horn of Africa gave Hughes an outlet for his compulsion to discover and bear witness to black resistance and accomplishment. When fascist Italy invaded Ethiopia in 1935, Mussolini's forces met fierce resistance from Ethiopian troops before eventually seizing Addis Ababa and forcing Emperor Haile Selassie and his family into exile. Selassie would return and lead forces loyal to him to oust the Italian army in 1941, making Ethiopia a rare black-governed country on an African continent ruled by Europe.

As an indicator of how profoundly these events shaped Hughes's perception of Africa, consider that out of fourteen poems that Hughes published between 1935 and 1943 that evoke Africa directly or indirectly, eight of them specifically mention Ethiopia. Typical in its lament is "Broadcast on Ethiopia" (1936), which begins with a mixture of outrage and resignation: "The little fox is still / The dogs of war have made their kill."[10] The radio metaphor in the title prefigures the poet's use of the same trope in "Broadcast to the West Indies," which I discussed in scale enlargement A. The body of the poem extends the radio news metaphor by excerpting actual Associated Press and United Press newswire stories, including one narrating Selassie and his family's "flight from his crumbling empire."[11] In short, Hughes immediately subsumed Selassie's struggle into his narrative of pan-African entanglement and resistance, where for a while it assumed a place of importance rivaling the Haitian Revolution.

"Broadcast on Ethiopia" also hints that Ethiopia's struggle was entangled within larger webs of colonial and capitalist power: one of the newswire excerpts concerns French elections in which the Communist Party swept to power and the Minister of Colonies lost his seat. As the poem nears its finale, the tone becomes satirical:

Station XYZW broadcasting:
MISTER CHRISTOPHER COLOMBO
Just made a splendid kill.
The British Legation stands solid on its hill.[12]

The Columbus reference evokes the Italian figure who arguably inaugurated the era of Europe's obsession with colonizing the rest of the world, thereby establishing a line of continuity between 1492 and the poem's present. The reference to the "British Legation," meanwhile, broadens the net of complicity that the poem casts over European colonialism. Most specifically, it seems to criticize the British and French position in the Hoare-Laval Pact of December 1935, which tried unsuccessfully to end the war in Ethiopia by partitioning the country. More generally, the poem hints at Great Britain's own position as colonial hegemon. After all, as the poem implicitly reminds us, while the invasion of Ethiopia marked a new phase of military aggression for Italy in 1935, England had laid claim to African territory centuries earlier and spent the nineteenth and early twentieth centuries expanding and consolidating power over its global empire.

The path of Hughes's relationship to an imagined Africa, then, was from youthful romantic idealization to disappointment and muted frustration and then to recognition of an emerging anticolonial spirit in twentieth-century Africa. This rebellious spirit resonated satisfyingly with his desire for a global black community. But for the most part, until the 1950s Africa remained to him more of a distant abstraction learned about through reading than it was a living place with artists and intellectuals he might engage in his ever-growing pan-African network. After that first journey along the African coast in 1923–24, he would not return to the continent again until 1960, when he attended the inauguration of Benjamin Nnamdi "Zik" Azikiwe, whom he knew through Lincoln University, as governor-general of Nigeria.[13] Indeed, as the era of African decolonization dawned in the late 1950s, Hughes found himself well connected to the leaders of those struggles: in addition to Azikiwe, who would become the first president of independent Nigeria in 1963, Hughes corresponded with another Lincoln alumnus, Kwame Nkrumah of the Gold Coast, later prime minister of Ghana, and he had carried on an irregular correspondence with Léopold Sédar Senghor of Senegal since 1950 and with J. B. Danquah of the Gold Coast since 1954.

Hughes began expanding his pan-African network to South Africa beginning in the early 1950s. In the next chapter I tell the story of his correspondence with novelist Peter Abrahams, of how judging a short story competition for *Drum* magazine alerted him to the existence of a younger generation of African writers, and of how he later compiled two important anthologies of African writing in the 1960s. What is more, the 1960 visit to Nigeria was only the first of a flurry of trips to Africa: he returned to Lagos in 1961 for the American Society of African Culture (AMSAC) conference, and he was a guest of honor at the celebrated Mbari writers conference in Uganda in 1962. Between those two gatherings, he met the West Africans Chinua Achebe, George Awoonor-Williams, John Pepper Clark, Cyprian Ekwensi, Gabriel Okara, Christopher Okigbo, Wole Soyinka, and the sculptor Ben Enwonwu, among others; from South Africa he met Es'kia Mphahlele, Bloke Modisane, Arthur Maimane, and Lewis Nkosi.[14] In the summer of 1962 he returned to West Africa to speak at the opening of a US library in Accra, Ghana. Finally, Hughes was appointed as the official US representative to the First World Festival of Negro Arts in Dakar, Senegal, in April 1966, where he was publicly feted by President Senghor among others.[15]

To some extent these were all vanity trips, and Hughes most likely relished the honors and the lionization. But I would argue that he also approached these travels pragmatically, seeing them as opportunities to extend and increase pan-African entanglements and facilitate cultural exchange. A speech he gave at the AMSAC conference in Lagos in 1961, representing the African American delegation, illustrates his thinking clearly enough to quote it at length:

> We have come through the air and across the ocean seven thousand miles to exchange with you our gifts, to exchange with your artists our art, and to give to you, this audience, in all humbleness and love and sincerity. In a sense, we feel we are coming *home,* to our ancestral home, back to the roots of our culture. Of course, in the Americas—North and South, the United States, the West Indies, Brazil—other cultures have mingled with those of the peoples of Africa, other bloods have mingled with your blood. But all of [us] here tonight have in our veins, to some degree, the blood of Africa, and in our hearts, the love of Africa. We come back to you, the land from which our forefathers came, to this great continent in its mighty march toward the future, to bring you our music and our songs.[16]

As with his speech a year later at the opening of the US library in Accra (quoted in my introduction), Hughes by the 1960s was seeing Africa simultaneously on two different planes: as ancestral homeland, to which he felt linked through "the roots of our culture" and "the blood of Africa," and also as a source of contemporary vitality, inspiration, and solidarity in the modern world and the "mighty march toward the future." On this contemporary plane, established in the first sentence by the reference to air travel, the emphasis was on *cultural exchange*—"to exchange with your artists our art."

A first reading of the above speech might give the impression that Hughes, muddled in his thinking, contradicted himself within this short paragraph, wavering between essentialist assertions of black kinship and constructivist understandings of race and identity. I would argue to the contrary that he was actually navigating those imperatives quite precisely and self-consciously: he attempted to imagine into existence memories of pan-African ancestral connection, even as he used the speech to advocate for fruitful channels of cultural exchange in the twentieth century. He had used a similar rhetorical move in a speech he gave some five years earlier in New York: "The blood of Africa and the rhythms of Africa are very much a part of American life today. But we here in the United States have developed a new race, the American Negro, with a great variety of beauties, skin colors, and hair texture."[17] Hughes executed this double move, of asserting (ancestral) kinship while negotiating (contemporary) difference, just as deliberately in his poetry from this late period, as I discuss at greater length in chapter 5. In the process, Hughes positioned himself as facilitator and promoter of African literature and as interpreter of Africa for American readers. His anthologies and books for children did both jobs at once, including *An African Treasury, Poems from Black Africa, The First Book of Africa,* and the anthology he unsuccessfully shopped around to publishers circa 1955, *Big Ghost and Little Ghost and Other Stories: An Anthology of African Short Stories of Today,* edited for teenagers.[18]

As with all the relationships that are the focus of this book, the effects of the transatlantic contact, both fleeting and sustained, were deeply and mutually felt. On the African side, a burgeoning generation of young African writers benefited from Hughes's mentorship, promotion, and power to legitimize. My next chapter makes this case at length for the South African writers loosely associated with *Drum* magazine, but Hughes left his mark on West Africa as well. Chinua Achebe in 1988 recalled the American's presence at the Mbari conference in Kampala a quarter century before: "An American visitor walked into our deliberations—venerable, even avuncular.... His name was Langston Hughes. Without saying much, he seemed to preside naturally over our debate and bless our youthful zealousness with a wise benevolence."[19] Achebe credited this encounter with his decision, upon receiving an open travel fellowship from UNESCO in 1962, to visit the United States and Brazil: "I think that the strong impression made on me by Langston Hughes—his deus ex machina appearance at that critical moment in the intellectual and literary history of modern Africa, and that unspoken message of support and solidarity after three hundred years of brutal expatriation—I think all that played a part in my choice of countries to visit. I wanted to see something of the situation of the African diaspora in its two major concentrations in the New World."[20] Achebe's homage gives credence to my claim that Hughes should be considered a central figure in the rise of postcolonial literature in Africa and the diaspora. Certainly Achebe's essay makes explicit that the encounter with Hughes expanded the scope of his and other writers' thinking about African identity and collectivity and sent him toward the path of his own lifelong project of facilitating pan-African entanglement.

For Hughes, too, the new connections to African writers and artists, and the new recognition his work received from those quarters, must have been enormously gratifying. The web of contacts was certainly extensive, as Hughes's correspondence preserved in the Langston Hughes Papers at Yale reveals: beyond his extensive correspondence with several South African writers, described in the next chapter, Hughes corresponded at least once with writers John Akar, Adeboye Babalola, Adelaide Casely-Hayford, Gladys May Casely-Hayford, John Pepper Clark, Mabel Dove Danquah, Alioune Diop, Cyprian Ekwensi, Matei Markwei, Davidson Nicol, Gabriel Okara, Francis Ernest Parkes, Léopold Senghor, Wole Soyinka, Efua Theodora Sutherland, Tchicaya U Tam'si, and Amos Tutuola.

In chapter 5 I will devote considerable attention to the question of how extended contact with this rapidly expanding literary and political network shaped and colored Hughes's literary writings about Africa—particularly in the late poem *Ask Your Mama*. For now, let me offer as a simpler example the lyrics he wrote to accompany his friend the musician Randy Weston's song "African Lady" in 1960, around the same time as *Ask Your Mama*:

> Sunrise at dawn, night is gone,
> I hear your song, African Lady.
> The dark fades away, now it's day,
> A new morning breaks.
> The birds in the sky
> All sing for Africa awakes.
> Bright light floods the land,
> And tomorrow's in your hand,
>   African lady.[21]

There are traces in these lyrics of the old primitivism of the 1920s and of Senghor's personifications of Negritude as an idealized black woman. But this is not a celebration of an ancient, lost Africa but rather of a forward-looking Africa that "awakes" at the dawn of a "new morning." By this point Ghana and Nigeria were both independent nations, "flood[ing] the land" with the bright light of their examples. And if South Africa in the wake of the Sharpeville Massacre in March of 1960 was caught more tightly than ever in the grip of white minority rule and racist apartheid laws, Hughes knew that at least there was a generation of revolutionary young black and mixed-race writers using their art in opposition to those laws. The story of that thread in his web of pan-African interconnection is the subject of the next chapter.

4 A "Song of Africa across Oceans and Centuries"

Langston Hughes, Negritude, and South Africa

SCOTT MALCOLMSON regards certain entertainment figures such as Bruce Lee, Michael Jackson, and Bob Marley as the vehicles for "actually existing cosmopolitanisms," which "involve individuals with limited choices deciding to enter into something larger than their immediate cultures."[1] Malcolmson expresses concern about the limited range of choices available to those in poor countries who celebrate such global cultural icons. The case of South Africa in the 1950s, however, would seem to complicate this picture: blacks and "coloureds" (people of mixed race), who certainly had limited choices, defiantly adopted an American-flavored cosmopolitanism as an alternative to a stultifying and essentializing vision of their "immediate cultures" being promulgated by the white minority apartheid government that had been elected in 1948. Or to shift to my own terminology, South Africans sought out entanglements with black America to counter white nationalism's ethos of separation.

Take, for example, a comment by Es'kia Mphahlele that *Ebony* magazine showed to black South Africans the "achievements of the black race. Something to celebrate. And oh, how badly *we* needed that in our corner of Africa."[2] As Mphahlele's remark implies, African American culture deeply inspired and influenced the generation of black South Africans who came of age in the mid-twentieth century.[3] The art and writing of the Harlem Renaissance was especially important to the rise of a new generation of black South African writers. The very first issue of the highly influential *Drum* magazine, for example, began by reprinting Countee Cullen's poem "Heritage" (which begins with the question "What is Africa to me?"). Going back a bit further, we know from Peter Abrahams's autobiography *Tell Freedom* that his adolescent discovery of *The New Negro* anthology and other works of African American literature in the 1930s provided an almost epiphanic moment for him: to those authors, Abrahams wrote, "I owe a great debt for crystallizing my vague yearnings to write and for showing me the long dream was attainable."[4] One of the authors he quoted was Langston Hughes, whom Mphahlele and Richard Rive also admired in print and described as a friend.[5]

Yet the full extent of Hughes's role in launching the literary movement around *Drum* magazine has begun to come clear only more recently, with the publication of *Langston Hughes and the South African Drum Generation: The Correspondence,* edited by myself and John Walters (2010), and of Hughes's brief correspondence with a young Bessie Emery—soon Bessie Head—edited by David Chioni Moore and published in *Research in African Literatures* (2010). These letters help reveal how profoundly the relationship with Langston Hughes contributed to the South African writers' development of an urban, transnational identity at a time when the apartheid government was determined to "fossilize" Africans into "tribal inventions," in Can Themba's phrase.[6] A careful analysis of their exchange of letters contributes to a deeper, richer understanding of the ethos and aesthetics of entanglement that underpinned this emerging cosmopolitan identity. The condition of transnational entanglement was at first eagerly desired by black South African intellectuals in the 1950s and then was forced upon many of them by the vicissitudes of exile. The letters also show Hughes connecting the South Africans to a larger pan-African network that could both rival and, when necessary, replace the nation as a staging ground for gaining literary access, legitimacy, and prestige.

These relationships were not without tensions, however. Although Hughes was both an inspiration as a poet and an invaluable contact in terms of getting African writing published and promoted internationally, his work caused considerable ambivalence for the South African writers. This is because much of his writing, especially the poetry from the 1920s for which he was best known at the time, painted a romanticized portrait of a primitive, tribal Africa that in many ways appeared to corroborate the "separate development" rationale for the apartheid policies implemented in South Africa following the National Party's electoral victory in 1948. Hughes's romantic evocation of a primitive Africa through palm trees and tom-tom drums came uncomfortably close to the apartheid vision of fixed racial identities kept "pure" by quarantine. Most often, though, the South African writers channeled their discomfort with such depictions of Africa as we see in Hughes's work into their quarrels with Negritude.

My intentions for this chapter are, first, to explore the web of connections linking Langston Hughes to the aforementioned South African writers (Abrahams, Head, Mphahlele, and Rive) as well as Peter Clarke, Todd Matshikiza, Bloke Modisane, Phyllis Ntantala, Henry Nxumalo, and others. Second, I intend to survey the various and evolving attitudes and approaches in the South African writers' engagements with Negritude and other modes of cultural pan-Africanism, especially as many of them went into exile and experienced the alienation of diaspora more directly. Most importantly, building on my account in earlier chapters of a transatlantic conversation happening throughout much of the twentieth century over the meaning of blackness and what it means to be African, I will investigate how this conversation was transformed when South African authors and intellectuals were brought into the debate. Specifically, what are the implications of the South African critique of Negritude for Hughes's ethos and aesthetics of pan-African entanglement and for his vision of a transnational black literary community? And, inversely, what did South African writers gain from their contacts with the African diaspora, both through the written word and through the frequent experience of leaving South Africa and living in exile abroad?

By way of answering these questions, I will focus especially on the lives and works of two men, Peter Abrahams and Es'kia Mphahlele. Both left South Africa to spend decades in exile: Abrahams left in 1939 and eventually moved to Jamaica, where he lived until his murder in 2017; Mphahlele left southern Africa in 1957 and spent two decades moving frequently among the newly independent nations of West and East Africa as well as around Europe and the United States before repatriating to South Africa permanently in 1977. Their different pathways in part reflect differing views of the national and the local: while Mphahlele felt himself bound by the "tyranny of place" to the land of his ancestors, Abrahams's loyalties were more fluid, and he was able to put down roots in Jamaica by building a career as a radio and newspaper journalist there. While both writers were skeptical of assumptions of kinship or similarity based on race, the experience of living in the West as, respectively, a man of mixed race and a black African man nevertheless rendered them both increasingly receptive to ideas of a transnational black identity and culture. Increasingly, too, they assimilated tropes and images from African American and West Indian history, literature, and art—especially those involving slavery—into their own writings, thus drawing on and perpetuating the lexicon of pan-African entanglement that Hughes and many others had pioneered before them.

With this in mind, I will read Abrahams's and Mphahlele's fictional and nonfiction works extending into the 1980s and beyond as, in part, extensions of Hughes's ethos of pan-African entanglement devoted to facilitating cultural exchange and transnational solidarity. Yet Abrahams and Mphahlele took very different views of this project. Abrahams, in his last novel, *The View from Coyaba,* and his memoir, *The Black Experience in the Twentieth Century,* pessimistically regarded black people as so embattled and mentally subjugated that the only solution was withdrawal and a kind of self-segregation, at least for the short term. Mphahlele, for his part, spent his later years developing a philosophy he called "African Humanism," which likewise called for people of African descent to invest in their heritage and traditions but to do so in the service of elevating Africa onto the global stage as equal partner, with its own culture to share with the world.

In contrasting Abrahams and Mphahlele, we can see both of them wrestling with the same paradoxical tensions that run through all of Hughes's writing, but Mphahlele, I will argue, more successfully reconciled the competing tensions. Especially in his later writing, Mphahlele increasingly used the symbolic palette that circulates in narratives of slavery in the Americas, but he coupled this embrace of the lexicon of pan-African entanglement with a simultaneous turn to rural tradition in Africa itself. Put another way, Mphahlele urged Africans on their native soil to look inward to their specific local cultural practices for universal values that, subjected to careful synthesis, could lay the groundwork for pan-African solidarity. Mphahlele's work, then, shows us that constructing any sort of unity out of the far-flung cultures of the black Atlantic required the continual negotiation and translation of cultural *difference*. This emphasis marks a departure from the strategic essentialism we saw in the Negritude poets' adoption of the rhetoric of racial kinship and from the assumptions of Kwame Nkrumah's brand of pan-Africanism regarding an essential "African personality." For Mphahlele, the challenge was to nurture indigenous local aesthetics and traditions that could be parlayed into currency for cultural exchange, without crudely commodifying them or allowing them to be reduced to lyrical museum pieces.

Weaving South Africa into Black Atlantic Literature

In the world of literature, to speak of a "black Atlantic" web of interconnections between South Africa and the United States in the mid-twentieth century is not to retrospectively impose order on random happenstance, as academic labels often do.[7] Rather, a group of black writers from both countries deliberately and determinedly forged a network with each other, sustained by newly accessible travel and communication technologies and carried out through a steady trade of airmail letters and postcards, books, magazines, records, paintings, photographs, and other material channels for cultural exchange. Langston Hughes was the hub of this conversation on the American side. Beginning in 1953 when he accepted an invitation to judge an African short story competition for *Drum* magazine, he began corresponding with a group of South African writers and thereby entangled them in his black Atlantic network—putting them in touch, for example, with agents, publishers, radio show producers, and other key figures in Europe and North America.

Drum magazine, launched in 1951, gave ample attention to pin-up girls, sports, and entertainment, yet its writers and photographers also carried out important muckraking journalism. For a time in the 1950s, *Drum* was also a crucial outlet for publishing literary short fiction from across anglophone Africa, but especially from South Africa itself. The magazine both documented and fueled the outpouring of cultural creativity that has sometimes been dubbed the "Sophiatown Renaissance," named for the Johannesburg neighborhood at the heart of midcentury bohemian urban identity, by analogy with the Harlem Renaissance of some three decades before.

Like their American predecessors, the South African writers loosely associated with *Drum* were intent on establishing a modern, urban, cosmopolitan identity for themselves. They therefore sought out entanglements with other cultures at every opportunity and at every scale. In the 1960s, for example, Es'kia Mphahlele would insist on the existence of a "proletarian culture . . . in the making" in South Africa's cities.[8] This culture was fomenting in opposition to the government's insistence that "all Africans belong in the rural areas and are merely in the city because the white man needs their labour. The city is never to be regarded as their natural home," as the protagonist-narrator Timi complains in *The Wanderers*.[9] This speech echoes the author's own complaint that the Afrikaner publishing companies that controlled African-language publishing for the schools accepted only fiction that, "whenever it portrays a non-white character who comes into the city, shows him up as a wretched picture of frustration. The hero must return to the rural areas"—a policy Mphahlele correlated with attempts to impose influx controls on the cities and to cement black Africans in an imagined racial essence.[10] The taint of association with Bantu education and other apartheid policies caused a backlash against rural and tribal identifications among urban black South Africans, many of whose families had been settled in the cities for generations.

Moreover, Mphahlele would later write in *Voices in the Whirlwind*, urban black culture "is the only virile culture in South Africa, beside which the derivative and fragmented one of the whites (English and Afrikaans) looks sterile; it is something that sustains the black man" in the face of what Mphahlele regarded as the stagnation of rural African culture under apartheid.[11] More generally, urbanism and modernity offered access to potentially liberating cross-cultural exchanges. For example, he saw in television (not introduced in South Africa until the 1970s) a threat "that non-whites will—even more than the radio and cinema make it possible at present—form part of an ever-growing *world audience;* an audience that is absorbing more and more entertainment and becoming more and more involved in a cross-breeding of ideas. A dangerous antidote to apartheid!"[12]

Because he saw popular culture and not just high art playing a role in this international crossbreeding, the transnational entanglement that Mphahlele identified was especially shaped by US culture: "It may be startling to a non–South African to notice how much of our cultural life is American. It won't be so startling when one considers that 5,000,000 Africans are urbanized and therefore detribalized."[13] The link Mphahlele took for granted between American cultural life and urbanization is telling: in the face of a white minority government determined to lock Africans into ethno-linguistic tribal identities and confine them to rural reservations (later supposedly independent countries called Bantustans or Homelands), many black city dwellers saw an antidote in a cosmopolitan urban identity heavily inflected with cultural borrowings from America, especially black America.[14] Thus when the Englishman Anthony Sampson took over the editorship of *Drum* magazine and conducted informal surveys of potential readers in Johannesburg, they told him contemptuously what was wrong with the issues published to date: "Tribal music! Tribal history! Chiefs! We don't care about chiefs! Give us jazz and film stars, man! We want Duke Ellington, Satchmo, and hot dames! Yes, brother, anything American."[15]

Thus, even if the South Africans found much to suspect and criticize in Langston Hughes's more romantic evocations of Africa, as I argue below, they were also primed to receive other aspects of his work with great enthusiasm. For instance, the urban thrust of so much of his writing no doubt explains its appeal to the South Africans: the character Jesse B. Semple, nicknamed "Simple," was in a sense the embodiment of a "detribalized" and refugee black American who drifted in and out of Harlem, and the Simple stories were widely read in 1950s South Africa.[16] Moreover, the political and racial focus of virtually all of Hughes's writing resonated powerfully with black and mixed-race South Africans confronting the intensification of racial segregation. Rive remarks in his first letter to Hughes, "The first literature of this [racial] nature which I read was your *Ways of White Folks* which I read when I was ten years old."[17] Abrahams made a similar declaration about discovering Hughes's work in Alain Locke's *New Negro* anthology as a "semi-literate youngster in Johannesburg": "That discovery made all the difference in the world to my life because till then literature, like so much else had seemed to me to be 'Reserved for Europeans only.'"[18] Both authors would repeat this sentiment in their autobiographies: in *Tell Freedom*, Abrahams describes coming across *The New Negro* in the Bantu Men's Social Centre and thinking: "These poems and stories were written by Negroes! Something burst deep inside me. The world could never again belong to white people only!"[19] In *Writing Black,* Rive similarly recounts the revelatory impact of discovering black American literature: "Then I read Richard Wright, Langston Hughes and Countee Cullen, and discovered Bigger Thomas and Cora who was unashamed and Big Boy who left home, and Simple."[20]

The South Africans, then, were certainly acquainted with the work of Langston Hughes. Hughes had the opportunity to encounter their work in turn when he agreed to judge the *Drum* story competition for three consecutive years in 1953–55. Through the submissions, Hughes encountered fiction by Can Themba, Bloke Modisane, Richard Rive, Peter Clarke (under the pen name Peter Kumalo), and Es'kia Mphahlele (then known by his given name Ezekiel but publishing initially under the pen name Bruno Esekie), among others. In Hughes's own words, these stories "moved, surprised, and quite delighted" him,[21] and they inspired him to edit first the collection *An African Treasury* (1960) and later *Poems from Black Africa* (1963). He began corresponding with African writers from all over the continent, mostly to solicit material for these anthologies. From South Africa, that list of correspondents eventually included Abrahams, Clarke, Bessie Head (then Bessie Emery), Tennyson Makiwane, Todd Matshikiza, Modisane, Mphahlele, Phyllis Ntantala, and Rive, most of whom contributed stories, poems, or essays to *An African Treasury.*[22] And he began avidly promoting this contemporary cultural output from South Africa in his highly visible weekly column in the *Chicago Defender.* He was especially excited by South Africa's embrace of jazz music, which he described in 1955 as "Africa's own music born in the rhythms of its drums centuries ago, developed in America, and now going back to Africa again."[23]

In some cases, Hughes's correspondence with the African writers was brief and businesslike, focused on the logistics of editing the anthology and obtaining permissions. In other instances, the South African writers were clearly eager to solidify this valuable new connection. When Hughes wired to ask permission to use his column, for example, Matshikiza replied, "Shucks, it's great for me to hear from someone whom I have admired for ages. Your wire of course sent me completely, and when your letter came, well, I just went 'gone.'"[24] Richard Rive's enthusiasm to develop the correspondence was shown in the more than fourteen thousand words that he wrote to Hughes across twenty-four letters between 1954 and 1966. The American clearly welcomed the correspondence with Rive, in turn writing: "That was a wonderful letter, yours, telling me more about South Africa, or at least the Cape Town area, than I've gotten before from any source."[25] And in his letters to Bloke Modisane, Hughes grew as affectionate and informal as he seemingly ever became with anyone, jokingly calling him "my favorite Bantu"[26]—to which Modisane responded by calling Hughes "the greatest American Bantu I know."[27] Modisane also wrote: "You have always made me feel that maybe something good will come out of me yet; when I think I'm going mad, you tell me: nuts."[28]

As further expression of his ethos of pan-African entanglement, Hughes sent more than letters to his correspondents abroad, and when Rive wrote that Hughes "picked me up as a literary orphan and fathered me," he was pointing to more than just words of encouragement.[29] Hughes sent copies of books and records, magazines, and other expressions of American culture to Rive and several other South African writers. After visiting Modisane in England, Hughes even shipped him two boxes of coats, sweaters, scarves, and other clothes, along with a box of his own records and some books.[30] Especially for the writers who remained in Africa, Hughes's generosity provided an important link to the world outside and to models of black accomplishment, as Mphahlele's first letter to him in 1954 revealed: "It is indeed very flattering to me to have such warm complimentary comments from a great writer like you on my amateurish attempt (as I regard it)—for that matter, from a Negro to another. Believe me, we this end are starved for Negro literature, and I should like to grasp this opportunity of asking you if one can procure regularly some periodical Negro literature of a high standard in America."[31] Moreover, this cultural exchange was never limited to African American culture on Hughes's side. He sent Peter Clarke his translations of the work of Federico García Lorca, for instance, and Clarke responded gratefully: "Thanks a great deal for the Lorca books too. I was, at one time, intensely interested in him, when I came across the book *Garcia Lorca* by Edwin Honig, some time back, in a small second-hand bookshop in Cape Town. I was absolutely enthralled and always looked for more books on his writing but without success."[32] Clarke's letter gives us a glimpse into a fascinating tangle of transnational exchanges and flows: a Spanish poet and playwright, translated by an African American writer, was being avidly read by a mixed-race South African painter and writer. As Dimock notes, "Territorial sovereignty is poor prophylactic"[33] in the face of such transnational exchanges, even when national boundaries, media, and publications are as strictly policed as they were in 1950s South Africa.

David Chioni Moore, in his introduction to Hughes's correspondence with the young Bessie Head, notes that the time gap between their letters "is stunning; forty years ago, international mail seems to have run much faster."[34] Indeed, the rapid exchange of letters between Hughes and many of his correspondents in Africa and Europe would not have been possible without the relatively new technology of airmail. And his black Atlantic network was also facilitated by the increasing affordability of air travel throughout the twentieth century, enabling Hughes's several trips to Africa for conferences, festivals, and inaugurations. He met many of the South African writers in London, Paris, and New York on numerous occasions. He traveled with Modisane to Italy in 1962 for the Spoleto Festival of Two Worlds, where a production of Hughes's play *Black Nativity* was being staged.[35] He met Rive in London in 1963, a meeting the South African writer later recounted in his autobiography.[36] Later when Rive was studying for an MA degree at Columbia University, Hughes invited him for dinner with Arna Bontemps in Harlem to discuss the poems the two Americans had assembled for a new edition of *The Poetry of the Negro*. In a talk Rive gave at Columbia as part of his MA requirements, he described this as "a meeting with the two greatest black writers in the world."[37]

All of these personal connections naturally enabled an ongoing network of opportunities for mutual publication and promotion and thus generated further strands in the skein entangling Harlem with South Africa. Hughes himself published or allowed his work to be reprinted in various African journals and magazines, including in *Drum,* its sister publication, *Africa!,* and in Ronald Segal's *Africa South*.[38] After years of controversy over his radical poems of the 1930s and his summons to appear before Joseph McCarthy's Senate subcommittee in 1953, such opportunities to create a new audience for his work among a new generation of readers in a far-off land, and thus to reinvent himself as a writer, were no doubt highly welcome to Hughes. The tributes from the South African writers must have also been gratifying: Rive dedicated his first single-author collection of short stories, entitled *African Songs,* to the American poet and would use Hughes's poem "Our Land" as an epigraph, because "you have through your letters done a helluva lot to encourage me to continue writing" and because he felt that "Our Land" was "so appropriate to South Africa as well."[39] Abrahams dedicated his 1956 novel *A Wreath for Udomo* to Hughes,[40] a favor Hughes repaid in 1963 when he dedicated *Poems from Black Africa* to "Peter Abrahams of South Africa." Long after the American poet's death, Abrahams still sang his praises in print, claiming that Hughes seemed "to have broken free of the dependence on the white literary establishment for survival and progress as a writer. . . . He wrote for his own black audience and in the process he helped to create that audience."[41]

In turn, in another manifestation of his ethos of pan-African entanglement, Hughes often went out of his way to help the African writers make names for themselves in the United States and Europe.[42] The most important links arose from Hughes's efforts to compile the anthology *An African Treasury;* he conceived of it soon after judging the first *Drum* competition but did not publish it until 1960. It was not the first anthology of

African literature. In fact, it was preceded some two years earlier by a book under *Drum*'s own imprint, edited by Peggy Rutherfoord, called *Darkness and Light* (released in the United States under the title *African Voices*), which overlapped with Hughes's collection insofar as it included stories by Modisane, Rive, and Themba.

If Rutherfoord beat Hughes to press with her anthology, however, *An African Treasury* was the more groundbreaking and well-received of the two, in part because it emphasized contemporary Africa over traditional or ancestral Africa. Much of *Darkness and Light* was devoted to praise poems, folktales, fables, and other artifacts of traditional African culture, and Mphahlele criticized it in a review in *Black Orpheus* for falling victim to "an excessive love of the exotic for its own sake."[43] Hughes, by contrast, determined early on that his anthology would highlight contemporary Africa. As he wrote to Mphahlele in 1954, many of the submissions he received were "animal tales or folk stories, which is not the kind of material we can use in this anthology, since it is to be a book purely of creative fiction in the shorter form."[44] Eventually the scope of *An African Treasury* would widen to include poems and nonfiction essays as well as a small handful of folktales and proverbs, but overall the selections succeeded in painting a portrait of a modernizing Africa at a moment of great social-political change and turmoil. Mphahlele reviewed Hughes's collection and called it a "robust little packet, the best collection of contemporary African writing."[45] Privately he wrote to Hughes that "you have captured African writing which resounds through and through like the footsteps of a giant rubbing his eyes as he walks, just from a deep sleep."[46]

The South African government promptly banned *An African Treasury* after its publication, probably precisely because it depicted contemporary Africa as a modern, urbanizing continent locked in a fierce anticolonial struggle. Daniel Wong-Gu Kim points out that in its structure—beginning with articles outlining political situations around the continent and essays about cultural life in Africa before moving on to more traditional "literary" texts—the anthology illustrates the broader sweep of Hughes's pan-African coalition building in the late 1950s: "Beginning with the state of the Pan-African polity (the leaders and then the masses in the anthology's first two sections), then moving to the state of Pan-African national culture within it (a third section on literary and cultural criticism), and then closing with the actual practice of that national culture, the anthology drives to redefine black aesthetic praxis for a modem African scene in which anti-colonial resistance and national liberation struggles are re-shaping society."[47] For the South African writers, inclusion in the anthology (and thus by extension inclusion in Hughes's efforts to build a "Pan-African polity") meant immediate international exposure and visibility. Perhaps the emergence on the global stage of such writers as Rive, Mphahlele, and Alex La Guma was inevitable: *Drum* magazine was already winning international attention, many of those writers would soon live abroad in exile, and interest in African literature exploded following Chinua Achebe's *Things Fall Apart* in 1958. Certainly, though, their association with Hughes gave those writers immediate credibility and visibility. Consider, for example, that soon after *An African Treasury* was published by Crown Publishers, Rive began publishing prolifically with presses in Europe and the United States, including with Crown.

This kind of access to an international readership and cultural exchange at a transnational scale was made all the more important for the South African writers by the apartheid government's heavy-handed censorship of books, movies, music, and art. It banned not only Hughes's *An African Treasury* but also books by Abrahams, Matshikiza, Modisane, Mphahlele, and Rive at various times.[48] As Rive complained repeatedly and bitterly,[49] possessing a copy of his own book was punishable with jail time and heavy fines. White writers like Alan Paton and Nadine Gordimer often had international connections and could circumvent such censorship by publishing their books in London and New York. Black writers were rarely so fortunate and sometimes had to leave the country altogether before their works could be published. These censorship policies under apartheid thus partly explain why so many of the writers Hughes corresponded with were forced to go into exile and why Clarke, Mphahlele, and others wrote for *Drum* under pseudonyms.

Censored at home and precluded from competing on the world literary stage on the basis of a national tradition, Abrahams, Mphahlele, and other black and mixed-race South African writers were eager to enter into an already emergent transnational literary space created by black writers from America, Europe, the Caribbean, and the rest of Africa—the space of pan-African entanglement, and of black Atlantic literature. Yet forging anything like a unified community of artists across the ocean did not come naturally or easily; it required the negotiation of key differences over the meaning of Africa and its traditions.

Peter Abrahams and Pan-African Entanglement

As part of her campaign against what she regards as contemporary cultural theory's overly sweeping valorization of transnationalism and its corollary denigration of nationalism, Laura Chrisman singles out Peter Abrahams in one article for his "preference for an Americanized 'Negro' identity" and for embracing "an exclusively modern racial identity at the expense of national and nationalist identity."[50] It is true that the Abrahams who wrote *Tell Freedom* (1954) rejected both nationalism and apartheid racial categories, interlinked as they were in his experience, and searched for a more universal aesthetic and ethos: "Perhaps life had a meaning that transcended race and colour. If it had, I could not find it in South Africa. Also, there was the need to write, to tell freedom, and for this I needed to be personally free."[51]

In response to Chrisman's argument, I want to emphasize how deeply hybridized and transnational coloured identity already was in South Africa. Richard Rive gave us one example of how a uniquely Capetonian celebration was entangled with far-off cultures when he wrote to Langston Hughes about the Coon Carnival. He described it as "a spectacle in Cape Town rivaling Mardi Gras or those of the South of France. New Year's Eve thousands of them dressed in rich satins dance and sing their way through the streets of Cape Town to the accompaniment of guitars and banjos. They have unfortunately become very American with such names as 'the Dixiana Minstrels' or 'the Oklahoma Broadway darkies.' They are exclusively Coloured."[52] Rive went on to describe the bands of Cape Malays (descendants of Asian slaves brought to the early Cape colony by Dutch settlers), whose repertoire included a song about the *Alabama*, "a Confederate ship used during the American Civil War that called at the Cape and was immortalised in song by the local peoples."[53] This account of a mixed-raced population, descended in part from former slaves of Asian descent, singing odes to a Confederate States of America navy ship and participating in a parody of a blackface minstrel show, reflects the complicated and unpredictable ironies of transatlantic entanglement.

In the face of the apartheid state's obsession with achieving and protecting cultural purity for all racial and linguistic groups, its ethos of separation, the "contamination" of Cape Town life (already dangerously mongrel in the eyes of white nationalists) by American cultural imports takes on a potentially subversive dimension. If Rive's descriptions of the New Year's celebrations show us how largely a mythologized America came to figure in the imagination of South Africans, those descriptions likewise clearly fascinated Hughes and showed him a modern, cosmopolitan Africa, one *not* trapped in an idealized past of tom-toms and palm trees. In other words, he increasingly came to value strands of entanglement with Africa on the plane of contemporary cultural exchange, not only on the plane of ancestry and kinship.

While not a Capetonian, Peter Abrahams himself represented a complicated tangle of racial and national threads. Born in 1919, he was raised in the slums of Johannesburg, born of an Ethiopian father he never met and a mother who was Cape Malay or coloured, a group he described as "an essentially urban community" with "no past, no tradition that goes to a time beyond the coming of the White man. They lack, as a group, the cohesive stability of the other groups."[54] It was seemingly an easy decision, then, for him to leave South Africa in 1939 and return only once for a visit of a few months in the early 1950s to write *Return to Goli*. In that book he inveighed against African nationalists who would counter racism with a color bar of their own: "They go counter to the timeless, raceless, and nationless aspirations, that lie dormant in most men everywhere."[55] Abrahams lived several years in England and France before making his first trips to the United States and the West Indies in 1955 and settling in Jamaica in 1957. In light of the sense of alienation and rootlessness he so often expressed before that move, it hardly seems a moral failing for Abrahams to have chosen a "transnational black identity" in lieu of an African nationalism that was in his day divided over the role that mixed-race people would play in a future black-ruled South Africa. Perhaps it is not surprising, either, that Abrahams eventually made a home in the Caribbean, where everybody "comes from somewhere else. . . . That is to say, their true cultures, the places they really come from, the traditions that really formed them, are somewhere else."[56]

For Abrahams, though, the basis for transnational black community was not an imagined racial essence or African personality but instead the hard work of institution building and cultural exchange. And his vision of transnational blackness was not hostile to or incompatible with national allegiances so long as they were of a less narrow and exclusive variety than he found in South Africa in the 1930s. Unlike Claude McKay, who died resolutely uncommitted to any national identity, Abrahams lived in Jamaica from the late 1950s until his death. During Jamaica's push for independence and its early years as a nation, he contributed significantly to the creation of structures to support national media, culture, and art. In 1956–57, for example, he briefly edited the newspaper *Public Opinion*—"an independent nationalist paper to serve the cause of Jamaican nationalism"[57]—and founded the magazine *West Indian Economist* in 1957, both at a time when Jamaica's political leaders were working toward an independent federation of British Caribbean islands. Later, after Jamaica declared its independence, he worked for Radio Jamaica and then the Jamaica Broadcasting Corporation. Abrahams's voluntary commitment to his adopted country—where, he wrote, "I had sunk new roots; I was accepted as Jamaican"[58]—might lead us to soften the damning conclusions Chrisman draws from a handful of very early poems about Abrahams's "failure of social vision . . . [and] of his political vision: he cannot envision black collectivity as a creative nationalist force."[59]

To the contrary, I would concur with Kgomotso Masemola: even in the early autobiography *Tell Freedom,* Abrahams stakes a claim of belonging "to a unifiable multiplicity called the Black Atlantic, organizable by the principle of the double consciousness."[60] But this web of multiplicity is flexible enough to contain national allegiances within it and to use the mechanisms of the democratic nation-state to advance an "unfolding vision ... toward the acceptance of our common humanity."[61] Furthermore, in his late writings Abrahams does offer us multiple models of a black collectivity. When *The View from Coyaba* was published in 1985, it was Abrahams's first new novel in almost twenty years; like *This Island, Now* (1966) before it, *The View* is set initially in Jamaica, though the narrative ultimately travels to Atlanta, Liberia, Uganda, and elsewhere. The novel begins with a group of runaway slaves forming a community in the foothills high above Kingston and follows four generations of their descendants. It is also an imagined history of Coyaba estate, the name Abrahams gave to the land he and his wife bought and built their house on. The name, from the Arawak word for their ancient burial sites, means "place of tranquility." Thus, beginning with the place name and the title, the novel lays bare or imaginatively reconstructs the layered history of the land, emphasizes the strength of the community, and invests symbolically in that particular place, the author's attachment to which was no less real and deeply felt for not being in the country of his birth.

The View from Coyaba

If his attachment to Jamaica showed him investing in a local and national identity, part of what appealed to Abrahams about Jamaica was "its openness and cosmopolitanness," which he says is the nearest thing "to Soweto, and what used to be Sophiatown."[62] He also felt that "the African connection for [African Americans] is much further away than it is here in Jamaica."[63] Moreover, the kind of black community that he dwelt on most frequently in his writing crossed borders fluidly. In *The View from Coyaba,* for example, he held up the independent black church of his Jamaican missionary character Jacob Brown as a counterexample of a transnational institution contributing to the global advancement of black people and universal democracy. The church operates a network of mission stations throughout Africa; the one in Liberia where Jacob Brown is stationed as a young man, for instance, exerts a subversive influence on local politics, encouraging the indigenous Africans to assert their rights against the Americo-Liberian hegemony.[64] Furthermore, when the Ugandan government violently cracks down on Christian churches, Jacob's church acts much as a national embassy or consulate might, utilizing its transnational network to whisk the elderly bishop across the border and then to safety in his native Jamaica. A speech by Jacob's revolutionary son David hints at the pan-African potential of his father's church: "Your people, your church, have always had the answer to the problem which obsessed your friend DuBois and so many generations of black folk."[65]

Such careful attention to the institutional avenues through which cultural exchange is carried out and sustained suggests that Abrahams envisioned a transnational black community based not (or at least not solely) on romantic ideas about black blood but rather on the negotiation of real cultural differences and the forging of a new language of black identity. This project could work in tandem with nationalist agendas, but in contexts where nationalism represented an undesirable foreclosure of identities, a black Atlantic collectivity could also serve as an effective substitute: it provided its own moral gauges of behavior and human worth, alternative structures for collective belonging, and the opportunity for immigrants and wanderers to build new communities and find new allies in distant lands.

In *The View from Coyaba*, Abrahams dramatized the process by which pan-African entanglements are formed through both performative assertions of ancestral connection and the careful navigation of cultural difference. In one scene, the Jamaican missionary Jacob Brown is visited by a group of Mende elders who want him to intercede with the Liberian government to stop the army from extorting their village for more taxes. When Jacob agrees to help them, they give him a bag full of diamonds in gratitude:

"It is not necessary," Jacob murmured.

"Not for you, perhaps; for us, yes. There is a need to show thanks. That is our way."

"I know."

"You do? That is good. Not many who are not born here do."

"My grandmother told us. She knew your ways."

"She came from this land?"

"I do not know. She was a slave. Perhaps she did. She knew your ways."[66]

This scene shows us the power of human dialogue to create amity and connection among very different peoples; in this case, cultural negotiation also reveals continuities and similarities through the persistence of African folkways in Jamaica and the larger African diaspora.

For Abrahams, then, conversation serves an important function at the level of interpersonal relations between individuals but also at the macro level of geopolitics. We can see the latter at work in the rhetoric of revolutionary physician David Brown, Jacob's son, who gets caught up in the Algerian struggle against French colonialism, alongside Frantz Fanon. David hopes that Algeria will initiate an "alliance of the exploited of the earth."[67] To a large extent, of course, all this cross-cultural exchange and conversation is made necessary by centuries of global migration, but Abrahams makes a virtue of this necessity and sees the movement of peoples across artificial borders as a necessary precondition for the emergence of true pan-African entanglement.[68]

The novel embeds this universal narrative of human migration and adaptability in the story of Jacob Brown, whose situation inverts Abrahams's own: whereas the author left South Africa for a life in Jamaica, his character leaves Jamaica and ultimately settles in Uganda, where he had served as a bishop for his church. The roots he puts down there are so deep that, when he is forced by Idi Amin's persecution of Christians to flee Uganda for seven years, he finds himself unable to connect with the place in Jamaica where he was raised. The high mountain valley has radically changed since his youth, and he and his son David are both aghast at the violent turn Jamaican politics has taken. When he receives word that it is safe to return to Uganda, he exclaims to his beloved dog, "We're going home again!"[69] The deep connections that Abrahams clearly felt for Jamaica and that Jacob Brown feels for Uganda are testament to the power of cultural entanglements, under the right conditions, to alleviate the alienation of life in exile.

Broadcasting Entanglement

Abrahams lived through a period in which conditions were ideal for building diasporic communities, thanks largely to emerging technologies. Earlier I mentioned airmail and the easy accessibility of commercial air travel. Another crucial technology was radio, which facilitated the dispersal of information and cultural production to far-flung locations.[70] For Abrahams in particular, radio played an important role in his career as a journalist after his move to Jamaica: once settled in Jamaica, he worked first for a British-owned radio station, then for Radio Jamaica, which he helped found under Norman Manley's presidency in the early 1960s. Abrahams regarded this as an experiment in democratic freedom of expression and political discourse; for a while, at least, he and his colleagues succeeded in creating a media house that was "independent of foreign money or narrowly-based local capital, and at the same time ... independent of political control."[71] John Chitole, who succeeds Jacob Brown as the bishop of East Africa in *The View from Coyaba*, has similar designs for a radio station run by the mission, a need he identifies out of his dismay at recognizing a "huge continent of black people and the only sounds in the African air were the sounds made by whites."[72]

With its potential for reaching large numbers of people, including poor and illiterate audiences, across vast distances and national borders, radio has the ability, Abrahams showed us, for generating black pride and mutual understanding across the Atlantic, if only it falls into the right hands—black hands, hands that can counter the overweening message of European superiority broadcast on the stations sponsored by the white colonial rulers. Incidentally, in the second letters that Hughes and Abrahams wrote to each other in 1954, they wrote about radio—specifically about the opera *The Barrier*, for which Hughes wrote the libretto, which was being performed by Dutch actors on Radio Vara in Holland, and which Abrahams listened to in England via shortwave radio.[73] In this moment, we see a single clear example of radio serving as the vehicle for cultural exchange and the dissemination of art across national borders.

Through these various media and channels of exchange, Hughes disseminated his vision of pan-African entanglement, with its Afrocentric but not exclusionary lexicon and repertoire. This gave the writers connected to his network access to a broader palette of symbols and cultural raw materials. Casanova describes how throughout Africa and the postcolonial world, as newly independent nations began to forge new national literatures, "popular tales collected, edited, reworked, and published by patriotic writers became the first quantifiable resource of a nascent literary space,"[74] quickly followed by the use of vernacular languages and other indigenizing techniques. But writers who looked beyond the nation of their birth for literary inspiration and community had a different, larger selection of diasporic imagery and source material to choose from. Thus, even writers like Abrahams, born and raised in Africa, began to adopt tropes and images from slavery in the Americas in their writing.

Abrahams, Slavery, and Primitivism

The widespread experience of exile and life in the African diaspora led many midcentury South African authors to begin incorporating imagery from the history of slavery into their own writings, just as Hughes, Césaire, and others had done before them. One of the most frequently recurring of these images is the figure of the fugitive slave, which embodies both oppression and resistance at once. Abrahams, especially, used fugitive imagery in his late work: after a short prelude, *The View from Coyaba* begins with a group of runaway slaves hacking a path through the mountainous jungles of Jamaica in the 1820s. Through flashbacks and recounted memories, the narrator goes on to depict the dehumanizing brutality of slavery in the West Indies and thereby draws from a deep lexicon derived from the literature of slavery, from Olaudah Equiano and Frederick Douglass to Alex Haley's *Roots*. When Abrahams adopted the imagery of Caribbean slavery in his writing, he simultaneously tried to enter into a diasporic identity and accepted the obligations and possibilities of Hughes's ethos and aesthetics of pan-African entanglement.

The novel also makes visible an older layer, the partially erased traces of African and Native American presence on the island, and draws attention to its erasure, as with the runaway slaves early in the novel: "They cut a narrow path through the bush under the big trees and as they passed through . . . those who made up the rear replaced the bush again, covering their tracks."[75] When Samson and the boy find the place where they settle, the narrator remarks: "Then the man and the boy walked down to the water, re-opening the path that another group of now-vanished people had trod when they tried to escape from slavery and the slavers' whips."[76] Abrahams found in Jamaica, then, much of what Hughes and Césaire had found in Haiti: a space of pan-African entanglement, where Africa's legacy was partially erased or obscured but still preserved, and where a history of resistance and self-assertion was inscribed on the very land.

Yet, as we have seen, in the American context, imagined reconstructions of slavery were deeply intertwined with evocations of Africa, and often tinged with the rhetoric of modern primitivism. For the South African writers, the assertion of a black identity rooted in ancient and primitive Africa posed awkward problems, in part because from the middle of the century, the white minority apartheid government espoused a policy of "separate development" that confined Africans to rural spaces and to conservative notions of a "traditional" African identity. The intellectual project of African writers during this period, then, was largely devoted to staking a claim for Africans as equals in a modern, urban South Africa—that is, they made the case for Africans as modern people and thus chafed at representations of Africa as the embodiment of an atavistic essence of blackness. Rhetoric to that effect in the hands of Hughes and the Negritude writers might have been strategically calculated, but it nevertheless resonated with the rhetoric of the apartheid state to an uncomfortable degree.

We can see Abrahams's rejection of apartheid rhetoric, and his insistence on recognizing the existence of modern black South Africans, in *Return to Goli* (1953), his journalistic account of his only return to South Africa. He repeatedly emphasized that black people who were born and raised in Johannesburg and other cities were urban and "detribalised":[77] "There is in the Union today a Black community that is completely urban and completely Westernised. And there is evolving, too, a Black culture of the cities. The tribal content of this culture is subconscious, what the people carry within themselves of their tribal past. But their conscious orientation is away from the tribe and to the new, semi-universal culture-forms of the cities."[78] Such was the rhetoric that black writers wanted in South Africa in the 1950s: not tropes of tom-toms and palm trees but a "Black culture of the cities" that could counteract apartheid's vision of rural, traditional roles for black Africans.

In his long decades in exile, however, while inhabiting the black diaspora in Europe and the West Indies, Abrahams continually came into contact with the psychological need for Africa as cultural root and spiritual motherland. In *The Black Experience,* he narrated a visit to Coyaba by a group of Rastafarians from Kingston, who traveled halfway up the mountain to ask the journalist from Africa why he left the mother continent: "The idea of a black man not finding a place of peace in his own continent shocked them. Africa, by their folk myth, was the home of all black people, the one place on earth where all black people could be free of Babylon and in control of their own lives. For most it was a land of milk and honey as in the Bible."[79] Abrahams was sympathetic to this view and understood the motivation behind it as well as the motives driving Marcus Garvey's "Back to Africa" movement: "The escapism of 'Back to Africa' was as much an emotional and psychic support system as were the otherworldly spirituals of the black slaves. To dream of freedom, to sing of freedom, to conjure up a land of freedom, is part of the holding on to that human will to be free."[80] For all its absurdities and excesses, Abrahams came to see Garveyism as "the seedbed of the later unity of African, American, and Caribbean black folk."[81]

If Abrahams nevertheless refused to subscribe to the mythologization of Africa, that was partly because he himself had lived there and partly because, in his view, traces of the best of African communal life survived in Jamaica through its folkways, food, and oral culture, just as Hughes found correspondences and echoes of African cultural traditions in the peasants of Haiti and in poor sharecroppers in the southern United States. In *The View from Coyaba,* the omniscient narrator tells us that after slavery was abolished in the 1830s, many newly freed men and women founded communities in the hills and mountain valleys: "Each community, each village, each family shared life co-operatively, in an old remembered way whose unknown roots were lost in the distant past that went back to times beyond the days of slavery."[82] In the travel book *Jamaica: An Island Mosaic,* written after his first visit to Jamaica in the mid-1950s, Abrahams recounted visiting the Maroons in the high mountains and being struck by the similarity in physical appearance and mannerisms between the descendants of

Jamaica's guerilla army of runaway slaves and the people he had met earlier in West Africa: "Physique, features and that dusty, matt near-blackness sang a song of Africa across oceans and centuries."[83] He similarly recognized the movements of Jamaican women who carry heavy loads on their heads as uncannily resembling those of African women.[84]

Abrahams, then, exhibited the same fascination that Langston Hughes always did for the remnants of African culture in West Indian life, and he engaged in a similar project of recuperating and documenting African cultural values and practices in the Americas. For Abrahams, the process of taking the shards and fragments of recorded memory of Africa, slavery, and the Middle Passage and piecing them together into a collective diasporic memory provided a partial antidote to what he calls the "colonization" of the African mind.[85]

Black Nationalism as the Path to Transnational Entanglement

Yet even as Abrahams appeared to pay tribute to the ethos and aesthetics of pan-African entanglement and to accept its obligations, his late writings suggest that he increasingly tended to make the black scale of interconnection and exchange exclusive rather than accepting the fact of entanglement with other cultures, including the cultures of the white colonizers. Already in the 1980s, *The View from Coyaba* was ambivalent on this score: David decides that the next step in the ongoing process of black self-liberation must be "withdrawal" from the world at large. His solution is not a total rejection of Western thinking or Western genres but a synthesis that nevertheless requires the withdrawal from the West for some time: "It is not being against anything or anybody; it is not anti-Westernism, not anti-capitalist or anti-Marxist. It is, quite simply, being for us, first, second, third and last. And to be for us, we must withdraw from all this as fully as is humanly possible, and for as long as it is necessary, in order to free ourselves from that long occupation of our minds."[86]

This withdrawal might appear to express an ethos of separation, but David insists that it will be a temporary state of affairs, as "decolonizing the mind" is prerequisite to black people's entry into true cultural exchange. As he declares to his wife, "What is urgent is to lay the groundwork and set up the new structures, and give them time to root and grow."[87] Moreover, if the retreat into blackness that David (and, implicitly, Abrahams) calls for is essentially a form of black nationalism, it is nevertheless a deeply *trans*national phenomenon. One model is the ocean-spanning influence Abrahams saw Marcus Garvey continuing to exert late into the twentieth century: "Is it any wonder that the Cubans, at a critical stage of the Southern African struggle, sent soldiers and military support to stop the racist South African army [in Angola] . . . ? The earlier influences of the Garvey movement in Cuba surely had a bearing."[88] The novel also gives us a fictional model in Jacob Brown's church, which refuses to be co-opted either by the mainstream white churches or by the governments of the nations to which it sends missionaries.

Abrahams elsewhere pointed to secular versions of these structures of black empowerment for which David Brown expresses admiration. For example, one of the things he admired about Langston Hughes is that he seemed "to have broken free of the dependence on the white literary establishment for survival and progress as a writer. . . . He wrote for his own black audience and in the process he helped to create that audience."[89] Here again we see a practical benefit of Hughes's and Abrahams's transatlantic network building—it helped to create new readers for their work and for countless other writers across the Black Atlantic.

Far from a retreat into a narrow ethnic nationalism, then, the separatism that Abrahams implicitly called for in *The View from Coyaba* was prelude to an alternative universalism based not on Eurocentrism but on a simple question: "If all human life as we know it today began in Africa, as the scholars tell us, then who is, and who is not, an African?"[90] Significantly, though, he did not look to his native Africa for metaphors and examples of African-grounded transnational entanglement but to the history and culture of his adopted homeland. In the dancehall reggae singer Junior Reid's song "One Blood," for example, he discovered an expression of an "unfolding vision, especially among the young, . . . toward the acceptance of our common humanity."[91] Furthermore, Abrahams hoped to make acknowledgment of slavery central to modernity's self-conception when he called for "a memorial to slavery as a permanent reminder of the human capacity . . . for cruelty and wickedness"[92] and for "a judicial ruling from the International Court of Justice on the crime of slavery."[93] Building a memorial "as a lasting warning and reminder of where the drive for power and profit can lead, will be choosing the direction which may help turn us into the caring creative humans history shows us capable of being."[94] In short, then, in the memoir with which Abrahams concluded his publishing career, he saw lessons in the history of Africans in the Americas that can guide humanity toward unity and solidarity. Es'kia Mphahlele, Abrahams's schoolmate, would derive similar lessons over many years of refining his philosophy of African humanism while remaining more cognizant than Abrahams seemed to be of the need to continually reanimate and regenerate the channels of pan-African entanglement. Before either author could reach such conclusions, however, both had to navigate their suspicions and antipathies toward the rhetoric of racial essence or kinship that Negritude and apartheid exhibited in common.

Entanglements between Abrahams, Mphahlele, Hughes, and Negritude

If, as I have been arguing, the separatism that Abrahams arrived at late in his writing career was ultimately reconcilable with the ethos of transnational entanglement that he had long espoused, it did nevertheless mark a kind of defeat or concession: in his view, black people in the diaspora were too embattled to successfully stake their claim to belonging in the modern world. He differed in this regard from Es'kia Mphahlele, who also called for black people to cultivate their own traditions and cultural practices and products, while conceding far less about the degradation of African values. In contrast likewise to Bloke Modisane, who sought "a universalizing art that would transcend rather than incorporate the local,"[95] Mphahlele aimed not only to incorporate the particularly (South) African into the universal but also to make African aesthetics and values the basis for an alternative universalism, a counterweight to Eurocentrism. But Mphahlele, too, arrived at his conception of African humanism and reassessed his skepticism toward rural African traditions only after years of intellectual struggle to disassociate those traditions from the racial essentialism he perceived in so much writing from the African diaspora, including that of Hughes and the Negritude poets.

Earlier I discussed the intellectual debt that Abrahams acknowledged to Langston Hughes and other African American authors. He himself then disseminated this influence among others from a young age, including Mphahlele when they met as classmates at St. Peter's Secondary School in Johannesburg. Mphahlele recalled the poetry that Abrahams was writing even then as "the first version of the black-is-beautiful theme that came my way during my youth."[96] Indeed, Mphahlele and other midcentury South African writers found much to admire in the aspects of Negritude and African American literature that emphasized pride in one's blackness and African origins. For example, when Todd Matshikiza wrote to Hughes in November 1960 to congratulate him on the publication of *An African Treasury,* he favorably contrasted it to efforts by "white hands" to pay tribute to African writing: "The whites I know have no feeling. They could never understand 'negritude' which I'd love to discuss with you one day."[97] Even the skeptic Mphahlele, at the height of his public feud with Negritude in 1963, accepted as valid "the historical fact of *négritude* as both a protest and a positive assertion of African cultural values."[98]

In the next breath, however, Mphahlele went on to criticize the way so much Negritude poetry "romanticizes Africa—as a symbol of innocence, purity and artless primitiveness."[99] More generally, as Mark Sanders puts it, Mphahlele and other writers kept their distance from Negritude because "for South African intellectuals to embrace Négritude was to embrace apartheid. . . . In South Africa after 1948 Négritude appeared to mean submitting to an ethnic-national worldview that foreclosed, on racial grounds, any prospect of a larger humanity."[100] Thus Richard Rive rejected the idea of a common style or personality in black art around the world and took the historical view of Negritude as "a literary phenomenon observable in particular ethnic groups, in particular geographic areas, brought about by a unique set of experiences." He also rejected what he called the sophistry of Senghor's "non-racist racism," concluding: "The Black who abstracts himself and seeks protection within race, no matter how valid his reason, is a racist racist."[101]

Mphahlele was harsher still in his repeated and full-throated critiques of Negritude. In the first edition of *An African Image* he called it "just so much intellectual talk, a cult."[102] He also disparaged the "rhythm boys" of the Harlem Renaissance, including Hughes, with their "hankering for old Africa and its kraals and jungles and tom-toms."[103] Mphahlele's analysis of both cultural movements was not without sympathy for those in France or America "living through a series of crises," but he rejected the romanticism and nostalgia of Negritude as irrelevant to the lives of the vast majority of Africans: "We who grew up and were educated in Africa do not find anything new" in Senghor's "philosophic musings."[104] Like the younger Abrahams, Mphahlele in the early 1960s emphasized pan-African entanglement on the plane of contemporary cultural exchange among modern, urbanized black people, while rejecting and even attacking assertions of ancestral entanglements as essentialist and retrograde.

In the decades to follow, however, Mphahlele took a winding path in his intellectual relationship with Negritude—and with Hughes and the Harlem Renaissance. Ten years after *An African Image*, in *Voices in the Whirlwind*, he was more careful to distinguish, on the one hand, Caribbean writers such as Roumain, McKay, and Césaire and African American writers such as Hughes from, on the other hand, West African poets such as Senghor. Nevertheless, Mphahlele still maintained that Hughes (at that time not long deceased) "was intellectually lightweight, and had a very limited capacity for the passionate rendering of sensuous impressions."[105] Moreover, like Rive, Mphahlele suggested that Negritude belonged to a particular time, place, and context and emphasized again its irrelevance for South Africa: at first blacks there assimilated European culture, but then they "consolidated their urban culture, thus creating their own music, dance, and communal life at once new, indigenous, and virulent."[106] In a 1964 interview with Lewis Nkosi and Richard Rive, Mphahlele likewise insisted that in South Africa, the African and the European "ways of living" are "much more integrated than you will find outside South Africa. . . . The black tar has rubbed off on to the white man and the white tar has rubbed off on to the [black]."[107] The tar metaphor suggests his favorable attitude toward the "contamination" effect of being entangled with the Other. Certainly he did not see it as compromising his African values, which "continue to remain a top, solid thing inside me, the African humanism,"[108] and so he saw little need for Negritude's recuperation of an imagined African past.

By the time Mphahlele published the dramatically revised edition of *The African Image* in 1974, however, his positions on Negritude and the Harlem Renaissance had begun to soften and would continue to do so throughout the next decade. At times in the 1960s his quarrel with the editors of the flagship publication of the Negritude movement, *Présence africaine*, for example, had come to seem personal as much as ideological or aesthetic. His revised critique, though, was based on pragmatic grounds: "Modern African problems require solutions for which negritude in its traditional sense is too simple an answer. As a literary creed it produces poetry that does not tell us the whole truth about Africa or even falsifies in part present-day realities."[109] In 1976 he wrote a tribute to Senghor for *Présence africaine* on the Senegalese president's seventieth birthday, claiming that when he first found himself in exile in West Africa, Senghor's voice among others "did something to steady me, to measure the energy of Africa in me, the thing we had taken for granted in ghettos where you could never efface your blackness, where you've got to feel the tyranny of place and time."[110] And in *Afrika My Music* (1984), while he still felt more instinctively sympathetic to the passionately drawn emotions in Richard Wright's fiction, Mphahlele now recognized that "in their own gentle and almost unobtrusive manner Langston's short fiction and poetry did things to me. I realised later that I had needed them both—those two antithetical idioms of black American expression, Wright's and Langston's."[111] It seems, then, that by the time Mphahlele revised *The African Image*, and certainly by the mid-1980s, he had begun to reconcile in his own mind and in his writing the tensions between traditional and modern; ancestral and contemporary; rural and urban; local and global; and national, tribal, and global. How he achieved that reconciliation between the different scales and planes of transnational entanglement is the subject of the next section.

Mphahlele and African Tradition

As I argued above, whereas many black South Africans of the 1950s saw modernization as an antidote to apartheid's odious and reductive conception of rural African tradition, Langston Hughes frequently held out African tradition as the antidote to modern urban alienation. This difference accounts for Mphahlele's suspicion of Hughes's work in the early 1960s, despite having written in 1961 that said work might allow the black American to "retain his cultural identity and avoid being swallowed up by the American mainstream."[112] But in Mphahlele's writing of the 1970s and early 1980s, we can see him struggling with the tension between his cosmopolitan proclivities and his increasing submission to the "tyranny of place" that South Africa exerted over him. Ruth Obee claims that of the black South African writers of his generation, only he and Bessie Head "chose to document rural African culture," and only Mphahlele "effectively attempts to bridge the gap between rural and urban cultures," particularly after his return to South Africa in 1977.[113] In bridging this gap, Mphahlele attempted to counter what he saw as one of the great shortcomings of the pan-Africanism shared by Hughes and the Negritude poets: its appeal rested primarily among the urbanized and alienated, whether Africans educated in the West or the descendants of African slaves raised in the diaspora. It was Mphahlele, in short, who synthesized most successfully the cosmopolitan and urban with the living traditions of rural Africans and, by extension, the ancestral and contemporary planes of pan-African entanglement.

We can see glimpses of this emerging synthesis in the revised 1974 edition of *The African Image,* in which he called for an intensification of cultural exchange between Africa and the New World as an antidote to misconceptions of the mother continent and of its diaspora: "What do we want from one another, we blacks of the world? . . . Before we can answer these questions, we shall have to know each other better. Africa knows very little about its diaspora. . . . More Afro-Americans and Caribbeans must visit Africa; Africa must open her doors to them. They should get to know Africa as she is, not as a mere grand idea."[114] As if to advance this goal of mutual understanding between Africa and its diaspora, Mphahlele increasingly deployed tropes borrowed from the Americas to make sense of his situation and the broader historical condition of blackness. Chief among those tropes was the figure of the runagate, as when he quoted Haitian poet René Depestre: "Negritude is the modern (cultural) equivalent of the old condition of the fugitive slave."[115] Later, in *Afrika My Music,* Mphahlele described black South Africa as a "survival culture, a fugitive culture."[116] David Attwell notes that through the figure of the fugitive slave, "Mphahlele's South African and diasporic selves could become one."[117]

Mphahlele's writing about South Africa from the early 1970s onward, furthermore, was full of other evocations of the African American historical experience. For example, allusions to the black diaspora recurred throughout *Afrika My Music:* the author studded his memories of South Africa and his descriptions of his return with metaphors and references to the American context. One lyrical passage quoted extensively from songs made famous by American singers Nina Simone, Dinah Washington, Billie Holiday, and Sophie Tucker—who collectively sang "a long black song. They sang it centuries ago, our ancestors"—interspersed between elegies to the historical sufferings of Africans: of Makhanda, for example, the first black prisoner to be exiled to Robben Island, and of the women who "cry for men and sons taken away in droves to the mines."[118] When he visited his former home in Soweto, Mphahlele found that it now stood across the street from Uncle Tom's Hall. When he visited Alexandra Township, he thought of James Baldwin, "who said that those who debase others are also debasing themselves." When he met his childhood friend Danie in Atteridgeville, he remembered him singing Paul Robeson songs years before.[119] Like his use of fugitive slave imagery, such allusions to African American culture and history reflect the "influence of diasporic thinking."[120] As Attwell observes, "When he left South Africa Mphahlele sought to interpret the diaspora via home; by the time he writes [*Afrika My Music*], he is interpreting South Africa via the diaspora."[121] Indeed, when Mphahlele returned home, his perception of his native land was indelibly overlaid with his experiences during two decades of exile and alienation.

By the 1970s, in short, Mphahlele was, in a conscious way, borrowing from, adapting, and contributing to the aesthetics of pan-African entanglement that he had earlier criticized in the Harlem Renaissance and Negritude. Furthermore, perhaps liberated from the need to stake out a modern, urban identity for black Africans by the profound impact Black Consciousness thinking had exerted in South Africa by the time of his homecoming, Mphahlele also became gradually more open to exploring rural African identities and traditions and began to borrow from his own indigenous folk traditions. The Mphahlele who published *Chirundu* in 1979 seemed largely to agree with the character Tirenje in her lament for the plight of the modernized African: "Something has touched us who live in the city or have read books at school—some strange magic—or it is as if we were caught in a net and ripped away from the teaching of our elders and now loneliness comes easy to us."[122] Given that I have been using tropes involving webs and networks to discuss Langston Hughes's ethos of pan-African entanglement, it is interesting that Tirenje here uses a net as a metaphor for urbanization and Western education: a net can catch you if you fall, but it can also trap you, as slavers once snared Africans in nets. The contamination effect that a younger Mphahlele had celebrated is now the source of ambivalence: contact with European culture, Tirenje implies, has robbed Africans of something vital in their own culture.

Five years later in *Afrika My Music,* Mphahlele suggested a remedy for the loneliness that Tirenje describes: recuperating Africa's "traditional myths" without allowing the "master mind" that designed apartheid and colonialism to co-opt them: "Where are the African heroes—in the memory? Where are the institutions that could assert a collective consciousness in the African? We are teetering on the edge of somewhere between what the master mind has designed for us and the self-censored memory of our past heroes, between our resistance against the design and the need to recreate traditional myths, lest they consolidate a separateness."[123] It is perhaps because he felt the need to reconnect with his own traditional myths and to try to register them in the collective memory of the black Atlantic that Mphahlele returned to South Africa despite the controversy the move caused.[124] What motivated the move, he explained to his biographer, was the realization that "the search for self was really a search for a community to which I could abandon myself in terms of what I could give as a writer and teacher. . . . I needed the community so much because much of what I could give depended on what I could get from it."[125] Once returned to South Africa, he and his wife did indeed find solace in their native land: "We sought community, we found it. We sought an identifiable culture, we found it. We sought relevance, we found it. We sought a return to ancestral ground, this is it, and it cuts across all man-made boundaries."[126] More concretely, Mphahlele also "discovered jogging routes that restored a full acquaintance with the landscape."[127] In his private correspondence he was more emphatic about the joy this renewed acquaintance brought him: "I've been jogging a lot and retracing the goat-and-cattle trails of my boyhood—1924–1931. It's powerful therapy for me. Down south—Soweto, Pretoria etc. breathes turmoil and the cruelty of the times, but here in these valleys is a more serene affirmation of life."[128]

Clearly, then, the Mphahlele who returned to South Africa at the age of fifty-seven was less resistant than his younger self to the notion (implicit in the work of Hughes and the Negritude poets) that connecting to the landscapes and cultural wisdom of ancient Africa could serve as antidote to the alienation of diaspora. Peter McDonald attributes the softening in Mphahlele's criticism to his increasing skepticism of "the universalizing assumptions underlying both liberal and socialist forms of [European] humanism."[129] By the 1970s Mphahlele did indeed recognize the necessity of Negritude—or pan-Africanism, or Black Consciousness, or his own evolving notion of African humanism—to help combat the dehumanizing effects of racism and to create alternative channels of cultural exchange and renewal. In 1978, for example, he wrote that poems by Damas, Senghor, Césaire, and Birago Diop, among others, were "some of the most eloquent rebuttals of Western rationalism—that one-dimensional ideology that had been used to put down the Black race. They are a celebration of the total being—emotional and intuitive—embracing those humanistic elements that European modernity had sought to erase."[130]

To a large extent, then, the new value that Mphahlele found in Negritude and other expressions of pan-African entanglement derived implicitly from their ability to counter Western racism and to give people of African descent their own frames of reference for understanding the world. Thus in 1995, when he formulated his ideal curriculum for teaching African literature in South African secondary and tertiary schools, he emphasized oral tradition first and foremost and then such thematic components as "Negritude, Pan-Africanism, Black Consciousness, assertion of Africanism (indigenous values)" and "assertion of our right to take charge of our cultural synthesis that has so far always happened on the White man's terms."[131] In short, Mphahlele late in life was motivated most strongly by the desire to give African students images of their own cultures that emphasized their humanity and could help recharge and reinvent their cultural traditions. The ethos of pan-African entanglement, he had realized, was needed and relevant in South Africa every bit as much as in the diaspora.

David Attwell attributes Mphahlele's shifts in attitude between the two editions of *The African Image* first to the fact that he had spent well over a decade living in Europe and America as "a member of a racial minority that has to look deep within itself to find the resources to survive" and second to his careful study while in exile of Fanon and Césaire.[132] Indeed, whereas the first edition of *The African Image* mentioned Césaire only in passing, in both the revised edition and in *Voices in the Whirlwind* Mphahlele took the Martinican poet's work much more seriously: the Harlem Renaissance, he wrote, "helped Césaire to form a picture in his mind of a black consciousness; a black civilization spread all over the world. He arrived at the idea that there was a 'Negro situation' which expressed itself in various parts of the world. Negritude became for him the meeting point of Africa, the Caribbean, and the black Americas."[133] In other words, careful study revealed to Mphahlele Césaire's vision of Negritude not as essentialism or "anti-racist racism," but as a transnational web consisting of ancestral links and channels of cultural exchange.

To recap: by the 1970s, rather than continuing to critique Negritude for its romanticism and prescriptive imperatives, Mphahlele was more inclined to emphasize its potential to create solidarity and interconnection among far-flung peoples sharing similar circumstances of historical oppression. He had also begun to see more clearly the big picture of the global conversation happening throughout the twentieth century over the meaning of blackness and the role of Africa in the collective memories of the black diaspora. His contribution to that conversation, I would submit, was a model of African humanism rooted in the past and the world of the ancestors, but not trapped there, and able to adapt and make new alliances.

In *Global Matters,* Paul Jay cautions us against the temptation to regard the local as an antidote to the homogenizing tendencies of globalization: "The trap here is that we may perpetuate a simple-minded binarism that facilely and uncritically celebrates the local as pure culture opposed to rapacious and homogenizing westernization. The stress, rather, ought to be on the multidirectionality of cultural flows, on the appropriation and transformation of globalized cultural forms wherever they settle in."[134] This is precisely the point I wish to emphasize by way of concluding this chapter: neither Abrahams nor Mphahlele late in their careers advocated a full retreat from the global into local African traditions; rather, they sought to recuperate elements of those traditions in order to have something to offer within a network of global cultural exchange.

Moreover, in their respective paths—Abrahams making a new home for himself and finding the raw materials for a greater black identity in the Caribbean diaspora, Mphahlele returning home but bringing with him those same imaginative resources from his decades spent in exile in Africa, Europe, and the United States—the two writers explored different avenues for resolving the tensions Hughes had long struggled to balance. His ethos of transnational entanglement had to strike a balance, for example, between his desire for black unity and his recognition of real cultural differences within the black Atlantic network he helped to build, between that same black unity and his recognition of cultural entanglements on a larger scale, and between the need to endow black identity with its own unique qualities and the danger of letting those African-derived cultural practices and styles be exploited and commodified. It would take Abrahams and Mphahlele a long time to recognize the power and motility of Hughes's flexible conception of pan-African and transnational entanglements. Perhaps this was because they, like most of the world, paid too little attention to Hughes's late masterpiece, *Ask Your Mama,* which I argue in the next chapter offered the fullest expression of his aesthetics of transnational entanglement.

5 Cultural Exchange in *Ask Your Mama*

IN THE previous chapter, I focused on how Hughes pulled two generations of South African writers into his ever-expanding black Atlantic network and how they extended his ethos and aesthetics of pan-African entanglement decades after Hughes himself was gone. In this chapter, I will assess how Hughes's lifelong efforts to establish connections and build solidarity with black writers across national and oceanic borders cumulatively affected his own work in the last fifteen years of life—after he established contact with the *Drum* writers in South Africa and during the period when he was traveling to Africa regularly as a cultural ambassador from black America. In both his nonfiction writings and in his underrecognized 1961 masterpiece *Ask Your Mama*, Hughes offered a complex vision of vernacular, transnational entanglements in which Africa served as symbol of ancestral roots and spiritual homeland for those living in the diaspora, while still existing as a modernizing continent engaged in a long process of decolonization and cultural nation building. In other words, Hughes came to emphasize modern Africa's potential contributions to a global network of cultural exchange and in the process redeemed the more romantic facets of his depictions of Africa from primitivist commodification.

Throughout this book I have repeatedly contended that Hughes's dedication to what he called the Negro people was by no means exclusionary or chauvinistic but rather existed within the author's larger ethos of transnational entanglement that delighted in traveling, encountering other cultures, finding unexpected similarities, and learning to negotiate difference. This sensibility was fully displayed and articulated in Hughes's second autobiography, *I Wonder as I Wander* (1956), which is as much travelogue as life story. The book opens with an epigraph taken from Romans 1:14: "I am debtor both to the Greeks and to the barbarians; both to the wise and to the unwise."[1] Paul's declaration of the universality of Christ's message, in the context of Hughes's memoir, represents a cosmopolitan confession of indebtedness to the European enlightenment (heirs to the Greeks) as well as to the global peasantry ("barbarians" in the King James Version). This epigraph suggests that the "unwise" and the "barbarians" have something of value to offer the educated citizen of the world. It confirms that Hughes in his fifties was still operating within the ethos and aesthetic of transnational entanglement that his younger self had cultivated in conversation with Claude McKay and Jacques Roumain, among others.

This cosmopolitan sentiment is confirmed in the book's last chapter, where Hughes wrote: "My interests had broadened from Harlem and the American Negro to include an interest in all the colored peoples of the world—in fact, in *all the people* of the world, as I related to them and they to me."[2] The last clause is important: it is the emphasis on *relation* and fellow feeling that distinguishes Hughes's ethos from a universal humanism based in intellectual and scriptural heritage. That emphasis puts us in the realm of the "Poetics of Relation," which Édouard Glissant characterizes in terms of the Deleuzian rhizome.[3] It "maintains . . . the idea of rootedness but challenges that of a totalitarian root. Rhizomatic thought is the principle behind what I call the Poetics of Relation, in which each and every identity is extended through a relationship with the Other."[4] Indeed, while part of my method in *Cultural Entanglements* has been to study material links and exchanges between the various authors, the end goal of Hughes's network building was to generate precisely such feelings of relation, as we see in *I Wonder as I Wander* through his travels from the United States and West Indies to Spain, Russia, Central Asia, and Japan.

It bears reiterating that this ethos of entanglement at a global or universal scale was fully compatible in Hughes's mind with an ethos of *pan-African* entanglement, which prioritized the art and cultures of what he called the "Negro race." Appiah helps us understand this by identifying local and family affiliations as "circles among the many circles narrower than the human horizon that are appropriate spheres of moral concern" for the liberal cosmopolitan.[5] Similarly, Hughes in *I Wonder* thought of human kinship and solidarity in terms of concentric circles, or at least of overlapping fields. He felt closest to African Americans, then to people of African descent throughout the diaspora, and then to people of color in, for example, Asia. Indeed, that is the trajectory of the autobiography itself, which begins with Hughes traveling south from New York to New Orleans, then to Cuba and Haiti, and then later venturing east to the Soviet Union and Japan and later still to war-torn Spain.

Over the course of *I Wonder* it becomes evident that Hughes's "first loyalties" to his race did not interfere with his capacity or willingness to relate to people throughout the world. So, for example, in Spain he saw a performance by a Romany singer and found the "strange, high, wild crying of her flamenco in some ways much like the primitive Negro blues of the deep South."⁶ In Japan he found that a translation of his own poems had "attracted considerable attention in Tokyo."⁷ And traveling with a phonograph player and a crate of records in tow, he learned that "everywhere, around the world, folks are attracted by American jazz. A good old Dixieland stomp can break down almost any language barriers."⁸ Hughes, in short, proved receptive both to the linguistic and cultural differences that made such acts of literal and figurative translation necessary and to the unexpected similarities he found in the midst of such difference. This receptivity, in turn, made it possible for Hughes to generate solidarity with ideological and artistic allies around the world and thus facilitate new clusters of pan-African entanglement.

In pursuing those ends, Hughes proved willing to forge pragmatic alliances with various other scales of transnational interconnection, including Soviet communism. Hughes spent several months in Russia and Soviet Asia in 1932–33 as a guest of the Soviet government. His writings expressed admiration (if not entirely uncritical) for the USSR's support for workers, for its having abolished all racial codes in the legal systems of its republics, and for the global scope of its ambitions. Yet this admiration was notably muted in *I Wonder as I Wander,* which Hughes wrote throughout the early to mid-1950s, much of it in the aftermath of his appearance before Joseph McCarthy's Senate subcommittee investigating supposedly subversive political activities. That hearing took place in 1953, and the autobiography was published in 1956. Many critics have noted the noncommittal, subdued tone the author used to mask the political views he espoused during the Great Depression. In this regard, the book might be read as an implicit renunciation of the communist sympathies he so avidly proclaimed in such lines as "Put one more s in the U.S.A. / To make it Soviet."⁹ The evidence suggests to me, however, that Hughes's enthusiasm for international communism was always rooted in two things— the Soviet Union's relatively progressive views and policies on race issues and the very fact that it was international in its aims and scope. So while it is true that he grew more cautious in putting forward avowedly socialist political sentiments—a caution fully evident in *I Wonder as I Wander*—he never lost sight of the underlying goal of establishing an international community in which black artists and intellectuals were accepted, treated as equals, and allowed to engage with global networks of modern cultural exchange. This goal derived from his ethos of pan-African entanglement, which found its fullest poetic expression in the long narrative poem *Ask Your Mama,* which he published five years after the autobiography.

In this late poem, Hughes more fully integrated the ancestral and contemporary planes of pan-African entanglement than he ever had before. That is, he made his narrative of a collective, transnational black past—from primitive Africa to slavery to revolution—the raw material for an aesthetic that was shared across Africa and the diaspora through modern circuits of cultural exchange. Indeed, *cultural exchange* is a key theme in Hughes's late writings, and I argue that it is crucial to understanding both his motives for continuing his extensive network-building efforts and the themes and formal experimentation that characterize some of his late poetry.

We can see the importance cultural exchange held for Hughes in a speech he gave at the opening of the US library in Accra, Ghana, in 1962—already excerpted in my introduction, but worth quoting here more fully: "Today, when America comes to Africa, as through these library shelves, to offer an *exchange* of knowledge (not merely to *give* in the old patronizing sense), America is bolstering her *own* basic dreams, and finding here in Africa a new strengthening of the old concept of freedom in your liberated lands. Black Africa today is sending rejuvenating currents of liberty over all the earth reaching even as far as Little Rock, Birmingham and Jackson, Mississippi."[10] Hughes's romanticization of Africa on this occasion celebrating his friend Nkrumah's project of cultural nationalism was both good ambassadorship and an opportunity to pursue his own project of validating black achievement and forging black solidarity across the Atlantic. Notice in this regard the emphasis in Hughes's speech on reciprocity and exchange and on Africa as a *modern* source of inspiration and political direction. Both, Hughes felt, were badly needed among African Americans in a South still terrorized by Jim Crow.

"Cultural Exchange" is also the title of the first section of *Ask Your Mama,* and as the speaker of the poem reminds us, "CULTURE, THEY SAY, IS A TWO-WAY STREET."[11] I will argue further, then, that cultural exchange is the operative metaphor that explains both the eclectic musical accompaniment and the seemingly random jumps in space and time that characterize the structure of the poem. Its principal poetic method consists of allusive entanglements of people, places, and cultural practices. In Hughes's hands, cultural exchange became not a simple give-and-take but a flexible, complex, and multidirectional ebb and flow across national borders, oceans, and time periods, involving a complex process of mixture, synthesis, and creolization. Cultural exchange yielded the threads that Hughes saw connecting people and crossing national divides and cultural differences across the pan-African world, while also asserting a larger kinship with all humankind.

Expressions of Entanglement in *Ask Your Mama*

Rampersad calls *Ask Your Mama: 12 Moods for Jazz* "by far the most ambitious single poem of [Hughes's] life" and notes that at around eight hundred lines it is "by far his longest single effort in verse."[12] Hughes began writing *Ask Your Mama* on 4 July 1960, in the immediate aftermath of the civil unrest that had broken out at the Newport Jazz Festival two days earlier between the local police and a crowd of mostly white concertgoers and led to intervention by the National Guard. For Hughes, this was a momentous event: "The descendants of masters now danced to the music of the descendants of slaves; American 'civilization' had begun, in however modest a degree, a fateful slide toward revolution."[13] Despite decades of attempts by the white establishment to impose separation and segregation of the races, the inevitable entanglements of European and African cultures in North America had "contaminated" both, in ways that Hughes saw sometimes as stifling but at other times, as with young white Americans' embrace of jazz music, as productively transgressive. Hughes therefore wrote *Ask Your Mama* to give voice to the complex and ambivalent entanglements between blacks and whites but also between African Americans and black people throughout the pan-African world. Scott Saul calls it "an experimental poetic sequence that set out to bewilder the rioters and white America generally through well-crafted mockery."[14]

Unlike his shorter lyric poems, which Hughes often wrote in a single surge of inspiration and then revised only lightly, *Ask Your Mama* went through over a dozen drafts, involving significant structural revision and expansion from one version to the next, including the title, which began as *Show Fare, Mama: Notes for Jazz*. It was published in the autumn of 1961 to mixed reviews: one reviewer warned that "lovers of real poetry" would not be among its admirers;[15] another called it the work of "a man being harmed by his intellectually impotent adversary."[16] Lewis Nkosi of South Africa called it "merely shouting and name-dropping."[17] Dudley Fitts seemed torn, calling it "stunt poetry" but also "insistent and strong in what is clearly a parallel development" to the work of Nicolás Guillén and Luis Pales Matos,[18] while J. Saunders Redding declared it proof that Hughes was "far from through" as a writer and praised it for its "range of subtle nuances" that he regarded as a new development in Hughes's work.[19]

The title takes its cue from playing the dozens—African American "verbal insult rituals," which Henry Louis Gates Jr. classifies as "an especially compelling subset of Signifyin(g)."[20] According to the primary source Hughes consulted in doing the research for this poem, the dozens is "a valve for aggression in a depressed group. . . . It is undoubtedly set in motion by aggressive tendencies which have been mobilized in other situations and are ready for expression."[21] Yet in Hughes's poem, playing the dozens happens not merely among African Americans, nor is it simply a psychological coping mechanism for them. Rather, it becomes a weapon the speaker wields in response to insulting or patronizing questions from a white person:

> AND THEY ASKED ME RIGHT AT CHRISTMAS
> IF MY BLACKNESS, WOULD I RUB OFF?
> I SAID, ASK YOUR MAMA.
>
> . . . .
> THEY ASKED ME AT THE PTA
> IS IT TRUE THAT NEGROES—?
> I SAID, ASK YOUR MAMA.[22]

Dollard notes that "in verbalizing the forbidden notions the speaker [of the insult] experiences a triumph over repressive forces in himself, a triumph sweet to the child-animal in all of us."[23] This triumph must be all the sweeter when it is wielded not against a fellow African American playing the game but by a black "migrant" to the suburbs against his white neighbors and against his white readers.[24] At the same time, given the United States' long history of lynching black men accused of sexual crimes or intentions toward white women, the vulgar sexual subtext of the speaker's response in that white-dominated context has a decidedly more potent charge and carries sharper risks. The speaker's blunt, even crude, disregard for white sensibilities establishes from the title onward the poem's vernacular register, much as Roumain used such language as "we will fuck them one in the ass, the bastards"[25] in *Gouverneurs de la rosée* to establish the defiant persistence of his Haitian peasants. The poem's use of the dozens also reinforces its adoption of a posture of black rebellion, one that emanates from Europe's colonies (as we saw in his Accra speech, and as we will see in the repeated references in *Ask Your Mama* to anticolonial and postcolonial leaders in Africa, the Caribbean, and elsewhere) and extends across the borders of nations and continents.

Ask Your Mama is not only Hughes's longest single poem but also his most structurally complex one. It consists of twelve sections or "moods," each featuring a column with the text of the poem in all capital letters, a sidebar providing prose instructions for musical accompaniment, and a prose endnote, or "Liner Note," providing sarcastic commentary and counterpoint to the themes of the individual moods. Those notes were one of the principle sources of critical displeasure for the poem's reviewers and also one of its most misunderstood features: one reviewer complained that the notes are "pretty useless"[26] and another that they "don't always clarify."[27] More astutely, Rampersad reads the notes as written "no doubt in insulting parody of T. S. Eliot's celebrated notes to *The Waste Land*."[28] Seen in this light, Hughes's notes position *Ask Your Mama* as an overtly modernist poem, or at least one that reacts ambivalently to the high-art aspirations of Eliot's modernism. At the same time, the fact that he titled them "Liner Notes for the poetically unhep" links the poem to jazz and perhaps implies that jazz is an intrinsically modernist art form in itself. Yet I would argue that the principal function of the liner notes is neither to clarify the individual moods nor solely to mock and parody but to open up still more of the circuits of cultural exchange that Hughes used throughout the poem to establish continuity between past and present and to make visible the threads of pan-African entanglement. We see this happening, for example, in the liner note for "Ride, Red, Ride," which begins, "In the restless Caribbean there are the same shadows as in Mississippi," and for "Ode To Dinah," which opens with "Hard times endure from slavery to freedom—to Harlem."[29]

While the liner notes and the main body of the poem braid these various strands together at the thematic level, Hughes's notes in the sidebar that runs alongside the text perform a similar feat through musical form. These notes have been compared to the stage directions that are interspersed throughout Vachel Lindsay's long poem *The Congo*.[30] Lindsay's notes, however, take the form of guidelines for a performance of the poem: "To be read or sung in a rolling bass, with some deliberation," for example, or "With pomposity." By contrast, interplay between the "framed" and "framing" texts in *Ask Your Mama* achieves, as Baxter Miller notes, an artistic fusion between "the voice of the personal narrator who retells history"—that is to say, the "I" who speaks so many of Hughes's poems—and "the sonorous complement of a communal narrative. . . . *Ask Your Mama* is, in other words, Hughes's finally sustained rapprochement between the Black intellectual as a talented individual and the Black community at large."[31]

To Miller's reading I would add Gunter Lenz's observation that the black community Hughes imagines the poem speaking for, and to, exists within "the transnational, global context of the postcolonial world."[32] The musical accompaniment dictated by the sidebar plays an important role in establishing the scope of such transnational entanglements, drawing as it does from a nearly global repertoire of musical styles and instruments. In doing so, it performs the much more complex function, to recall a phrase from an earlier poem, of making visible "the maze of patterns / Woven by democracy and me."[33] Indeed, Hughes used the complex multilayered structure of the poem to lay bare the circuits of cultural exchange on which he based a vision of flexibly federated black Atlantic community, rallying around (and generating) similarity, but welcoming of difference.

In *Ask Your Mama* Hughes emphasized a particular mode of cultural exchange and entanglement that he sometimes represented through metaphors of weaving. In the sidebar accompanying the ninth mood, "Ask Your Mama," we find these musical cues: "Delicate post-bop suggests pleasant evenings and flirtatious youth as it gradually weaves into its pattern a musical echo of Paris which continues until very softly the silver call of a hunting horn is heard far away. African drums begin a softly mounting rumble."[34] This brief example reveals the musical accompaniment to be in itself a tapestry woven out of numerous threads of transnational musical origin. The weaving of this web of transnational musical references, rooted in Africa, begins with the opening lines of music in the first mood, tellingly titled "Cultural Exchange": "The rhythmically rough scraping of a guira continues monotonously until a lonely flute call, high and far away, merges into piano variations on German lieder gradually changing into old-time traditional twelve-bar blues up strong between verses until African drums throb against blues."[35] Hughes's typescripts at the Beinecke show that he added the reference to the guira—a scraped metal or wood percussion instrument from the Hispanic Caribbean—only in the last author's copy he sent to the publisher, Knopf. This suggests that, right up to his publication deadline, he was consciously seeking to expand the transnational scope of his cultural references in the poem and to tie the West Indies into his model of pan-African entanglement.

For Hughes, the quintessential embodiment of the aesthetics of pan-African entanglement was jazz music, and indeed *Ask Your Mama* takes jazz as both a theme and a source of poetic forms. The poem is subtitled *12 Moods for Jazz,* and Hughes's directions for musical accompaniment draw principally from jazz and the blues; even the decision to write twelve sections reads as an homage to the blues with its typical twelve-bar chord progressions. African American music, for Hughes, had always "remembered Africa, the ships of the Middle Passage, whips, chains, blood hounds, the slave markets."[36] In other words, jazz, blues, gospel, and other black musical forms linked the modern world to the ancestral plane of pan-African connections and embodied the collective memory of pan-African entanglement, from the African past and American slavery to freedom. Jazz thus provided a much-needed sense of rootedness, even as it opened up African American culture and made it accessible to the world: "The Negroes of the New World created jazz, but now it belongs to everybody—our gift of rhythm to all the peoples of the earth."[37] But the poet also acknowledged the inevitable influence of European cultures, represented in "Cultural Exchange" by the "piano variations on German lieder," which are quickly entangled with references in the text to the African American soprano Leontyne Price. The central knot in this great transnational skein, as the poem depicts it, is the beat of those "African drums," evolved in his American context into the "old-time traditional twelve-bar blues." The essence of all music is stripped bare in these opening lines of the poem and shown to be the drumming of humanity's shared African ancestors.

On a thematic level, too, the poem positions Africa at the center of the great global web of cultural entanglements. Unlike in so much Western writing about Africa (including, sometimes, Hughes's own work), the Africa that emerges in *Ask Your Mama* is modern and vibrant, not fixed in the amber of primitive essence. The poem celebrates the anticolonial movements that had, by late 1960, begun to win victories in their struggles for national independence from their European colonizers. Furthermore, "Cultural Exchange" inverts the common narrative of the Westerner who travels to a benighted and primitive Africa by having the opening mood tell of an African dignitary who visits an unnamed American city to see the "QUARTER OF THE NEGROES."[38] That phrase recurs as a leitmotif throughout the poem. The liner notes explain: "Negroes often live either by the river or the railroad, and for most there is not much chance of going anywhere else. Yet *always* one of them has been away and has come home. The door has opened to admit something strange and foreign, yet tied by destiny to a regional past nourished by a way of life in common."[39]

Stagnation, Commodification, and Cultural Exchange

Throughout the remainder of "Cultural Exchange" and the eleven other sections of *Ask Your Mama,* the poet explores the tensions between the foreign and the familiar and between the stationary lives of those trapped in poverty and the mobility of those wanderers who take their culture into the world and bring the world back with them. The second stanza continues:

BY THE RIVER AND THE RAILROAD
WITH FLUID FAR-OFF GOING
BOUNDARIES BIND UNBINDING
A WHIRL OF WHISTLES BLOWING
NO TRAINS OR STEAMBOATS GOING.[40]

The "fluid far-off going" happens to other people; for those who live in the poor neighborhoods within earshot of the railroad tracks and rivers, ironically, there are "no trains or steamboats going." This image is repeated in a later section, entitled "Ode to Dinah," whose liner notes tell a story about Harriet Tubman crossing from Buffalo into Canada by train with a band of fugitive slaves.[41] The main text of the mood includes the refrain "Niagara Falls is frozen,"[42] implying that the old route to freedom, via the Underground Railroad and flight to Canada, is frozen and blocked, leaving poor black Americans cut off from the circuits of transnational entanglement. Their cultural stagnation can be seen in the modern residents of a housing project who are described as "TRIBAL NOW NO LONGER / SAVE IN MEMORIES OF GANGRENOUS ICING."[43]

These passages imply recognition of a basic limitation of Hughes's ethos of pan-African entanglement: it relied to a large degree on a border-crossing mobility that was denied to a majority of the poor whose practices and values were the bedrock of the transnational community he envisioned yet whose memories of a tribal African past are frozen in "gangrenous icing." Moreover, the poem's speaker later voices self-reflexive criticism (or at least acknowledges other perspectives) of himself and other black writers who chose international travel and cosmopolitanism over attachment to the land of their birth:

> THEY KNOW ME, TOO, DOWNTOWN,
> ALL ACROSS THE COUNTRY, EUROPE—
> ME WHO USED TO BE NOBODY,
> NOTHING BUT ANOTHER SHADOW
> IN THE QUARTER OF THE NEGROES,
> NOW A NAME! MY NAME—A NAME!
>
> . . . .
>
> AND WHY DID RICHARD WRIGHT
> LIVE ALL THAT WHILE IN PARIS
> INSTEAD OF COMING HOME TO DECENT DIE
> IN HARLEM OR THE SOUTH SIDE OF CHICAGO
> OR THE WOMB OF MISSISSIPPI?
> AND ONE SHOULD LOVE ONE'S COUNTRY
> FOR ONE'S COUNTRY IS YOUR MAMA.[44]

The speaker—who in some respects resembles, but is not, Langston Hughes, having vacated Harlem for a house in the white suburbs, an unthinkable move for Hughes—feels defensive ambivalence about his own international stature. On the one hand, it is a source of pride that he has risen from being just another "shadow / in the quarter of the negroes" to be a "name," like the dozens of other successful African American personalities he catalogs over the course of this poem. On the other hand, the speaker feels that his role, and Richard Wright's, as citizens of the world and as international writers, has come to some extent at the price of their identity as Americans, and as African Americans. The insistence that Mississippi is "the womb" for black Americans, and that "one's country is your mama," poses a conflict to Hughes's lifelong efforts to center black American identity instead in an imagined Africa.

In the same vein of self-conscious interrogation of the limitations and possibilities of cultural exchange, the poem depicts the black American celebrities sent to the "quarter of the Negroes" to meet the African dignitary as commodities, offered up for the visitor's "consumption" in a kind of cultural supermarket:

> THERE, FORBID US TO REMEMBER,
> COMES AN AFRICAN IN MID-DECEMBER
> SENT BY THE STATE DEPARTMENT
> AMONG THE SHACKS TO MEET THE BLACKS:
> LEONTYNE SAMMY HARRY POITIER
> LOVELY LENA MARIAN LOUIS PEARLIE MAE
>
> GEORGE S. SCHUYLER MOLTO BENE
> COME WHAT MAY LANGSTON HUGHES
>
> . . . .
> PUSHCARTS FOLD AND UNFOLD
> IN A SUPERMARKET SEA.[45]

The liner notes explain the African visitor's discovery that "in the American social supermarket blacks for sale range from intellectuals to entertainers."[46] Even "high artists" such as Leontyne Price and Marian Anderson and poets such as Hughes himself are simply part of a marketplace of commodified black bodies. This idea interplays ironically with the phantom history of slavery that haunts this poem and much of Hughes's late work. Here again, then, Hughes complicated his conceptualization of pan-African entanglement: he called into question whether the material basis of a transnational black culture was inextricable from the systems of global finance and commodity exchange that had so often enslaved and exploited black bodies.

Even as the poem acknowledges all these complications, it also seems to espouse an "If you can't beat 'em, join 'em" attitude by resorting to naked marketing tactics. The catalog of musicians, actors, and writers in the above passage, for example is very typical of Hughes's method throughout *Ask Your Mama*. The publicity team at Knopf identified in the poem the names of or references to some 115 people (some of them historical but most of them alive and active in 1961) and wrote to the living people on the list to offer them a discount.[47] At the same time, they anticipated the charge of gratuitous name dropping, with one early publicity note quoting Hughes's response to an advance review:

Langston Hughes countered, "Why not use the names of recognizable people in today's poetry—names everybody knows like Patti Page and Ralph Bunche and Governor Faubus. Poets are always using nature names like the violet and the rose, the shumach and the willow, and Dylan Thomas wrote a whole book about the milkwood. I use names like *the* Harry Belafonte and *the* Martha Roundtree and *the* Duke and *the* George Sokolsky, the great Louis and Lena Horne, almost as well known to most Americans as the names of flowers and trees. These human beings are certainly better known than milkwood."[48]

Hughes thereby suggested that black personalities were part of the fabric and the backdrop of American cultural life and part of what gave America a cultural originality that could be exchanged in a global market, just as Thomas turned the milkwood into a symbol of Welsh identity in *Under Milk Wood*. The botanical metaphor also carries connotations of rootedness and transplantation, evoking a common set of tropes in diasporic discourse of all sorts.

If the poet's catalog of notable figures positions them as emblems of African American identity, they are quickly woven into a larger pan-African identity conjoined with the Caribbean and Africa. That pan-African skein is then woven in turn into global circuits of cultural exchange and thus inevitably entangled amid the racist structures of global power. For example, in the fantasia that opens the third mood, "Shades of Pigmeat," the speaker intones:

IN THE QUARTER OF THE NEGROES
BELGIUM SHADOW LEOPOLD
PREMIER DOWNING AGING
GENERAL BOURSE BELEAGUERED
EASTLAND AND MALAN DECEASED
DEAD OR LIVE THEIR GHOSTS CAST SHADOWS.[49]

Lines 2 through 4 envision the decline of the great European colonial powers: the Belgian King Leopold's control over the Congo and the colonial holdings of England (Downing Street) and France (the *Bourse de commerce,* or commodities exchange). South Africa is evoked in the specter of D. F. Malan, one of the architects of apartheid who died in 1959; Mississippi, more puzzlingly, is associated with the "ghost" of segregationist Senator James Eastland, who was alive and still in office when Hughes published this poem. But as the next line notes, "Dead or live their ghosts cast shadows" over the "quarter of the negroes." These lines come not long after the fantasy sequence that closes "Cultural Exchange," in which the speaker imagines Martin Luther King Jr. as governor of Georgia and the wives of Eastland and other prominent segregationists work as mammies in black homes (this inversion being perhaps another attempt, like turning the dozens against white people, to shock the sensibilities of a readership accustomed to deferential behavior from black people). The implication, then, is that in the poet's imagination, the upending of Jim Crow in the American South would be part of an international revolution, of which the "aging" and "beleaguered" state of European rule in Africa was an early sign. Hughes anticipated that this revolution would allow black people to participate in an increasingly globalizing modern culture as equals and would enable a fruitful, multidirectional entanglement within an emerging transnational black community.

In the meantime, however, black writers and artists found themselves in a marginalized position that made them dependent on capitalist markets to disseminate their work to a global audience. The poem hints at this compulsory commodification in the line quoted earlier about pushcarts folding and unfolding "in a supermarket sea." In most of Hughes's work, including the autobiography *The Big Sea,* oceans and seas symbolize newness, amnesia, and a space in which entanglements with the Other can form. In this instance, reinforced by the commodification of black bodies and black minds, the sea further connotes the history of slavery and the Middle Passage. Through this complex layering of symbols and associations, Hughes acknowledges that, given the context of uneven power dynamics, distilling a culture to a few totemic representations for the purposes of cultural exchange is always on some level an act of commodification:

> CONCENTRATED TO THE ESSENCE
> OF THE SHADOW OF THE DOLLAR
> PAID AT THE BOX OFFICE.[50]

The title of this opening section likewise makes clear that these circuits of cultural exchange, like passenger trains, were available only to those who had the money or status to afford them.

Interweaving the Ancestral and Contemporary Planes of Entanglement

What redeems the cultural exchange between the African sent by the state department and the African American cultural ambassadors chosen to meet him is the spark of kinship and similarity—what the liner notes, again, refer to as "a regional past nourished by a way of life in common—in this case collard greens."[51] Just as the drums connote African musical heritage, the greens cooking in the pot behind the "PAPER DOORS" represent African foodways, a link to the ancestral plane of pan-African entanglement otherwise lost in historical amnesia. Hughes saw the ancestral plane, then, as a necessary but insufficient ingredient for generating solidarity and community among black people globally.

That ancestral plane manifests itself in various ways, including devotion to the ancient deities of Vodou and other African-derived religious practices, including the Afro-Jamaican sects of Bedwardism and Pocomania and the Nañigo sect of Cuba and Haiti. Allusions to all these religions and movements arrive in a particularly dense cluster in the seventh mood, "Gospel Cha-Cha":

> IN THE QUARTER OF THE NEGROES
> WHERE THE PALMS AND COCONUTS
> CHA-CHA LIKE CASTANETS
>
> . . . .
> ERZULIE PLAYS A TUNE
> ON THE BONGO OF THE MOON
> . . . .
> MAMA MAMACITA PAPA PAPIAMENTO
> DAMBALLA WEDO OGOUN AND THE HORSE
> THAT LUGGED THE FIRST WHITE
> FIRST WHITE TOURIST UP THE MOUNTAIN
> TO THE CITADELLE OF SHADOWS SHADOWS
>
> . . . .
> MAMACITA! PAPA LEGBA! SHANGO!
> BEDWARD! POCOMANIA! WEDO! OGOUN!
> THE BOAT BEYOND THE FORTALEZA
> TO THE VILLE OF NAÑIGO.
> A LONG WAY TO BAHIA—
> HOW I GOT THERE I DON'T KNOW.
> WHAT'S HIS NAME, MY COUSIN,
> WHO SEDUCED MARIE LAVEAU?[52]

I quote such extended excerpts to show how densely the poet imbricates the allusions to ancient Africa, to slavery and the fight against it, and to black communities and cultures throughout the twentieth-century diaspora. The palms and coconuts could place the "quarter of the negroes" equally well in Africa, the West Indies, or Florida. Likewise, the loas Erzulie, Wedo, Legba, Shango, and Ogoun are common to the Ifa religion of the Yoruba people in West Africa; to any number of Caribbean islands where Vodou, Obeah, or Santería is practiced; and to New Orleans (home to the famous Vodou priestess Marie Laveau). With each line in the poem, the cluster of entanglements within this black Atlantic triangle grows denser.

At times, the evocations of ancestral Africa in *Ask Your Mama* seem like throwbacks to Hughes's primitivist phase. In "Blues in Stereo" he links a barefoot dance to familiar imagery of ancient rivers:

> SHOUTS FROM THE EARTH ITSELF
> BARE FEET TO BEAT THE GREAT DRUMBEAT
> OF GLORY TO YOUR NAME AND MINE
> ONE AND THE SAME:
> YOU BAREFOOT, TOO,
> IN THE QUARTER OF THE NEGROES
> WHERE AN ANCIENT RIVER FLOWS.[53]

In these lines, the barefoot dance offers a promise of recovering the lost unity of the African past—of "your name and mine / one and the same." At the same time, the lines also recall Hughes's focus on West Indian peasants, the "people without shoes," in the Haiti and Cuba chapters of *I Wonder as I Wander*.

Clearly, then, Hughes in 1961 was still invested in forging a memory of pan-African entanglement where primitive huts and ancient rivers could serve as anchors for diasporic identity. But he also traced that ancestral narrative through the Americas and brought its repertoire into the modern world, thus redeeming passages like the one above from pure romantic primitivism. The vision of the pan-African world he presented in *Ask Your Mama* is notable, then, first for its emphasis on anticolonial resistance, past and present; and second for its reliance not on some imagined essence of blackness but on mixture, synthesis, and creolization. The title of "Gospel Cha-Cha," for instance, combines African American religious music with a lively Cuban dance, and the first stanza alludes to Papiamento, a Spanish Creole spoken on a handful of Caribbean islands. Hughes, then, used musical fusions, linguistic creolization, and strategic juxtapositions of names to make visible the processes of cultural contamination and grafting that result in such hybrids.

Ask Your Mama derives its hybrid qualities and its multidirectional flexibility from its methods of imbricating and interweaving past and present, local and global, mythological and political. Thus it makes use of narratives of ancestral Africa, Middle Passage, slavery, and revolt to evoke, comment upon, and make sense of Hughes's own present day. In the other direction, meanwhile, it uses the twentieth-century situation of people of African descent worldwide to recall key elements of their forgotten, collective past. We see how this multidirectional move illuminates the spectral past in "Cultural Exchange," where the simple act of crossing the bridge into New York City is overlaid both with the history of the slave trade and with contemporary revolutions happening in Africa:

> COME WHAT MAY—THE SIGNS POINT:
>   GHANA   GUINEA
> AND THE TOLL BRIDGE FROM WESTCHESTER
> IS A GANGPLANK ROCKING RISKY
> BETWEEN THE DECK AND SHORE
> OF A BOAT THAT NEVER QUITE
> KNEW ITS DESTINATION.[54]

What is now Ghana, on the Gulf of Guinea, was a key outpost of the slave trade through the eighteenth century; the reference to a "boat that never quite / knew its destination" suggests that the survivors of the Middle Passage, and their descendants ever since, have been wandering lost, "between the deck and shore," looking for signs to point them home. Yet, in 1961, the place names also evoked anticolonial revolutions with distinct socialist leanings: the Gold Coast became the first British colony in Africa to win its independence in 1957 and, under the socialist leadership of Kwame Nkrumah, became Ghana; French rule in Guinea collapsed in 1958 and gave way to Sekou Touré's Soviet-backed leadership.

By overlaying those recent events with references to slavery and the existential dislocation of diaspora, the poem implies that the accomplishments of these men are themselves signs pointing the way to solutions and the possible restoration of a unitary pan-African identity. This is part of "Hughes's African (Re)Turn 1954–1960," which Kim argues was for Hughes a second radical phase and "an equally important vector of black radicalism—anticolonialism, nationalism—that demands its own consideration."[55] Given that this "vector of black radicalism" emanated from Africa, the larger implication is that the continent for Hughes was no longer simply a symbolic source of succor and roots but a living, modern place with lessons that African Americans would benefit from learning. That Hughes emphasized both black political liberation and black cultural nationalism explains the curiously political character of the selections in the anthology *An African Treasury*, which he published just a few months before *Ask Your Mama*: the first nine selections consisted of nonfiction articles about the contemporary state of various countries in Africa.

The excerpt from "Cultural Exchange" above appears in the context of the African dignitary's visit to the US "quarter of the Negroes." This implies that, in a setting of such squalor and seeming hopelessness, it requires the perspective of the foreigner, the African dignitary, to see in black American ghettoes glimpses of the same spirit of insurrection that was rocking Europe's African and Caribbean colonies (and the de facto US colony of Cuba) in 1960. More glimpses follow three stanzas later:

IN THE SHADOW OF THE NEGROES
    NKRUMAH
IN THE SHADOW OF THE NEGROES
    NASSER NASSER
IN THE SHADOW OF THE NEGROES
    ZIK AZIKIWE
CUBA CASTRO GUINEA TOURÉ
FOR NEED OR PROPAGANDA
    KENYATTA
AND THE TOM DOGS OF THE CABIN
THE COCOA AND THE CANE BRAKE
THE CHAIN GANG AND THE SLAVE BLOCK
TARRED AND FEATHERED NATIONS
SEAGRAM'S AND FOUR ROSES
$5.00 BAGS A DECK OR DAGGA.[56]

The almost frantic shuttling we see here between places and times throughout the history and expanse of the African diaspora traces lines of entanglement between anticolonial movements in Africa, Castro's revolution in Cuba, slavery in the American South (represented via Stowe's *Uncle Tom's Cabin,* slyly evoked through the phrase "the tom dogs of the cabin"), heroin addiction in Harlem ("$5.00 bags a deck"), and apartheid in South Africa, through the sly introduction of the foreign word "dagga"—the South African term for marijuana, which Hughes had encountered in his correspondence with Richard Rive and his reading of South African fiction. Such juxtapositions of culturally specific slang function analogously to the vernacular constructions that Brent Hayes Edwards identifies in Hughes's poems about the Spanish Civil War from the 1930s: when Hughes uses "seed" instead of the simple past tense "saw," for example, "it is the vernacular 'mistake' that inserts the spore, the principle of unification, into [the poet's] gaze across the Mediterranean" from Spain to Moorish Africa.[57] Similarly, Larry Scanlon argues in relation to *Ask Your Mama* "that the durability of the vernacular lies precisely in its incompletion, and that this incompletion gives the vernacular the syncretic power to appropriate and redefine other traditions."[58]

To extrapolate from Edwards's and Scanlon's arguments: especially when he juxtaposed slang from different countries and cultures, Hughes deployed the vernacular as a vehicle for cultivating transnational entanglements, helping to establish fellow feeling and networks of cultural exchange across great distances, language barriers, and national borders. Such exchanges illustrate Gilroy's claim for "the existence of fractal patterns of cultural and political affiliation."[59] They do not assert a simple racial genealogy connecting the New World to Africa, but they do establish rhizomatic and densely interlinked affiliations between the cocoa plantations of West Africa, the settler colony of Kenya, Nasser's recently independent Egypt, the cane brakes of the West Indies, the prisons in South Africa, lynchings and chain gangs in the American South, and the drug-littered streets of Hughes's own Harlem. That this web of references is not confined to sub-Saharan Africa and its diaspora testifies to the concentricity and flexibility of Hughes's ethos and aesthetics of pan-African entanglement, able to prioritize racial relation while still welcoming cultural exchange with the Other.

The juxtapositions we see in this opening section of *Ask Your Mama* imply correspondence between and solidarity among the "tarred and feathered nations." More importantly, they also point to a network of multidirectional cultural exchange between the various black Atlantic coordinates, which the poem sketches again in the section "Ask Your Mama": "BAHIA LAGOS DAKAR LENOX / KINGSTON TOO GOD WILLING."[60] The speaker imagines a scene where "AZIKIWE'S SON, AMEKA, / SHAKES HANDS WITH EMMETT TILL."[61] This image quite explicitly links the anticolonial politics of West Africa (specifically Hughes's friend, the governor general of Nigeria, Nnamdi Azikiwe) to the civil rights struggle and the fight against lynching in the US South. Baxter Miller remarks that the "Ask Your Mama" section of the poem "exposes the repressed memory of the Black middle class,"[62] but this repressed memory clearly exceeds the national context of African Americans. Indeed, for Hughes it became the raw material for imagining into existence a border-crossing, ocean-spanning community of black intellectuals.

Hughes continued this allusive shuttling between, and thereby weaving together of, various points in the black Atlantic in "Bird in Orbit." The title simultaneously positions us in black American culture with its reference to jazz saxophonist Charlie "Bird" Parker and in the global position of a ship orbiting the earth. The speaker then connects the Negritude movement (evoked through a composite of the names Alioune Diop, Aimé Césaire, and Léopold Sédar Senghor) to the civil rights movement in the United States in three satirical lines:

ALIOUNE AIMÉ SEDAR SIPS HIS NEGRITUDE.
THE REVEREND MARTIN LUTHER
KING MOUNTS HIS UNICORN.[63]

This is followed in the middle section of the mood by an apostrophe to the speaker's allegorical grandfather, asking if he had heard

THE OLD FOLKS SAY HOW
HOW TALL HOW TALL THE CANE GREW
SAY HOW WHITE THE COTTON COTTON
SPEAK OF RICE DOWN IN THE MARSHLAND.[64]

The allegorical figure of the speaker's black ancestors is by turns associated with the cane fields of the West Indies, the cotton plantations of the Deep South, and the rice paddies of Southeast Asia. The latter hints at the possibilities of solidarity and political coalitions between the black Atlantic community the poem envisions and other dispossessed peoples around the world, possibilities that result from the flexibility of Hughes's model, with its overlapping clusters of entanglement.

Once again, the connections that Hughes emphasized and valued were focused on vernacular entanglements, especially those embedded in the cultures of oppressed peoples. And here again, the narrative of a pan-African past that the poem evokes and imagines gives strong emphasis to the constant manifestations of resistance: King's nonviolent protest, as miraculous as the unicorn he is described as riding; Douglass's abolitionist oratory; John Brown's armed uprising; the references to Toussaint and the Haitian Revolution quoted earlier. And because mutual entanglement is the chief poetic method of *Ask Your Mama*, these historical references are quickly brought into alignment with the contemporary plane through the many references to twentieth-century revolutionary and anticolonial leaders. These allusions, then, are more than "totemic, inspirational presences";[65] they are instrumental to the narrative of a black past that Hughes spun. His aesthetic of pan-African entanglement, emphasizing as it did stories about black figures of resistance, thus became a form of resistance in itself by providing connection, solidarity, and inspiration to communities isolated by colonialism, segregation, and apartheid.

The complexity of the poem's vision of pan-African entanglement is equally on display in the second mood, entitled "Ride, Red, Ride." The musical accompaniment specifies maracas to the rhythms of "When the Saints Go Marching In" and then a piano playing a calypso tune. Musically, then, the mood establishes implicit links between African American gospel and the musical forms (calypso) and instruments (maracas) of the English- and Spanish-speaking Caribbean. The leitmotif that pulses through all of *Ask Your Mama*, the question "How long must I hesitate?" from the traditional folk song "Hesitation Blues," is introduced in the left-side text:

208 *Cultural Entanglements*

> TELL ME HOW LONG—
> MUST I WAIT?
> CAN I GET IT NOW?
> ÇA IRA! ÇA IRA!
> OR MUST I HESITATE?
> IRA! BOY, IRA!
>
> IN THE QUARTER OF THE NEGROES
> TU ABUELA, ¿DÓNDE ESTÁ?
> LOST IN CASTRO'S BEARD?
> TU ABUELA, ¿DÓNDE ESTÁ?
> BLOWN SKY HIGH BY MONT PELÉE?
> ¿DÓNDE ESTÁ? ¿DÓNDE ESTÁ?
> WAS SHE FLEEING WITH LUMUMBA?[66]

The speaker, through relentless juxtaposition, weaves postrevolutionary Cuba and the Congo into a larger network of black solidarity. This transnational web also includes the French island of Martinique, associated closely with its native sons Aimé Césaire and Frantz Fanon, and home to the active volcano Mount Pelée; the legacy of the French Revolution, evoked through the song "Ça Ira"; and the American context of a people's dream deferred, which the poet has by now closely linked to the phrase "quarter of the Negroes." The trilingual wordplay in the above passage further reflects Hughes's awareness late in life that any sort of black Atlantic network would necessarily have to be multilingual and capable of code switching and crossing borders smoothly. The earlier reference to Bahia in Portuguese-speaking Brazil might also serve as a reminder that efforts to forge an encompassing network across the African diaspora will require navigating languages beyond the three dominant tongues of the Caribbean and North America. Finally, as it did in Césaire's poetry, the image of the erupting volcano suggests endless possibilities for destruction, newness, and regeneration, all necessary to preserving the plasticity, motility, and relevance of their models of black identity.

Hughes's aesthetic practice in *Ask Your Mama*—the speaker's rapid shuttling around the planet tying together the Black Atlantic in a dizzying catalog of people and places around the world—mimicked his pursuit of pan-African entanglements in "real life." For him, the ethical and the aesthetic, the political and the artistic, were too deeply knotted together to separate. His published poetry should therefore be regarded as part of the same larger impulse as his restless traveling, his vast and carefully preserved body of correspondence with people around the world, and his tireless efforts to mentor younger writers from Africa and the diaspora. All of these were expressions or products of his ethos of pan-African entanglement, the ultimate aim of which was to generate a sense of community and fellow feeling among black people around the world.

I have been emphasizing the flexibility and adaptability of Hughes's model, woven equally out of past and present, perceived kinship and cultural difference. As the 1960s wore on, Hughes and his network of pan-African writers would be overshadowed in the public discourse to a large extent by the Black Arts and Black Power movements. Moreover, of course, after Hughes's death in early 1967 the network he had brought together into a loose literary confederation lost its hub. Nevertheless, as we saw in chapter 4, writers such as Richard Rive, Es'kia Mphahlele, and Peter Abrahams continued to explore and adapt the aesthetics of pan-African entanglement that Hughes had cultivated and to develop transnational literary and intellectual networks of their own.

Unfortunately, if *Ask Your Mama* was the crowning poetic expression of Hughes's aesthetic, it also reflected many of the blind spots in his vision that I have discussed elsewhere. Most glaringly, while the moods in *Ask Your Mama* frequently allude to African American women (mostly singers and entertainers but also historical and political figures such as Sojourner Truth and Mary McLeod Bethune), the only African or Caribbean figures they mention by name are men. The effect of this gendering is to once again relegate African and black West Indian women to keepers of the collective memory of the ancestral plane of entanglement. The crucial work of reanimating that memory and setting it into motion in the contemporary plane of cultural exchange was seemingly left to male writers and artists, at least on the Caribbean and African sides of the diasporic triangle.

In pointing out Hughes's blind spot toward the agency of black women in Africa and the Caribbean, I do not mean to sit in retrospective judgment but simply to point out some of the limits of his ethos of entanglement and its universalizing tendencies. Certainly, his failure to depict black women as purposeful agents in his own writing about Africa and the Caribbean and the imbalance of his correspondence toward male authors were not, I believe, born of animosity toward women and women writers in general. At least his collaborations with his contemporaries Zora Neale Hurston and Gwendolyn Bennett would suggest otherwise (though the play Hughes cowrote with Hurston, *Mule Bone,* did lead to an acrimonious fall out between the two, as recently narrated by Yuval Taylor),[67] as did his later vigorous support for younger African American women such as Maya Angelou, Gwendolyn Brooks, Lorraine Hansberry, and Alice Walker.

When it came to his travels, his correspondence, his translations, and other manifestations of his campaign of pan-African cultural exchange, however, Hughes mostly made contact with male writers, artists, and intellectuals—perhaps inevitably so, given the conservatism of the time and the strict gender segregation practiced in many of the countries where he traveled. The limitations that this imposed on his vision of black Atlantic intellectual community is clear from the overtly masculinist web of connections he sketched in *Ask Your Mama.* Yet, despite the limitations of his own particular pursuit of transnational entanglement, in the coda that concludes *Cultural Entanglements* I argue that the gendered blind spot in Hughes's model of black Atlantic literature was remediable and that his ethos and aesthetics of pan-African entanglement continued to prove vital and productive for younger writers long after his death. To make my case, I turn to the African American writer of Caribbean descent, Paule Marshall, to study her own vision of black Atlantic interconnection.

Coda
Paule Marshall and Langston Hughes

IN HER family history, her biography, and her writing, Paule Marshall is the perfect heir to Hughes's ethos and aesthetics of pan-African entanglement. Marshall was born in Brooklyn in 1929 to first-generation immigrants from Barbados (who call themselves "Bajans"). When she was nine years old, she went to visit her maternal grandmother, who still lived in Barbados; later, when she received a publisher's advance for her first novel, *Brown Girl, Brownstones* (1959), she took her newborn son to Barbados for several months while she revised the manuscript. Her second book, *Soul Clap Hands and Sing* (1961), was a collection of four novellas named for four different points in the African diaspora—"Barbados," "Brooklyn," "British Guiana," and "Brazil"—revealing already what she later called in her memoir her "tripartite self," a life "divided in three" between Brooklyn, the Caribbean, and "the colossus of ancestral Africa."[1] Later, while working on her second novel, Marshall again took up residence for a year in the Caribbean, this time in Grenada.

In her autobiographical memoir *Triangular Road,* Marshall recounted her childhood in the Bajan community of Brooklyn, her early development as a writer, and her early travels in the West Indies, but none of these stories appeared in her opening chapter. That honor went to a chapter about her friendship with and mentorship by Langston Hughes, entitled "Homage to Mr. Hughes." The aging poet had attended the book launch for *Brown Girl* in 1959 and wrote to congratulate Marshall when *Soul Clap Hands* was published two years later.[2] Hughes's correspondence with her reveals multiple attempts in the early 1960s to meet in New York, but their busy travel schedules seem to have prohibited it.[3] But then in 1965 Hughes invited Marshall and another young African American writer, William Kelley, to join him for a month-long cultural tour of Europe, sponsored by the US State Department.

Marshall was an outspoken activist in the civil rights movement and was interviewed by a State Department official who presented her with a considerably thick FBI file on her activities and writings. The fact that she was cleared nevertheless to join Hughes on the speaking tour made her suspect that she was being used by the US government as propaganda, to prove to European audiences America's commitment to the democratic principles of free speech and tolerance of political dissent. She concluded that her opportunity to go abroad and shed light on the racial situation in the USA outweighed whatever compromises the government sponsorship might entail: "Speaking out would be a way of making use of being used—if, indeed, such was the case."[4] Hughes might similarly have justified his decision to represent the US government as cultural ambassador in terms of the opportunity to disseminate his work and promote the writings of other black writers such as Marshall and Kelley. Yet when asked about the civil rights movement and segregation in the United States, Hughes stayed mostly quiet and let the younger writers field those questions.

Marshall's memoir briefly addressed the perception many African Americans had in the 1960s that, after the McCarthy hearings, Hughes had "disavowed his socialist and communist principles" to save his career, yet she also notes the "contradiction and irony, the illogic" of his situation, concluding that he had endured such injuries to his reputation only to be "once again embraced by black America as well as called upon by the government to serve as a cultural ambassador around the world."[5] For her own part, Marshall wrote that when she saw Hughes at the airport in New York, "I felt like bowing before his royal presence," and she called him "a loving taskmaster, mentor, teacher, griot, literary sponsor and treasured elder friend."[6]

Marshall extended the homage of her first chapter through the titles of subsequent chapters, which riff on the opening line of Hughes's most famous poem: "I've Known Rivers: The James River"; "I've Known Seas: The Caribbean Sea"; and "I've Known Oceans: The Atlantic." Like Hughes in so many of his works, then, Marshall used water as a symbol of the interconnected African diaspora. Moreover, just as Hughes conceived of his loyalties in terms of concentric circles, the organization of Marshall's memoir begins with the James River in Richmond, Virginia, where she lived for many years in the 1980s and 1990s and where the first African slaves were brought to American shores from the West Indies; it proceeds to the Caribbean, where she explored her roots and new routes; and then it culminates in Africa, where she attended a pan-African festival of the arts. Her narration of those travels highlighted the tangled threads and arteries connecting the various locations across the pan-African world.

To conclude this book, then, I will turn to the novel that Marshall published some sixteen years after Hughes's death: *Praisesong for the Widow*

(1983). I will build on Lisa McGill's argument that Marshall used African American and Caribbean cultures in her fiction to imagine "a recuperation of a black diasporic identity as a source of spiritual and political power for blacks," a project that developed in conversation with Marshall's black radical political activism.[7] I will argue more specifically that not only is *Praisesong* packed with direct allusions to Langston Hughes and other African American writers but it draws from the same lexicon and repertoire of pan-African entanglement that Hughes and his network of African and diasporic writers helped develop. The novel, for example, exhibits a similar method of "weaving" threads of similarity and difference and of past and present. It shows Marshall continuing Hughes's lifelong project of both exposing ties of kinship and continuity and cultivating cultural exchange. Furthermore, like Hughes, she regarded ordinary folk as keepers of African cultural tradition, to whom she turned in her efforts to reclaim "African culture for black diasporan peoples."[8] But her vision of pan-African interconnection arguably improved upon and corrected the limitations of Hughes's own vision: the peasants and rum shop owners Marshall depicted—especially her women characters—are not passive reservoirs of cultural knowledge but rather are active in the propagation and dissemination of African-derived folk practice.

Pan-African Entanglements in *Praisesong for the Widow*

The widow referred to in the title of *Praisesong for the Widow* is Avey Johnson. Her name is short for "Avatara," hinting from the outset that she is a kind of avatar of an African archetype. The plot takes the form of a quest for healing—what Joyce Pettis calls a "movement toward spiritual wholeness."[9] Avey, at first unconsciously, is seeking an antidote to her alienation from her roots, a "fractured psyche"[10] that the novel links to her marriage to an African American man who equated success with material comfort and assimilation to mainstream white society. In this regard the novel continues a theme in Marshall's work going back to her first novel, which she has described as "an attempt to articulate feelings I had long held about the acquisitive nature of the society and what I feel to be its devastating impact on human relationships. . . . Overemphasis on the material which is the national ethic often destroys the ability of people to feel and care for each other."[11] And so, as Simone Alexander puts it, the quest for material gain "precipitates [Avey's and Jay's] 'fall,' the neglecting of their spiritual side and their not adhering to or answering the call of their ancestors."[12]

Avey's attachment to the materialist world is dramatized right from the in medias res opening chapter, where we find her packing six enormous suitcases full of clothes and shoes for a Caribbean cruise with two friends, which she has suddenly decided to abandon. (By contrast, when she later leaves for the life-changing excursion to Carriacou from Grenada, she takes only a small bag with a single change of clothes.) The opening scene implicitly links Avey's sudden unease to the overpowering whiteness embodied by the cruise ship: named the *Bianca Pride*, it seems the embodiment of Euro-American postindustrial modernism, impressing the viewer with "All that dazzling white steel! . . . The precision and power of her lines! . . . Huge, sleek, imperial, a glacial presence in the warm waters of the Caribbean."[13] The ship's association with white power is confirmed by the fact that Avey's friends prefer to dine in the Versailles Room, a name that outraged Avey's daughter Marion when she mentioned it after a previous cruise: "*Do you know how many treaties were signed there, in that infamous Hall of Mirrors, divvying up India, the West Indies, the world?*"[14]

Marion is equally disturbed by the transformation of her father, Avey's husband, from a poor but hardworking "race man" to a financially successful accountant with disdain for other African Americans who fail to assimilate to white social norms. Avey recalls early in their marriage dancing barefoot to jazz music in their Brooklyn apartment: the hardwood floor would be "like a rich nurturing ground from which she had sprung and to which she could always return for sustenance."[15] The dancing barefoot motif is significant to my discussion in part because of Hughes's frequently declared sympathies for what he called "people without shoes" and in part because Avey experiences the same sensation at the end of the novel when she dances at the Big Drum ritual.[16] Her husband of those early days she called "Jay," and he loved listening to jazz and blues and quoting poetry by Hughes and Dunbar. When he came home from work he would play records by Coleman Hawkins, Lester Young, Duke Ellington, Ma Rainey, or Bill Broonzy, and "under their ministrations, the fatigue and strain of the long day spent doing the two jobs—his and his boss's—would ease from his face."[17]

This jazz-loving Jay of their Brooklyn years, whom Avey remembers with longing and affection, is gradually replaced by Jerome Johnson, who internalizes a judgmental and self-loathing attitude toward black people. Avey begins to spy a "stranger" in her husband, "who had slipped in when he wasn't looking and taken up residency behind his dark skin; someone who from the remarks he made viewed the world and his fellow man according to a harsh and joyless ethic." He says, "If it was left to me I'd close down every dancehall in Harlem and burn every drum! That's the only way these Negroes out here'll begin making any progress!"[18] In this speech Jerome Johnson sounds hauntingly like Dessalines in Hughes's play *Emperor of*

Haiti, disavowing his African heritage as embodied in the figure of the drums. Marshall might never have read or seen Hughes's rather obscure play, but if this echo does not indicate direct influence, it does show both authors tapping into a symbolic repertoire of pan-African memory, the shared web of associations around such imagery as the drum.

Marshall, in other words, used *Praisesong* to highlight the threads connecting contemporary African Americans to their African heritage and to the larger black diaspora. One such thread is expressed through the sexual connection that Avey feels to Jay but loses to Jerome. It is explicitly characterized as a channeling of ancient Yoruba gods: "Erzulie. . . . Yemoja. . . . Oya. . . . A pantheon of the most ancient deities who had made their temple the tunneled darkness of his wife's flesh."[19] Later, though, she remembers Jerome presenting his love "like a burden he wanted rid of. Like a leg-iron which slowed him in the course he had set for himself."[20] The trajectory of their conjugal life, then, mirrors the narrative of pan-African entanglement we have seen so often in *Cultural Entanglements,* beginning with an imagined African unity and proceeding through the "leg-iron" of slavery.

The transformation of Jay into Jerome perfectly embodies the existential alienation that, according to Marshall, results from assimilation to Western cultural practice. That transformation is closely entangled with another such symbol: his and Avey's move from Brooklyn to the predominantly white suburb of North White Plains. I am reminded of the speaker of Hughes's "Horn of Plenty" in *Ask Your Mama,* who sees his move to Long Island, where "I'M THE ONLY COLORED," as a sign that he has "GOT THERE! YES, I MADE IT!"[21] Jerome similarly sees his move to Westchester County as a triumph, the culmination of his bitterly hard-fought battle to establish himself as a self-employed accountant. Avey, however, remembers thinking "not so much of the new life awaiting them but of the early years back on Halsey Street, of the small rituals and private pleasures that had lasted through the birth of Sis. And in the face of Jay's marathon effort and her own crowded wearying days, such thoughts seemed a betrayal."[22] The novel ultimately shows us, though, that her real betrayal is moving away from the African American community, both literally and symbolically through Jerome's newfound contempt for the culture of ordinary black people. As Irele notes, a black person in the Americas "suffered a negation of his human being. . . . In order to be acceptable socially in the Western world, it was necessary for him to deny a part of himself."[23] Such certainly seems to be true for Avey's husband.

Jerome's transformation is inevitably paralleled by a change in Avey also, one she now rues and laments. The small rituals she once shared with Jay—reciting poetry, dancing to jazz records—had served "to join them to the vast unknown lineage that had made their being possible. And this link, these connections, heard in the music and in the praisesongs of a Sunday: '. . . *I bathed in the Euphrates when dawns were / young . . ,*' had both protected them and put them in possession of a kind of power."²⁴ Avey wishes that they had been able to leave Halsey Street in Brooklyn while still "preserving, safeguarding, treasuring those things that had come down to them over the generations, which had defined them in a particular way. The most vivid, the most valuable part of themselves!"²⁵ The quotation from "The Negro Speaks of Rivers" in the above passage effectively positions Hughes as the embodiment and the preserver of the "vast unknown lineage" that defined African Americans "in a particular way"—that is, in a way that preserves and valorizes African-derived cultures' particularities and differences from Western culture and establishes pan-African entanglement on an ancestral plane. Instead, Avey finds herself so alienated from herself and her own cultural roots at the novel's beginning that when she introduces herself to the rum shop owner Lebert Joseph in Grenada, she momentarily forgets her name: "When it did come to her and she said it aloud, it sounded strange, almost like someone else's name."²⁶

The plot of the novel, then, depicts Avey's quest to recover her name and her "nation"²⁷ and to purge herself of her internalized self-loathing. At the same time, it sketches the same pathway as the narrative of ancestral pan-African entanglement that Hughes, Césaire, and others had done: from African unity to slavery and then to liberation and self-reclamation. The latter phases of this quest are outlined in the titles of the four sections: part 1 is "Runagate," evoking a fugitive slave (and also Robert Hayden's poem "Runagate Runagate," which Marshall excerpts in the section's epigraph); part 2 is "Sleeper's Wake," which implies both a funeral and an awakening; part 3 is "Lavé Tête," literally meaning "cleansed head" but referring to a Vodou ceremony in which the mind is cleansed in preparation for contact with the spirit world; and the final section is entitled "Beg Pardon," which is the part of the Big Drum ceremony in which the ancestors are asked for forgiveness on behalf of the singer as well as those who, as Lebert Joseph puts it to Avey, "don' know your nation."²⁸ The islanders' repertoire of performed and performative memories of the collective diasporic experience includes not just ancestral Africa but also bondage in the Americas, as with the Bongo dance: "The song to it tells what happened to a Carriacou man and his wife during the slave time."²⁹ Once again Diana Taylor's concept of the repertoire as a mode of preserving and transmitting knowledge proves useful, as it helps us understand Lebert Joseph as a kind of Caribbean griot, whose embodied performance has the power not just to relate the past but to reanimate it and fill it with new meaning and resonance. In that way,

Marshall is able to weave the ancestral plane of pan-African entanglement into the contemporary plane, where it facilitates further connections across Africa and its diaspora.

For Avey, the Lavé Tête purging comes both literally and figuratively on the volcano-roiled channel between Grenada and Carriacou. In a fit of vomiting and diarrhea, she has a vision of being on a slave ship during the Middle Passage: "She was alone in the deckhouse. . . . Yet she had the impression as her mind flickered on briefly of other bodies lying crowded in with her in the hot, airless dark. A multitude it felt like lay packed around her in the filth and stench of themselves, just as she was. Their moans, rising and falling with each rise and plunge of the schooner, enlarged upon the one filling her head. Their suffering—the depth of it, the weight of it in the cramped space—made hers of no consequence."[30] On one level what is being purged from Avey's soul is the degradation and dehumanization that haunts her people's collective memory. On another level, though, this scene also shows Avey making an almost mystical connection to ancestors who might have crossed these very waters in captivity centuries before. This is part of the "spiritual return to Africa" that Marshall says is "absolutely necessary for the reintegration of what was lost in our collective historical past"[31] but also part of a project of establishing both ancestral kinship and contemporary connection across the modern diaspora.[32]

Crossing the Kick'em Jenny Channel, then, functions like a Lavé Tête ritual and leaves Avey receptive to connection with the ancestors and spirits but also with her contemporary "cousins" in the West Indies. First, though, she must find her way through a maze of cultural difference that she finds bewildering. When Avey disembarks from the cruise ship at St. George's, for example, she finds herself on the docks, overwhelmed by crowds of people boarding outbound ships. She later learns they are natives of Carriacou, one of the "outer islands" north of Grenada, going home for their annual excursion to take part in the Big Drum ritual. During the excursion they speak only their native patois, which a Grenadian taxi driver calls "just some African mix-up something."[33] It is this language, together with the closeness and curious intensity of the crowd, that Avey finds so unsettling: "The small island of space she had managed to secure around herself and the suitcases was shrinking by the minute. . . . She experienced that special panic of the traveler who finds himself sealed-off, stranded in a sea of incomprehensible sound."[34] The island and sea images, which will later come to symbolize the interconnectedness and entanglement of the African diaspora, at this point in Avey's character arc instead convey the paradox of her situation: she feels alone, almost shipwrecked, even in the midst of this "sea" of people she cannot understand.

On the one hand, then, the sounds of the locals speaking creole are initially unnerving to Avey because they use "unintelligible words" and her interactions with them were "one-way conversations."[35] On the other hand, though, the novel implies that the language seems to Avey not quite alien but uncanny, precisely because it also contains vestiges of the familiar. After all, a few days earlier it had been the sound of Martinicans speaking their own French Creole, the "peculiar cadence and lilt of the Patois," that triggered Avey's memories and dreams of South Carolina and her great-aunt: "There had been the same vivid, slightly atonal music underscoring the words. She had heard it and that night from out of nowhere her great-aunt had stood waiting in her sleep.... The vaguely familiar sound of the Patois might have resurrected Tatem and the old woman."[36]

Earlier we saw Hughes use vernacular black English and slang as rough stand-ins for creolized dialects elsewhere in the black Atlantic, as when he rendered the speech of Haitian peasants in *Emperor of Haiti* and in his translation of Roumain's *Masters of the Dew,* where he used rural African American dialects. In Marshall's novel, such connections run deeper: the creoles of Martinique and Carriacou, even as they confound Avey in her attempts to find a taxi, serve to cement the connections in her mind between these Caribbean islands and the coastal South Carolina village of her childhood, connections that extend as well to the black community in Brooklyn. Marshall has declared this her aim in writing *Praisesong*: while acknowledging that there were tensions and animosities between African Americans and Caribbean migrants in the New York of her childhood, she nevertheless stresses that "what my work certainly tries to do, is to touch upon what the similarities and commonalities are. One of the things that impelled me, for example, to write *Praisesong for the Widow,* was to deal with those linkages, those connections."[37]

As Avey's awakening plays out, it becomes increasingly clear that the cultural differences she had previously felt to be so unbridgeable were mostly material and superficial and that the ancestral pan-African entanglements had always been there—were in fact ubiquitous—no matter how she had previously tried to disavow them. As early as her arrival on the docks in Grenada, Avey is surprised that the locals respond to her black skin rather than to the clothes and luggage that to her mind so clearly mark her as an outsider: "None of them seemed aware of the fact that she was a stranger, a visitor, a tourist, although this should have been obvious from the way she was dressed and the set of matching luggage at her side. But from the way they were acting she could have been simply one of them there on the wharf."[38] The suitcases and clothes signal her status as American, modern, and different; the luggage signifies the materialistic world of North

White Plains, which she arrays around herself like a barricade. Yet with the Carriacou islanders embarking on their excursion, "their eyes immediately stripped her of everything she had on and dressed her in one of the homemade cotton prints the women were wearing."[39]

From that moment on, Avey's experiences in Grenada and Carriacou reveal to her countless small vernacular entanglements between African American, Caribbean, and African cultures. This begins with the taxi driver she finally does find, who is delighted that she knows the colloquial expression that black people are like crabs in a barrel: "So you has it among the black people in America too!"[40] The discovery of relation, in Glissant's sense, intensifies when Avey stumbles into Lebert Joseph's rum shop after a long walk in the hot sun. The man himself emblemizes kinship and relation: "Near everybody in Ti Morne is family to me. They all got to call me father or uncle or grandfather, granduncle or great-grandfather or cousin or something."[41] Avey is surprised that the man who had been in a hurry to get her out of the shop just a moment before was now "telling her his family history, going on like some Old Testament prophet chronicling the lineage of his tribe."[42] This passage positions Joseph as a kind of African griot, keeper of ancient traditions. That impression is reinforced and generalized to the entire African continent by the "lines etched over his face like the scarification marks of a thousand tribes."[43]

Lebert Joseph is crucial to the narrative of Avey's recuperation of her ancestral legacy. Accordingly, Pettis reads Joseph along with Avey's great-aunt Cuney as ancestor figures: "mythical, timeless, sage, androgynous, and futuristic visionaries."[44] Furthermore, both Pettis and Dorothy Denniston treat him as a male West Indian counterpart to Cuney, and they both (following Eugenia Collier) see Joseph as representing Legba, the loa of Vodou who acts as intermediary between the human and spirit worlds.[45] It is Joseph who unwittingly diagnoses the likely cause of Avey's malaise: the "Old Parents. . . . The Long-time People. Each year this time they does look for us to come and give them their remembrance. . . . You best remember them! . . . If not they'll get vex and cause you nothing but trouble."[46] It is Joseph, likewise, who introduces Avey to the concept of the "nation dance" and attempts to help her find her own nation: he wants to know if she is "Arada . . . Cromanti . . . Yarraba . . . Moko." The names "made her head ache all the more. She thought she heard in them the faint rattle of the necklace of cowrie shells and amber Marion always wore. Africa? Did they have something to do with Africa?"[47] When Lebert Joseph asks if she knows the Juba, she acknowledges a faint memory of "hearing or reading about it somewhere," and he responds with immense relief: "It was as if he meant more than just the dance. He might have been also referring to the place that bore the name: Juba, the legendary city at the foot of the White Nile.... He remembered it from memories that had come down to him in the blood: as Juba, the once-proud, imperial seat at the heart of the equatoria."[48]

Avey initially dismisses the old man as senile, especially when he begins to demonstrate the various nation dances. But she soon experiences other uncanny flashes of ancestral pan-African entanglement. Throughout the novel she experiences flashbacks to her childhood visits to South Carolina, especially to the quasi-religious Ring Shouts that her aunt Cuney took her to in a wood "filled with every kind of ha'nt there was, according to the children she played with in Tatem."[49] It consists of "the handful of elderly men and women still left, and who still held to the old ways, [who] could be seen slowly circling the room in a loose ring"; they do "a curious gliding shuffle which did not permit the soles of the heavy work shoes they had on to ever once lift from the floor."[50] The climax to Avey's journey to reconnection comes during the dance following the Big Drum performance, when she realizes in effect that her own "nation dance" is the Ring Shout shuffle; the locals recognize in her dance what they call the "Carriacou Tramp, the shuffle designed to stay the course of history."[51]

The Big Drum ceremony illuminates another of Avey's memories of Tatem: her aunt Cuney's tale about the place called the Landing, once known as Ibo Landing. According to the story, the first African slaves to arrive on the island had a vision of the future of slavery, war, emancipation, and redoubled oppression; their response was to turn and walk on river and ocean back across the Atlantic to Africa, singing as they walked. As Cuney's grandmother recalled it, "Chains didn't stop those Ibos none. Neither iron.... Those Ibos! Just upped and walked on away not two minutes after getting here!"[52] This tale echoes throughout *Praisesong* and poses a powerful alternative to the narratives of armed resistance that Hughes, Césaire, and Abrahams, among many others, used so extensively. Marshall, borrowing from the miraculous and magical possibilities in folk narratives, furnishes us with a less violent and less masculinist narrative of resistance through refusal—in the case of the story of Ibo Landing, a refusal to abide by the laws of slavery, or even the laws of physics.

Avey's entire struggle to reclaim her African heritage is written in microcosm through her struggle with the obligation she feels her aunt Cuney visited upon her: "In instilling the story of the Ibos in her child's mind, the old woman had entrusted her with a mission she couldn't even name yet had felt duty-bound to fulfill. It had taken her years to rid herself of the notion."[53] Even as a child, she fought against the compulsion to claim the collective past. She remembers one visit as an obstinate teenager, when she refused to accompany her aunt to the Landing: "In seconds a hand with the feel of a manacle had closed around her wrist."[54] Waking up from a dream on the cruise ship, Avey feels "even now her left wrist retained something of the pressure of the old woman's iron grip."[55] The words "manacle" and "iron," of course, have inextricable associations with slavery. What Avey is resisting, these figures imply, is the cultural memory of slavery, with all its agony and humiliation, but which the ancestors (and Lebert Joseph) are telling her she must acknowledge and commemorate.

Despite her childhood resistance to her aunt's "mission," Avey as an adult has not always shunned Cuney's rituals of remembrance. Early in her marriage to Jay she tells him the story of the Ibos, and he declares, "I'm with your aunt Cuney and the old woman [Cuney's grandmother] you were named for. I believe it, Avey. Every word."[56] The trip to the Landing becomes an annual excursion for them, akin to the excursion of the out-islanders from Grenada. This is one of the rituals that Avey and Jerome later let disappear from their life in Westchester County; the resolution of the novel's central conflict, then, comes when she decides to retire to Tatem. There she will demand that her grandchildren be sent to her every summer so she can lead them to the Landing and tell them the story of the Ibo who refused to be slaves, "as had been ordained."[57] Thus Avey determines to become, like Lebert Joseph, a griot figure handing down ancestral knowledge and values to future generations.

What is it about the Big Drum that triggers such a life-changing epiphany for Avey? First of all, the novel emphasizes both the expansiveness and the adaptability of the ritual. Seeing Lebert Joseph dance the Beg Pardon, Avey Johnson understands that he is asking the ancestors for benevolent intercession: "not only for themselves and for the friends and neighbors present in the yard, but for all their far-flung kin as well—the sons and daughters, grands and great-grands in Trinidad, Toronto, New York, London. . . . She remembers him back in Grenada explaining to her that he asked for pardon '*for tout moun.*' And his little truncated arms had opened in a gesture wide enough to take in the world."[58] This image perfectly encapsulates the ethos and aesthetics of pan-African entanglement that Marshall inherited from Hughes: encompassing much of the globe but embedded in African cultural practice. Avey recognizes that in the nation dances, "it was the essence of something rather than the thing itself she was witnessing. . . . All that was left were a few names of what they called nations which they could no longer even pronounce properly, the fragments of a dozen or so songs, the shadowy forms of long-ago dances and rum kegs for drums. . . . And they clung to them with a tenacity she suddenly loved in them and longed for in herself."[59] What brings about this passionate response in Avey is a dance; this confirms Marshall's professed view of dance "as ritual celebration, as renewal, as perhaps the most profound expression of the confraternity" of people of African descent.⁶⁰

Moreover, despite the above implication that it taps into an essence of Africa, the Big Drum has the sort of syncretic and organic flexibility to accommodate modernity that we have seen in Negritude poetry, in the late works of Langston Hughes, and in the South African writers. Far from an atavistic throwback or an attempt to restore ancient African practices to some previously pure state and preserve them behind glass, the ritual shows the islanders to be resourceful and open to cross-pollination as they incorporate elements of the modern world into their dance: "One muscular fellow in a red T-shirt had appeared carrying the heavy iron hub of a car wheel in the crook of his arm. And this he was striking with a thin metal rod that became a blur in his hand each time the tempo of the music increased."⁶¹ The image of the drummer appropriating a hubcap—the detritus of an automobile, a characteristic fixture of twentieth-century modernity—suggests that the sense of kinship and historical continuity generated by the ritual does not rely on some fixed, if deeply repressed, cultural or racial essence, but rather is constantly evolving and capable of absorbing the technologies associated with Western scientific rationalism into its own African-derived collective consciousness.

For Avey Johnson, the capacity of the repertoire of performances such as the Big Drum ceremony to reanimate the past goes further. With an almost mystical clarity it illuminates for her the myriad connections between the triangle of the black United States, the black Caribbean, and Africa. Her understanding of why she finds the folkways of the Carriacou migrants so uncannily familiar dawns at the beginning of the excursion, where the docks bustling with out-islanders in their Sunday best remind her (on her second encounter, now knowing where the people are going) of both Africa and the Harlem of her childhood: "The milling, moving tide of bodies, the colors and sounds, the pageantry of the umbrellas were like frames from a home movie she remembered [her daughter] Marion had made her last trip to Ghana.... Moreover, the scene in front of her also vaguely called to mind something from her own life... the annual boat ride up the Hudson River to Bear Mountain!"⁶² Once she arrives on the island of Carriacou and meets Lebert Joseph's daughter, Rosalie Parvay, her mind goes "swinging like a pendulum back in time—as it had been doing ever since she awakened—it was the ruined field of sea-island cotton she and her great-aunt used to cross on the way to the Landing."⁶³ When she arrives at the site of the Big Drum, "she felt to be dwelling in any number of places at once and in a score of different time frames."⁶⁴ One experiences a similar effect of being unmoored in time from reading Hughes's *Ask Your Mama*. The diasporic consciousness that both texts attempt to imagine into existence is one that encompasses and traverses not just space but also time—that is, she comes to perceive pan-African entanglements at different scales and on different temporal planes. And so when Parvay's maid Milda joins the dance, her stride "was that, Avey Johnson thought, of her great-aunt striking out across the fields toward the Landing, and of the taxi driver two days ago.... A stride designed to cover an entire continent in a day"[65]—just as Avey's own newly raised consciousness of the interconnected black diaspora allows her thoughts and memories to jump across continents and decades.

Marshall's themes and narrative methods most closely resemble Langston Hughes's aesthetics of pan-African entanglement when she explicitly introduces *threads* and *weaving* into the novel as metaphors for diasporic connection. She remembers the community boat rides up the Hudson as a child: "She would feel what seemed to be hundreds of slender threads streaming out from her navel and from the place where her heart was to enter those around her. And the threads went out not only to people she recognized from the neighborhood but to those she didn't know as well, such as the roomers just up from the South and the small group of West Indians whose odd accent called to mind Gullah talk."[66] Here we see one of Hughes's favorite techniques at work, as the stream of Avey's consciousness moves seamlessly from Harlem to the West Indies to coastal South Carolina. The narrator continues: although the threads "were thin to the point of invisibility, they felt as strong entering her as the *lifelines of woven hemp* that trailed out into the water at Coney Island.... for those moments, she became part of, indeed the center of, a huge wide confraternity."[67] Marshall's phrasing here seems as apt a description as any of the vision of pan-African entanglement and exchange that earlier motivated so much work by Hughes and his network of Caribbean and African writers.

By the end of the Big Drum and the nation dances, Avey has recovered the ability to detect such threads of kinship, this time those connecting her to the people of Carriacou: Lebert Joseph scraping his thumb across a drum skin produced a note that "sounded like the distillation of a thousand sorrow songs"[68] and stirred up "feelings and a host of subliminal memories that over the years had proven more durable and trustworthy than the history with its trauma and pain out of which they had come. After centuries of forgetfulness and even denial, they refused to go away. The note was a lamentation that could hardly have come from the rum keg of a drum. Its source had to be the heart, the bruised still-bleeding innermost chamber of the collective heart."[69] Performative traditions such as Big Drum prevent narratives of pan-African entanglement from being frozen in the archive. It brings them into the living repertoire, making them feel like they come from "the bruised still-bleeding innermost chamber of the collective heart." And this process is continual, rather than being a simple matter of a one-off healing ritual. As Mbembe explains, "No Black identity exists in the form of a book of Revelation. There exists instead an identity in the process of becoming, nourished by the ethnic, geographic, and linguistic differences among Blacks."[70]

Weaving Women into the Black Atlantic Network

Hughes, as we have seen, cultivated the nourishing flows of cultural exchange avidly and purposively through, among other vehicles, overseas arts and literary festivals and conferences of black writers. Marshall followed his lead in this respect also. She concluded *Triangular Road* with an account of her participation at the Second World Festival of Black and African Arts, or FESTAC '77, held in Lagos in 1977 (Hughes had been a central figure in the first FESTAC in Dakar in 1966). She also mentions FESTAC in an interview with Maryse Condé: "This was the first time I had ever been to Africa, and, also was the first time I had ever encountered Black writers from Africa and the Black diaspora."[71] Marshall describes this festival as "nearly four weeks . . . of meeting, conversing and interacting with fellow artists in a spirit of confraternity."[72]

Significantly, this description echoes the language used by the narrator of *Praisesong for the Widow* to describe the feeling Avey gets from the novel's various excursion ceremonies: "She became part of, indeed the center of, a huge wide confraternity."[73] Insofar as the etymology of the word "confraternity" connotes a specifically male kinship, it seems fitting to describe the sort of community that developed in male-dominated spaces and discourses like those cultivated at the FESTACs. But the term feels inadequate to describe the more feminine and mystical sense of interconnection that Marshall shows us in *Praisesong*. Though it is the male figure of Lebert Joseph who convinces Avey to undertake the excursion, his performance of his nation dance seems to strip away his male identity and reveal a feminine essence: "Out of his stooped and winnowed body had come the illusion of height, *femininity* and power."[74] Moreover, once Joseph has helped Avey board their ship for Carriacou, he hands her over to the care of a community of women, who "took charge" and, when she grows seasick, "held her. Hedging her around with their bodies . . . they tried cushioning her as much as possible from the repeated shocks of the turbulence."[75] On arrival at the outer island, he again leaves her in the hands of capable women, in this case his daughter and her maid, who serve as translators and tour guides for her benefit throughout the Big Drum.

The importance of this community of women confirms something that Marshall emphasizes about her fiction in her 1973 essay "Shaping the World of My Art." Tasked with writing about "the important early influences which shape my work," here she stresses not the influence of Langston Hughes or other Harlem Renaissance writers but rather that of her mother and her circle of West Indian women friends who would gather at their kitchen table after work to tell stories.[76] These "rap sessions" were "a kind of magic rite, a form of juju, for it was their way to exorcise the day's humiliations and restore them to themselves."[77] She admires the "poet's skill with words" exhibited by the women and the "seemingly effortless way they had mastered the form of storytelling. They ... were carrying on a tradition as ancient as Africa, [a] centuries old oral mode by which the culture and history, the wisdom of the race had been transmitted."[78] Here again, the ancestral plane of pan-African entanglement is brought into line with the contemporary black Atlantic through a repertoire of performative devices derived from Africa.

It is significant that Marshall, in her essay and her fictional works alike, positions women not only as keepers of the ancestral pan-African repertoire but also as active agents in its weaving into the modern world. We have seen the male poets within Langston Hughes's orbit, such as Roumain and Senghor, deploy black women as symbols of the "motherland" of Africa and its ancient cultural traditions, while little acknowledging women's active roles in preserving, recrafting, and renewing those traditions in the authors' own time. Likewise, although Hughes himself depicted black Caribbean and American women as repositories of African folk wisdom, when it came to depicting a modern, decolonizing Africa in the late poem *Ask Your Mama*, he almost exclusively named male writers and politicians, who likewise constituted most of his intellectual network in Africa and the Caribbean.

It seems to me, then, that Paule Marshall's work, even more than that of Peter Abrahams and Es'kia Mphahlele, which I discussed in chapter 4, makes her the proper heir to Langston Hughes's ethos and aesthetics of black entanglement. Her work, like Abrahams's, shows the flexibility made possible when one defines one's identity in transnational "black Atlantic" terms, as well as the possibility of putting down "roots" and finding similarity and solidarity in new places. Unlike Abrahams, though, Marshall did not retreat late in life into resignation and racial separatism but rather adopted Hughes's vision of black identity as a series of concentric circles of loyalty and relation, expanding outward to include the human race. Arguably, too, her model of the black Atlantic is more inclusive and successful than her mentor's, as it more fully recognizes the role of women in preserving, transmitting, and exchanging knowledge and values across the great pan-African skein of cultural entanglement.

Notes

Abbreviations

AAKR   Alfred A. Knopf, Inc. Records, Harry Ransom Center, University of Texas at Austin
CMC   Claude McKay Collection, Beinecke Rare Book and Manuscript Library, Yale University, JWJ MSS 27
JWJ   James Weldon Johnson and Grace Nail Johnson Papers, Beinecke Library, Yale University, JWJ MSS 49
LGDP   Léon-Gontran Damas Papers, Schomburg Center for Research in Black Culture, New York Public Library, MG 302
LHC   Langston Hughes Collection, Schomburg Center for Research in Black Culture, New York Public Library, Sc MG 129
LHP   Langston Hughes Papers, Beinecke Rare Book and Manuscript Library, Yale University, JWJ MSS 26
TCR   Transcription Centre Records, Harry Ransom Center, University of Texas at Austin

Introduction

1. Throughout this book I observe the time-honored practice instituted by George Shepperson in 1962 of reserving "Pan-Africanism" with a capital *P* to refer to the political movement associated with W. E. B. Du Bois, George Padmore, and Kwame Nkrumah. Lowercase "pan-Africanism," then, refers not to "a clearly recognizable movement, with a single nucleus such as the nonagenarian DuBois. . . . It is rather a group of movements, many very ephemeral. The cultural element often predominates" (Shepperson, "Pan-Africanism and 'Pan-Africanism,'" 346).

2. I discuss the general "transnational turn" in literary and cultural studies below. Among noteworthy examples specific to Langston Hughes studies: Thomas Hale speaks of a "literary triangle trade between Afro-American, Afro-Caribbean, and African writers" beginning in the 1920s ("From Afro-America to Afro-France," 1089); Brent Hayes Edwards has attempted to recuperate Hughes's radical work from the Spanish Civil War in the 1930s ("Langston Hughes and the Futures of Diaspora"); Daniel Wong-gu Kim has posited an "African (Re-)turn" in Hughes's intellectual work of his last two decades ("We, Too, Rise with You"); James de Jongh

discusses appropriations of the Harlem Renaissance figures' works by African and Caribbean writers (*Vicious Modernism*); Richard Jackson discusses the influence of Hughes and other black American writers on Latin American literature (*Black Writers and Latin America*); Vera Kutzinski discusses Hughes's translations of works by Spanish-speaking writers, and vice versa (*The Worlds of Langston Hughes*); and Ryan Kernan's doctoral dissertation likewise considers issues of translation in Hughes's black internationalism ("Lost and Found in Black Translation").

3. That Hughes was both aware and proud of the web of influence that he had helped create becomes clear from an essay he wrote less than a year before his death: "Léopold Sédar Senghor of Senegal and Aimé Césaire of Martinique, the great poets of *négritude*, while still students at the Sorbonne, had read the Harlem poets and felt a bond between themselves and us. In faraway South Africa, Peter Abrahams, who became one of Africa's most distinguished authors, wrote in his autobiography, *Tell Freedom*, how, as a teenager . . . he discovered the Harlem poets of the twenties" (Hughes, "The Twenties," 17).

4. James de Jongh describes Africa, "the unremembered place of origin," as one of three places in the "legacy language of place" that "cohere and give order to Langston Hughes's literary vocabulary" throughout his career. The other two places in this triangular self-identification were "the unrealized yet perfectible social space of America, and the unprecedented yet perfectible enclave of black Harlem" (de Jongh, "The Poet Speaks of Places," 66).

5. The date of Hughes's birth was long accepted as 1 February 1902, but a researcher in Kansas recently came across a reference in the African American weekly the *Topeka Plaindealer* to "Little Langston Hughes" from December 1901. The most plausible explanation is that Hughes's mother delayed his school enrollment to give him an advantage, and the later birth date she put down in school records was the date that stuck. See Schuessler, "Langston Hughes Just Got a Year Older."

6. See Graham, introduction to Graham and Walters, *Langston Hughes and the South African* Drum *Generation*, 11.

7. In November 1960, Hughes seized his first opportunity to visit Africa since 1924, when his old friend Benjamin Nnamdi Azikiwe invited Hughes to his inauguration as governor-general of Nigeria (letter from Nnamdi Azikiwe to Langston Hughes, 26 October 1960, LHP, Box 9, Folder 221). Over the next six years, Hughes visited Africa four more times for various conferences and lectures and would meet a virtual who's who of African writers of the day.

8. Robolin, *Grounds of Engagement*, 144.

9. Like the jazz tropes that Chinitz discusses, these figures drawn from an imagined past in Africa and slavery helped "to formulate a synthesis between the poles of sameness and radical difference" (Chinitz, "Rejuvenation through Joy," 67).

10. Hughes is therefore a quintessential example of the "cross-cultural engagements" that later happened between South Africans and black Americans in the 1980s, according to Robolin: "Themselves the result of earlier exchanges or connections, [they] represent a new set, which prefigure future engagements, as well—a

new batch of texts that would explicitly meditate on South African and U.S. relationships" (Robolin, *Grounds of Engagement*, 164).

11. Nuttall, *Entanglement*, 1.

12. Ibid., 20.

13. Halbwachs, *On Collective Memory*, 172. According to Halbwachs, "It is language, and the whole system of social conventions attached to it, that allows us at every moment to reconstruct our past" (173). Halbwachs discusses frameworks of collective memory at the scales of family, church, or a given society. A similarly materialist conception of group memory, Ron Eyerman's "cultural trauma," focuses on the simultaneously national and racial scale of African American identity (Eyerman, *Cultural Trauma*). My thinking has also been influenced by Marianne Hirsch and her term "postmemory," which she uses to describe the experience of the children, like herself, of Holocaust survivors. It describes "experiences they 'remember' only by means of the stories, images, and behaviors among which they grew up. But these experiences were transmitted to them so deeply and affectively as to *seem* to constitute memories in their own right" (Hirsch, *The Generation of Postmemory*, 5). Hirsch's concept is valuable for understanding Marshall, Hughes, and other writers who evoked a collective diasporic consciousness: "postmemory" provides a nonmystical explanation for how narratives of a diasporic past can be transmitted intergenerationally.

14. Bulson, *Little Magazine, World Form*, 34.

15. For an illuminating reading of Hughes's work, from his openly socialist agitprop verse and theater to his Simple stories, see Michael Denning's *Cultural Front*, especially chapter 5. In brief, Denning reads Hughes in relation to the "structure of feeling" he calls the Popular Front (26).

16. In chapter 1 I discuss Edwards's notion of "vagabond internationalism," which has shaped and informed my own conception of vagabond entanglements (Edwards, *The Practice of Diaspora*, 187).

17. Hughes, "Always the Same," in *The Collected Poems*, 165–66.

18. Hughes, "Danse Africaine," in *The Collected Poems*, 28.

19. Hughes, "Nude Young Dancer," in *The Collected Poems*, 61.

20. Chinitz, "Rejuvenation through Joy," 60–61.

21. Hughes would surely have been open to cultivating entanglements with black Brazilians and other South Americans as well, but so far as I have been able to determine, he had few such opportunities.

22. Fisher, *Habitations of the Veil*, 5, 1.

23. Mbembe, *Critique of Black Reason*, 85.

24. Hale, "From Afro-America to Afro-France," 1089.

25. Mary Louise Pratt uses the term "contact zones" to describe "social spaces where cultures meet, clash, and grapple with each other, often in contexts of highly asymmetrical relations of power, such as colonialism, slavery, or their aftermaths as they are lived out in many parts of the world today" (Pratt, "Arts of the Contact Zone," 34).

26. Appiah, *Ethics of Identity*, 271.

27. Appiah, *Cosmopolitanism*, 111.

28. Appiah, "Cosmopolitan Patriots," 91. Bruce Robbins similarly insists that the new cosmopolitanism is not necessarily or intrinsically opposed to nationalism (Robbins, *Perpetual War*, 17).

29. Hughes confirmed my sense of the flexibility of his allegiances in a panel discussion on the question "What is African literature?" at the Conference for African Writers of English Expression in Kampala, Uganda, in 1962: "There are, of course, even larger categories than African literature or American literature—there's English literature in general—. . . if you're writing English it would come under the big heading of English literature. And then you would come down to your national heading, and I myself see no harm in nationalistic identifications, it seems to me in the first place . . . it helps librarians to catalogue your books! And it helps yourself to be, sort of, orientated within yourself" (Mbari Writers Conference Records, TCR, Folder 1.3). Hughes makes the case for this flexibility of literary identity in both practical terms (getting one's books into libraries) and psychological identity terms (being "orientated within yourself").

30. Mbembe, *Critique of Black Reason*, 34.

31. Beal, *Networks of Modernism*, 16.

32. Bulson, *Little Magazine, World Form*, 34.

33. Paul Jay argues that this transnational turn "began in earnest when the study of minority, multicultural, and postcolonial literatures began to intersect with work done under the auspices of the emerging study of globalization" (Jay, *Global Matters*, 2). My view is that it merely constitutes a long-overdue recognition that literary traditions, genres, and artistic sensibilities have always promiscuously crossed borders, mixed, and produced hybrids, creoles, and mongrels that have been under accounted for in nationalist models of literary study. As Jahan Ramazani puts it, "Under modernity, even a 'national poet' turns out, on closer inspection, to be also a transnational poet," and in the twentieth century, "even localist poems evince the contracted space and time of transnational flows and imaginaries" (Ramazani, *A Transnational Poetics*, 14, 15).

34. Dimock, *Through Other Continents*, 55.

35. Ibid., 78. Ramazani uses a metaphor from genetics in place of Dimock's fractal geometry, but they come to similar conclusions: "Because of the interconnecting cultural traces wound into the DNA of poetic forms and poetic language, poetry's cross-national molecular structure betrays the national imaginary on behalf of which it is sometimes made to speak" (Ramazani, *A Transnational Poetics*, 13). And Dimock's discussion of a "tangle of relations" evokes Glissant's concept of "the Poetics of Relation, in which each and every identity is extended through a relationship with the Other" (Glissant, *Poetics of Relation*, 11).

36. Seyhan, *Writing outside the Nation*, 15.

37. Hall, "Negotiating Caribbean Identities," 284.

38. Davis, "Rearticulations, Reconnections and Refigurations," 276.

39. As Hall emphasizes, the "African diasporas of the New World have been in one way or another incapable of finding a place in modern history without the symbolic return to Africa" (Hall, "Negotiating Caribbean Identities," 286). And in writing about that return, as Mbembe says, "Africa was a transformative force, almost mytho-poetic" (Mbembe, *Critique of Black Reason*, 26).

40. Ron Eyerman makes a similar argument when he posits slavery as the "primal scene" that has the potential to "unite all 'African Americans' in the United States" (Eyerman, *Cultural Trauma*, 1). Like the narrative of a return to Africa, the collectively conjured memory of a traumatic past makes that past usable and potentially productive. I also see similarities here to what Ifeoma Nwankwo calls "black cosmopolitanism," which is "born of the interstices and intersections between two mutually constitutive cosmopolitanisms—a hegemonic cosmopolitanism, exemplified by the material and psychological violence of imperialism and slavery . . . and a cosmopolitanism that is rooted in a common knowledge and memory of that violence" (Nwankwo, *Black Cosmopolitanism*, 13). Mbembe discusses the latter as part of the "*Black consciousness of Blackness*," which he sees as part of the same constellation of "Black reason" as the racist ideologies that made its evolution necessary. See his discussion of the "second narrative" of Black reason that seeks to "create community" and "exorcise the demon of the first [racist] narrative" (Mbembe, *Critique of Black Reason*, 29–30).

41. Mbembe, *Critique of Black Reason*, 18.

42. This corroborates Clare Corbould's argument that in the 1920s and 1930s, the "pursuit of the study of black history became one of the central planks of black public life. Africa's status as the cradle of civilization served as the basis for black claims to a rightful place as citizens in the American polity. . . . 'Negroes' thus began to imagine themselves much more self-consciously as members of a modern black diaspora" (Corbould, *Becoming African Americans*, 13).

43. Gilroy, *The Black Atlantic*, 36.

44. Ibid., 29.

45. Ibid., 15.

46. Paul Jay concurs, seeing the black Atlantic as "a space between national borders where identity and culture evolve in syncretic patterns traceable in literature and other forms of cultural expression. . . . Technologies of travel and communication, crude as they were compared to our own time, converged with the three-way flow of people, knowledge, and commodities to produce early economic forms of globalization that had a profound effect on the production and transformation of personal and cultural identities" (Jay, *Global Matters*, 85). Annalisa Oboe and Anna Scacchi, in their introduction to *Recharting the Black Atlantic*, similarly call for a "circumatlantic perspective" that helps us represent and account for "an area of shared and discrepant meanings, neighboring maps, and tangential histories—a fluid domain that is often a palimpsest of places and times, of different seas that are separate and yet flow into each other" (Oboe and Scacchi, introduction to *Recharting the Black Atlantic*, 2). In his more recent pronouncements about

the black Atlantic as a unit of analysis, Gilroy himself argues for its continuing significance well beyond his original concerns: "I am convinced that the archives of the black Atlantic can contribute significantly to those tasks that are not undertaken on behalf of racism's victims alone" (Gilroy, "The Black Atlantic and the Re-enchantment of Humanism," 22).

47. Edwards, "Langston Hughes and the Futures of Diaspora," 691–92.

48. McKay, *Banjo*, 45.

49. Edwards, *The Practice of Diaspora*, 5.

50. McKay, *Banjo*, 45.

51. Such a study might focus especially on Wright's 1954 memoir *Black Power*, about a journey to the Nkrumah-led Gold Coast; his association with the journal *Présence africaine*; and his extended correspondence with Peter Abrahams and many other African and Caribbean intellectuals, much of which survives intact in Wright's papers at Yale's Beinecke Library.

52. In his chapter "On National Culture," Fanon writes, "The nation is not only a precondition for culture.... It is a necessity.... [It] is the nation that will provide culture with the conditions and framework for expression. The nation satisfies all those indispensable requirements for culture which alone can give it credibility, validity, dynamism, and creativity" (Fanon, *Wretched of the Earth*, 177). Hughes, to the contrary, spent his career demonstrating that culture was a syncretic, ever-proliferating product of a process of cultural exchange and took a pragmatic view of national identifications.

53. As Nwankwo points out, "Positing national identity and cosmopolitan subjectivity as polar opposites presumes that national identity is available to all individuals" (Nwankwo, *Black Cosmopolitanism*, 12). The insistence on the totalizing necessity of national culture also poorly accounts for the situation of many black writers participating in the construction of postcolonial national identities, trying to establish something independent of the metropolis, with all its colonial baggage and its competitive ethos, even as they inevitably borrowed from the traditions of the former colonizers and created hybrids of European, African, and American.

54. Casanova, *World Republic of Letters*, 17. Jessica Berman critiques Casanova's model on the grounds that it "can serve as a vehicle for the homogenization of literature . . . rather than a realm in which various world texts and scenes of reading come in contact with each other" (Berman, "Imagining World Literatures," 61). I would argue that such homogenization is a product of the larger modernist literary project itself rather than of Casanova's descriptive account of that project. Hughes and his associates, indeed, reacted against this homogenizing model by writing works that defiantly established a different, putatively African-derived aesthetic, by developing their own global networks of influence and readership, and by emphasizing cooperation over competition.

55. *Présence africaine* 64 (1967): 33–58.

56. In Hughes's 15 December 1951, column for the *Chicago Defender*, for example, he wrote: "When you buy the books of Negro authors, you help build up the literary culture of the race, you help publishers realize that there is an ever growing

market for Negro writing—and thereby you encourage them to publish more such books. Also, by aiding in disseminating Negro literature, you help build up race pride and race knowledge" (Hughes, "Christmas Comes but Once a Year," 10).

57. Mbembe, *Critique of Black Reason*, 54. As Mark Sanders argues about apartheid, it was at its core a disavowal of "foldedness with the other" (Sanders, *Complicities*, 4). An ethos of entanglement, then, is analogous to Sanders's concept of "responsibility-in-complicity," which affirms human interfoldedness.

58. Moreover, this ethos urges those who adopt it to foster new interconnections and exchanges, to bridge differences while also respecting and preserving them, and to make the overall skein of transnational culture productive and invigorating rather than constricting. Appiah speaks of a "cosmopolitan project," which he distills to the slogan "universality plus difference" (Appiah, *Cosmopolitanism*, 18, 151). That is to say, cosmopolitanism asserts the universal humanity of all peoples and their cultures while also recognizing "that human beings are different and that we can learn from each other's differences" (4). Appiah's formulation is useful to understanding the particular ethos of pan-African entanglement shared by Hughes and many of the writers I will be considering.

59. Paul Jay, for instance, points to a "shift in our attention from sameness to difference" and the "breakdown of a late nineteenth-century Arnoldian model of literary study" in favor of deconstructive theories of difference and critical attention to previously neglected groups (Jay, *Global Matters*, 17). David Palumbo-Liu similarly observes a tension between a "sameness requirement" in such thinkers as Aristotle and Adam Smith and "literature's privileging of difference" (Palumbo-Liu, *The Deliverance of Others*, 6, 10).

60. Hughes, *I Wonder as I Wander*, 2.
61. Ibid., 114.
62. Ibid., 400; emphasis in original.
63. Hughes, "I, Too," in *The Collected Poems*, 46.
64. Hughes, "Freedom's Plow," in *The Collected Poems*, 263–68, 267.
65. Hughes, "Prelude to Our Age," in *The Collected Poems*, 384.
66. Ibid., 379.
67. Eyerman, *Cultural Trauma*, 91.
68. Hughes, "Prelude to Our Age," in *The Collected Poems*, 380.
69. Ibid., 381.
70. Taylor, *The Archive and the Repertoire*, 20, 23.
71. Hughes, "Prelude to Our Age," 379.
72. Ibid., 383.
73. Hughes, "Prelude to Our Age," hand-corrected typescripts, LHC.
74. Hughes, "Prelude to Our Age," 383.
75. In an interview with Nicolás Guillén, Hughes rather grandly proclaimed that his "greatest ambition is to be the poet of the blacks. The black poet" (quoted and translated in Mullen, *Langston Hughes in the Hispanic World and Haiti*, 28).
76. Hughes, "A New Song," in *The Collected Poems*, 170.
77. Mbembe, "The New Africans," 109.

78. Marx himself was dismissive, even scornful, of the poorest of the poor: "They belonged for the most part to the lumpenproletariat, which in all big towns forms a mass sharply differentiated from the industrial proletariat, a recruiting ground for thieves and criminals of all kinds living on the crumbs of society, people without a definite trade, vagabonds, *gens sans feu et sans aveu,* varying according to the degree of civilization of the nation to which they belong, but never renouncing their lazzaroni character" (Marx, *Class Struggles in France,* 56).

79. Like Hughes, Du Bois gave voice to a feeling of kinship with Africa, of which he asked, "What is it between us that constitutes a tie which I can feel better than I can explain? . . . Since the fifteenth century these ancestors of mine and their other descendants have had a common history; have suffered a common disaster and have one long memory" (Du Bois, "What Is Africa to Me?," 655). But unlike Hughes, Du Bois gave special prominence to a "Talented Tenth" of black people who might lead the rest to freedom. Writing about the Pan-African Congress of 1919 with the hindsight of a couple of years, for example, he concluded that one of its principal accomplishments was bringing "face to face and in personal contact a group of educated Negroes of the calibre that might lead black men to emancipation in the modern world" (Du Bois, "A Second Journey to Pan-Africa," 667).

80. Johnny Washington notes Locke's conscious efforts to cultivate cultural understanding among people of African origins throughout the American hemisphere: "He believed that through the appreciation of the cultural values of various peoples, mutual understanding would be achieved, and that this cultural dimension was needed to supplement the economic dimension" of a hemispheric "good-neighbor" policy (Washington, *A Journey into the Philosophy of Alain Locke,* 43). Such rhetoric resembles what we will see from Hughes on cultural exchange, though Locke never expanded his efforts to include the modern African continent itself, as both Hughes and Du Bois would eventually do. Nor did he seem to perceive Africa as a living place from which modern cultural expression might arise, as is implied in the title of his essay "The Legacy of the Ancestral Arts," where he writes: "Even if the present vogue of African art should pass . . . for the Negro artist [it] ought still to have the import and influence of classics in whatever art expression is consciously and representatively racial" (Locke, "The Legacy of the Ancestral Arts," 267). Nevertheless, Locke's cultural pluralism and opposition to absolutist ideologies made his ideas resonate with Hughes's ethos of entanglement. But Locke gave at least as much emphasis to the notion of a black elite as did Du Bois: "The Elite has a duty to lead the masses; in turn, he suggested that the masses have a duty to follow the Elite, who points the way." Yet "the Elite remains loyal to the Black masses and vice versa" (Washington, *Alain Locke and Philosophy,* 89–90). We can see Locke striking a balance in a 1942 essay: "Even as we stress the right of the mass Negro to his important place in the picture, artistically and sociologically, we must become aware of the class structure of the Negro population, and expect to see, hear and understand the intellectual elite, the black bourgeoisie as well as the black masses" (Locke, "Who and What Is 'Negro'?," 210). Yet as Anna Pochmara points out, in "Locke's intertextual travels . . . most of the

destinations are in Europe and most of the discourses he appropriates do not foreground the race issue." His model of male comradeship and mentorship, moreover, "is deeply ingrained in classical (white) European discourses" (Pochmara, *The Making of the New Negro*, 91). For an illuminating discussion of the "paradigm of affinity" between Locke and Paul Gilroy, see Garcia, "Dynamic Nominalism in Alain Locke and Paul Gilroy."

81. Fanon, *The Wretched of the Earth*, 23. It is worth anticipating here that the revolutionary potential of the peasantry is a central theme of Roumain's *Masters of the Dew* and worth noting that Fanon drew the title of his book from a poem by Roumain.

82. Though he begins by claiming that "any national liberation movement should give this lumpenproletariat maximum attention," Fanon soon explains that the oppressor "is only too willing to exploit those characteristic flaws of the lumpenproletariat, namely its lack of political consciousness and ignorance. If this readily available human reserve is not immediately organized by the insurrection, it will join the colonialist troops as mercenaries" (Fanon, *The Wretched of the Earth*, 87). As we will see in the first chapter, Hughes and McKay took a far more benign, even affectionate, view of the urban poor.

83. Bhabha, "Foreword: Framing Fanon," x.

84. For an exhaustive history of the Bandung Afro-Asian Conference and its political ramifications, see Lee, *Making a World after Empire*. One of the most famous contemporary accounts of the conference appeared in Richard Wright's *The Color Curtain: A Report on the Bandung Conference*, reprinted in Wright, *Black Power*.

85. Hughes, *The Big Sea*, 10, 11.

86. Hughes, *I Wonder as I Wander*, 28.

87. Saunders, *The Cultural Cold War*, 1.

88. Ibid., 98, 99.

89. My research has not produced evidence to answer whether Hughes was even aware of the extent to which the CCF and the Transcription Centre, for example, were fronts for CIA cultural activities. On the one hand, Frances Stonor Saunders tells us that the General Assembly of the Congress for Cultural Freedom, which included Mphahlele, was apparently unaware of the congress's covert CIA backing until May 1967, just a couple of weeks before Hughes's death (Saunders, *The Cultural Cold War*, 391–92). Thus it is plausible that Hughes himself was likewise ignorant of CIA involvement in these cultural organizations. On the other hand, after having had his works removed from the United States Information Agency libraries around the world in 1953 under pressure from right-wing anticommunist groups, Hughes went on to represent the US Department of State in the 1960s at the opening of an USIA library in Ghana and on lecture tours of Europe. It is therefore equally plausible to speculate that, perhaps to get himself removed from unofficial blacklists, Hughes might have collaborated with agents of the US government in this and other capacities without asking too many questions about their "cultural cold war" agenda.

90. Hughes, "American Interest in African Culture," LHP, Box 483, Folder 12221, quoted in Rampersad, *The Life of Langston Hughes*, 2:355; emphasis in original.

91. Studying the correspondence between Hughes and the South African writers, Stéphane Robolin claims they "attest to the centrality of Hughes as an ardent, if humble, engineer of transnational black literary circulation. Perhaps more importantly, this correspondence underscores how significant cross-cultural connections have been for black writers' personal and professional development the world over" (Robolin, *Grounds of Engagement*, 1).

92. Hughes, "The Negro Speaks of Rivers," in *The Collected Poems*, 23.

93. Hughes, *Ask Your Mama*, in *The Collected Poems*, 481; capitalization and italics in original.

94. Beal describes the short story collection "as a nodal construction of autonomous units whose complete meaning can only be understood in relation to an array of other texts" (Beal, *Networks of Modernism*, 20).

95. Most of this archival material is in the Langston Hughes Papers at the Beinecke Rare Book and Manuscript Library at Yale University, with other holdings at the Schomburg Center for Research in Black Culture at the New York Public Library; the New York Library for the Performing Arts; the Harry Ransom Center at the University of Texas; and the Huntington Library in San Marino, California. See my key to the archival collection codes at the beginning of my bibliography.

96. Fanon, *Wretched of the Earth*, 177.

97. Graham and Walters, *Langston Hughes and the South African* Drum *Generation*.

98. Graham, "'This Curious Thing.'"

99. The turn to Marshall at the end risks the appearance of tokenism, but it stems from the especially masculinist character of Hughes's international black network. Certainly, many African American women writers benefited from Hughes's generosity, mentoring, and promotion, but he had apparently much less contact with women writers on his travels abroad. Even when Hughes did know women writers in the Caribbean, such as Louise Bennett and Una Marson, there is usually a paucity of surviving correspondence to ground our understanding of the relationship between them, as I have tried to do with the writers examined herein. In part this gender imbalance simply reflects the strict gender roles of Haiti, Cuba, Jamaica, and many countries in Africa, where women had few opportunities to write and publish, and interactions between a woman and a single man might have been frowned upon.

100. Marshall, *Triangular Road*, 29.

1. Vernacular Pan-African Entanglements

1. Homi Bhabha coins the term "vernacular cosmopolitanism" to describe "cosmopolitan community envisaged in a *marginality*" (Bhabha, "Unsatisfied," 195; emphasis in original). When I speak of an "aesthetic of vernacular pan-African entanglement," I mean "vernacular" to similarly emphasize the liminality and marginality of the people who make up the imagined community, but I would also stress

a more literal sense of "vernacular" to refer to the everyday language and cultural practices of ordinary people.

2. Robbins, *Feeling Global*, 100.
3. McKay, *A Long Way from Home*, 168.
4. Rampersad, *The Life of Langston Hughes*, 2:144.
5. Hughes, "Negro Art and Claude McKay," 46.
6. Hughes, "Claude McKay," 53.
7. Berry, *Langston Hughes*, 52.
8. Letter from Claude McKay to Langston Hughes, 27 April 1934, LHP, Box 109, Folder 2044.
9. Rampersad, *The Life of Langston Hughes*, 2:74.
10. Letter from Langston Hughes to Claude McKay, 5 March 1928, CMC, Box 3, Folder 98.
11. Letter from Claude McKay to Langston Hughes, 22 September 1924, LHP, Box 109, Folder 2042.
12. CMC, Box 13, Folder 426.
13. Hughes, "Twelve Favorite Negro Poems," 26 July 1951, LHC, Box 1, Folder 1, SC Micro R-977.
14. Letter from Langston Hughes to Carl Cowl, 24 July 1952, LHP, Box 370, Folder 5981.
15. McKay, *A Long Way from Home*, 13; emphasis added.
16. Letter from Claude McKay to Langston Hughes, 30 April 1927. LHP, Box 109, Folder 2042.
17. Letter from Langston Hughes to Claude McKay, 5 March 1928, CMC, Box 3, Folder 98; first emphasis mine.
18. Letter from Claude McKay to Langston Hughes, 30 March 1928, LHP, Box 109, Folder 2042.
19. Baldwin, *Beyond the Color Line*, 28.
20. Cooper, section introduction in McKay, *The Passion of Claude McKay*, 131.
21. Letter from Claude McKay to James Weldon Johnson, 20 April 1928, JWJ, Box 13, Folder 308.
22. Letter from Langston Hughes to Claude McKay, 5 March 1928, CMC, Box 3, Folder 98.
23. Du Bois, "Two Novels," 202.
24. Letter from Claude McKay to Langston Hughes, 13 June 1928, LHP, Box 109, Folder 2043.
25. The most public disagreement between Hughes and a more conservative black intellectual was the debate in 1926 between him and George Schuyler in the pages of *The Nation*, where Hughes published his landmark essay "The Negro Artist and the Racial Mountain."
26. McKay, *My Green Hills*, 69.
27. Letter from Claude McKay to Langston Hughes, 22 September 1924, LHP, Box 109, Folder 2042. Hughes's defense of this technique is missing from

the archives, but it seems to me that what McKay complained about is an early manifestation of the dialogic narrative form that would later characterize so much of Hughes's fiction and poetry, from Simple's banter with his bookish straight-man narrator to the call-and-response structure of many of the poems in *Montage of a Dream Deferred* (1951) to *Ask Your Mama*'s (1961) mischievous second speaker's playing the dozens.

28. Letter from Claude McKay to Langston Hughes, 30 March 1928, LHP, Box 109, Folder 2042.
29. McKay, *A Long Way from Home*, 4.
30. Glissant, *Poetics of Relation*, 11–12.
31. Edwards, *The Practice of Diaspora*, 187.
32. McKay, *Banjo*, 137.
33. McKay, *A Long Way from Home*, 300.
34. Letter from Claude McKay to William Bradley, 2 October 1929, William A. Bradley Literary Agency Records, Harry Ransom Center, University of Texas at Austin, Box 43, Folder 8.
35. McKay, *Banjo*, 136.
36. Ibid., 312.
37. Ibid.
38. The pun between "roots" and "routes" is fully exploited by James Clifford, who calls for a study of intercultural connection that focuses "on hybrid cosmopolitan experiences as much as on rooted, native ones" (Clifford, *Routes*, 24). Elizabeth DeLoughrey also takes up the pun, using it to describe the "tidalectic between sea and land. . . . Attention to movement offers a paradigm of rooted routes, of a mobile, flexible, and voyaging subject who is not physically or culturally circumscribed by the terrestrial boundaries of island space" (DeLoughrey, *Routes and Roots*, 3).
39. Mbembe, *Critique of Black Reason*, 100.
40. McKay, *Harlem*, 16.
41. Hughes, "Good Morning," in *The Collected Poems*, 426.
42. Ibid., 427.
43. McKay, *A Long Way from Home*, 20.
44. McKay, *My Green Hills*, 46; emphasis added.
45. Ibid., 20.
46. Hughes, *The Big Sea*, 97.
47. Letter from Claude McKay to Langston Hughes, 30 April 1927, LHP, Box 109, Folder 2042; emphasis added.
48. McKay, *A Long Way from Home*, 277.
49. Ibid.
50. Gilroy, *The Black Atlantic*, 4.
51. Marianna Torgovnick usefully defines the set of images and ideas that define primitivist discourse: "Primitives are like children, the tropes say. Primitives are our untamed selves, our id forces—libidinous, irrational, violent, dangerous. Primitives are mystics, in tune with nature, part of its harmonies. Primitives are free. . . . The ensemble of tropes . . . forms the basic grammar and vocabulary of

what I call primitivist discourse, a discourse fundamental to the Western sense of self and Other" (Torgovnick, *Gone Primitive*, 8).

52. Hughes credited Lawrence's short stories with their "psychologically powerful account of folks in England" as inspiration for his own first attempts at short fiction (Hughes, *I Wonder as I Wander*, 213). And Cooper notes that McKay shared with Lawrence "a deep faith in the primitive life forces in human nature, as opposed to the artificial constraints imposed upon humanity by modern industrial society" (Cooper, *Claude McKay*, xiii). For more on the influence of D. H. Lawrence on McKay, see Paul De Barros, who ascribes McKay's celebration of the "primitive African sex feeling" to Lawrence's belief in "a powerful 'life-force' that would eventually, through animal instinct, repair what was a broken civilization" (De Barros, "'The Loud Music of Life,'" 315). And see Mervyn Morris's introduction to *My Green Hills of Jamaica and Five Jamaican Short Stories*, which refers to Lawrence as an "evident influence" on McKay (ix).

53. Donna Jones goes further and claims that Henri Bergson's notion of an *élan vital* given its purist expression among "primitive" people actually contributed to the generation of "racial modernism" in the early twentieth century: "Once race is understood as the Bergsonian God of the evolutionary process, vitalism is no longer a form of primitivism; it is rather a form of reactionary—nay racial—modernism" (Jones, *The Racial Discourses of Life Philosophy*, 121).

54. McKay, "In Bondage," in *Complete Poems*, 165.
55. McKay, "Heritage," in *Complete Poems*, 166.
56. McKay, "Africa," in *Complete Poems*, 169.
57. Hughes, "Lament for Dark Peoples," in *The Collected Poems*, 39.
58. McKay, "In Bondage," in *Complete Poems*, 165.
59. McKay, *Banjo*, 49.
60. Hathaway, *Caribbean Waves*, 35.
61. McKay, "Enslaved," in *Complete Poems*, 167.
62. Hughes, "Poem [1]," in *The Collected Poems*, 32.
63. Hughes, "Lament for Dark Peoples," in *The Collected Poems*, 39.
64. Hughes, "Afraid," in *The Collected Poems*, 41.
65. Hughes, "Danse Africaine," in *The Collected Poems*, 28.
66. Hughes, "Poem [1]," in *The Collected Poems*, 32.
67. Quoted in Lewis, *When Harlem Was in Vogue*, 154.
68. Ibid., 153.
69. Hughes, *The Big Sea*, 325.
70. Hughes, "Slave on a Block," 19.
71. See for example Shields, "'Never Cross the Divide.'"
72. Chinitz, "Rejuvenation through Joy."
73. Hughes, "The Negro Mother," in *The Collected Poems*, 155–56.
74. Hughes, *The Big Sea*, 102.
75. Ibid., 11.
76. Ibid., 118.
77. Hughes, "Afro-American Fragment," in *The Collected Poems*, 129.

78. Hughes, "Johannesburg Mines," in *The Collected Poems*, 43.

79. Onwuchekwa Jemie concurs that Hughes's personal contact with the continent was "too brief to save his early evocations of Africa wholly from the romanticism which characterized, for instance, Countee Cullen's 'Heritage' or Claude McKay's 'In Bondage,' 'Outcast,' and 'Africa'" (Jemie, "Or Does It Explode?," 136). And Chinitz argues that well into the 1930s, "Hughes continues to believe, at times almost mystically, that jazz expresses and addresses a realm of the human psyche that Western civilization has suppressed; that the African American retains easier and more immediate access to this spirit" (Chinitz, "Rejuvenation through Joy," 69).

80. McKay, "How Black Sees Green and Red," in *The Passion of Claude McKay*, 58.

81. Letter from Claude McKay to Langston Hughes, 8 April 1925, LHP, Box 109, Folder 2042.

82. Cooper, *Claude McKay*, 101.

83. McKay, *A Long Way from Home*, 245; emphasis added.

84. McKay, *Banjo*, 49.

85. McKay, *Home to Harlem*, 308–9; emphasis added.

86. McKay, *A Long Way from Home*, 111.

87. Letter from Claude McKay to Nancy Cunard, 1 December 1931, Nancy Cunard Collection, Harry Ransom Center, University of Texas at Austin, Box 17, Folder 1.

88. Claude McKay, "North Africa and the Spanish Civil War," in *The Passion of Claude McKay*, 285.

89. Hathaway, *Caribbean Waves*, 53.

90. McKay, *Banjo*, 105.

91. Hughes, "Spirituals," in *The Collected Poems*, 102.

92. McKay, *Banjo*, 200.

93. Ibid., 201.

94. McKay, *A Long Way from Home*, 28.

95. Spivak, "Subaltern Studies," 214; emphasis in original. Spivak has complained that her concept of strategic essentialism has been misunderstood and misused by other critics; her chief complaint is that they fail to ask "what is meant by strategy" and overlook the "visible political interest" that justifies the tactical deployment of essentialist claims and representations. Spivak continues, "So I don't go with the strategic use of essentialism anymore. I'm much more interested in seeing the differences among these so-called essences in various cultural inscriptions" (Spivak, "An Interview with Gayatri Chakravorty Spivak," 35–36). I nevertheless continue to find her original use of the term illuminating in relation to writers such as Hughes, Césaire, and to some extent McKay, who indeed seemed to deploy racial essentialism with conscious and strategic intent.

96. McKay, *A Long Way from Home*, 76.

97. Kate Baldwin summarizes McKay's early hopes for Soviet internationalism: it promised the opportunity "to foster connections across the parameters of nationhood and create productive alliances among those similarly excluded

by the conventional bounds of national identity" (Baldwin, *Beyond the Color Line*, 79).

98. Letter from Claude McKay to Max Eastman, 16 October 1944, in *The Passion of Claude McKay*, 305.
99. McKay, "Socialism and the Negro," in *The Passion of Claude McKay*, 54.
100. McKay, "Garvey as a Negro Moses," in *The Passion of Claude McKay*, 67.
101. McKay, *A Long Way from Home*, 354.
102. McKay, *Harlem*, 143.
103. Ibid., 177.
104. Ibid.
105. Hughes, *The Big Sea*, 102.
106. McKay, "A Circular Letter for the Creation of a Negro Writers' Guild," in *The Passion of Claude McKay*, 233.
107. Letter from Claude McKay to James Weldon Johnson, 15 April 1934, JWJ, Box 13, Folder 308.
108. McKay, *A Long Way from Home*, 178.
109. McKay, "For Group Survival," in *The Passion of Claude McKay*, 235.
110. McKay, *A Long Way from Home*, 90–91.
111. Edwards, *The Practice of Diaspora*, 215.
112. Ibid., 217, 219.
113. Michelle Stephens's characterization of *Banjo* sheds more light on this subject: "The novel represents McKay's attempt to explore internationalism as an alternative source for black identity. It also represents his effort to imagine an alternative site of home for the black male subject migrating within and moving across transnational boundaries" (Stephens, *Black Empire*, 178).
114. McKay, "A Negro Writer to His Critics," in *The Passion of Claude McKay*, 137.
115. Letter from Claude McKay to William Bradley, 1 August 1927, William A. Bradley Literary Agency Records, Harry Ransom Center, University of Texas at Austin, Box 43, Folder 7.
116. McKay, *A Long Way from Home*, 20; emphasis added.
117. Robbins, *Feeling Global*, 170.
118. McKay, *Banjo*, 307.
119. Ibid., 66.
120. Jay, *Global Matters*, 55–56.
121. McKay, *Banjo*, 208.
122. Ibid.
123. McKay, "A Negro Writer to His Critics," in *The Passion of Claude McKay*, 139.
124. McKay, *A Long Way from Home*, 9.
125. Ibid., 173.; emphasis added.

Scale Enlargement A

1. Dimock, *Through Other Continents*, 28.

2. A letter Hughes wrote to Harold Jackman on 1 August 1924 refers to a review Walrond had written of Jessie Fauset's first novel as "Eric's review." In *Selected Letters*, 38.

3. Letter from Langston Hughes to Countee Cullen, 4 July 1924, in *Selected Letters*, 36.

4. Michel Fabre explains that Maran's salon in Paris was visited in the 1920s and 1930s by, among others, Hughes, McKay, Cullen, Walter White, Gwendolyn Bennett, Jessie Fauset, Mercer Cook, and W. E. B. Du Bois (Fabre, *From Harlem to Paris*, 150).

5. Hughes, "Brothers," in *The Collected Poems*, 424.

6. Hughes, "Caribbean Sunset," in *The Collected Poems*, 98.

7. The so-called Scottsboro Boys were nine black teenagers falsely accused of raping two young white women on a train near Scottsboro, Alabama, in 1931. For a thorough analysis of Hughes's engagement with the issue, see Thurston, "Black Christ, Red Flag."

8. Hughes, *Scottsboro, Limited*, 129.

9. Hughes, "Merry Christmas," in *The Collected Poems*, 132.

10. Hughes, "Always the Same," in *The Collected Poems*, 165–66.

11. Hughes, "Ballad of the Seven Songs," in *The Collected Poems*, 344.

12. Hughes, "Memo to Non-White Peoples," in *The Collected Poems*, 457.

13. Hughes, "Broadcast to the West Indies," in *The Collected Poems*, 275.

14. Ibid., 273.

15. Robolin, *Grounds of Engagement*, 12.

16. Gilroy, *The Black Atlantic*, 6.

17. Hughes, "Broadcast to the West Indies," in *The Collected Poems*, 273.

18. Appiah, "Cosmopolitan Patriots," 91.

19. Beal, *Networks of Modernism*, 10.

20. Hughes, "Broadcast to the West Indies," in *The Collected Poems*, 273.

21. Ibid., 274; manuscript in LHP, Box 375, Folder 6217.

22. Hughes, "To the Little Fort of San Lazaro on the Ocean Front, Havana," in *The Collected Poems*, 136.

23. Ibid.

24. Nora, "Between Memory and History," 7–8.

25. Ibid., 8.

26. Halbwachs, *On Collective Memory*, 106.

27. Nora, "Between Memory and History," 8.

28. Hughes, "Notes at Summer's End," 14.

29. The original: "Cuando apareció Mr. Hughes nos encontramos con un jovencito de veintisiete años, menudo y delgado, de color trigueño, y que no usa bigote a la inglesa ni a la moda de ninguna otra nación. Parece justamente un 'mulatico' cubano" (Hughes, "Conversación con Langston Hughes," 16; my translation).

30. Letter from Langston Hughes to Claude McKay, 30 September 1930, in *Selected Letters*, 98.

31. Edward Mullen notes that at the time of Hughes's death in 1967, "he was more widely known in the Hispanic world than in the country of his birth" (Mullen, *Langston Hughes in the Hispanic World and Haiti*, 15). For a comprehensive account of prominent translations of Hughes's work into Spanish, see Kutzinski, *The Worlds of Langston Hughes*, 56–85.

32. Griffith, *The BBC and the Development of Anglophone Caribbean Literature*, 52–53.

33. Hughes got to know Bennett in New York later, as he noted in a letter to Salkey: "Louise Bennett is here in New York now and was at my house the other day for a party." Letter from Langston Hughes to Andrew Salkey, 16 September 1953, LHP, Box 142, Folder 2647. Later he wrote to Peter Abrahams that "Louise Bennett (that most amusing woman) spent a year or so here, got married, and just recently departed for her native Jamaica leaving behind with me a copy of her hilarious poem, 'Colonizing in Reverse,' and her delightful record." Letter from Langston Hughes to Peter Abrahams, 28 February 1955, in Graham and Walters, *Langston Hughes and the South African* Drum *Generation*, 68.

34. Rampersad, *The Life of Langston Hughes*, 2:138–39.

35. Griffith, *The BBC and the Development of Anglophone Caribbean Literature*, 53.

36. Bennett, "Jamaica Oman," 145.

37. For Hughes's and Brière's correspondence, see LHP, Box 23, Folder 471. Note that Brière also wrote a poem called "Me Revoici, Harlem," or "Here I Am Again, Harlem," dedicated to Langston Hughes. Hughes's translation of Anthony Lespes's "Song for Youth" appears in LHP, Box 425, Folder 9452.

38. Rampersad, *The Life of Langston Hughes*, 2:304.

39. Ibid.

40. Letter from Langston Hughes to Jimmy Davis, 9 October 1965, in *Selected Letters*, 402.

41. Fowler, *A Knot in the Thread*, 252.

42. Guillén, "Sobre Jacques Roumain."

2. "Marks of a Rebellious Slave"

1. Hughes, *I Wonder as I Wander*, 5.
2. Chinitz, "Rejuvenation through Joy," 69.
3. Hughes, *I Wonder as I Wander*, 3, 7, 22.
4. Largey, *Vodou Nation*, 7.
5. Corbould, *Becoming African Americans*, 15, 165.
6. Hughes, *I Wonder as I Wander*, 15.
7. Largey, *Vodou Nation*, 21.
8. Taylor, *The Archive and the Repertoire*.
9. Rothberg, *Multidirectional Memory*, 29.
10. Hughes, "An Appeal for Jacques Roumain," *New Republic*, 12 December 1934, 130, reprinted in *Essays on Art, Race, Politics, and World Affairs*, vol. 9 of *Collected Works of Langston Hughes*, 555.

11. Berry, *Langston Hughes*, 121.
12. Jackson and Bacon, introduction to *African Americans and the Haitian Revolution*, 2.
13. Kaisary, *The Haitian Revolution*, 3, 1–2.
14. Mbembe, *Critique of Black Reason*, 15.
15. James, *Black Jacobins*, ix.
16. Dash, introduction to Roumain, *Masters of the Dew*, 6.
17. Kaussen, *Migrant Revolutions*, 3.
18. Quoted in Kennedy, *The Negritude Poets*, 17.
19. Kaussen, *Migrant Revolutions*, 27.
20. Quoted in Kaussen, *Migrant Revolutions*, 30.
21. Ibid., 28–29.
22. Cobb, *Harlem, Haiti, and Havana*, 84.
23. Quoted in Cobb, *Harlem, Haiti, and Havana*, 81.
24. Smith, *Red & Black in Haiti*, 25.
25. Mullen, *Langston Hughes in the Hispanic World and Haiti*, 33.
26. Hughes, "People without Shoes."
27. Hughes, "Scottsboro," in *The Collected Poems*, 142.
28. Hughes, "The Need for Heroes," 184. Oddly, Hughes does not mention the seminal history of the Haitian Revolution, C. L. R. James's *The Black Jacobins*, published only three years before this essay. Nor have I found any mention of James elsewhere in Hughes's writings, though Rampersad mentions that they met once in Trinidad (Rampersad, *The Life of Langston Hughes*, 2:304).
29. Kaussen, *Migrant Revolutions*, 34.
30. McClintock, "Imperial Ghosting and National Tragedy," 821.
31. Hughes, *I Wonder as I Wander*, 17.
32. Hughes, "A Letter from Haiti," 554.
33. Hughes, *I Wonder as I Wander*, 16, 27.
34. Ibid., 16.
35. Nora, "Between Memory and History," 7.
36. Taylor, *The Archive and the Repertoire*, 22.
37. Ibid., 19, 20.
38. Hughes, "White Shadows in a Black Land," 52.
39. Hughes, *The Big Sea*, 325.
40. Hughes, *Emperor of Haiti*, 282.
41. Ibid.
42. Hughes, "Afro-American Fragment," in *The Collected Poems*, 129.
43. Nora, "Between Memory and History," 9.
44. Ibid., 7–8.
45. Taylor, *The Archive and the Repertoire*, 21.
46. Hughes, *Emperor of Haiti*, 282.
47. Ibid., 283.
48. See for example the "silver moons" that the speaker of "Lament for Dark Peoples" has lost (Hughes, "Lament for Dark Peoples," in *The Collected Poems*, 39).

49. Hughes, *Emperor of Haiti*, 291.
50. Ibid., 296.
51. Hughes, *Troubled Island*, 22.
52. Hughes, *Emperor of Haiti*, 310.
53. Ibid., 317.
54. Ibid., 318.
55. Ibid., 317.
56. Ibid., 319.
57. Ibid., 321.
58. Hughes, *I Wonder as I Wander*, 21.
59. Kaisary, *The Haitian Revolution*, 41.
60. Chatterjee, *The Nation and Its Fragments*, 117.
61. Hughes, *Emperor of Haiti*, 323.
62. *Emperor of Haiti* had a short run at the Karamu Theatre in Cleveland beginning in November 1936 and a brief run in Detroit in April 1937 under the title *Drums of Haiti* (McLaren, *Langston Hughes*, 101).
63. Smith, *Red & Black in Haiti*, 2.
64. Ibid., 16–17.
65. Largey, *Vodou Nation*, 152.
66. Kaisary, *The Haitian Revolution*, 42.
67. Hughes, *Emperor of Haiti*, 297.
68. Ibid., 298.
69. Ibid., 310.
70. Ibid., 331, 332.
71. McClintock, "Imperial Ghosting and National Tragedy."
72. Hughes, *Emperor of Haiti*, 288.
73. Ibid., 289.
74. Hughes, "Afro-American Fragment," in *The Collected Poems*, 129.
75. Hughes, *I Wonder as I Wander*, 30.
76. Ibid., 31.
77. Garrett, *The Renaissance of Haitian Poetry*, 107.
78. Quoted in Fowler, *A Knot in the Thread*, 274.
79. Ibid., 140.
80. Cobb, *Harlem, Haiti, and Havana*, 90.
81. Garrett writes of Hughes and Roumain that "their themes and emotions are the same. Both are preoccupied with the masses instead of with the individual and recognize that the problems of all the underprivileged are similar. They shared a friendship based upon a common cause" (Garrett, *The Renaissance of Haitian Poetry*, 116).
82. Quoted in Fowler, *A Knot in the Thread*, 308; emphasis in original.
83. Ibid., 142.
84. Cobb, *Harlem, Haiti, and Havana*, 84.
85. Fowler, *A Knot in the Thread*, 134.
86. Hughes's translation of "When the Tom-Tom Beats" appeared in Nancy Cunard's *Negro: An Anthology* in 1934. The same poem along with Hughes's

translation of "Guinea" was published in the 1942 edition of Dudley Fitts's *Anthology of Contemporary Latin-American Poetry* and again in Hughes's own anthology coedited with Arna Bontemps, *The Poetry of the Negro* (1949). The two translations were reanthologized as recently as 1989 with the publication of Ellen Conroy Kennedy's *The Negritude Poets*.

87. Letter from Jacques Roumain to Langston Hughes, 13 November 1931, LHP, Box 138, Folder 2589.

88. Roumain, "Guinea," in Hughes and Bontemps, *Poetry of the Negro*, 365–66.

89. Roumain, "When the Tom-Tom Beats," in Hughes and Bontemps, *Poetry of the Negro*, 364.

90. Anita Patterson likewise argues that in this poem Roumain "conjoins elements from Hughes's 'The Negro Speaks of Rivers' with the revisionist primitivism of Hughes's 'Danse africaine'" (Patterson, *Race, American Literature and Transnational Modernisms*, 126).

91. Dimock, *Through Other Continents*, 3.

92. Fowler, *A Knot in the Thread*, 136.

93. Roumain, *Le sacrifice du tambour-assoto(r)*. This translation is by Amy Spingarn, from a typescript in Joel and Amy Spingarn Papers, Schomburg Center for Research in Black Culture, New York Public Library, MG174, Box 1, Folder 10, page 73.

94. The original reads "le doux sortilege du souvenir" (Roumain, "Quand bat le tam-tam," in *When the Tom-Tom Beats*, 24; Fungaroli and Sauer's translation, 25). Hughes's translation appears in Kennedy, *The Negritude Poets*, 22.

95. Roumain, "Langston Hughes," in *When the Tom-Tom Beats*, 21.

96. Ibid.; emphasis in original.

97. Fowler, *A Knot in the Thread*, 155–56.

98. For example, Hughes wrote numerous articles protesting "the uncalled for and unmerited sentence to prison of Jacques Roumain, one of the few, and by far the most talented, of the literary men of Haiti" (Hughes, "An Appeal for Jacques Roumain," 555). He was in regular contact throughout 1935 and 1936 with Francine Bradley, a New Yorker who established the Committee for the Release of Jacques Roumain (letters from Francine Bradley to Langston Hughes, 1935–46, LHP, Box 22, Folder 454). On at least one occasion, in February 1936 at the Harlem YMCA, Hughes read his poetry at an event Bradley organized to protest the imprisonment of Roumain and other opposition figures in Haiti (letter from Francine Bradley to Jean Toomer, 20 February 1936, Jean Toomer Papers, Beinecke Rare Book and Manuscript Library, Yale University, JWJ MSS 1, Box 1, Folder 33).

99. Fowler, *A Knot in the Thread*, 177.

100. Hughes, "Too Much of Race," 272.

101. Rampersad, *The Life of Langston Hughes*, 1:345.

102. Ibid., 1:206.

103. Fowler, *A Knot in the Thread*, 133.

104. Roumain, "Ebony Wood," in *When the Tom-Tom Beats*, 79.

105. Roumain, "Filthy Negroes," in *When the Tom-Tom Beats*, 95.
106. Kennedy, *The Negritude Poets*, 19.
107. Fowler, *A Knot in the Thread*, 193.
108. Ibid., 195.
109. Roumain, "Ebony Wood," in *When the Tom-Tom Beats*, 77–79.
110. Ibid., 73.
111. Ibid.
112. Ibid., 75–77.
113. Roumain, "Filthy Negroes," in *When the Tom-Tom Beats*, 89.
114. Rothberg, *Multidirectional Memory*, 14.
115. Ibid., 71.
116. Roumain, "New Negro Sermon," in *When the Tom-Tom Beats*, 101–3.
117. Hughes, "One More 'S' in the U.S.A," in *The Collected Poems*, 176–77. For a cogent contextualization of Hughes's poetry from the 1930s against the Popular Front and "the legacy of earlier modernist art and literature," see Smethurst, *The New Red Negro*. Smethurst argues that to dismiss Hughes's revolutionary poems as mere sloganeering "misses the sly voice inhabiting the poems. This voice usually means what it says, but never quite says all that it means in a straightforward way" (Smethurst, *The New Red Negro*, 102).
118. Hughes, "Chant for Tom Mooney," in *The Collected Poems*, 164.
119. Hughes began to draw right-wing protests at speaking engagements around the country as early as the 1930s, especially because of his 1931 poem "Christ in Alabama," which includes the lines "Christ is a nigger, / Beaten and black" (in *The Collected Poems*, 143). Hughes was named in the magazine *Life* in 1949 as one of fifty supposedly communist "dupes and fellow travelers," he was repeatedly investigated by the House Un-American Activities Committee, and in the early 1950s he was summoned to appear before Joseph McCarthy's Senate subcommittee investigating purportedly subversive activities.
120. Roumain, "Filthy Negroes," in *When the Tom-Tom Beats*, 93–95.
121. For example, in a letter to Blanche Knopf from autumn 1946, Hughes tried to convince her to publish his and Benjamin Carruthers's translations of Guillén's poetry, which ended up being published by Ward Ritchie under the title *Cuba Libre* (letter from Langston Hughes to Blanche Knopf, 25 September 1946, AAKR, Box 1.6). Hughes persevered in these efforts despite being privately pessimistic, to the extent that he was reluctant to undertake the translation of *Gouverneurs de la rosée* without a contract from a publisher, because "Latin American books have not sold very well here, and ... now most of the publishing houses are averse to accepting new ones" (letter from Langston Hughes to Mercer Cook, 16 March 1945, in *Selected Letters*, 262). Once *Masters of the Dew* was published by Reynal and Hitchcock, Hughes used his column in the *Chicago Defender* on at least two different occasions to promote the translation (19 July 1947 and 3 June 1950).
122. Kutzinski, *The Worlds of Langston Hughes*, 10.
123. For an extended discussion of Hughes's writings in Spanish translation, see ibid., 56–85.

124. Patterson, *Race, American Literature and Transnational Modernisms*, 95.
125. Goyal, *Romance, Diaspora, and Black Atlantic Literature*, 13.
126. Ibid.
127. Fowler mentions several conflicting explanations for Roumain's sudden death at a young age, from the death certificate attributing it to an inflammation of the gall bladder to reports of sclerosis of the liver and even to rumors that he was poisoned.
128. My translation. Original: "Vous ne pouvez vous imaginer avec quelle emotion et quelle fierté, j'ai appris cette nouvelle: ce rêve que Jacques a fait à Mexico en achevant son roman, le voir traduit in anglais et présenté au public par Langston, devient une réalité." Letter from Nicole Roumain to Langston Hughes, 6 March 1946, LHP, Box 138, Folder 2589.
129. Dash, introduction to Roumain, *Masters of the Dew*, 11, 13.
130. Roumain, *Masters of the Dew*, 183, 149.
131. Ibid., 28.
132. Ibid., 42.
133. Ibid., 176.
134. See Kaussen, *Migrant Revolutions*, 56.
135. Roumain, *Masters of the Dew*, 87.
136. Ibid., 88.
137. Ibid., 71–72.
138. Quoted in Fowler, *A Knot in the Thread*, 332.
139. Ibid., 217.
140. Ibid., 219.
141. Kaussen, *Migrant Revolutions*, 122.
142. Ibid., 127.
143. Cobb, *Harlem, Haiti, and Havana*, 102.
144. Roumain, *Masters of the Dew*, 29; emphasis added.
145. Roumain, *Gouverneurs de la rosée*, 19.
146. Ibid.
147. Roumain, "New Negro Sermon," in *When the Tom-Tom Beats*, 103.
148. Roumain, *Masters of the Dew*, 35.
149. Roumain, *Gouverneurs de la rosée*, 29.
150. Dash, introduction to Roumain, *Masters of the Dew*, 17–18.
151. Kutzinski, *The Worlds of Langston Hughes*, 223.
152. Roumain, "Langston Hughes," in *When the Tom-Tom Beats*, 21.
153. Roumain, *Masters of the Dew*, 44.
154. Ibid., 88.
155. Ibid., 89–90.
156. Kaussen, *Migrant Revolutions*, 106.
157. Kaisary, *The Haitian Revolution*, 54.
158. Roumain, *Masters of the Dew*, 103.
159. Ibid., 102.
160. Ibid., 144.

161. Ibid., 117.
162. Ibid., 188.
163. Ibid., 186.
164. Roumain, *Gouverneurs de la rosée*, 219.
165. Hughes, *Selected Letters*, 263n.
166. Hughes, "A Poem for Jacques Roumain," typescript, 1944–45 (n.d.), LHP, Box 383, Folder 6827, copy in Nancy Cunard Collection, Harry Ransom Center, University of Texas at Austin, Folder 33.7.
167. Ibid.
168. Ibid.

Scale Enlargement B

1. For more on the influence of Hughes and the Harlem Renaissance on the Negritude movement and other French-language writers, see Ako, "The Harlem Renaissance"; Ako, "Langston Hughes"; Arnold, *Modernism and Negritude*, 27–33; Badiane, *The Changing Face of Afro-Caribbean Cultural Identity*; Bamikunle, "The Harlem Renaissance and Negritude Poetry"; Brière, "The Harlem Renaissance and Négritude"; Dixon, "Rivers Remembering Their Source"; Edwards, "Aimé Césaire and the Syntax of Influence"; Edwards, *The Practice of Diaspora*; Fabre, "Du mouvement nouveau noir"; Fabre, *From Harlem to Paris*, 146–59; Feuser, "Afro-American Literature and Negritude"; Hale, "From Afro-America to Afro-France"; Irele, "The Harlem Renaissance and the Negritude Movement"; Kesteloot, *Black Writers in French*, 56–74; Rabaka, *The Negritude Movement*; and Shuttlesworth-Davidson, "Literary Collectives."

2. Fabre notes, for example, that Maran's salon was visited in the 1920s and early 1930s by Hughes, McKay, Cullen, Locke, Walter White, Gwendolyn Bennett, Jessie Fauset, Mercer Cook, W. E. B. Du Bois, and others (Fabre, *From Harlem to Paris*, 150).

3. Edwards, *The Practice of Diaspora*, 100.
4. Ibid., 195.
5. McKay, *Banjo*, 201.
6. Edwards, *The Practice of Diaspora*, 196.
7. Quoted and translated in Edwards, *The Practice of Diaspora*, 187. Original: "les deux poètes noirs révolutionnaires, nous ont apporté . . . la joie africaine de la vie, la joie africaine de l'amour, le rêve africain de la mort" (Léro, "Misère d'une poésie," 12).
8. Kesteloot, *Black Writers in French*, 18.
9. Damas, "Negritude in Retrospect," 17.
10. Kesteloot, *Black Writers in French*, 84.
11. Mbembe, *Critique of Black Reason*, 43.
12. Senghor, "L'humanisme," LGDP, Box 5; my translation. "Assimilons nous les cultures française, latine et grecque. Apprenons ainsi à nous découvrir et à nous exprimer. L'Humanisme, pour nous, ne peut avoir d'autre sens. *Plonger jusqu'aux racines de notre race*, écrit Mac Kay [sic], *et bâtir sur notre propre fond, ce n'est*

pas retourner à l'état sauvage, c'est la culture même!" Note how Senghor translates "native roots": "racines de notre race"—a pun that doesn't exist in the English original, emphasizing that for Senghor, one's cultural roots (racines) are inextricably linked to one's race. The quote from the novel is from McKay, *Banjo*, 200.

13. Ibid.

14. Senghor, "La poésie négro-américaine," 107–8; my translation. "La personnalité nègre s'est affirmée dans le passé; l'expérience d'esclavage n'a fait que l'enrichir en profondeur."

15. Ibid., 112. "Les chants africains, où une oreille musicale découvre, bientôt, sous l'apparente simplicité et monotonie, une richesse et une subtilité peu communes."

16. Ibid., 121, emphasis in original. "Depuis quelques années, la poésie négro-américaine s'efforce de dépasser le thème de la *Race,* par l'union avec *Dieu*—ou avec le *Prolétariat.* Claude MacKay [sic] et Langston Hughes sont les meilleurs représentants de cette nouvelle tendance."

17. Donna Jones offers the most nuanced intellectual genealogy of Senghor's racialism I have encountered: "Senghor's position is unique: he positively embraces the thesis that differential racial physiology makes impossible shared, universal assumptions, but he finds in the African mind the frames and schema necessary for absolute or universal knowledge. In other words, Senghor sought the possibility of absolute knowledge through Bergsonian intuition grounded in Nietzschean terms in differential African physiology" (Jones, *The Racial Discourses of Life Philosophy,* 123).

18. Damas, "Negritude in Retrospect," 18.

19. Ibid., 14.

20. Rabaka, *The Negritude Movement,* 80.

21. Damas, "Negritude in Retrospect," 14.

22. Ibid., 17.

23. Hughes, "Marry Black, New Credo," 10.

24. Kernan, "Lost and Found in Black Translation," 329.

25. An uncited, undated excerpt from an interview with Damas preserved in his papers mentions that he had met Hughes in 1938. LGDP, Box 9, Folder Aimé Césaire.

26. Letter from Léon Damas to Langston Hughes, May 1946, LHP, Box 51, Folder 955.

27. Kernan, "Lost and Found in Black Translation," 422.

28. Letter from Léopold Senghor to Langston Hughes, 22 January 1945, LHP, Box 144, Folder 2673.

29. Rampersad, *The Life of Langston Hughes,* 2:342–43.

30. Letter from Léopold Senghor to Langston Hughes, 20 June 1963, LHP, Box 144, Folder 2673. Brian Quinn's characterization of FESMAN's theatrical program in terms of weaving is significant to my concept of cultural entanglements: "Weaving the performance of text with multiple musical and dance interludes, each of the theatrical productions at FESMAN appealed to multivalent understandings of a new pan-African citizenship that included dialogical, visual and auditory forms of participation" (Quinn, "Staging Culture," 83).

31. Senghor, "Negritude and Americanism, or 'Let America Be America,'" speech given 27 May 1975 at the annual dinner of the PEN Club of American Writers, LGDP, Box 5, Folder Senghor—Speeches & writings.

32. Quoted in *Africa Abroad,* episode 9, TC/132, 26 June 1962, TCR, Folder 5.3.

33. Hughes, "The Twenties," 18.

34. Hughes, "Black Writers in a Troubled World," 477.

35. Jaji, *Africa in Stereo,* 101–2.

36. Damas, "Trite without Doubt," in Hughes and Bontemps, *The Poetry of the Negro,* 371–72.

37. Hughes, "Nude Young Dancer," in *The Collected Poems,* 61.

38. Senghor, "To the American Troops," in Hughes, *An African Treasury,* 199.

39. Senghor, "Congo," in *The Collected Poetry,* 76–78.

40. Senghor, "Night in Sine," in *The Collected Poetry,* 6–7.

41. Senghor, "Black Woman," in *The Collected Poetry,* 8–9.

42. Senghor, "To the Music of *Koras* and *Balaphon*," in *The Collected Poetry,* 24.

43. Dixon, introduction to *The Collected Poetry of Léopold Sédar Senghor,* xxx.

44. In *Rewriting the Return to Africa,* Anne François points out how fiction by francophone Caribbean women in the 1970s and 1980s "challenged the idea of returning to Africa" so prominent in the work of their male predecessors (ix). She writes that in "the women's novels, the continent is not represented as a propitious mother figure but rather as a disappointing father figure" (ix–x).

45. Senghor, "The African Road to Socialism," 86.

46. Senghor, "To the Music of *Koras* and *Balaphon*," in *The Collected Poetry,* 19.

47. Senghor, "Que M'Accompagnent Koras et Balafong," in *The Collected Poetry,* 284.

48. Senghor, "To New York," 142–43.

49. Jaji, *Africa in Stereo,* 66. Jaji elaborates that "jazz, for Senghor, captured something putatively unnameable and inexpressible . . . about blackness" (74).

50. Quoted in Jack, *Negritude and Literary Criticism,* 99.

51. McKay, "To the White Fiends," in *Complete Poems,* 132. The epigraph appears in Damas, *Pigments—névralgies,* 11.

52. Damas, "They Came That Night," in Kennedy, *The Negritude Poets,* 45. Original: "Ils sont venus ce soir où le / tam / tam/ roulait de / rythme / en / rythme / la frénésie / des yeux / la frénésie des mains / la frénésie / des pieds de statues" (Damas, "Ils sont venus ce soir," in *Pigments—névralgies,* 13).

3. "It Cancels the Slave Ship!"

1. I have tried to keep in mind while writing this chapter Edwards's caution "that one cannot presuppose 'influence' to be an overwhelming force, a model so defining and definitive that everything that follows is written under its shadow and in its debt. The invocation of 'influence' may have more to do with political strategy and historical

framing—the rhetoric with which a writer situates his work, in hindsight—than with the contextual pressures and reading habits that may have informed a particular scene of writing" (Edwards, "Aimé Césaire and the Syntax of Influence," 3).

2. Césaire, "Entretien avec Aimé Césaire," viii; my translation. "Avant la guerre, en 1938, 1939, Senghor et moi, nous fréquentions Langston Hughes, Countee Cullen, Claude McKay, en particulier, dont le roman *Banjo*.... Ils faisaient partie, si je puis dire, de nos bagages personnels."

3. Rabaka, *The Negritude Movement*, 154.

4. Bulson, *Little Magazine, World Form*, 183.

5. See my discussion of Spivak's concept of "strategic essentialism" in chapter 1.

6. Jones argues that in the *Notebook*, Césaire "assumes the 'wild and wilder' voice Bergson attributes to the primitive, for how else could he have been recognized and heard? . . . [Césaire] defends [his people's] mental capacities in the valorized Bergsonian terms as superbly intuitive," but Jones likewise regards this position as calculated and strategic rather than stemming from uncritical racial romanticism (Jones, *The Racial Discourses of Life Philosophy*, 127).

7. Davis, *Aimé Césaire*, 61.

8. Ibid., 49.

9. In a 2004 interview Césaire recalled that surrealism had "interested us, since it permitted us to break with reason, with artificial civilization, and to call out to the profound forces in mankind" (Césaire, *Nègre je suis, nègre je resterai*, 27; my translation). "Ce mouvement nous intéressait, parce qu'il nous permettait de rompre avec la raison, avec la civilisation artificielle, et de faire appel aux forces profondes de l'homme." Elsewhere he declared that surrealism was "a weapon that exploded the French language," and offered "a plunge into Africa for me" (Césaire, "An Interview with Aimé Césaire," 83, 84). Irele comments that "it was not so much the technical revolution as the social import of surrealism that came to have a meaning for Black intellectuals," referring to its aggressive iconoclasm and drawing attention to imperfections in Western culture (Irele, *The Negritude Moment*, 21).

10. Jonassaint, "Césaire et Haïti," 145–46; my translation. "Son théâtre . . . s'inscrit dans une double tradition caribéenne: celle du théâtre patriotique haïtien . . . et celle des écrivains de la Caraïbe toute langue confondue de puiser à même l'histoire d'Haïti."

11. Arnold, *Modernism and Negritude*, 25.

12. Césaire, "Entretien avec Aimé Césaire," xvii; my translation; emphasis in original. "Une culture naît, non pas quand l'homme *saisit*, mais quand l'homme *est saisi* . . . exactement comme dans le vaudou. Ce sont les rites de la possession. . . . On danse, on danse et, brusquement, 'le type' est possédé; il est passé à autre chose. Il n'est plus Monsieur un tel ou Mademoiselle une telle; il est Chango, il est Ogou, il est Erzulie."

13. Ibid., xviii; emphasis in original. "[Pas] comme *religion constitueé*, mais il existe, à mon avis, comme tendance, comme séquelle. . . . Il y a toute une attitude émotionnelle qui n'a rien à faire avec l'Europe et qui ressemble pendant le carnaval, pendant les élections . . . à ce qu'on voit dans le vaudou. Mais ce n'est pas un

vaudou véritable. Les Noirs furent beaucoup trop influencés par les Blancs. . . . Par contre, en Haïti, ils furent transportés en nombre, surtout au cours des dix dernières années qui précédèrent 1789. Ils représentaient, là-bas, les neuf-dixièmes de la population dans des provinces entières. C'est ainsi que les moeurs africaines ont pu y être conserves."

14. Césaire, "An Interview with Aimé Césaire," 90; my emphasis.

15. Ibid., 87.

16. Césaire, *Nègre je suis, nègre je resterai*, 25–26; my translation. "Les nègres américains ont été pour nous une révélation. . . . Ce qui comptait le plus pour nous, c'était de rencontrer une autre civilisation moderne, les Noirs et leur fierté, leur conscience d'appartenir à une culture."

17. Césaire, "Introduction à la poésie nègre américaine," 41; my translation. "Tout au plus du rythme, mais de primitif, de jazz ou de tam-tam c'est-à-dire enfonçant la résistance de l'homme en ce point de plus basse humanité."

18. Césaire, "Présentation," 5; my translation. "J'entends hurler l'acier, le tam-tam parmi la brousse, le temple prier parmi les banians."

19. Césaire, "Introduction à la poésie nègre américaine," 37; my translation. "C'est au cri que l'on reconnaît l'homme. Au cri fils aîné de la vie, ou plutôt la vie elle-même qui . . . s'incarne dans l'immédiateté de la voix."

20. Hughes, "Afraid," in *The Collected Poems*, 41.

21. Hughes, "A New Song," in *The Collected Poems*, 170.

22. Davis, *Aimé Césaire*, 20.

23. Césaire, *The Original 1939 Notebook*, 41.

24. Hughes, "A New Song," in *The Collected Poems*, 172.

25. Fanon, *Black Skin, White Masks*, 201.

26. Kernan, "Lost and Found in Black Translation," 342.

27. This is the spelling of McKay used throughout *Tropiques* as well as its Parisian predecessor *La revue du monde noir*. Their spelling of "Hugues" appears to be idiosyncratic, however.

28. Césaire et al., "Réponse de *Tropiques*," xxxix; my translation. "'Racistes,' 'sectaires,' 'révolutionnaires,' 'ingrats et traîtres à la Patrie.' . . . 'Ingrats et traîtres à notre si bonne Patrie' comme Zola. . . . 'Révolutionnaires' comme l'Hugo. . . . 'Racistes,' oui. Du racisme de Toussaint Louverture, de Claude Mac Kay [sic] et de Langston Hugues [sic]—contre celui de Drumont et de Hitler."

29. Sartre, "Black Orpheus," 223.

30. Irele, *The Negritude Moment*, 2; my emphasis. Gregson Davis likewise calls Negritude "a plastic concept in the process of construction" and quotes Césaire himself: "There is no predetermined négritude; there is no essence; there is only history—a living history" (Davis, *Aimé Césaire*, 5).

31. Rosello, introduction to *Notebook of a Return to My Native Land*, trans. Rosello and Pritchard, 26.

32. Parry, "Resistance Theory / Theorizing Resistance," 230.

33. My reading, then, is not quite the same as Kubayanda's, which takes Césaire's primitivism as more earnest: "The invented primitive becomes for these

Afrocentric poets [Césaire and Guillén] an auspicious, healing, and revitalizing consciousness" (Kubayanda, *The Poet's Africa*, 32).

34. Césaire, "An Interview with Aimé Césaire," 83; emphasis added.

35. Quoted in "Interview de Césaire à l'université Laval," in Kesteloot, *Césaire et Senghor*, 65; my translation. "C'était l'affirmation d'une solidarité, une solidarité à travers le temps, une solidarité à travers le monde. . . . Autrement dit, une sorte d'oecuménisme noir."

36. Césaire, "Entretien avec Aimé Césaire," xix; emphasis in original. "C'est cela, *primitive* tout court, pas forcément *africaine*!"

37. Ibid., xxi; emphasis in original; my translation. "Je ne peux pas dire que je ne crois pas du tout à l'importance de la race. Je pense que, effectivement, on naît blanc, on naît noir, etc. Mais ça se confond, pour moi, *très vite*, avec la culture. Quand je me revendique de l'Afrique, cela signifie que je me revendique des *valeurs culturelles africaines*."

38. Fabre, *From Harlem to Paris*, 155.

39. Césaire, *Discourse on Colonialism*, 78.

40. Césaire, *The Original 1939 Notebook*, 4–5; Césaire, *Notebook of a Return to the Native Land*, trans. Rosello and Pritchard, 75.

41. Césaire, *The Original 1939 Notebook*, 3–5, 11.

42. Arnold, introduction to Césaire, *The Original 1939 Notebook*, xii.

43. Césaire, *The Original 1939 Notebook*, 15.

44. Quoted in Davis, *Aimé Césaire*, 5. According to Davis, the grandmother attained "quasi-mythic status" in the boy's eyes, and "played a subliminal role in shaping the idealized conception of Africa that lies behind Césaire's version of négritude" (6).

45. Césaire, *Notebook of a Return to the Native Land*, trans. Rosello and Pritchard, 89–91.

46. Jonassaint notes that the recurring use of "debout" contains an echo of a 1927 poem by Carl Brouard and thus establishes another line of kinship between the *Notebook* and earlier generations of poetry from Haiti: "debout! / pour le grand coup de balai" (stand up! / for the great sweeping away). Quoted in Jonassaint, "Césaire et Haïti," 139; my translation.

47. Césaire, *Notebook of a Return to My Native Land*, trans. Rosello and Pritchard, 90.

48. Césaire, "Introduction à la poésie nègre américaine," 38; my translation. "La noire cour des miracles est debout. Tout ce qu'il y avait de souffrante humanité dans les slums de Harlem, dans les champs de maïs du Maryland, dans les plantations de coton des Caroline. . . . Et il y a ceux du chain-gang, et il y a les aigris, les optimistes, les débrouillards, les sots, ceux du Mississipi [sic], ceux de New-Orléans et d'Atlanta; les musiciens aux rythmes syncopés, les pikanninies sans souliers, les prostituées au teint du chocolat enluminé de rouge, les joueurs de Trombone épileptiques, les joueurs de jazz qui lancent leur baguettes à la lune."

49. Indeed, it is worth recalling Houston Baker Jr.'s observation that the etymology of the word "vernacular" derives from the Latin word for slave and that it

is the combination of "the material conditions of slavery in the United States and the rhythms of Afro-American blues" that produce "an ancestral matrix that has produced a forceful and indigenous American creativity" (Baker, *Blues, Ideology, and Afro-American Literature*, 2).

50. Césaire, *Notebook of a Return to My Native Land*, trans. Rosello and Pritchard, 95.
51. Ibid.
52. Ibid., 89.
53. Grantham, "Messianism in French Caribbean Literature," 19.
54. Césaire, *The Original 1939 Notebook*, 53.
55. Césaire, *Notebook of a Return to the Native Land*, trans. Rosello and Pritchard, 119.
56. Ibid., 133.
57. Arnold and Eshleman, appendix to Césaire, *The Original 1939 Notebook*, 62.
58. Césaire, *Notebook of a Return to the Native Land*, trans. Rosello and Pritchard, 77.
59. Hughes, "Fascination," in *The Collected Poems*, 39.
60. Senghor, "Black Woman," in *The Collected Poetry*, 8.
61. Césaire, *The Original 1939 Notebook*, 9.
62. Ibid., 35.
63. For a concise history of the submarine mountain theory of coral reef formation, see Stoddart, "Darwin, Lyell, and the Geological Significance of Coral Reefs."
64. Césaire, "Corps Perdu / Lost Body," in *The Collected Poetry*, 242–45.
65. Clifford, *The Predicament of Culture*, 175–76; emphasis in original.
66. Rosello, introduction to *Notebook of a Return to My Native Land*, trans. Rosello and Pritchard, 60.
67. For these closing lines I prefer this translation by Anthony Hurley. Césaire, "Lost Body," in *The Oxford Book of Caribbean Verse*, 39–40. "Je me lèverai un cri et si violent / que tout entier j'éclabousserai le ciel /. . . . je commanderai aux îles d'exister" (Césaire, "Corps perdu," in *La Poésie*, 228–30).
68. Arnold, *Modernism and Negritude*, 61.
69. Quoted in Rosello, introduction to *Notebook of a Return to My Native Land*, trans. Rosello and Pritchard, 60.
70. Césaire, *Notebook of a Return to My Native Land*, trans. Rosello and Pritchard, 73.
71. Ibid., 75.
72. Ibid., 123.
73. Ibid., 75.
74. Césaire, *The Original 1939 Notebook*, 41.
75. Arnold, introduction to Césaire, *The Original 1939 Notebook*, xix.
76. Césaire, *Discourse on Colonialism*, 73.
77. If an "Afrocentric humanism" seems just as oxymoronic and exclusionary as a Eurocentric humanism, I would argue that in fact it only made the case stronger

for the kind of cultural exchange for which Hughes and Césaire would both, in their different ways, advocate throughout their careers. If every ethnocentric humanism coexists concentrically within a larger universalism, then each is compatible with and capable of learning from the others. My thinking here thus dovetails with Kaisary's reading, which argues that Césaire's "historical/cultural négritude, in opposition to a Senghorian essentialist version, enabled the installation of black achievement. My interpretation thus ascribes to négritude a universalism that distinguishes it from mere identity politics" (Kaisary, *The Haitian Revolution*, 23–24).

78. Parry, "Resistance Theory / Theorizing Resistance," 226, 227.
79. Lee, *Frantz Fanon*, 196.
80. Fanon, *Wretched of the Earth*, 236.
81. Césaire, *Discourse on Colonialism*, 73.
82. Fanon, *Black Skin, White Masks*, 164.
83. Garcia, "*Home of the Brave*, Frantz Fanon and Cultural Pluralism," 54.
84. Fanon, *Black Skin, White Masks*, 200.
85. Ibid., 203.
86. Fanon, *Wretched of the Earth*, 148.
87. Ibid., 150.
88. Ibid., 151.
89. Ibid., 154.
90. Lee does acknowledge that Fanon's "nation-focused argument decisively contrasts with the civilizational paradigm espoused by Négritude" (Lee, *Frantz Fanon*, 170).
91. Alessandrini, "'Enough of This Scandal,'" 58.
92. Fanon, *Wretched of the Earth*, 178.
93. Ibid., 179.
94. Ibid. Fanon's final paragraph similarly begins: "If man is judged by his acts, then I would say that the most urgent thing today for the African intellectual is the building of his nation" (Fanon, *Wretched of the Earth*, 180).
95. Parry, "Resistance Theory / Theorizing Resistance," 244.
96. Lee, *Frantz Fanon*, 171.
97. Césaire's motivations for advocating departmentalization over Martinican independence fall outside the scope of this chapter. See Hale and Véron for an account of the complex confluence of forces—including "the difficulties posed by the economic conditions in Martinique, the challenges to Césaire of obtaining aid from the government in Paris, the long history of the island's relationship to France, and the contemporary geopolitical situation in the Caribbean at the time"—that shaped both his political positions and his poetic practice (Hale and Véron, "Is There Unity in the Writings of Aimé Césaire?," 54).
98. Jack, *Negritude and Literary Criticism*, 58.
99. Louis, *Conversation avec Aimé Césaire*, 58–59; my translation. "J'ai toujours vu et senti qu'il y avait une douleur antillaise, une nostalgie antillaise. Il y a un moi antillais, un moi profond, recouvert de toutes sortes de couches plus ou moins superficielles, et c'est ce moi profond que je voulais retrouver. . . . Pour

moi, martiniquais, retrouver le moi profond, c'était me dépouiller de toutes les défroques occidentales et françaises, et retrouver l'Afrique. C'était ça, pour moi, le moi profond."

100. My investigation into whether Césaire had read or seen *Emperor of Haiti* or its adaptation into the opera *Troubled Island* at the time he wrote *Christophe* has been inconclusive. Hughes mentioned to Léon Damas in 1953 that he had recently sent him a copy of *Troubled Island* (the play had at one time used that title, but Hughes probably meant the more recent opera libretto; letter from Langston Hughes to Léon Gontrans-Damas, 1 March 1953, LHP, Box 51, Folder 955). It is possible that Hughes also sent Césaire a copy or that Césaire obtained a copy from Damas or elsewhere. It certainly seems probable that Hughes would have sent Césaire a copy after they met in 1964 and Hughes saw *Christophe* performed, and it is conceivable that the revisions Césaire made to the play before its publication in the canonical 1970 *Présence africaine* edition were made partly with Hughes's pieces in mind.

101. I agree with Kaisary on this point when he writes that Césaire's writings "should be considered for their qualities of radical universalism and that if they have sought to represent figures or episodes of 'mysterious' or 'heroic uniqueness' that emerged in the unfolding of the Haitian Revolution, it was only in order to vindicate the actuality of black agency in colonial history" (Kaisary, *The Haitian Revolution*, 10).

102. Davis, *Aimé Césaire*, 138.
103. Arnold, *Modernism and Negritude*, 14.
104. Césaire, quoted in Davis, *Aimé Césaire*, 139.
105. Césaire, *Toussaint Louverture*, 313. Quoted and translated in Davis, *Aimé Césaire*, 140.
106. Césaire, *Toussaint Louverture*, 344. Quoted and translated in Davis, *Aimé Césaire*, 141.
107. Césaire, *The Tragedy of King Christophe*, 10.
108. Quoted in Mbom, *Le théâtre d'Aimé Césaire*, 64; my translation. "Il incarne la négritude. . . . Il en assume la responsabilité selon son idéal. Au point de vue mythologique il représente le Dieu Tonnerre, la volonté de puissance, tout à la fois destructeur et bienveillant."
109. Césaire, *The Tragedy of King Christophe*, 9.
110. Ibid., 21.
111. Ibid., 40.
112. Ibid.
113. Ibid., 81.
114. Ibid., 82.
115. Ibid., 96.
116. Ibid., 97. *La tragédie du roi Christophe*, 152.
117. Huyssen, *Present Pasts*, 23–24.
118. Ibid., 14.
119. Breslin notes that "Césaire's Christophe remains a self-divided figure almost to the very end of the play; it is not always easy to judge the proportions of

contempt and affirmation in his references to blackness" (Breslin, "Intertextuality, Translation, and Postcolonial Misrecognition in Aimé Césaire," 260). In one interview Césaire acknowledged that the "character of Christophe is extremely complex. There is in him Prometheus, Pierre le Grand, the Bourgeois Gentleman. . . . This tyrant, who bases his tyranny on ambition for the collective good, forms a *binomial* with Hugonin. It is the classic Shakespearean coupling of the king and the fool. Christophe embodies the force, Hugonin the joke. These are two complementary aspects" (quoted in Harris, *L'humanisme dans le théâtre d'Aimé Césaire*, 76; my translation). "Le personnage de Christophe est extrêmement complexe. Il y a chez lui du Prométhée, du Pierre le Grand, du Bourgeois gentilhomme . . . Ce tyran, qui fonde la tyrannie sur l'ambition de la grandeur collective, forme un *binôme* avec Hugonin. C'est le couple shakespearien classique du roi et du bouffon. Christophe incarne la force, Hugonin la plaisanterie. Il s'agit de deux aspects vitaux complémentaires." Harris also points out the many explicit textual parallels in the play between Christophe and the Yoruba deity Shango, who is "a valorous warrior but also a tyrannical despot" who eventually sacrifices himself for the people who have abandoned him (ibid., 111). "Shango fut un guerrier valeureux mais aussi un despote tyrannique."

120. Césaire, *The Tragedy of King Christophe*, 49.

121. Ibid., 50; my emphasis.

122. This is the paradox that Figueroa sees at the heart of Césaire's tragedy: "Christophe attempts to vindicate Africa in the Americas *by mimicking the splendor of imperial Europe*" (Figueroa, *Prophetic Visions of the Past*, 105; emphasis in original).

123. Césaire, *The Tragedy of King Christophe*, 15.

124. Ibid.

125. Ibid., 52.

126. Ibid., 38. Césaire, *La tragédie du roi Christophe*, 60.

127. Roumain, "Quand bat le tam-tam," in *When the Tom-Tom Beats*, 25.

128. Césaire, *The Tragedy of King Christophe*, 63; emphasis added; Césaire, *La tragédie du roi Christophe*, 99.

129. Recalling Césaire's claim in his interview with Leiner that he found elements of the primitive in Greek drama, perhaps the chorus was one element he had in mind.

130. Césaire, *The Tragedy of King Christophe*, 7–8.

131. Ibid., 41.

132. Ibid., 43.

133. Ibid., 23; emphasis added.

134. Ibid., 30.

135. Ibid., 46.

136. Ibid., 54. Césaire, *La tragédie du roi Christophe*, 88.

137. Césaire, *The Tragedy of King Christophe*, 61.

138. Perhaps the most unsparing take on the relationship between Césaire as poet and Césaire as politician comes from Raphaël Confiant in *Aimé Césaire*. Rosello succinctly summarizes Confiant's critique: Césaire "completely ignored the revolutionary

potential of creole language and culture, always privileged France and Frenchness, and consistently treated his fellow Martinicans as colonised subjects whose welfare was dependent on the generosity of the metropole" (Rosello, introduction to *Notebook of a Return to My Native Land*, trans. Rosello and Pritchard, 44).

139. Césaire, *The Tragedy of King Christophe*, 68.

140. Ibid., 26.

141. Césaire, *Notebook of a Return to the Native Land*, trans. Rosello and Pritchard, 115.

142. Césaire, *The Tragedy of King Christophe*, 26; my emphasis.

143. Perhaps this is an expression of the "*tension, a source of anxious concern*" that Figueroa sees in Césaire's attempts to balance "the universal and the particular": "The reason for Césaire's discomfort, I venture, is that he was trying to dismantle from the inside a colonial logic that ontologizes Europe's claim as sole or main possessor of the universal and the human" (Figueroa, *Prophetic Visions of the Past*, 99).

144. Confiant, *Aimé Césaire*, 146; my translation. "Césaire s'est donc posé en Christ, en saveur non seulement du peuple Martiniquais, mais de la race noire tout entière."

145. Césaire, *The Tragedy of King Christophe*, 45; my emphasis.

146. Shohat, "Imaging Terra Incognita," 57.

147. Césaire, *La tragédie du roi Christophe,* undated typescript, Fond Michel Leiris, Bibliothèque Littéraire Jacques Doucet, Paris-Sorbonne University, France, LRS Ms 168.

148. The stage directions make this connection explicit toward the end of act 2 when they describe "*The Citadel. Pharaonic labors*" (Césaire, *The Tragedy of King Christophe*, 64).

149. Breslin, "Intertextuality, Translation, and Postcolonial Misrecognition in Aimé Césaire," 263.

150. Césaire, *The Tragedy of King Christophe*, 22.

151. Ibid., 31.

152. Ibid., 61.

153. Hughes, "The Negro Speaks of Rivers," in *The Collected Poems*, 23.

154. Césaire, *The Tragedy of King Christophe*, 41.

155. Roumain, *Masters of the Dew,* 117.

156. Césaire, *The Tragedy of King Christophe*, 72; Césaire, *La tragédie du roi Christophe*, 118.

157. Breslin, "Intertextuality, Translation, and Postcolonial Misrecognition in Aimé Césaire," 263.

158. Césaire, *The Tragedy of King Christophe*, 92.

159. Césaire, *La tragédie du roi Christophe,* 146. Compare this to Piquion's translation of the last line of "The Negro Speaks of Rivers": "Mon âme a grandi en profondeur comme ces fleuves" (Piquion, *Langston Hughes*, 80).

160. Césaire, *The Tragedy of King Christophe*, 79.

161. Ibid., 90.

162. Hale and Véron, "Is There Unity in the Writings of Aimé Césaire?," 63.
163. Césaire, *The Tragedy of King Christophe*, 15.
164. Fanon, *The Wretched of the Earth*, 97.
165. Césaire, *The Tragedy of King Christophe*, 82.
166. Jack, *Negritude and Literary Criticism*, 86.
167. In *Wretched of the Earth*, for example, Fanon criticized both the Negritude movement and the New Negro movement for placing ideas about race above national culture: "'Negro' or 'Negro-African' culture broke up because the men who set out to embody it realized that every culture is first and foremost national, and that the problems for which Richard Wright or Langston Hughes had to be on the alert were fundamentally different from those faced by Léopold Senghor or Jomo Kenyatta" (154).
168. Césaire, "Entretien avec Aimé Césaire," xxi; my translation. "Papa Doc me choque, me choque profondément."
169. For readings of Christophe's despotism as allegorical commentary on the emerging dictatorships in postcolonial Africa in the 1960s, see for example Mbom's chapter on *Christophe* in *Le théâtre d'Aimé Césaire* and Ojo-Ade's treatment of the play in *Aimé Césaire's African Theater*. Ojo-Ade disputes the validity of the comparison to modern Haiti, claiming that unlike Papa Doc, a "monster to the marrow," Césaire's Christophe "never ceases to be committed to [the people's] cause" (146). But just as Hughes used *Emperor of Haiti* as a veiled critique of the neocolonial regime of Sténio Vincent in the 1930s, I see Césaire's *Christophe* working as a commentary on Duvalierism, "a nationalist ideology, which gave top priority to the psycho-cultural aspects of the Haitian situation, [but] found itself unable to understand and solve the problems of the most deprived sectors of the black masses" (Remy, "The Duvalier Phenomenon," 50).
170. Quoted in Rampersad, *The Life of Langston Hughes*, 2:385.
171. Quoted in Arnold, *Modernism and Negritude*, 33.
172. Quoted in Jahn, *Neo-African Literature*, 265.

Scale Enlargement C

1. Hughes, "Our Land," in *The Collected Poems*, 32–33.
2. Hughes, *The Big Sea*, 10–11.
3. Hughes, "The Negro Speaks of Rivers," in *The Collected Poems*, 23.
4. Hughes, "Our Land," in *The Collected Poems*, 32.
5. Hughes, *The Big Sea*, 113.
6. Hughes, "Ships, Sea and Africa," 26–27.
7. Hughes, *The Big Sea*, 11.
8. Hughes, "I Thought It Was Tangiers I Wanted," in *The Collected Poems*, 110–11.
9. Hughes, "Johannesburg Mines," in *The Collected Poems*, 43.
10. Hughes, "Broadcast on Ethiopia," in *The Collected Poems*, 192–93.
11. Ibid., 192.
12. Ibid., 193.

13. For an extended discussion of the connection between Hughes and Zik, see OBIWU, "The Pan-African Brotherhood of Langston Hughes and Nnamdi Azikiwe."

14. For Hughes's records from the AMSAC Conference, see LHP, Box 483, Folder 12205. I found the Mbari writers conference program in TCR, Box 1.3. For Mphahlele's report on the Mbari conference, see Mphahlele, "The Makerere Writers Conference."

15. Rampersad, *The Life of Langston Hughes*, 2:400–403.

16. Hughes, draft of speech at AMSAC conference, Lagos, Nigeria, 1961, LHP, Box 483, Folder 12210.

17. Hughes, "A Talk for the Afro-Arts Theatre at Colonial Park Amphitheatre in New York City, August 31, 1956," LHP, Box 329, Folder 5372.

18. Hughes's notes toward an anthology of African stories for teenagers appear in his materials collected for *An African Treasury*, LHP, Box 269, Folder 4414.

19. Achebe, "Spelling Our Proper Name," 54–55. In a later memoir, Achebe recalled a visit to his home in Lagos by "the great African American poet Langston Hughes, who stopped by during one of his famous African tours" (Achebe, *There Was a Country*, 67).

20. Achebe, "Spelling Our Proper Name," 55.

21. Hughes, "African Lady." Song lyrics written for Randy Weston, 1–3 November 1960, LHC, MG129, Folder 12.

4. A "Song of Africa across Oceans and Centuries"

1. Malcolmson, "The Varieties of Cosmopolitan Experience," 240.

2. Mphahlele, "Your History Demands Your Heartbeat," 161.

3. The connection between South Africa and black America in the early and mid-twentieth century has been comprehensively explored in recent scholarship. See especially Masilela, "The 'Black Atlantic' and African Modernity in South Africa"; Mphahlele, "Your History Demands Your Heartbeat"; Nixon, *Homelands, Harlem and Hollywood*; Titlestad, *Making the Changes*; and Vinson, *The Americans Are Coming!* For more on the "Sophiatown Renaissance" of the 1950s, see also Chapman, "More Than Telling a Story"; Driver, "*Drum* Magazine"; Gready, "The Sophiatown Writers"; Nicol, *A Good-Looking Corpse*; and Sampson, *Drum*.

4. Abrahams, *Tell Freedom*, 230.

5. See Rive, "Taos in Harlem"; Rive, *Writing Black*, 102–4; Mphahlele, "Your History Demands Your Heartbeat," 173; and Mphahlele, *Afrika My Music*, 19. See also Viljoen, "Proclamations and Silences"; and Viljoen, "Langston Hughes and Richard Rive."

6. Quoted in Nixon, *Homelands, Harlem and Hollywood*, 28.

7. Nor is my positioning of South African literature within a black Atlantic frame meant to discount other important recent scholarship that shifts the transnational focus away from the Atlantic world altogether and instead situates South Africa within the Indian Ocean and/or its intracontinental cultural exchanges with sub-Saharan Africa. For work on south-south connections between South Africa and

India, see among others: Frenkel, *Reconsiderations;* Hofmeyr, "The Black Atlantic"; Rastogi, *Afrindian Fictions*; and Samuelson, "Textual Circuits." See also Helgesson, *Transnationalism in Southern African Literature,* which links South Africa to its Lusophone neighbors. This work all confirms my premise that pan-African entanglement is not exclusive but overlaps with ties and circuits connecting it with the world at large.

8. Mphahlele, *The African Image* (1962), 34.
9. Mphahlele, *The Wanderers,* 49.
10. Mphahlele, *The African Image* (1962), 37.
11. Mphahlele, *Voices in the Whirlwind,* 154.
12. Mphahlele, *The African Image* (1962), 32.
13. Ibid., 30.
14. Michael Chapman writes, "In grasping at chances to escape the demeaning strictures of apartheid, the writer aimed to realise himself abroad as a worldly citizen: as a man of culture who could appreciate Beethoven as effortlessly as pennywhistle street music" (Chapman, *Southern African Literature,* 243).
15. Sampson, *Drum,* 20.
16. To name only three examples: Hughes's correspondence with Abrahams began when the South African writer sent a letter to Hughes's publisher saying that he liked *Simple Takes a Wife* (letter from Langston Hughes to Peter Abrahams, 9 January 1954, in Graham and Walters, *Langston Hughes and the South African* Drum *Generation,* 27). Later that year, Rive would write that he had just met a "Coloured University student who was appalled because I had not read *Simple Speaks His Mind*" (letter from Richard Rive to Langston Hughes, 30 July 1954, in Graham and Walters, *Langston Hughes and the South African* Drum *Generation,* 43). And in the periodical *African Forum* in 1965, Nat Nakasa wrote that a book he was reviewing "took me right back to the days when Johannesburg was thrilled by Jesse B. Semple" (Nakasa, "Harlem," 137).
17. Letter from Richard Rive to Langston Hughes, not dated (circa July 1954), in Graham and Walters, *Langston Hughes and the South African* Drum *Generation,* 38.
18. Letter from Peter Abrahams to Langston Hughes, 14 January 1954, in Graham and Walters, *Langston Hughes and the South African* Drum *Generation,* 27.
19. Abrahams, *Tell Freedom,* 226.
20. Rive, *Writing Black,* 10.
21. Hughes, introduction to *An African Treasury,* 9.
22. The original correspondence is held in the Langston Hughes Papers at the Beinecke Rare Book and Manuscript Library. Photocopies of many of the South Africans' side of the correspondence can be found at the National English Literary Museum in Grahamstown, South Africa. Poems by Abrahams, Clarke, Modisane, Mphahlele, and Rive would appear in *Poems from Black Africa,* along with a poem by Ntantala's husband, A. C. Jordan. Hughes also traded letters with Ruth First in her capacity as editor of *Fighting Talk* and with Ronald Segal, editor of *Africa South.*
23. Hughes, "Jazz from Africa via America Now Goes Back to Africa," 9.

24. Letter from Todd Matshikiza to Langston Hughes, 8 February 1960, in Graham and Walters, *Langston Hughes and the South African* Drum *Generation*, 103.

25. Letter from Langston Hughes to Richard Rive, 6 October 1954, in Graham and Walters, *Langston Hughes and the South African* Drum *Generation*, 46.

26. Letter from Langston Hughes to Bloke Modisane, 4 December 1960, in Graham and Walters, *Langston Hughes and the South African* Drum *Generation*, 119. "Bantu" is a word for black Africans (literally "people" in isiZulu), made into a derogatory term by its apartheid associations but reclaimed by Hughes and Modisane and transformed into a term of affection.

27. Letter from Bloke Modisane to Langston Hughes, 18 January 1961, in Graham and Walters, *Langston Hughes and the South African* Drum *Generation*, 123.

28. Letter from Bloke Modisane to Langston Hughes, 31 May 1962, in Graham and Walters, *Langston Hughes and the South African* Drum *Generation*, 149.

29. Letter from Richard Rive to Langston Hughes, 10 March 1955, in Graham and Walters, *Langston Hughes and the South African* Drum *Generation*, 79.

30. Mentioned in letter from Langston Hughes to Bloke Modisane, 4 December 1960, in Graham and Walters, *Langston Hughes and the South African* Drum *Generation*, 119.

31. Letter from Es'kia Mphahlele to Langston Hughes, 18 June 1954, in Graham and Walters, *Langston Hughes and the South African* Drum *Generation*, 35–36.

32. Letter from Peter Clarke to Langston Hughes, 20 June 1962, in Graham and Walters, *Langston Hughes and the South African* Drum *Generation*, 150.

33. Dimock, *Through Other Continents*, 4.

34. Moore, "The Bessie Head–Langston Hughes Correspondence," 5.

35. Hughes invited Modisane to join him at Spoleto in a letter from 27 May 1962, in Graham and Walters, *Langston Hughes and the South African* Drum *Generation*, 147.

36. Rive, *Writing Black*, 102–4.

37. Rive, "An Interview with Langston Hughes and Arna Bontemps: A Paper Presented to 3601 Education and Professional Writing Class, Teachers College, Columbia University in Partial Fulfillment of the Requirements for the Degree Master of Arts," 2 April 1966, Richard Rive Papers, National English Literary Museum, Grahamstown, South Africa.

38. Despite *Africa South*'s general policy not to publish material already available elsewhere, it did publish two poems by Hughes that were revised versions of previously published poems, as well as one poem, "Memo to the Non-White Peoples," published there for the first time (letter from Ronald Segal to Langston Hughes, 8 January 1957, LHP, Box 3, Folder 43). The poems were "Johannesburg Mines," "Memo," and "In Explanation of Our Times" and appeared in *Africa South* 1, no. 3 (1957). Two of Hughes's short stories ("Slice Him Down!" and "Cora Unashamed") were reprinted in *Drum* in 1954 and 1955, and in those same years more than a dozen of his "Simple" stories were republished in *Africa!* It is worth

further noting that Hughes allowed his work to be republished in Nigeria's *Black Orpheus* in 1959, when Mphahlele was on the board.

39. Letter from Richard Rive to Langston Hughes, 5 January 1962, in Graham and Walters, *Langston Hughes and the South African* Drum *Generation*, 138.

40. In a letter to Hughes on 11 June 1956, Abrahams asked, "Do I apologise for inscribing the controversial *Udomo* to you?" In Graham and Walters, *Langston Hughes and the South African* Drum *Generation*, 98.

41. Abrahams, *The Black Experience*, 145–46.

42. A few examples: Hughes often referred the South Africans to his well-connected friend Rosey Pool and to the Transcription Centre in London, which produced radio programs about Africa. He put Rive in touch with his literary agent in New York City, just as Rive was entering his most productive period as a fiction writer (letter from Langston Hughes to Richard Rive, 10 December 1963, in Graham and Walters, *Langston Hughes and the South African* Drum *Generation*, 135). He attempted to help Phyllis Ntantala place articles with American magazines after she and her husband moved to Wisconsin (letter from Langston Hughes to Phyllis Ntantala Jordan, 10 August 1964, LHP, Box 121, Folder 2288). He wrote an endorsement of Abrahams's autobiography *Tell Freedom* for Knopf in 1954: "*Tell Freedom* is as engrossing as fiction and as moving as poetry—only it is real. . . . It illuminates the contemporary news stories from South Africa better than any other book I've read about that troubled land, fact or fiction" (letter from Langston Hughes to Alfred A. Knopf Publishers, 16 May 1954, AAKR, Box 142, Folder 2). Later he promoted *Tell Freedom* in no fewer than four of his columns in the *Chicago Defender* (24 July 1954, 18 December 1954, 2 April 1955, and 10 December 1955). He also mentioned and promoted *Drum* magazine in two different columns (7 May 1955 and 12 September 1959). The American edition of Modisane's *Blame Me on History* boasted a quotation from Hughes calling it "an intensely readable auto-narrative" and "an important addition to the recorded truths of our time."

43. Mphahlele, review of *Darkness and Light*, 55.

44. Letter from Langston Hughes to Ezekiel Mphahlele, 6 October 1954, in Graham and Walters, *Langston Hughes and the South African* Drum *Generation*, 45.

45. Mphahlele, "An African Treasury," 67.

46. Letter from Ezekiel Mphahlele to Langston Hughes, 27 July 1960, in Graham and Walters, *Langston Hughes and the South African* Drum *Generation*, 109.

47. Kim, "We, Too, Rise with You," 424.

48. For a complete database of publications censored under apartheid, see the Beacon for Freedom of Expression website: www.beaconforfreedom.org.

49. See, for example, letter from Richard Rive to Langston Hughes, 7 September 1963, in Graham and Walters, *Langston Hughes and the South African* Drum *Generation*, 170.

50. Chrisman, "Beyond Black Atlantic and Postcolonial Studies," 253–54.

51. Abrahams, *Tell Freedom*, 370.

52. Letter from Richard Rive to Langston Hughes, 17 December 1954, in Graham and Walters, *Langston Hughes and the South African* Drum *Generation*, 57.

53. Ibid.
54. Abrahams, *Return to Goli,* 57.
55. Ibid., 25.
56. Hall, "Negotiating Caribbean Identities," 283–84.
57. Abrahams, *The Black Experience,* 184.
58. Ibid., 221.
59. Chrisman, "Beyond Black Atlantic and Postcolonial Studies," 267.
60. Masemola, "Of Belonging and Becoming," 69.
61. Abrahams, *The Black Experience,* 384.
62. Abrahams, "An Interview with Peter Abrahams," typescript in the National English Literary Museum, Grahamstown, South Africa.
63. Ibid.
64. Abrahams, *The View from Coyaba,* 185–86.
65. Ibid., 412.
66. Ibid., 197.
67. Ibid., 275.
68. Elsewhere Abrahams depicts transplantation as a phenomenon both exceptional and recurring through the ages: "Throughout human history, there have been the minorities who have found themselves in faraway places in different cultures and who have met and fallen in love and married men and women outside their own group. . . . These minority exceptions to the norm are as old as the story of human migration" (Abrahams, *The Black Experience,* 217).
69. Abrahams, *The View from Coyaba,* 425.
70. For an incisive study of the role of radio in renegotiating South African identities in a diasporic context, see Gunner, "Reconfiguring Diaspora."
71. Abrahams, *The Black Experience,* 287.
72. Abrahams, *The View from Coyaba,* 294.
73. Letter from Langston Hughes to Peter Abrahams, 1 February 1954, and letter from Peter Abrahams to Langston Hughes, 20 February 1954, in Graham and Walters, *Langston Hughes and the South African* Drum *Generation,* 28–29.
74. Casanova, *The World Republic of Letters,* 225.
75. Abrahams, *The View from Coyaba,* 27.
76. Ibid., 37.
77. Abrahams, *Return to Goli,* 139.
78. Ibid., 159.
79. Abrahams, *The Black Experience,* 247.
80. Ibid., 365.
81. Ibid., 36.
82. Abrahams, *The View from Coyaba,* 83.
83. Abrahams, *Jamaica,* 53.
84. Ibid.
85. Abrahams, *The View from Coyaba,* 434.
86. Ibid., 435.
87. Ibid., 437.

88. Abrahams, *The Black Experience*, 14.
89. Ibid., 145–46.
90. Ibid., 408.
91. Ibid., 384.
92. Ibid., 400.
93. Ibid., 403.
94. Ibid., 402.
95. Gready, *Writing as Resistance*, 157.
96. Quoted in Manganyi, *Exiles and Homecomings*, 56.
97. Letter from Todd Matshikiza to Langston Hughes, 24 November 1960, in Graham and Walters, *Langston Hughes and the South African* Drum *Generation*, 118.
98. Mphahlele, "Negritude—a Phase," 83.
99. Ibid.
100. Sanders, *Complicities*, 94.
101. Rive, "Senghor and Negritude," 137–38.
102. Mphahlele, *The African Image* (1962), 40.
103. Ibid., 43.
104. Ibid., 51, 53.
105. Mphahlele, *Voices in the Whirlwind*, 47.
106. Ibid., 52.
107. Mphahlele, "Interview with Ezekiel Mphahlele," by Lewis Nkosi and Richard Rive, *African Writers of Today*, program 3 (New York: National Educational Television, 1964), typescript, Lewis Nkosi Collection, National English Literary Museum, Grahamstown, South Africa.
108. Ibid.
109. Mphahlele, *The African Image* (1974), 80.
110. Mphahlele, "Homage to Léopold Sédar Senghor," 292.
111. Mphahlele, *Afrika My Music*, 19.
112. Mphahlele, "Langston Hughes," 21.
113. Obee, *Es'kia Mphahlele*, 9.
114. Mphahlele, *The African Image* (1974), 121–22.
115. Ibid., 95.
116. Mphahlele, *Afrika My Music*, 256.
117. Attwell, *Rewriting Modernity*, 130.
118. Mphahlele, *Afrika My Music*, 133, 135.
119. Ibid., 185, 189, 190.
120. Attwell, *Rewriting Modernity*, 135.
121. Ibid., 136.
122. Mphahlele, *Chirundu*, 89.
123. Mphahlele, *Afrika My Music*, 218–19.
124. The most common implication was that Mphahlele had made concessions to the apartheid state to be allowed to teach in South African universities and have the ban on his writings lifted. Daniel Kunene, for example, wrote in 1981 that

Mphahlele "was returning not on his own terms, but on those of the South African government" (Kunene, "Ideas under Arrest," 433).

125. Manganyi, *Exiles and Homecomings,* 290.

126. Mphahlele, *Afrika My Music,* 250.

127. Ibid., 197.

128. Letter from Es'kia Mphahlele to Bernth Lindfors, 6 December 1977, in *Research in African Literatures* Records, Harry Ransom Center, University of Texas at Austin, Folder 18.

129. McDonald, *The Literature Police,* 244.

130. Mphahlele, "African Identity," 63.

131. Mphahlele, "Notes Towards the Rationale for the Necessary Inclusion of Africa," 127.

132. Attwell, *Rewriting Modernity,* 128–29.

133. Mphahlele, *The African Image* (1974), 93.

134. Jay, *Global Matters,* 71.

5. Cultural Exchange in *Ask Your Mama*

1. Hughes, *I Wonder as I Wander,* 2.

2. Ibid., 400; emphasis in original.

3. See Deleuze and Guattari, *A Thousand Plateaus,* 3–25.

4. Glissant, *Poetics of Relation,* 11.

5. Appiah, *The Ethics of Identity,* 246.

6. Hughes, *I Wonder as I Wander,* 333.

7. Ibid., 242.

8. Ibid., 114.

9. Hughes, "One More 'S' in the U.S.A.," in *The Collected Poems,* 176–77.

10. Hughes, "American Interest in African Culture" (official transcript of speech in Accra, Ghana), 29 June 1962, LHP, Box 483, Folder 12221, quoted in Rampersad, *The Life of Langston Hughes,* 2:355; emphasis in original.

11. Hughes, *Ask Your Mama,* in *The Collected Poems,* 481; italics and capitalization in original.

12. Rampersad, *The Life of Langston Hughes,* 2:316.

13. Ibid.

14. Saul, *Freedom Is, Freedom Ain't,* 123.

15. "Ask Your Mama," *Virginia Kirkus Bulletin* 29 (15 August 1961): 767, in Dace, *Langston Hughes,* 635.

16. Allen Thornton, "The Loss of Beauty," *Dallas Times Herald,* 22 October 1961, E9, in Dace, *Langston Hughes,* 635.

17. Nkosi, *Africa Abroad,* episode 3, TC/108, 3 May 1962, TCR, Folder 5.3.

18. Dudley Fitts, "A Trio of Singers in Varied Keys," *New York Times Book Review,* 29 October 1961, 16, in Dace, *Langston Hughes,* 636.

19. J. Saunders Redding, "Book Review: Hughes Scores Again," *Afro-American Magazine,* 28 November 1961, 2, in Dace, *Langston Hughes,* 637–38.

20. Gates, *The Signifying Monkey,* 69, 71.

21. Dollard, "The Dozens," 22. This is one of the typed excerpts that appears in Hughes's "Research articles and notes" folder for *Ask Your Mama*, LHP, Box 269, Folder 4452.

22. Hughes, *Ask Your Mama*, in *The Collected Poems*, 480, 509.

23. Dollard, "The Dozens," 24.

24. Saul's description of the poem is apt: *Ask Your Mama* "played the Dozens with and around its reader, attacking a white interlocutor and pummeling older poetic models" (Saul, *Freedom Is, Freedom Ain't*, 124).

25. Roumain, *Gouverneurs de la rosée*, 19.

26. Clark Collin, "New Books Appraised," *Library Journal* 86 (1 December 1961): 4190–91, in Dace, *Langston Hughes*, 638.

27. Thomas McGrath, "Poems Just for Jazz," *National Guardian*, 19 February 1962, 9, in Dace, *Langston Hughes*, 644.

28. Rampersad, *The Life of Langston Hughes*, 2:319.

29. Hughes, *Ask Your Mama*, in *The Collected Poems*, 528.

30. Dudley Fitts drew the comparison to Lindsay in a contemporary review, "A Trio of Singers in Varied Keys," *New York Times Book Review*, 29 October 1961, 16, in Dace, *Langston Hughes*, 636. Rampersad claims that Hughes was "consciously taking his lead" from Lindsay's *The Congo* when he wrote the musical cues (Rampersad, *The Life of Langston Hughes*, 2:317).

31. Miller, "Framing and Framed Languages," 3.

32. Lenz, "'The Riffs, Runs, Breaks, and Distortions,'" 278.

33. Hughes, "Prelude to Our Age," in *The Collected Poems*, 383.

34. Hughes, *Ask Your Mama*, in *The Collected Poems*, 512–13; italics in original.

35. Ibid., 477–78.

36. Hughes, "That Sad, Happy Music Called Jazz," in *Langston Hughes and the* Chicago Defender, 216.

37. Ibid., 217.

38. Hughes, *Ask Your Mama*, in *The Collected Poems*, 477.

39. Ibid., 527; emphasis in original.

40. Ibid., 477.

41. Ibid., 528–29.

42. Ibid., 490–91.

43. Ibid., 491.

44. Ibid., 499–500.

45. Ibid., 478.

46. Ibid., 527.

47. "Discount to Names Mentioned in *Ask Your Mama*," AAKR, 1380.3.

48. "Publicity note on *Ask Your Mama*," LHP, Box 272, Folder 4472.

49. Hughes, *Ask Your Mama*, in *The Collected Poems*, 486.

50. Ibid., 524.

51. Ibid., 527.

52. Ibid., 503–4.

53. Ibid., 495.
54. Ibid., 479.
55. Kim, "We, Too, Rise with You," 435.
56. Hughes, *Ask Your Mama,* in *The Collected Poems,* 479–80.
57. Edwards, "Langston Hughes and the Futures of Diaspora," 695.
58. Scanlon, "News from Heaven," 47.
59. Gilroy, *The Black Atlantic,* 88.
60. Hughes, *Ask Your Mama,* in *The Collected Poems,* 513.
61. Ibid.
62. Miller, *The Art and Imagination of Langston Hughes,* 93.
63. Hughes, *Ask Your Mama,* in *The Collected Poems,* 517.
64. Ibid.
65. Saul, *Freedom Is, Freedom Ain't,* 138.
66. Hughes, *Ask Your Mama,* in *The Collected Poems,* 483.
67. Taylor, *Zora and Langston.*

Coda

1. Marshall, *Triangular Road,* 163. This tripartite self represented "the widespread nature of fracturing that originated with a displaced West African population during the slave trade" (Pettis, *Toward Wholeness,* 2).
2. Marshall, *Triangular Road,* 3–4.
3. Hughes's correspondence with Marshall over an eight-year period is preserved in LHP, Box 110, 2071.
4. Marshall, *Triangular Road,* 11.
5. Ibid., 17–18.
6. Ibid., 13, 29, 33.
7. McGill, *Constructing Black Selves,* 76.
8. Denniston, *The Fiction of Paule Marshall,* xiv.
9. Pettis, *Toward Wholeness,* 3.
10. Ibid., 2.
11. Marshall, "Shaping the World of My Art," 108–9.
12. Alexander, *Mother Imagery in the Novels of Afro-Caribbean Women,* 170.
13. Marshall, *Praisesong for the Widow,* 15–17.
14. Ibid., 47; italics in original.
15. Ibid., 12.
16. Ibid., 237.
17. Ibid., 94.
18. Ibid., 131, 132.
19. Ibid., 127.
20. Ibid., 129.
21. Hughes, *Ask Your Mama,* in *The Collected Poems,* 499.
22. Marshall, *Praisesong for the Widow,* 122.
23. Irele, *The Negritude Moment,* 42.
24. Marshall, *Praisesong for the Widow,* 137.

25. Ibid., 139.
26. Ibid., 186.
27. Meredith Gadsby reads Avey as "a woman who must achieve wholeness via return" and usefully points out how fluid Marshall's conception of "nation" seems to be in the novel: "In the Big Drum performance, 'nation' is made at the level of identification with origins, and with a history in constant danger of erasure" (Gadsby, *Sucking Salt*, 156, 158).
28. Marshall, *Praisesong for the Widow*, 175.
29. Ibid., 176.
30. Ibid., 209.
31. Marshall and Condé, "Return of a Native Daughter," 53.
32. Denniston provides book-length support for her thesis that "the cultural space surrounding Marshall's characters also includes her imaginative reconstruction of African history and culture to establish an underlying unity that links all peoples of African descent" (Denniston, *The Fiction of Paule Marshall*, xii).
33. Marshall, *Praisesong for the Widow*, 75.
34. Ibid., 70.
35. Ibid., 69.
36. Ibid., 67. The idea that hearing the language sparked Avey's dream about her great-aunt is repeated on page 196.
37. Marshall, "Interview with Paule Marshall," 15. In this regard, see Davis, who argues that Marshall's aim as a writer is "to facilitate healing by encouraging cultural interconnections, by emphasizing contact zones, by spiritually reconnecting New World blacks to Africa" (Davis, "Rearticulations, Reconnections and Refigurations," 282). Later Davis elaborates: "By dancing the Big Drum, Avey has inserted herself in a wide spiritual community that has the ability to sustain her by reconnecting her to the parts of herself that really matter" (285).
38. Marshall, *Praisesong for the Widow*, 69.
39. Ibid., 72.
40. Ibid., 78.
41. Ibid., 163.
42. Ibid.
43. Ibid., 161.
44. Pettis, *Toward Wholeness*, 118.
45. Ibid., 121–22; Denniston, *The Fiction of Paule Marshall*, 139.
46. Marshall, *Praisesong for the Widow*, 165.
47. Ibid., 167.
48. Ibid., 178.
49. Ibid., 33.
50. Ibid., 34. Alexander calls the dance "indicative of the ancestors whose movements were limited because of the chains that restrained them, yet in spite of these chains they danced and celebrated life" (Alexander, *Mother Imagery in the Novels of Afro-Caribbean Women*, 184).
51. Marshall, *Praisesong for the Widow*, 250.

52. Ibid., 39.
53. Ibid., 42.
54. Ibid., 43.
55. Ibid., 47.
56. Ibid., 115.
57. Ibid., 256.
58. Ibid., 236.
59. Ibid., 240.
60. Quoted in Pettis, *Toward Wholeness*, 131. Marshall's description of the dance also confirms Denniston's observation that "form and content merge to foster unity in a personal, communal, and national sense" that then expands "to include an international or global sense" (Denniston, *The Fiction of Paule Marshall*, xviii).
61. Marshall, *Praisesong for the Widow*, 242.
62. Ibid., 187–88.
63. Ibid., 227.
64. Ibid., 232.
65. Ibid., 241–42.
66. Ibid., 190.
67. Ibid., 191; emphasis added. The same idea is repeated in very similar language on 249.
68. Ibid., 244.
69. Ibid., 245.
70. Mbembe, *Critique of Black Reason*, 95.
71. Marshall and Condé, "Return of a Native Daughter," 52.
72. Marshall, *Triangular Road*, 152.
73. Marshall, *Praisesong for the Widow*, 191.
74. Ibid., 243; emphasis added.
75. Ibid., 194, 205.
76. Marshall, "Shaping the World of My Art," 97.
77. Ibid., 98.
78. Ibid., 103.

Bibliography

Archival Sources

Beinecke Rare Book and Manuscript Library, Yale University
Langston Hughes Papers
James Weldon Johnson and Grace Nail Johnson Papers
Claude McKay Collection
Jean Toomer Papers

Bibliothèque Littéraire Jacques Doucet, Paris-Sorbonne University
Fond Michel Leiris

Bibliothèque Nationale de France à Richelieu, Paris
Fond Jean-Marie Serreau

Harry Ransom Center, University of Texas at Austin
Alfred A. Knopf, Inc. Records
Nancy Cunard Collection
Research in African Literatures Records
Transcription Centre Records
William A. Bradley Literary Agency Records

National English Literary Museum, Grahamstown, South Africa
Lewis Nkosi Collection
Richard Rive Papers

New York Library for the Performing Arts
Black Nativity Papers

Schomburg Center for Research in Black Culture, New York Public Library
Léon-Gontran Damas Papers
Langston Hughes Collection
Joel and Amy Spingarn Papers

Published Sources

Abrahams, Peter. *The Black Experience in the Twentieth Century: An Autobiography and Meditation.* Bloomington: Indiana University Press, 2000.

———. "An Interview with Peter Abrahams." By Itala Vivana. Coyaba, Jamaica, February 1989. National English Literary Museum, Grahamstown, South Africa.

———. *Jamaica: An Island Mosaic.* London: Her Majesty's Stationery Office, 1957.

———. *Return to Goli.* London: Faber and Faber, 1953.

———. *Tell Freedom: Memories of Africa.* New York: Alfred A. Knopf, 1963.

———. *This Island, Now.* London: Faber and Faber, 1966.

———. *The View from Coyaba.* London: Faber and Faber, 1985.

Achebe, Chinua. "Spelling Our Proper Name." In *The Education of a British-Protected Child: Essays,* 54–67. New York: Alfred A. Knopf, 2009.

———. *There Was a Country: A Personal History of Nigeria.* New York: Penguin, 2012.

Ako, Edward O. "The Harlem Renaissance and the Negritude Movement: Literary Relations and Influences." PhD diss., University of Illinois, 1982.

———. "Langston Hughes and the Négritude Movement: A Study in Literary Influences." *College Language Association Journal* 28, no. 1 (1984): 46–56.

Alessandrini, Anthony. "'Enough of This Scandal': Reading Gilroy through Fanon, or Who Comes after 'Race'?" In *Retrieving the Human: Rereading Paul Gilroy,* edited by Rebecka Rutledge Fisher and Jay Garcia, 53–93. Albany: SUNY Press, 2014.

Alexander, Simone A. James. *Mother Imagery in the Novels of Afro-Caribbean Women.* Columbia: University of Missouri Press, 2001.

Appadurai, Arjun. *Modernity at Large: Cultural Dimensions of Globalization.* Minneapolis: University of Minnesota Press, 1996.

Appiah, Kwame Anthony. "Cosmopolitan Patriots." In *Cosmopolitics: Thinking and Feeling beyond the Nation,* edited by Pheng Cheah and Bruce Robbins, 91–114. Minneapolis: University of Minnesota Press, 1998.

———. *Cosmopolitanism: Ethics in a World of Strangers.* New York: W. W. Norton, 2006.

———. *The Ethics of Identity.* Princeton, NJ: Princeton University Press, 2005.

Arnold, A. James. Introduction to *The Original 1939 Notebook of a Return to the Native Land,* by Aimé Césaire, xi–xxii. Middletown, CT: Wesleyan University Press, 2013.

———. *Modernism and Negritude: The Poetry and Poetics of Aimé Césaire.* Cambridge, MA: Harvard University Press, 1981.

Attwell, David. *Rewriting Modernity: Studies in Black South African Literary History.* Pietermaritzburg: University of KwaZulu-Natal Press, 2005.

Badiane, Mamadou. *The Changing Face of Afro-Caribbean Cultural Identity: Negrismo and Négritude.* Lanham, MD: Lexington Books, 2010.

Baker, Houston, Jr. *Blues, Ideology, and Afro-American Literature: A Vernacular Theory.* Chicago: University of Chicago Press, 1984.

Baldwin, Kate A. *Beyond the Color Line and the Iron Curtain: Reading Encounters between Black and Red, 1922–1963*. Durham, NC: Duke University Press, 2002.
Bamikunle, Aderemi James. "The Harlem Renaissance and Negritude Poetry: The Development of Black Written Literature." PhD diss., University of Wisconsin, 1983.
Beal, Wesley. *Networks of Modernism: Reorganizing American Narrative*. Iowa City: University of Iowa Press, 2015.
Bennett, Louise. "Jamaica Oman." In *The Routledge Reader in Caribbean Literature*, edited by Alison Donnell and Sarah Lawson Welsh, 145–46. New York: Routledge, 1996.
Berman, Jessica. "Imagining World Literatures: Modernism and Comparative Literature." In *Disciplining Modernism*, edited by Pamela Caughie, 53–70. New York: Palgrave Macmillan, 2009.
Berry, Faith. *Langston Hughes: Before and beyond Harlem*. Westport, CT: Lawrence Hill, 1983.
Bhabha, Homi K. "Foreword: Framing Fanon." In *The Wretched of the Earth*, vii–xli. New York: Grove, 2004.
———. "Unsatisfied: Notes on Vernacular Cosmopolitanism." In *Text and Nation: Cross-Disciplinary Essays on Cultural and National Identities*, edited by Laura García-Moreno and Peter C. Pfeiffer, 191–207. Columbia, SC: Camden House, 1996.
Breslin, Paul. "Intertextuality, Translation, and Postcolonial Misrecognition in Aimé Césaire." In *Analyzing World Fiction: New Horizons in Narrative Theory*, edited by Frederick Luis Aldama, 245–67. Austin: University of Texas Press, 2011.
Brière, Eloise. "The Harlem Renaissance and Négritude: The Transmission of Modernism." In *Texte africain et voies-voix critiques: Littératures africaines et antillaises (maghreb, Afrique noire, antilles, immigration)*, edited by Claude Bouygues, 55–71. Paris: L'Harmattan, 1992.
Bulson, Eric. *Little Magazine, World Form*. New York: Columbia University Press, 2017.
Casanova, Pascale. *The World Republic of Letters*. Translated by M. B. Debevoise. Cambridge, MA: Harvard University Press, 2004.
Césaire, Aimé. *Discourse on Colonialism*. Translated by Joan Pinkham. New York: Monthly Review, 1972.
———. "Entretien avec Aimé Césaire." Interview by Jacqueline Leiner. In *Tropiques Numbers 1–5, 1941–1942*, v–xxxv. Paris: Éditions Jean-Michel Place, 1978.
———. "An Interview with Aimé Césaire." By René Depestre. In *Discourse on Colonialism*, translated by Joan Pinkham, 79–94. New York: Monthly Review Press, 1972.
———. "Introduction à la poésie nègre américaine." *Tropiques* 2 (1941): 37–42.
———. *La Poésie*. Edited by Daniel Maximin and Gilles Carpentier. Paris: Éditions du Seuil, 1994.
———. *La tragédie du roi Christophe*. Rev. ed. Paris: Présence Africaine, 1970.

———. "Lost Body." In *The Oxford Book of Caribbean Verse*, edited by Stewart Brown and Mark McWatt, translated by Anthony Hurley, 39–40. Oxford: Oxford University Press, 2005.

———. *Nègre je suis, nègre je resterai: Entretiens avec Françoise Vergès*. Paris: Éditions Albin Michel, 2005.

———. *Notebook of a Return to My Native Land / Cahier d'un retour au pays natal*. Translated by Mireille Rosello and Annie Pritchard. Tarset, UK: Bloodaxe Books, 1995.

———. *The Original 1939 Notebook of a Return to the Native Land*. Translated by A. James Arnold and Clayton Eshleman. Middletown, CT: Wesleyan University Press, 2013.

———. "Présentation." *Tropiques* 1 (1941): 5–6.

———. *Toussaint Louverture*. Paris: Présence Africaine, 1961.

———. *The Tragedy of King Christophe: A Play*. Translated by Paul Breslin and Rachel Ney. Evanston, IL: Northwestern University Press, 2015.

Césaire, Aimé, Suzanne Césaire, Georges Gratiant, Aristide Maugée, René Ménil, and Lucie Thésée. "Réponse de *Tropiques*." In *Tropiques Numbers 1–5, 1941–1942*, xxxix. Paris: Éditions Jean-Michel Place, 1978.

Chapman, Michael, ed. "More Than Telling a Story: *Drum* and Its Significance in Black South African Writing." In *The Drum Decade: Stories from the 1950s*, 183–227. Pietermaritzburg: University of Natal Press, 2001.

———. *Southern African Literature*. London: Longman, 1996.

Chatterjee, Partha. *The Nation and Its Fragments: Colonial and Postcolonial Histories*. Princeton, NJ: Princeton University Press, 1993.

Chinitz, David. "Rejuvenation through Joy: Langston Hughes, Primitivism, and Jazz." *American Literary History* 9, no. 1 (1997): 60–78.

Chrisman, Laura. "Beyond Black Atlantic and Postcolonial Studies: The South African Differences of Sol Plaatje and Peter Abrahams." In *Postcolonial Studies and Beyond*, edited by Ania Loomba, Suvir Kaul, Matti Bunzl, Antoinette Burton, and Jed Esty, 252–71. Durham, NC: Duke University Press, 2005.

Clifford, James. *The Predicament of Culture: Twentieth-Century Ethnography, Literature, and Art*. Cambridge, MA: Harvard University Press, 1988.

———. *Routes: Travel and Translation in the Late Twentieth Century*. Cambridge, MA: Harvard University Press, 1997.

Cobb, Martha. *Harlem, Haiti, and Havana: A Comparative Critical Study of Langston Hughes, Jacques Roumain, Nicolás Guillén*. Washington, DC: Three Continents, 1979.

Confiant, Raphaël. *Aimé Césaire, une traversée paradoxale du siècle*. Paris: Écriture, 2006.

Cooper, Wayne. *Claude McKay: Rebel Sojourner in the Harlem Renaissance*. Baton Rouge: Louisiana State University Press, 1987.

Corbould, Clare. *Becoming African Americans: Black Public Life in Harlem, 1919–1939*. Cambridge, MA: Harvard University Press, 2009.

Cunard, Nancy, ed. *Negro: An Anthology.* London: Wishart & Co., 1934.
Dace, Tish. *Langston Hughes: The Contemporary Reviews.* Cambridge: Cambridge University Press, 1997.
Damas, Léon Gontran. "Negritude in Retrospect." *Continuities: Journal from the Black Studies Department of the City College of New York* (1974). LGDP, Box 2.
———. *Pigments—névralgies.* Paris: Présence Africaine, 1972.
Dash, J. Michael. Introduction to *Masters of the Dew,* by Jacques Roumain, 5–21. Oxford: Heinemann, 1978.
Davis, Andrea. "Rearticulations, Reconnections and Refigurations: Writing Africa through the Americas." In *Africa and Trans-Atlantic Memories: Literary and Aesthetic Manifestations of Diaspora and History,* edited by Naana Opoku-Agyemang, Paul E. Lovejoy, and David V. Trotman, 275–90. Trenton, NJ: Africa World Press, 2008.
Davis, Gregson. *Aimé Césaire.* Cambridge: Cambridge University Press, 2008.
De Barros, Paul. "'The Loud Music of Life': Representations of Jazz in the Novels of Claude McKay." *Antioch Review* 57, no. 3 (1999): 306–17.
De Jongh, James. "The Poet Speaks of Places: A Close Reading of Langston Hughes's Literary Use of Place." In *A Historical Guide to Langston Hughes,* edited by Steven C. Tracy, 65–84. Oxford: Oxford University Press, 2004.
———. *Vicious Modernism: Black Harlem and the Literary Imagination.* Cambridge: Cambridge University Press, 1990.
DeLoughrey, Elizabeth. *Routes and Roots: Navigating Caribbean and Pacific Island Literatures.* Honolulu: University of Hawai'i Press, 2007.
Deleuze, Gilles, and Felix Guattari. *A Thousand Plateaus: Capitalism and Schizophrenia.* Translated by Brian Massumi. Minneapolis: University of Minnesota Press, 1987.
Denning, Michael. *The Cultural Front: The Laboring of American Culture in the Twentieth Century.* London: Verso, 1997.
Denniston, Dorothy Hamer. *The Fiction of Paule Marshall: Reconstructions of History, Culture, and Gender.* Knoxville: University of Tennessee Press, 1995.
Dimock, Wai Chee. *Through Other Continents: American Literature across Deep Time.* Princeton, NJ: Princeton University Press, 2006.
Dixon, Melvin. Introduction to *The Collected Poetry of Léopold Sédar Senghor,* xxiii–xli. Charlottesville: University Press of Virginia, 1991.
———. "Rivers Remembering Their Source: Comparative Studies in Black Literary History—Langston Hughes, Jacques Roumain, and Negritude." In *Afro-American Literature: The Reconstruction of Instruction,* edited by Dexter Fisher and Robert B. Stepto, 25–43. New York: Modern Language Association, 1979.
Dollard, John. "The Dozens: Dialectic of Insult." *American Imago* 1 (November 1939): 3–25.
Donnell, Alison. *Twentieth-Century Caribbean Literature: Critical Moments in Anglophone Literary History.* London: Routledge, 2006.

Driver, Dorothy. "*Drum* Magazine (1951–99) and the Spatial Configurations of Gender." In *Text, Theory, Space: Land, Literature and History in South Africa and Australia*, edited by Kate Darian-Smith, Liz Gunner, and Sarah Nuttall, 231–42. London: Routledge, 1996.

Du Bois, W. E. B. "A Second Journey to Pan-Africa." In *W. E. B. Du Bois: A Reader*, edited by David Levering Lewis, 662–67. New York: Henry Holt, 1995.

———. "Two Novels: Nella Larsen, *Quicksand* and Claude McKay, *Home to Harlem*." *Crisis* 35 (June 1928): 202.

———. "What Is Africa to Me?" In *W. E. B. Du Bois: A Reader*, edited by David Levering Lewis, 655–59. New York: Henry Holt, 1995.

Edwards, Brent Hayes. "Aimé Césaire and the Syntax of Influence." *Research in African Literatures* 36, no. 2 (2005): 1–18.

———. "Langston Hughes and the Futures of Diaspora." *American Literary History* 19, no. 3 (2007): 689–711.

———. *The Practice of Diaspora: Literature, Translation, and the Rise of Black Internationalism*. Cambridge, MA: Harvard University Press, 2003.

Eyerman, Ron. *Cultural Trauma: Slavery and the Formation of African American Identity*. Cambridge: Cambridge University Press, 2001.

Fabre, Michel. "Du mouvement nouveau noir à la négritude Césairienne." In *Soleil éclateé: Mélanges offerts à Aimé Césaire a' l'occasion de son soixante-dixième anniversaire*, edited by Jacqueline Leiner, 149–59. Tübingen: Narr, 1984.

———. *From Harlem to Paris: Black American Writers in France, 1840–1980*. Urbana: University of Illinois Press, 1993.

Fanon, Frantz. *Black Skin, White Masks*. Translated by Richard Philcox. New York: Grove, 2008.

———. *The Wretched of the Earth*. Translated by Richard Philcox. New York: Grove, 2004.

Feuser, W. F. "Afro-American Literature and Negritude." *Comparative Literature* 28, no. 4 (1976): 289–308.

Figueroa, Víctor. *Prophetic Visions of the Past: Pan-Caribbean Representations of the Haitian Revolution*. Columbus: Ohio State University Press, 2015.

Fisher, Rebecka Rutledge. *Habitations of the Veil: Metaphor and the Poetics of Black Being in African American Literature*. Albany: SUNY Press, 2014.

Fitts, Dudley, and H. R. Hays, eds. *Anthology of Contemporary Latin-American Poetry*. Norfolk, CT: New Directions, 1942.

Fowler, Carolyn. *A Knot in the Thread: The Life and Work of Jacques Roumain*. Washington, DC: Howard University Press, 1980.

François, Anne M. *Rewriting the Return to Africa: Voices of Francophone Caribbean Women Writers*. Lanham, MD: Lexington Books, 2011.

Frenkel, Ronit. *Reconsiderations: South African Indian Fiction and the Making of Race in Postcolonial Culture*. Pretoria: Unisa Press, 2010.

Gadsby, Meredith M. *Sucking Salt: Caribbean Women Writers, Migration, and Survival*. Columbia: University of Missouri Press, 2006.

Garcia, Jay. "Dynamic Nominalism in Alain Locke and Paul Gilroy." In *Retrieving the Human: Rereading Paul Gilroy*, edited by Rebecka Rutledge Fisher and Jay Garcia, 161–86. Albany: SUNY Press, 2014.

———. "*Home of the Brave*, Frantz Fanon and Cultural Pluralism." *Comparative American Studies: An International Journal* 4, no. 1 (2006): 49–65.

Garrett, Naomi. *The Renaissance of Haitian Poetry*. Paris: Présence Africaine, 1963.

Gates, Henry Louis, Jr. *The Signifying Monkey: A Theory of Afro-American Literary Criticism*. New York: Oxford University Press, 1988.

Gilroy, Paul. *The Black Atlantic: Modernity and Double Consciousness*. Cambridge, MA: Harvard University Press, 1993.

———. "The Black Atlantic and the Re-enchantment of Humanism." Tanner Lecture on Human Values, Yale University, 21 February 2014. Tanner Humanities Center Lecture Library, University of Utah. https://tannerlectures.utah.edu/Gilroy%20manuscript%20PDF.pdf.

———. "A Dialogue on the Human: An Interview with Paul Gilroy." In *Retrieving the Human: Rereading Paul Gilroy*, edited by Rebecka Rutledge Fisher and Jay Garcia, 207–26. Albany: SUNY Press, 2014.

Glissant, Édouard. *Poetics of Relation*. Translated by Betsy Wing. Ann Arbor: University of Michigan Press, 1997.

Goyal, Yogita. *Romance, Diaspora, and Black Atlantic Literature*. Cambridge: Cambridge University Press, 2010.

Graham, Shane. "Black Atlantic Literature as Transnational Cultural Space." *Literature Compass* 10, no. 6 (2013): 508–18.

———. "'This Curious Thing': Richard Rive, the Harlem Renaissance, and the Commodification of the Black Atlantic." *Safundi: The Journal of South African and American Studies* 18, no. 3 (2017): 205–20.

Graham, Shane, and John Walters, eds. *Langston Hughes and the South African Drum Generation: The Correspondence*. New York: Palgrave Macmillan, 2010.

Grantham, Awendela Oni. "Messianism in French Caribbean Literature: Césaire, Roumain, Glissant, and Schwarz-Bart." PhD diss., Yale University, 2012.

Gready, Paul. "The Sophiatown Writers of the Fifties: The Unreal Reality of Their World." *Journal of Southern African Studies* 16, no. 1 (1990): 139–64.

———. *Writing as Resistance: Life Stories of Imprisonment, Exile, and Homecoming from Apartheid South Africa*. Lanham, MD: Lexington Books, 2003.

Griffith, Glyne. *The BBC and the Development of Anglophone Caribbean Literature, 1943–1958*. New York: Palgrave Macmillan, 2016.

Guillén, Nicolás. *Cuba Libre: Poems by Nicolás Guillén*. Translated by Langston Hughes and Ben Frederic Carruthers. Los Angeles: Anderson and Ritchie, 1948.

———. "Sobre Jacques Roumain." In *Prosa de prisa: 1929–1972*, edited by Angel Augier, 391–94. Havana: Universidad de La Habana, 1975.

Gunner, Liz. "Reconfiguring Diaspora: Africa on the Rise and the Radio Voices of Lewis Nkosi and Bloke Modisane." *Social Dynamics* 36, no. 2 (2010): 256–71.

Halbwachs, Maurice. *On Collective Memory.* Translated by Lewis A. Coser. Chicago: University of Chicago Press, 1992.
Hale, Thomas A. "From Afro-America to Afro-France: The Literary Triangle Trade." *French Review* 49, no. 6 (1976): 1089–96.
Hale, Thomas A., and Kora Véron. "Is There Unity in the Writings of Aimé Césaire?" *Research in African Literatures* 41, no. 1 (2010): 46–70.
Hall, Stuart. "Negotiating Caribbean Identities." In *Postcolonial Discourses: An Anthology*, edited by Gregory Castle, 280–92. Oxford: Blackwell, 2001.
Harris, Rodney E. *L'humanisme dans le théâtre d'Aimé Césaire.* Montreal: Éditions Naaman, 1973.
Harris, Wilson. *The Womb of Space: The Cross-Cultural Imagination.* Westport, CT: Greenwood, 1983.
Hathaway, Heather. *Caribbean Waves: Relocating Claude McKay and Paule Marshall.* Bloomington: Indiana University Press, 1999.
Helgesson, Stefan. *Transnationalism in Southern African Literature: Modernists, Realists, and the Inequality of Print Culture.* New York: Routledge, 2009.
Hirsch, Marianne. *The Generation of Postmemory: Writing and Visual Culture after the Holocaust.* New York: Columbia University Press, 2012.
Hofmeyr, Isabel. "The Black Atlantic Meets the Indian Ocean: Forging New Paradigms of Transnationalism for the Global South." *Social Dynamics* 33, no. 2 (2007): 3–32.
Hughes, Langston, ed. *An African Treasury: Articles/Essays/Stories/Poems by Black Africans.* New York: Pyramid Books, 1960.
———. "An Appeal for Jacques Roumain." In *Essays on Art, Race, Politics, and World Affairs*, vol. 9 of *Collected Works of Langston Hughes*, edited by Christopher De Santis, 554–55. Columbia: University of Missouri Press, 2002.
———. *The Big Sea.* New York: Hill and Wang, 1940.
———. "Black Writers in a Troubled World." In *Essays on Art, Race, Politics, and World Affairs*, vol. 9 of *Collected Works of Langston Hughes*, edited by Christopher De Santis, 474–79. Columbia: University of Missouri Press, 2002.
———. "Christmas Comes but Once a Year So Do Your Shopping with Good Cheer." *Chicago Defender*, 15 December 1951.
———. "Claude McKay: The Best." In *Essays on Art, Race, Politics, and World Affairs*, vol. 9 of *Collected Works of Langston Hughes*, edited by Christopher De Santis, 53–56. Columbia: University of Missouri Press, 2002.
———. *The Collected Poems of Langston Hughes.* Edited by Arnold Rampersad and David Roessel. New York: Vintage, 1994.
———. "Conversación con Langston Hughes." Interview by Nicolás Guillén. In *Prosa de prisa, 1929–1972*, edited by Angel I. Augier, 16–19. Havana: Universidad de La Habana, 1975.
———. *Emperor of Haiti.* In *The Plays to 1942: "Mulatto" to "The Sun Do Move,"*, vol. 5 of *Collected Works of Langston Hughes*, edited by Leslie Catherine Sanders and Nancy Johnston, 278–332. Columbia: University of Missouri Press, 2002.

———. *I Wonder as I Wander: An Autobiographical Journey.* New York: Hill and Wang, 1956.
———. "Jazz from Africa via America Now Goes Back to Africa." *Chicago Defender,* 7 May 1955.
———. *Langston Hughes and the* Chicago Defender: *Essays on Race, Politics, and Culture, 1942–62.* Edited by Christopher C. Santis. Urbana: University of Illinois Press, 1995.
———. "A Letter from Haiti." *New Masses* 7 (July 1931): 9.
———. "Marry Black, New Credo." *Chicago Defender,* 31 July 1965, 10.
———. "The Need for Heroes." *Crisis,* June 1941, 184–85.
———. "Negro Art and Claude McKay." In *Essays on Art, Race, Politics, and World Affairs,* vol. 9 of *Collected Works of Langston Hughes,* edited by Christopher De Santis, 46. Columbia: University of Missouri Press, 2002.
———. "The Negro Artist and the Racial Mountain." In *Essays on Art, Race, Politics, and World Affairs,* vol. 9 of *Collected Works of Langston Hughes,* edited by Christopher De Santis, 31–36. Columbia: University of Missouri Press, 2002.
———. *Not without Laughter.* New York: Alfred A. Knopf, 1930.
———. "Notes at Summer's End." *Chicago Defender,* 9 October 1948.
———. "Passing." In *Ways of White Folks,* 51–56. New York: Alfred A. Knopf, 1934.
———. "People without Shoes." *New Masses* 12 (1931): 12.
———, ed. *Poems from Black Africa.* Bloomington: Indiana University Press, 1963.
———. *Scottsboro, Limited: A One Act Play.* In *The Plays to 1942: "Mulatto" to "The Sun Do Move,"* vol. 5 of *Collected Works of Langston Hughes,* edited by Leslie Catherine Sanders and Nancy Johnston, 106–29. Columbia: University of Missouri Press, 2002.
———. *Selected Letters of Langston Hughes.* Edited by Arnold Rampersad, David Roessel, and Christa Fratantoro. New York: Alfred A. Knopf, 2015.
———. "Ships, Sea and Africa: Random Impressions of a Sailor on His First Trip down the West Coast of the Motherland." In *Essays on Art, Race, Politics, and World Affairs,* vol. 9 of *Collected Works of Langston Hughes,* edited by Christopher De Santis, 24–27. Columbia: University of Missouri Press, 2002.
———. "Slave on a Block." In *The Ways of White Folks,* 19–31. New York: Vintage, 1933.
———. "Too Much of Race." *Crisis,* September 1937, 272.
———. "The Twenties: Harlem and Its Negritude." *African Forum* 1, no. 4 (1966): 11–20.
———. *Troubled Island: An Opera in Three Acts.* In *Gospel Plays, Operas, and Later Dramatic Works,* vol. 6 of *Collected Works of Langston Hughes,* edited by Leslie Catherine Sanders, 15–51. Columbia: University of Missouri Press, 2004.
———. "White Shadows in a Black Land." In *Essays on Art, Race, Politics, and World Affairs,* vol. 9 of *Collected Works of Langston Hughes,* edited by Christopher De Santis, 51–53. Columbia: U of Missouri P, 2002.
———. "Who's Passing for Who?" In *Laughing to Keep from Crying,* 1–14. New York: Henry Holt, 1952.

Hughes, Langston, and Arna Bontemps, eds. *The Poetry of the Negro, 1746–1949.* New York: Doubleday, 1949.
Huyssen, Andreas. *Present Pasts: Urban Palimpsests and the Politics of Memory.* Stanford, CA: Stanford University Press, 2003.
Irele, F. Abiola. "The Harlem Renaissance and the Negritude Movement." In *The Cambridge History of African and Caribbean Literature,* edited by F. Abiola Irele and Simon Gikandi, 759–84. Cambridge: Cambridge University Press, 2003.
———. *The Negritude Moment: Explorations in Francophone African and Caribbean Literature and Thought.* Trenton, NJ: Africa World Press, 2011.
Jack, Belinda E. *Negritude and Literary Criticism: The History and Theory of "Negro-African" Literature in French.* Westport, CT: Greenwood, 1996.
Jackson, Richard L. *Black Writers and Latin America: Cross-Cultural Affinities.* Washington, DC: Howard University Press, 1998.
Jackson, Maurice, and Jacqueline Bacon, eds. *African Americans and the Haitian Revolution: Selected Essays and Historical Documents.* New York: Routledge, 2013.
Jahn, Janheinz. *Neo-African Literature: A History of Black Writing.* New York: Grove, 1968.
Jaji, Tsitsi Ella. *Africa in Stereo: Modernism, Music, and Pan-African Solidarity.* Oxford: Oxford University Press, 2014.
James, C. L. R. *The Black Jacobins: Toussaint Louverture and the San Domingo Revolution.* New York: Vintage, 1963.
Jay, Paul. *Global Matters: The Transnational Turn in Literary Studies.* Ithaca, NY: Cornell University Press, 2010.
Jemie, Onwuchekwa. "Or Does It Explode?" In *Langston Hughes: Critical Perspectives Past and Present,* edited by Henry Louis Gate Gates Jr. and Kwame Anthony Appiah, 69–93. New York: Amistad, 1993.
Jonassaint, Jean. "Césaire et Haïti, des apports à évaluer." *Francophonies d'Amérique* 36 (2013): 135–65.
Jones, Donna V. *The Racial Discourses of Life Philosophy: Négritude, Vitalism, and Modernity.* New York: Columbia University Press, 2010.
Kaisary, Philip. *The Haitian Revolution in the Literary Imagination: Radical Horizons, Conservative Constraints.* Charlottesville: University of Virginia Press, 2014.
Kaussen, Valerie. *Migrant Revolutions: Haitian Literature, Globalization, and U.S. Imperialism.* Lanham, MD: Lexington Books, 2008.
Kennedy, Ellen Conroy, ed. *The Negritude Poets: An Anthology of Translations from the French.* New York: Thunder's Mouth, 1989.
Kernan, Ryan J. "Lost and Found in Black Translation: Langston Hughes's Translations of French- and Spanish-Language Poetry, His Hispanic and Francophone Translators, and the Fashioning of Radical Black Subjectivities." PhD diss., University of California, Los Angeles, 2007.
Kesteloot, Lilyan. *Black Writers in French: A Literary History of Negritude.* Translated by Ellen Conroy Kennedy. Washington, DC: Howard University Press, 1991.

———. *Césaire et Senghor: Un pont sur l'Atlantique.* Paris: L'Harmattan, 2006.
Kim, Daniel Won-gu. "'We, Too, Rise with You': Recovering Langston Hughes's African (Re)Turn 1954–1960 in *An African Treasury*, the *Chicago Defender*, and *Black Orpheus*." *African American Review* 41, no. 3 (2007): 419–41.
Kubayanda, Josaphat B. *The Poet's Africa: Africanness in the Poetry of Nicolás Guillén and Aimé Césaire.* New York: Greenwood, 1990.
Kunene, Daniel P. "Ideas under Arrest: Censorship in South Africa." *Research in African Literatures* 12, no. 4 (1981): 421–39.
Kutzinski, Vera M. *The Worlds of Langston Hughes: Modernism and Translation in the Americas.* Ithaca, NY: Cornell University Press, 2012.
Largey, Michael. *Vodou Nation: Haitian Art Music and Cultural Nationalism.* Chicago: University of Chicago Press, 2006.
Lee, Christopher J. *Frantz Fanon: Toward a Revolutionary Humanism.* Athens: Ohio University Press, 2015.
———. *Making a World after Empire: The Bandung Moment and Its Political Afterlives.* Athens: Ohio University Press, 2010.
Lenz, Gunter H. "'The Riffs, Runs, Breaks, and Distortions of the Music of a Community in Transition': Redefining African American Modernism and the Jazz Aesthetic in Langston Hughes' *Montage of a Dream Deferred* and *Ask Your Mama*." *Massachusetts Review: A Quarterly of Literature, the Arts and Public Affairs* 44, no. 1–2 (2003): 269–82.
Léro, Étienne. "Misère d'une poésie." *Légitime défense* 1 (1932): 10–12.
Lewis, David Levering. *When Harlem Was in Vogue.* New York: Penguin, 1981.
Locke, Alain. "The Legacy of the Ancestral Arts." In *The New Negro: Voices of the Harlem Renaissance*, edited by Alain Locke, 254–67. New York: Athenium, 1992.
———. "Who and What Is 'Negro'?" In *The Philosophy of Alain Locke: Harlem Renaissance and Beyond*, edited by Leonard Harris, 209–28. Philadelphia: Temple University Press, 1989.
Louis, Patrice. *Conversation avec Aimé Césaire.* Paris: Arléa, 2004.
Malcolmson, Scott L. "The Varieties of Cosmopolitan Experience." In *Cosmopolitics: Thinking and Feeling beyond the Nation*, edited by Pheng Cheah and Bruce Robbins, 233–45. Minneapolis: University of Minnesota Press, 1998.
Manganyi, N. Chabani. *Exiles and Homecomings: A Biography of Es'kia Mphahlele.* Johannesburg: Ravan, 1983.
Marshall, Paule. *Brown Girl, Brownstones.* New York: Random House, 1959.
———. "Interview with Paule Marshall." By Sandi Russell. *Wasafiri* 4, no. 8 (1988): 14–16.
———. *Praisesong for the Widow.* New York: Plume, 1983.
———. "Shaping the World of My Art." *New Letters* 40 (1973): 97–112.
———. *Soul Clap Hands and Sing.* Washington, DC: Howard University Press, 1961.
———. *Triangular Road: A Memoir.* New York: Basic Civitas, 2009.
Marshall, Paule, and Maryse Condé. "Return of a Native Daughter: An Interview with Paule Marshall and Maryse Conde." Translated by John Williams. *SAGE: A Scholarly Journal on Black Women* 3, no. 2 (1986): 52–53.

Marx, Karl. *Class Struggles in France, 1848–1850*. London: ElecBook, 2000.
Masemola, Kgomotso. "Of Belonging and Becoming: Black Atlantic (Inter-)Cultural Memory in the Early Autobiographies of Peter Abrahams and Es'kia Mphahlele." *Current Writing: Text and Reception in Southern Africa* 16, no. 2 (2004): 47–70.
Masilela, Ntongela. "The 'Black Atlantic' and African Modernity in South Africa." *Research in African Literatures* 27, no. 4 (1996): 88–96.
Mbembe, Achille. *Critique of Black Reason*. Translated by Laurent Dubois. Durham, NC: Duke University Press, 2017.
———. "The New Africans: Between Nativism and Cosmopolitanism." In *Readings in Modernity in Africa*, edited by Peter Geschiere, Birgit Meyer, and Peter Pels, 107–11. Bloomington: Indiana University Press, 2008.
Mbom, Clément. *Le théâtre d'Aimé Césaire: Ou, la primauté de l'universalité humaine*. Paris: Éditions Fernand Nathan, 1979.
McClintock, Anne. "Imperial Ghosting and National Tragedy: Revenants from Hiroshima and Indian Country in the War on Terror." *PMLA* 129, no. 4 (2014): 819–29.
McDonald, Peter D. *The Literature Police: Apartheid Censorship and Its Cultural Consequences*. Oxford: Oxford University Press, 2009.
McGill, Lisa D. *Constructing Black Selves: Caribbean American Narratives and the Second Generation*. New York: New York University Press, 2005.
McKay, Claude. *Banjo*. San Diego: Harcourt Brace Jovanovich, 1929.
———. *Complete Poems*. Edited by William Maxwell. Urbana: University of Illinois Press, 2008.
———. *Harlem: Negro Metropolis*. New York: E. P. Dutton, 1940.
———. *Home to Harlem*. Boston: Northeastern University Press, 1928.
———. *A Long Way from Home: An Autobiography*. San Diego: Harvest/HBJ, 1970.
———. *My Green Hills of Jamaica and Five Jamaican Short Stories*. Edited with and introduction by Mervyn Morris. Kingston: Heinemann Educational Books, 1979.
———. *The Passion of Claude McKay: Selected Prose and Poetry 1912–1948*. Edited by Wayne Cooper. New York: Alfred A. Knopf, 1976.
McLaren, Joseph. *Langston Hughes: Folk Dramatist in the Protest Tradition, 1921–1943*. Westport, CT: Greenwood, 1997.
Miller, R. Baxter. *The Art and Imagination of Langston Hughes*. Lexington: University Press of Kentucky, 1989.
———. "Framing and Framed Languages in Hughes's *Ask Your Mama: 12 Moods for Jazz*." *MELUS* 17, no. 4 (1991): 3–13.
Modisane, Bloke. *Blame Me on History*. New York: E. P. Dutton, 1963.
Moore, David Chioni, ed. "The Bessie Head–Langston Hughes Correspondence, 1960–1961." *Research in African Literatures* 41, no. 3 (2010): 1–20.
Mphahlele, Es'kia. "African Identity: Nationalism—The African Personality—Negritude." 1978. In *Es'kia Continued*, 43–63. Johannesburg: Stainbank and Associates, 2004.
———. *The African Image*. New York: Praeger, 1962.

———. *The African Image.* Rev. ed. New York: Praeger, 1974.
———. *Afrika My Music: An Autobiography, 1957–1983.* Johannesburg: Ravan, 1984.
———. *Chirundu.* Johannesburg: Ravan, 1979.
———. "Homage to Léopold Sédar Senghor." In *Es'kia,* 291–94. Cape Town: Kwela Books, 2002.
———. "Langston Hughes." *Black Orpheus,* no. 9 (1961): 16–21.
———. "The Makerere Writers Conference." *Africa Report,* July 1962.
———. "Negritude—a Phase." *New African* 8 (June 1963): 82–84.
———. "Notes Towards the Rationale for the Necessary Inclusion of Africa: Further Thoughts on an Ideal Programme of African Literature at Secondary and Tertiary Levels." In *Es'kia Continued,* 122–29. Johannesburg: Stainbank and Associates, 2004.
———. Review of *An African Treasury,* edited by Langston Hughes. *Black Orpheus* 9 (June 1961): 67–68.
———. Review of *Darkness and Light,* edited by Peggy Rutherfoord. *Black Orpheus* 6 (November 1959): 55.
———. *Voices in the Whirlwind and Other Essays.* New York: Hill and Wang, 1972.
———. *The Wanderers.* New York: Macmillan, 1971.
———. "Your History Demands Your Heartbeat: Historical Survey of the Encounter Between Africans and African Americans." In *Es'kia,* 157–82. Cape Town: Kwela Books, 2002.
Mullen, Edward J., ed. *Langston Hughes in the Hispanic World and Haiti.* Hamden, CT: Archon Books, 1977.
Murphy, Laura T. *Metaphor and the Slave Trade in West African Literature.* Athens: Ohio University Press, 2012.
Nakasa, Nat. "Harlem." *African Forum* 1, no. 1 (1965): 136–38.
Nicol, Mike. *A Good-Looking Corpse: The World of* Drum*—Jazz and Gangsters, Hope and Defiance in the Townships of South Africa.* London: Secker and Warburg, 1991.
Niles, Blair. *Black Haiti: A Biography of Africa's Eldest Daughter.* New York: Putnam's, 1926.
Nixon, Rob. *Homelands, Harlem and Hollywood: South African Culture and the World Beyond.* New York: Routledge, 1994.
Nora, Pierre. "Between Memory and History: Les Lieux de Mémoire." Translated by Marc Roudebush. *Representations* 26 (1989): 7–24.
Nuttall, Sarah. *Entanglement: Literary and Cultural Reflections on Post-Apartheid.* Johannesburg: Wits University Press, 2009.
Nwankwo, Ifeoma Kiddoe. *Black Cosmopolitanism: Racial Consciousness and Transnational Identity in the Nineteenth-Century Americas.* Philadelphia: University of Pennsylvania Press, 2005.
Obee, Ruth. *Es'kia Mphahlele: Themes of Alienation and African Humanism.* Athens: Ohio University Press, 1999.

OBIWU. "The Pan-African Brotherhood of Langston Hughes and Nnamdi Azikiwe." *Dialectical Anthropology* 31, no. 1–3 (2007): 143–65.
Oboe, Annalisa, and Anna Scacchi, eds. *Recharting the Black Atlantic: Modern Cultures, Local Communities, Global Connections.* New York: Routledge, 2008.
Ojo-Ade, Femi. *Aimé Césaire's African Theater: Of Poets, Prophets and Politicians.* Trenton, NJ: Africa World Press, 2010.
Palumbo-Liu, David. *The Deliverance of Others: Reading Literature in a Global Age.* Durham, NC: Duke University Press, 2012.
Parry, Benita. "Resistance Theory / Theorizing Resistance or Two Cheers for Nativism." In *Rethinking Fanon: The Continuing Dialogue,* edited by Nigel C. Gibson, 215–50. Amherst, NY: Humanity Books, 1999.
Patterson, Anita. *Race, American Literature and Transnational Modernisms.* Cambridge: Cambridge University Press, 2008.
Pettis, Joyce Owens. *Toward Wholeness in Paule Marshall's Fiction.* Charlottesville: University Press of Virginia, 1995.
Piot, Charles. "Atlantic Aporias: Africa and Gilroy's *Black Atlantic.*" *South Atlantic Quarterly* 100, no. 1 (2001): 155–70.
Piquion, Rene. *Langston Hughes: Un chant nouveau.* Port-au-Prince, Haiti: Imprimerie de l'Etat, 1940.
Pochmara, Anna. *The Making of the New Negro: Black Authorship, Masculinity, and Sexuality in the Harlem Renaissance.* Amsterdam: Amsterdam University Press, 2011.
Pratt, Mary Louise. "Arts of the Contact Zone." *Profession* (1991): 33–40.
Quinn, Brian. "Staging Culture: Senghor, Malroux and the Theatre Programme at the First World Festival of Negro Arts." In *The First World Festival of Negro Arts, Dakar 1966: Contexts and Legacies,* edited by David Murphy, 83–96. Liverpool: Liverpool University Press, 2016.
Rabaka, Reiland. *The Negritude Movement: W. E. B. Du Bois, Leon Damas, Aime Cesaire, Leopold Senghor, Frantz Fanon, and the Evolution of an Insurgent Idea.* Lanham, MD: Lexington Books, 2015.
Ramazani, Jahan. *A Transnational Poetics.* Chicago: University of Chicago Press, 2009.
Rampersad, Arnold. *The Life of Langston Hughes.* 2 vols. Oxford: Oxford University Press, 2002.
Rastogi, Pallavi. *Afrindian Fictions: Race, Diaspora, and National Desire in South Africa.* Columbus: Ohio State University Press, 2008.
Remy, Anselme. "The Duvalier Phenomenon." *Caribbean Studies* 14, no. 2 (1974): 38–65.
Rive, Richard. "Senghor and Negritude." In *Selected Writings: Stories, Essays, Plays,* 119–39. Johannesburg: Ad. Donker, 1977.
———. "Taos in Harlem: An Interview with Langston Hughes." In *Selected Writings: Stories, Essays, Plays,* 110–18. Johannesburg: Ad. Donker, 1977.
———. *Writing Black.* Cape Town: David Philip, 1981.

Robbins, Bruce. *Feeling Global: Internationalism in Distress*. New York: New York University Press, 1999.

———. *Perpetual War: Cosmopolitanism from the Viewpoint of Violence*. Durham, NC: Duke University Press, 2012.

Robolin, Stéphane. *Grounds of Engagement: Apartheid-Era African American and South African Writing*. Urbana: University of Illinois Press, 2015.

Rosello, Mireille. "Introduction: Aimé Césaire and the *Notebook of a Return to My Native Land* in the 1990s." In *Notebook of a Return to My Native Land*, 9–68. Tarset, UK: Bloodaxe Books, 1995.

Rothberg, Michael. *Multidirectional Memory: Remembering the Holocaust in the Age of Decolonization*. Stanford, CA: Stanford University Press, 2009.

Roumain, Jacques. *Gouverneurs de la rosée*. Coconut Creek, FL: Educa Vision, 1944.

———. *Masters of the Dew*. Translated by Langston Hughes and Will Mercer Cook. Oxford: Heinemann, 1944.

———. *Le sacrifice du tambour-assoto(r)*. Port-au-Prince: Bureau d'Ethnologie de la République d'Haiti, 1943.

———. *When the Tom-Tom Beats*. Translated by Joanne Fungaroli and Ronald Sauer. Washington, DC: Azul Editions, 1995.

Sampson, Anthony. *Drum: The Story of the Newspaper That Won the Heart of Africa*. Cambridge, MA: Houghton Mifflin, 1957.

Samuelson, Meg. "Textual Circuits and Intimate Relations: A Community of Letters across the Indian Ocean." In *Print, Text and Book Cultures in South Africa*, edited by Andrew van der Vlies, 87–108. Johannesburg: Wits University Press, 2012.

Sanders, Mark. *Complicities: The Intellectual and Apartheid*. Durham, NC: Duke University Press, 2002.

Sartre, Jean-Paul. "Black Orpheus." Translated by S. W. Allen. *Présence africaine* 10–11 (1951): 219–47.

Saul, Scott. *Freedom Is, Freedom Ain't: Jazz and the Making of the Sixties*. Cambridge, MA: Harvard University Press, 2003.

Saunders, Frances Stonor. *The Cultural Cold War: The CIA and the World of Arts and Letters*. New York: New Press, 1999.

Scanlon, Larry. "News from Heaven: Vernacular Time in Langston Hughes's *Ask Your Mama*." *Callaloo* 25, no. 1 (2002): 45–65.

Schuessler, Jennifer. "Langston Hughes Just Got a Year Older: How a Random Late-Night Online Search Led to New Discoveries about the Poet's Birth and Early Years." *New York Times*, 9 August 2018.

Senghor, Léopold Sédar. "The African Road to Socialism." In *Readings in Modernity in Africa*, edited by Peter Geschiere, Birgit Meyer, and Peter Pels, 85–86. Bloomington: Indiana University Press, 2008.

———. *The Collected Poetry of Léopold Sédar Senghor*. Translated by Melvin Dixon. Charlottesville: University Press of Virginia, 1991.

———. "La poésie négro-américaine." In *Liberté 1: Négritude et humanisme*, 104–21. Paris: Éditions du Seuil, 1964.

———. "To New York." In *Poems from Black Africa*, edited by Langston Hughes, translated by Ulli Beier, 141–43. Bloomington: Indiana University Press, 1963.

Seyhan, Azade. *Writing outside the Nation*. Princeton, NJ: Princeton University Press, 2001.

Shepperson, George. "Pan-Africanism and 'Pan-Africanism': Some Historical Notes." *Phylon* 23, no. 4 (1962): 346–58.

Shields, John P. "'Never Cross the Divide': Reconstructing Langston Hughes's *Not without Laughter*." *African American Review* 28, no. 4 (1994): 601–13.

Shohat, Ella. "Imaging Terra Incognita: The Disciplinary Gaze of Empire." *Public Culture* 3, no. 2 (1991): 41–70.

Shuttlesworth-Davidson, Carolyn Elizabeth. "Literary Collectives of the New Negro Renaissance and the Negritude Movement." PhD Dissertation, University of Michigan, 1980.

Smethurst, James Edward. *The New Red Negro: The Literary Left and African American Poetry, 1930–1946*. Oxford: Oxford University Press, 1999.

Smith, Matthew J. *Red & Black in Haiti: Radicalism, Conflict, and Political Change, 1934–1957*. Chapel Hill: University of North Carolina Press, 2009.

Spivak, Gayatri Chakravorty. "An Interview with Gayatri Chakravorty Spivak." By Sara Danius and Stefan Jonsson. *Boundary 2* 20, no. 2 (Summer 1993): 24–50.

———. "Subaltern Studies: Deconstructing Historiography." In *The Spivak Reader: Selected Works of Gayatri Chakravorty Spivak*, edited by Donna Landry and Gerald MacLean, 203–35. New York: Routledge, 1996.

Stephens, Michelle Ann. *Black Empire: The Masculine Global Imaginary of Caribbean Intellectuals in the United States, 1914–1962*. Durham, NC: Duke University Press, 2005.

Stoddart, D. R. "Darwin, Lyell, and the Geological Significance of Coral Reefs." *British Journal for the History of Science* 9, no. 2 (1976): 199–218.

Taylor, Diana. *The Archive and the Repertoire: Performing Cultural Memory in the Americas*. Durham, NC: Duke University Press, 2003.

Taylor, Yuval. *Zora and Langston: A Story of Friendship and Betrayal*. New York: W. W. Norton, 2019.

Thurston, Michael. "Black Christ, Red Flag: Langston Hughes on Scottsboro." *College Literature* 22, no. 3 (1995): 30–49.

Titlestad, Michael. *Making the Changes: Jazz in South African Literature and Reportage*. Pretoria: University Press of South Africa, 2004.

Torgovnick, Marianna. *Gone Primitive: Savage Intellects, Modern Lives*. Chicago: University of Chicago Press, 1990.

Vandercook, John W. *Black Majesty: The Life of Christophe, King of Haiti*. New York: Harper & Bros., 1928.

Viljoen, Shaun. "Langston Hughes and Richard Rive: Notes Towards a Biography of Richard Rive." *English Studies in Africa* 41, no. 2 (1998): 55–65.

———. "Proclamations and Silences: 'Race,' Self-Fashioning and Sexuality in the Trans-Atlantic Correspondence between Langston Hughes and Richard Rive." *Social Dynamics* 33, no. 2 (2007): 105–22.

Vinson, Robert T. *The Americans Are Coming! Dreams of African American Liberation in Segregationist South Africa.* Athens: Ohio University Press, 2012.

Washington, Johnny. *Alain Locke and Philosophy.* Westport, CT: Greenwood, 1986.

———. *A Journey into the Philosophy of Alain Locke.* Westport, CT: Greenwood, 1994.

Wright, Richard. *Black Power: Three Books from Exile.* New York: Harper Perennial, 2008.

Zeleza, Paul Tiyambe. "Rewriting the African Diaspora: Beyond the Black Atlantic." *African Affairs* 104, no. 414 (2005): 35–68.

Index

Abrahams, Peter, 3, 5, 17, 24, 32, 111, 156, 160–63, 165–66, 170–82, 188, 209, 220, 225, 228n3, 262n14, 262n22, 264nn40–42; and African tradition, 188; books dedicated to Hughes, 168, 264n40; *The Black Experience in the Twentieth Century,* 162, 168, 172–73, 175, 178, 180–81, 265n68; and black nationalism, 24, 179–81; and communism, 24; and Harlem Renaissance, 160, 228n3; and Hughes, vii, 3, 111, 156, 160–61, 165–66, 170, 176, 180–83, 188, 209, 220, 225, 228n3, 262n16, 264n40; influence of Hughes's work on, 168, 181; *Jamaica: An Island Mosaic,* 178–79; and Jamaican identity, 172; and Es'kia Mphahlele, 180–81; and Negritude, 32, 168, 181–83; and primitivism, 176–79; and race, 162, 171; *Return to Goli,* 172, 177–78; *Tell Freedom,* 160, 165–66, 171, 173, 228n3, 264n42; *This Island, Now,* 173; *The View from Coyaba,* 162–63, 173–80; *A Wreath for Udomo,* 168

Accra (Ghana/Gold Coast), 22, 28, 32, 128, 130, 156–57, 159, 192, 194, 204, 222, 235

Achebe, Chinua, 156, 158, 170, 261n19; "Spelling Our Proper Name," 158; *Things Fall Apart,* 170

Addis Ababa (Ethiopia), 155

Africa, 10, 18–19, 22, 26, 35–36, 38, 93, 153–59, 170, 196, 212, 222; as ancestral/spiritual homeland, 11–12, 16, 28, 45–48, 56, 60, 70, 74, 88, 96, 99, 115, 124, 130–31, 137, 140, 153–54, 156–57, 177–78, 184–86, 189, 203, 211, 219, 225, 251n44; cultural practices derived from, 24, 32, 47, 50, 110, 120–22, 142–43, 148, 154, 178–79, 188, 221, 225; dance derived from, 12, 33, 51, 76, 121, 131, 142, 216, 219–24 (*see also specific dances*); folklore and folk/peasant culture derived from, 71–72, 75, 98–100, 103, 169, 174, 178, 185, 213, 220, 225; foodways derived from, 12, 76, 121, 178, 201–2; as a foundation of black identity, 4, 31, 76, 79, 92, 122–24, 148–49, 154, 177–78, 181, 199, 231n42; literary representations of, 3, 5, 16, 46–49, 60, 88, 92, 96, 112, 153–55, 159, 161, 165, 177, 182, 189, 197, 228n4; as model of anticolonialism and resistance, 63, 155–56, 159, 169, 194, 197, 204–7, 225; modern, 11, 28, 63, 154–59, 169–71, 177–78, 183–85, 189, 192, 197, 204, 225; music derived from, 29, 70–71, 76, 84, 110, 121, 166, 196, 221–23; mythologizing and romanticizing of, 2, 5, 11, 16, 18, 28, 46–47, 70–71, 79, 85, 88, 103, 112, 153–54, 156, 165, 178, 182, 189, 192, 231n39; religions derived from, 80–81, 99, 121, 143, 149–50, 202 (*see also specific religions*); rejection of, 81–83, 85, 214–15; valorization of, 21, 94, 187, 192, 216; values derived from, 21, 32, 81, 85, 109, 115, 117, 120, 125–28, 134, 143, 146, 179–81, 183, 198. *See also specific places*

Africa!, 168, 263n38

Africa Forum, 262n16

African American literature and culture, 19, 38, 87, 107–10, 113, 117, 119, 122, 160–61, 165–67, 170–71, 181–85, 198–99, 209, 213

African diaspora: cultural differences within, 17, 72, 109, 208; kinship and ties across, 17, 31, 34–36, 39, 50–51, 63, 71–72, 86, 96, 126–27, 150, 215–17, 223–24; and memory/history/the past, 5, 64, 80, 92, 97, 100, 138, 148, 179, 188; as moral framework, 63; and its relationship to Africa, 4–5, 11–12, 16, 18, 21, 34, 46–48, 80, 138, 174, 184, 186, 189, 231n39; as source of tropes and imagery, 5, 116–17, 176, 185, 200; as transnational community, 15–16, 90, 100, 102, 105, 110, 175, 212, 231n42. *See also* diaspora

African humanism, 32, 163, 180–81, 183, 187–88, 255n77. *See also* Mphahlele, Es'kia

Africanism, 72, 91, 187

African literature, 1–3, 7, 19, 26–33, 104–5, 112–13, 117, 136, 156–58, 161, 166–70, 176–77, 187, 209, 223–25, 227n2

African nationalism, 126, 172, 192

African personality or originality, 4, 52, 56, 109, 126–27, 153, 163, 172, 182

African Treasury, An, 114, 158, 166, 168–70, 181, 204, 261n18

African Voices, 169

Africa South, 168, 262n22, 263n38

airmail, 2, 8, 112, 163, 167, 175

air travel, 2–3, 8–9, 43, 157, 163, 167–68, 175

Akar, John, 158

Ako, Edward, 249n1

Alabama (United States), 10, 60–61, 171, 242n7, 247n119

al-Sadi, Abd, 22

Alessandrini, Anthony, 137

Alexander, Simone A. James, 213, 270n50

Alexandra Township (South Africa), 185

Alfred A. Knopf, Publishers, 196, 199, 264n42

Algeria, 175

American Communist Party, 54

American Society of African Culture (AMSAC) Conference, 156–57, 261n14

Amin, Idi, 175

Anand, Raj, 90

Anderson, Marian, 199

Angelou, Maya, 209

Anthologie Africaine et Malgache, 114. *See also* Senghor, Léopold Sédar

anthologies, 7, 19, 26–27, 32, 38, 88, 91, 111–14, 156–58, 160, 165–66, 168–70, 204

Anthology of Contemporary Latin American Poetry, 246n86

anticolonialism, 26, 32–33, 78, 82, 84, 104, 150, 156, 169, 194, 197, 203–7

Antar, 55

apartheid, 3–4, 6, 20, 159–61, 164–65, 170–71, 177–78, 181–82, 184, 186, 205, 207, 233n57, 262n14, 266n124. *See also* segregation

apostrophe (rhetorical address), 46, 89, 92–93, 131, 207

Appadurai, Arjun, 13

Appiah, Kwame Anthony, 13–14, 20, 57, 62–63, 190, 233n58. *See also* cosmopolitanism

archive (mode of recording knowledge), 23, 64, 77–80, 152, 223. *See also* Taylor, Diana

archives (institutions), 2, 7, 22, 37, 64, 139, 232n46, 237–38n27

Aristotle, 85

Arnold, A. James, 121, 128, 131, 133–34, 138–39, 152, 249n1

Artibonite River, 143, 147. *See also* rivers and streams

Asia, 14, 20, 26, 33, 51, 57, 60, 88, 123, 190–91, 207

Atlantic Ocean, 16, 22, 88, 93, 144, 148, 176, 192, 220, 231n46. *See also* Black Atlantic; seas, oceans, and sea imagery

Attwell, David, 184–85, 187

Awoonor-Williams, George, 156

Azikiwe, Benjamin Nnamdi, 32, 156, 206, 228n7. *See also* Lincoln University; Nigeria

Babalola, Adeboye, 158

Back to Africa movement, 178. *See also* Garvey, Marcus

Bacon, Jacqueline, 73

Badiane, Mamadou, 249n1

Baker, Houston, Jr., 254–55n49

Baldwin, James, 18, 185

Baldwin, Kate, 38, 240–41n97

bamboula (dance), 142

Bamikunle, Aderemi James, 249n1

Bandung Conference of 1955, 26, 235n84

Bantu education policy, 164

Bantu Men's Social Center, 165

Bantustans, 165

Barbados, 68, 211
Barrow, Raymond, 68
batucada (dance), 110
Beal, Wesley, 15, 29, 63, 236n94
Bedwardism, 202
beguin (dance), 51
Belafonte, Harry, 68, 200
Beier, Ulli, 116
Beinecke Rare Book and Manuscript Library, 37, 63, 65, 68, 158, 236n95, 246n98, 262n22
Bennett, Gwendolyn, 209, 242n4, 249n2
Bennett, Louise, 67–68, 236n99, 243n33
Bennett, Wycliffe, 67
Bergson, Henri, 239n53, 252n6
Berman, Jessica, 232n54
Berry, Faith, 36, 73
Bhabha, Homi K., 26, 236n1
Bible, 20, 178, 189–90
Big Drum ritual, 131, 214, 216–17, 220–24, 270n27, 270n37
Black Atlantic, 13, 16, 27, 35, 43, 57–58, 62, 72, 74, 88, 120, 163, 173–74, 180, 186, 195, 203, 206–8, 218, 224–25, 231–32n46, 261n7. *See also* Gilroy, Paul
Black Atlantic literature, 12, 15–19, 28–30, 35, 54, 68, 97, 104, 137–38, 163, 167, 170, 179–80, 188–89, 208–10, 261–62n7
Black Arts Movement, 209
black consciousness, 63, 185, 187
black cosmopolitanism, 231n40, 232n53
black diaspora. *See* African diaspora
black heritage and past, 12, 21–22, 33, 52, 55, 76, 78, 80–83, 97, 109–10, 115–17, 126–27, 130, 135–36, 142–45, 151, 163, 177, 181, 183, 191, 207, 215, 220, 231n42
black nationalism, 24, 50, 53, 73, 83, 179–80, 204. *See also* African nationalism; nationalism
Black Orpheus, 27, 126, 169, 264n38
Black Power movement, 209
black women, 12, 50, 67–68, 71, 81–82, 85, 88, 103–4, 115, 131–32, 142–43, 146, 159, 179, 185, 209–10, 213, 219, 224–25
blues music, 29, 39, 40, 66–67, 89, 110, 112, 130, 191, 196–97, 203, 214, 255n49. *See also* jazz
bombé (dance), 51
Bonaparte, Napoleon, 73, 77, 140

Bontemps, Arna, 31, 38, 65–68, 111, 113–14, 119, 168, 246n86
Boukman, Dutty, 80, 89. *See also* Haitian Revolution
Bradley, Francine, 246n98
Brazil, 109–10, 157–58, 208, 211, 229n21
Breslin, Paul, 147–48, 257–58n119
Breton, André, 119, 121
Brière, Eloise, 249n1
Brière, Jean, 68, 243n37, 249n1
Brooklyn, 211, 214–16, 218
Brooks, Gwendolyn, 209
Broonzy, Bill, 214
Brouard, Carl, 121, 254n46
Brown, Dan, 12
Brown, David, 174, 180
Brown, Jacob, 173–75, 180
Brown, John, 75, 207
Brown, Sterling, 110
Bulson, Eric, 8, 15, 119
Bunche, Ralph, 200
Bureau d'Ethnologie (Haiti), 90
burru (dance), 51

"Ça Ira," 208
calypso (dance), 110
calypso (music), 68, 207
Camille, Roussan, 68
Campbell, George, 68
Cape Malays, 171
Cape Town (South Africa), 61, 62, 166–67, 171
capitalism, 17–18, 20, 28, 56, 60, 63–64, 86, 91, 102, 155, 175, 201
capoeira (dance), 110
Caribbean, 2, 5, 10, 19, 27, 29–30, 43–44, 59–70, 75, 83, 94, 102, 109, 130, 133, 148–49, 172, 176–78, 190, 196, 206–7, 211–12, 217–18, 223; folklore and folk culture of, 67, 90, 121, 174, 178, 222; literary representations of, 30, 43, 59–65, 116, 148. *See also specific places*
Caribbean literature, 1–3, 7, 26–30, 38, 65, 68, 104–5, 117, 121, 130, 209, 223–25, 227n2
Carriacou, 214, 216–19, 222–24
Carruthers, Benjamin, 66, 247n121
Carver, George Washington, 61
Casanova, Pascale, 19, 176, 232n54
Casely-Hayford, Adelaide, 158
Casely-Hayford, Gladys May, 158
Castro, Fidel, 205, 208

Catholic Church/Catholicism, 52, 82, 99, 106, 134
catalogs of people/places, 10, 23–24, 60–61, 67, 75, 95–96, 130, 154, 198–200, 208
chart of the world's principal international cables, 8
Central Asia, 14, 33, 51, 60, 190–91
Césaire, Aimé, 2, 11, 17, 25, 31, 48, 52, 73, 94, 107–8, 110–11, 113–14, 118–52, 122, 126, 139, 176–77, 182, 187, 206, 208, 216, 220; and Africa, 2, 11, 31, 120, 122, 125–32, 136–38, 146, 148, 150, 152; and communism, 128–29; *Discourse on Colonialism*, 94, 127–28, 134–35, 146, 252n9; and Frantz Fanon, 32, 120, 127, 134–38, 150–51; and Haiti, 31, 73, 120–22, 125, 128, 138–41, 151–52, 177, 257n100, 260n169; and Harlem Renaissance, 107–10, 119, 122–23, 133, 152, 187, 228n3; and Hughes, 2, 25, 31, 119, 113, 118–20, 123–26, 138, 149, 151–52, 206, 228n3, 255–56n77, 257n100; "Introduction à la poésie nègre américaine," 123, 129–30; "Lost Body," 132–33, 149; and Martinican independence, 137, 151, 228n3, 256n97; and nationalism, 137, 150–51; *Nègre je suis, nègre je resterai*, 122, 252n9; and Negritude, 31, 120, 123, 126–36, 140–41, 144, 146–51, 187, 253n30, 256n77; *Notebook of a Return to the Native Land*, 113, 121, 124, 126, 128–34, 138, 140, 145, 149; as politician, 134, 137, 144, 256n97, 258–59n138; presumption of speaking for the black masses, 124, 129–30, 146; and primitivism, 31, 118, 120–21, 123–27, 252n6, 253–54n33; and race, 120, 126–29, 149; and surrealism, 119, 121, 252n9; *The Tragedy of King Christophe*, 31, 118–21, 125, 128–29, 135, 137–51, 257n100, 257–58n119; *Toussaint Louverture*, 139; use of first-person pronouns, 124, 130, 133; and Vodou, 121–22. See also Negritude; *Tropiques*
Césaire, Suzanne, 126
Chapman, Michael, 261n3, 262n14
Chatterjee, Partha, 82
Chicago Defender, 66, 110, 166, 232n56, 247n121, 264n42
Chinitz, David, 11, 48, 70, 228n9, 240n79
Chrisman, Laura, 170–72

Christophe, Henri, 72–73, 77–78, 138–52, 257–58n119, 258n122, 260n169; *The Tragedy of King Christophe* (Césaire), 31, 118–21, 125, 128–29, 135, 137–51, 257n100, 257–58n119; . See also Citadelle Laferrière; Haitian Revolution
CIA, 27, 235n89
Citadelle Laferrière, 72, 77–79, 139–41, 147–48, 152, 202. See also Christophe, Henri
civil rights movement, 21, 28, 63, 206, 211–12
Clark, John Pepper, 7, 156, 158
Clarke, Peter, 161, 166–67, 170, 262n22
class, 27, 35, 49, 78, 81, 83, 91–92, 100–101, 104, 121
Clifford, James, 133, 238n38
Cobb, Martha, 75, 87, 100
collective memory. *See under* memory
Collier, Eugenia, 219
Collin, Clark, 194
Collymore, Frank, 68
colonialism, 8, 12, 15, 18–19, 26, 31, 33–34, 48–49, 57–58, 73, 76, 82, 86, 94, 96, 108, 126, 131, 136–37, 154–55, 175–76, 179, 186, 194, 197, 200, 205–7, 214. See also anticolonialism
coloured identity in South Africa, 171–72
Columbia University, 153, 168
Columbus, Christopher, 155
Committee for the Release of Jacques Roumain, 246n98. See also Bradley, Francine
communism, 24–25, 27, 36, 52–54, 72, 75, 87, 90–91, 95, 106, 129, 155, 191, 212
Condé, Maryse, 217, 224
Conference for African Writers of English Expression, 113, 152, 156, 158, 230n29, 261n14. See also Mbari Artists and Writers Club
conferences, 2–3, 6–7, 26, 32, 113, 152, 156–58, 224, 228n7, 230n29, 235n84
Confiant, Raphaël, 146, 258–59n138
conga (dance), 27
Congo, 71, 93, 96, 130, 200, 208
Congo-Océan Railroad, 93
Congo River, 10, 29, 89, 114, 130
Congress for Cultural Freedom, 27, 235n89
Continents, Les, 107
Cook, Mercer, 31, 98, 101, 105, 242n4, 247n121, 249n2
Coon Carnival (Cape Town), 171
Cooper, Wayne, 38, 50, 239n52

Corbould, Clare, 71, 231n42
cosmopolitanism, 13–14, 20, 24–25, 35, 41–43, 57, 94, 160–61, 164–65, 184, 189–90, 198, 230n28, 231n40, 232n53, 233n58, 238n38; rooted cosmopolitanism, 62; vernacular cosmopolitanism, 236–37n1. *See also* Appiah, Kwame Anthony; black cosmopolitanism; entanglements
Cowl, Carl, 37
creoles (languages), 25, 29, 82, 105, 203, 217–18, 230n33, 259n138. *See also* patois; vernacular language and cultures
creolization, 27, 29, 55, 81, 192, 203
Cri des nègres, le, 90
Crisis, 21, 23, 39, 59, 75–76, 78, 154
Cuba, 33, 43, 47, 60, 63–69, 74, 90, 96, 100, 102, 110, 180, 190, 202–3, 205, 208, 236n99
Cuban Revolution, 205, 208
Cudjoe, 61. *See also* Maroons
Cullen, Countee, 37, 59, 75, 107, 119, 160, 166, 240n79, 242n4, 249n2
cultural cold war, 27–28, 235n89. *See also* Congress of Cultural Freedom; Saunders, Frances Stonor; Transcription Centre
cultural exchange: and aesthetics of entanglement, 28–29, 75, 192, 195; with Africa, 153, 170–74, 184, 189, 199–201; between writers, 5, 8, 97, 110–12, 156–58, 167, 172, 190, 210, 224; and capitalism and commodification, 25, 28, 56–58, 86, 163, 199–201; as cultural sustenance and antidote to isolation, 13, 18, 25–27, 33–34, 156–57, 164, 170–72, 184–85, 187; as vehicle for transnational black culture/identity, 1, 6–8, 20, 23, 25–29, 56–58, 88, 98, 112, 156–57, 162–64, 192, 195, 201, 206, 213, 256n77
Cunard, Nancy, 50, 90, 105, 245–46n86

Dakar (Senegal), 89, 112, 119, 153, 156, 206, 224
Damas, Léon-Gontran, 2, 31, 107–11, 113–14, 117–19, 121–22, 187; and Africa, 117; and Hughes, 2, 111, 250n25, 257n100; "Negritude in Retrospect," 109–10; *Pigments*, 117; proposed translations of Hughes's work, 111, 114; and race, 117; "They Came That Night," 117; "Trite without Doubt," 113–14. *See also* Negritude

Dambala, 80, 106
Danquah, J. B., 156
Danquah, Mabel Dove, 158
Darkness and Light, 169
Dash, J. Michael, 74, 98, 101–2
Davis, Andrea, 16, 270n37
Davis, Gregson, 120, 124, 128, 138, 253n30, 254n44
De Barros, Paul, 239n52
deep time, 15, 59, 63. *See also* Dimock, Wai Chee
De Jongh, James, 8, 228n2, 228n4
Deleuze, Gilles, 190, 267n3. *See also* rhizome
DeLoughrey, Elizabeth, 238n38
Denning, Michael, 229n15
Denniston, Dorothy Hamer, 213, 219, 270n32, 271n60
Depestre, René, 73, 151, 184
Dessalines, Jean-Jacques, 31, 72–73, 75–76, 78–81, 83–85, 100, 129, 139, 143, 214; *Emperor of Haiti* (Hughes), 31, 65, 71–72, 78–86, 96, 100, 103, 152, 154, 214–15, 218, 245n62, 257n100, 260n169. *See also* Haitian Revolution
Diakhaté, Lamine, 19
diaspora, 15–16, 94, 102, 115, 162, 204, 229n13. *See also* African diaspora; Jewish diaspora
Dimock, Wai Chee, 15, 30, 59, 88, 167, 230n35. *See also* deep time; scale enlargement
Diop, Alioune, 110, 158, 206
Diop, Birago, 187
Dixon, Melvin, 115, 249n1
docks and ports, 17, 43–46, 56–58, 217–18, 222
Dodat, François, 19, 111–12, 115
Dollard, John, 193–94
Douglass, Frederick, 22, 61, 177, 207
dozens, the, 193–94, 201, 238n27, 268n21, 268n24
Driver, Dorothy, 261n3
Drum, 3, 27, 32, 156, 158, 160–61, 163–70, 189, 263n38, 264n42, 270n27, 270n37
drums: as calls to resistance, 22, 80, 84, 91, 96, 99; as symbols of Africa, 11–12, 22–23, 28–29, 33, 47, 70–71, 76, 80–81, 84–85, 88–89, 99, 123, 142–43, 153, 161, 196–97, 201, 214–15, 220–23; as symbols of slavery, 80, 99; and Vodou, 29, 60, 80–81, 89

Drumont, Édouard, 125–26
Du Bois, W. E. B., 23, 26, 38–39, 54, 109, 227n1, 234nn79–80, 242n4, 249n2
Dunbar, Paul Laurence, 1, 38, 214
Duvalier, François "Papa Doc," 151, 260n169
Dynamo, 90

Eastland, James, 200–201
Ebony, 160
Éditions Seghers, 111, 114
Edwards, Brent Hayes, 17, 41, 55, 107–8, 205, 227n2, 229n16, 249n1, 251–52n1
Egypt, 93–94, 147, 206
Ekwensi, Cyprian, 156, 158
Eliot, T. S., 194–95
Ellington, Duke, 165, 214
England, 16, 38, 67, 90, 155, 167, 172, 176, 200, 239n52
entanglements: aesthetics of (pan-African) entanglement, 2, 4–6, 12, 28–31, 35–36, 40, 67–68, 72, 100, 114, 138, 177–79, 185, 188–92, 206–11, 223, 225; ancestral plane of, 10–11, 21, 23, 31, 48–50, 71, 89, 99, 109, 117, 123, 148–53, 182–84, 196, 201–3, 209, 216–20, 225; with capitalism, 17–18, 28, 56–58, 64, 86, 155, 201; as channels of cultural exchange, 5, 7–8, 13–14, 18–20, 25, 39–40, 45, 98–99, 144, 157, 163, 176, 180, 187; concentricity of, 9, 14, 32–33, 45, 50–51, 55, 62–63, 108–9, 116, 120, 126–27, 142, 146, 172, 190, 206–7, 225; as condition, 13–15; contemporary plane of, 13–15, 65, 71, 123, 149, 153, 157, 171, 182, 184, 191, 201–2, 207, 209, 217, 225; cultural entanglements, 1, 5, 13, 74, 98, 100, 164, 175, 188, 197; and elitism, 24–25; ethos of (pan-African) entanglement, 5–7, 17–18, 20–21, 24–25, 32, 41, 47, 51–56, 61, 65, 67, 72, 77, 82, 87, 90–91, 95–96, 98, 102, 104, 108, 112, 116, 119, 127, 130, 133, 138, 143, 146, 150, 152, 154, 161–62, 167–68, 177, 179, 181, 185–91, 198, 202, 206, 209–11, 221, 225; intensification and acceleration in twentieth century, 5, 8, 42, 106; lexicon/repertoire of (pan-African) entanglement, 2, 4, 11–12, 15, 24, 29, 31–32, 72, 76, 80, 103, 113, 117, 121, 126, 162–63, 176, 213; material entanglements, 2–3, 6–7, 53–54, 163, 167; multidirectionality of, 18, 33, 40, 97, 188, 192, 201, 203; pan-African entanglements, 1, 3–6, 9–12, 14–18, 23, 28, 33–34, 35, 39, 48, 50, 55–56, 65, 71, 76, 91, 97–98, 109, 120, 126–27, 132, 138, 142–43, 146, 149–50, 155–59, 170, 175, 179, 187, 191, 199, 207–8, 213, 217–20, 223–25; planes of, 9, 100, 183, 222; proletarian entanglements, 10, 91, 98, 127–28; scales of, 9–10, 53, 91, 100, 183, 222; spaces of, 42, 44, 177; transnational entanglements, 1, 6, 8, 9–10, 14, 17, 20, 25, 109, 161, 164, 171, 180, 188–89, 198, 205–6, 210; tropes of, 6–7, 21–22, 98–99, 150, 185; vagabond entanglement, 10, 25, 41, 101–2; vernacular entanglements, 24–25, 30, 35, 40, 72, 98, 103, 116, 130, 143, 146, 150, 189, 207, 219, 236–37n1. *See also* Nuttall, Sarah
Enwonwu, Ben, 156
Equiano, Olaudah, 177
Erzulie, 106, 121, 202, 215. *See also* Vodou
Eshleman, Clayton, 131
essentialism, 2, 7, 11, 32, 48–52, 56, 58, 71, 82, 85–86, 92, 102–3, 109, 111, 113, 118, 120–23, 126, 135–37, 157, 163–64, 172, 177, 181–82, 187, 222, 240n95. *See also* strategic essentialism
Ethiopia, 84, 154–55, 171. *See also* Hoare-Laval Pact; Selassie, Haile
Etudiant noir, L', 108
Eyerman, Ron, 22, 229n13, 231n40

Fabre, Michael, 127, 242n4, 249nn1–2
Fanon, Frantz, 19, 26, 32, 120, 124–25, 127, 134–38, 150–51, 175, 187, 208, 232n52, 235nn81–82; *Black Skin, White Masks*, 124–25, 135–36; and Césaire, 32, 120, 127, 134–38, 150–51; and Hughes, 135–36, 260n167; and nationalism/national consciousness/culture, 26, 32, 120, 127, 134, 136–38, 150, 232n52, 256n90, 260n167; and Negritude, 120, 134–36, 138, 151, 256n90, 260n167; *The Wretched of the Earth*, 26, 31–32, 135–38, 150–51, 232n52, 235nn81–82, 256n94
fascism, 90, 125–26, 129, 154–55. *See also* Nazism
Fauset, Jessie, 90, 107, 242n2, 242n4, 249n2
FESMAN. *See* World Festival of Negro Arts

FESTAC'77. *See* Second World Festival of Black and African Arts
festivals, 2–3, 6–7, 32–33, 112–13, 119, 152, 156, 168, 212, 224
Feuser, W. F., 249n1
Fighting Talk, 262n22
Figueroa, Víctor, 258n122, 259n143
Fire!!, 27
First, Ruth, 262n22
Fisher, Rebecka Rutledge, 12
Fitts, Dudley, 193, 246n86, 268n30
Fort-de-France (Martinique), 123, 128, 135
Fowler, Carolyn, 69, 87–92, 96, 100, 102, 248n127
François, Anne, 251n44
French Guiana, 59, 107, 111
French Revolution, 208
Freud, Sigmund, 56
Frenkel, Ronit, 262n7
frevo (dance), 110
Frobenius, Léo, 121
fugitives, 5, 12, 61, 173, 176–79, 184–85, 197, 216. *See also* slavery
Fungaroli, Joanne, 88–89

Gadsby, Meredith, 270n27
Gandhi, Mohandas Karamchand, 60, 75, 87
Garcia, Jay, 135
García Lorca, Federico, 167
Garrett, Naomi, 86–87, 245n81
Garvey, Marcus, 16, 22, 53–54, 109, 178–80
Garveyism, 178. *See also* Back to Africa movement
Gates, Henry Louis, Jr., 193
Gauguin, Paul, 45, 47
Ghana, 22, 28, 32, 130, 156, 159, 192, 204, 222, 232n51, 235n89
Gilroy, Paul, 13, 16, 35, 43, 45, 56, 62, 206, 232n46, 235n80. *See also* Black Atlantic
Glissant, Édouard, 13, 41, 102, 190, 219, 230n35. *See also* Poetics of Relation
Gold Coast. *See* Ghana
Gordimer, Nadine, 170
Goyal, Yogita, 97
Graham, Shane, 32, 161, 228n6
Graham, Shane, and John Walters, *Langston Hughes and the South African Drum Generation*, 32, 161, 228n6, 243n33

Grantham, Awendela, 130
Gready, Paul, 181, 261n3
Great Depression, 60, 97, 191
Great Migration, 47, 74
Grenada, 211, 214, 216–19, 221
Griffith, Glyne, 67
Griots, Les, 75
Guillaume, Paul, 45
Guillén, Nicolás, 19, 65–66, 68–69, 90–91, 96–97, 151, 193, 233n75, 247n121; *Cuba Libre*, 66–67, 91, 247n121; "Elegía a Jacques Roumain," 69; and Hughes, 65–66, 151, 242n29, 254n33; "Sobre Jacques Roumain," 69
Guinea, 70, 89, 93, 99, 204–5
Gunner, Liz, 265n70
Guyana, 59, 68, 211

Haiti: and African heritage/cultural values, 31, 47, 70–71, 74–76, 79–82, 84–86, 88, 97–100, 103, 106, 120–22, 128–29, 144, 152, 177–78; and class/race divides, 27; Césaire and, 31, 73, 120–22, 125, 128, 138–41, 151–52, 177, 257n100, 260n169; as first black republic, 65, 71, 78; Hughes and, 27, 30, 33, 60–61, 65, 70–87, 117, 120, 131, 152, 177–78, 190; literary representations of or allusions to, 10, 12, 43, 60–61, 117, 129–31, 138–51, 194, 202–3, 218; literature of, 68, 74–75, 87, 97, 102, 113, 116, 120–22, 184, 254n46; as proxy for Africa, 71, 79, 120, 122, 154; and slavery, 31, 84, 97, 122; as symbol of resistance and black empowerment, 12, 31, 65, 71, 74–76, 122, 125, 131, 148; in twentieth century, 31, 60–61, 71–72, 78, 83–85, 94, 102, 151, 260n169; US occupation of, 31, 60, 65, 71–72, 75, 83, 87, 99. *See also* Hispaniola; Saint-Domingue
Haitian Communist Party, 90
Haitian Revolution: Hughes and, 31, 65, 73, 141, 244n28; literary representations of or allusions to, 31, 65, 71–86, 138, 152, 207; significance to black diaspora, 71–74; as symbol of resistance and black empowerment, 12, 31, 65, 71–72, 154–55, 257n101. *See also* Boukman, Dutty; Christophe, Henri; Dessalines, Jean-Jacques; Louverture, Toussaint
Halbwachs, Maurice, 6, 65, 229n13

Hale, Thomas, 13, 150, 227n2, 249n1, 256n97
Haley, Alex, 177
Hall, Stuart, 15–16, 172, 231n39
Hansberry, Lorraine, 209
Harlem: as Hughes's home and subject, 1, 9, 14, 20, 38, 70, 190, 198, 228n4; literary representations of, 10, 42–43, 50, 62–63, 165, 198, 205–6, 222–23; and Claude McKay, 42–43; as meeting place for black people and home to black migrants, 17, 42–43, 47, 58, 62, 165, 168, 222–23; and Negritude, 113, 116, 129, 152. *See also* New York City
Harlem Renaissance: and Africa, 16; and African literature, 18, 160, 164, 182–83, 185–87, 228n2; and black identity, 133; and Caribbean literature, 74–75, 87, 228nn2–3; and Hughes, 1, 30, 35, 41, 152, 182–83; international dimensions of, 8, 26, 38; and Claude McKay, 30, 35, 38, 41; and Negritude and francophone literature, 2, 107–10, 114, 116, 119, 122–23, 133, 152, 228nn2–3. *See also* Cullen, Countee; Hughes, Langston; McKay, Claude; Van Vechten, Carl
Harlem Renaissance Reader, The, 38
Harris, Rodney, 258n119
Harris, Wilson, 13, 68, 258n119
Hathaway, Heather, 46, 51
Hawkins, Coleman, 214
Havana (Cuba), 60, 63–65, 70
Hayden, Robert, 216
Head, Bessie, 161, 166–67, 184
Helgesson, Stefan, 262n7
Herndon, Angelo, 90
"Hesitation Blues," 207–8
Hirsch, Marianne, 229n13
Hispaniola, 129. *See also* Haiti; Saint-Domingue
Hitler, Adolf, 125–26
Hoare-Laval Pact, 155. *See also* Ethiopia
Holiday, Billie, 185
Holocaust, 20, 94, 229n13
"Homage to Langston Hughes," in *Présence africaine*, 19
Homelands, 165
Honig, Edwin, 167
Horne, Lena, 200
Horne, Louis, 200
Hughes, Langston: and Africa, 2–3, 5, 26, 32, 46–49, 53, 99, 112, 114, 153–59, 161, 165, 189, 199, 204, 209, 225, 228n7, 240n79; as anthologist, 1, 3, 19, 27, 32, 54, 66–68, 111, 113–14, 116, 119, 156–58, 166, 168–70, 204, 245–46n86, 261n18; birthdate of, 228n5; and blackness/black heritage, 14, 21, 55, 112–13, 233n75; and Caribbean, 14, 27, 30, 59–69, 83, 196, 209; and communism, 36, 63, 72, 95, 191, 212, 229n15, 247n119; and Ethiopia, 154–55; and Haiti, 27, 30, 33, 60–61, 65, 70–87, 117, 120, 131, 152, 177–78, 190; and Marcus Garvey, 52–53; and Haitian Revolution, 31, 65, 73, 141, 244n28; and Harlem, 1, 9, 14, 20, 43, 47, 62–63, 70, 113, 190, 198, 205–6; and Harlem Renaissance, 1, 35, 41, 113, 152, 228n3; and jazz and blues, 11, 20, 39–40, 55, 66–67, 89, 130, 166, 190–91, 193, 195–96, 228n9, 240n79; as cultural ambassador, 3, 18, 112, 189, 192, 211–12; influence on other writers, 1, 5, 18–19, 30–33, 36, 40, 67, 74–75, 88, 107, 110, 118–19, 158, 161, 165–68, 181, 215, 228n3, 249n1; and lumpenproletariat, 25; and nationalism/national identification, 14, 26, 45, 63–64, 204; and Negritude, 31, 36, 107–18, 151–52, 206, 228n3, 260n167; and pan-Africanism, 17; and political radicalism, 36, 60, 63, 73, 95, 111, 115, 124–25, 165, 168, 191, 204, 212, 247n117; presumption of speaking for the black masses, 37, 48, 58, 62, 82, 124, 129; and primitivism, 4, 30–33, 45–50, 58, 70–72, 74, 79, 85, 88, 97, 99, 103, 109, 113, 115, 117–18, 120, 124, 153, 159, 161, 189, 203, 239n52; as promoter and mentor of other artists, 3, 19, 26, 30, 157–58, 161, 168, 209, 211–12, 225, 264n42; and race, 14, 27, 50, 61, 111–13, 115, 157, 165, 191; relationship with Charlotte Mason Osgood, 36, 47–48, 70, 79; sexuality of, 36; and South Africa, 3–4, 27, 29, 32, 110–11, 156, 160–89, 205, 228n3, 262n42; translations of his work, 97, 107, 111, 114–15, 125, 191, 243n31, 247n123, 259n159; as translator, 2–3, 19, 27, 31, 54, 66, 68, 72, 86–89, 96–98, 101, 105, 111, 113–14, 167, 210, 218, 245–46n86, 247n121; travels of, 1–3, 8–9, 20, 24, 26–28, 30, 32–33, 41, 48–49, 51, 60, 65, 75, 81,

89, 153–54, 156–57, 168, 189–91, 198, 208, 210–11, 228n7; urban identity of, 47; use of first-person pronouns, 10, 22, 48, 62, 75–76, 116, 124, 130, 133, 195; and Vodou/Ju-ju, 27, 29, 49, 80–81, 84, 100, 103, 121, 202; and women, 81–82, 88, 104, 131–32, 159, 209–10, 225, 236n99. See also *Fire!!*; Harlem Renaissance; "Homage to Langston Hughes," in *Présence africaine*; Semple, Jesse B.

—, works of: "Afraid," 46, 124; "African Lady," 159; *An African Treasury*, 114, 158, 166, 168–70, 181, 204, 261n18; "Afro-American Fragment," 49, 79, 85; "Always the Same," 10, 61; "American Interest in African Culture," 28, 192; "An Appeal for Jacques Roumain," 72, 246n98; *Ask Your Mama*, 5, 11, 28–29, 32–33, 58, 78, 103, 188–89, 191–206, 215, 222, 225, 238n27, 268n24; "Ballad of Negro History," 55; "Ballad of the Seven Songs," 61; *The Barrier*, 176; "Beachcomber," 44–45; *Big Ghost and Little Ghost and Other Stories*, 158; *The Big Sea*, 26, 44–45, 47–49, 53, 79, 89, 153–54, 201; *Black Nativity*, 168; "Black Writers in a Troubled World," 113; "Broadcast on Ethiopia," 155; "Broadcast to the West Indies," 37, 61–63, 155; "Brothers," 59, 61; "Caribbean Sunset," 59; "Chant for Tom Mooney," 95, 154, 232–33n56; "Christ in Alabama," 247n119; "Christmas Comes but Once a Year," 232–33n56; "Claude McKay," 36; *The Collected Poems of Langston Hughes*, 105; "Congo," 114; "Cora, Unashamed," 166, 263n38; "Danse Africaine," 11, 47, 109, 246n90; *Emperor of Haiti*, 31, 65, 71–72, 78–86, 96, 100, 103, 152, 154, 214–15, 218, 245n62, 257n100, 260n169; "Fascination," 131–32; *Fine Clothes to the Jew*, 37; *The First Book of Africa*, 158; "Freedom's Plow," 21; "Good Morning," 43; "Good Morning Revolution," 154; "Here to Yonder" column, 66 (see also *Chicago Defender*); "Haunted Ship," 44; "I, Too," 1, 21, 109, 112; "In Explanation of Our Times," 263n38; "I Thought It Was Tangiers I Wanted," 154; *I Wonder as I Wander*, 20–21, 27, 32–33, 41, 44, 47, 51, 70–71, 75, 77, 81–82, 86, 102, 189–91, 203, 239n52; "Jazz from Africa via America Now Goes Back to Africa," 166; "Johannesburg Mines," 49, 154, 263n38; "Lament for Dark Peoples," 46–47, 244n48; "Let America Be America Again," 114–15; "A Letter from Haiti," 77; "Memo to Non-White Peoples," 61, 263n38; "Merry Christmas," 60; *Montage of a Dream Deferred*, 59, 238n27; "The Need for Heroes," 76, 244n28; "Negro Art and Claude McKay," 36; "The Negro Artist and the Racial Mountain," 109–10, 237n25; "The Negro Mother," 48; "The Negro Speaks of Rivers," 10, 21, 29, 48, 130, 143, 147, 149, 153, 212, 216, 246n90, 259n159; "A New Song," 24–25, 119, 124–25, 129; *Not without Laughter*, 39, 47; "Notes at Summer's End," 66; "Nude Young Dancer," 11, 114; "One More 'S' in the U.S.A.," 95, 191, 247n117; "Our Land," 153, 168; "Passing," 50; "People without Shoes," 75, 101; "Poem [1]," 46–47; *Poèmes*, 11 (*see also* Dodat, François); "A Poem for Jacques Roumain," 105–6; *Poems from Black Africa*, 114, 116, 158, 166, 168, 262n22; *Poetry of the Negro*, 38, 65–68, 111, 113–14, 119, 168, 246n86 (*see also* Bontemps, Arna); *Popo and Fifina*, 31 (*see also* Bontemps, Arna); "Prelude to Our Age," 21–24, 55, 105, 195, 217; "Questions and Answers," 62; "Scottsboro," 75–76; *Scottsboro, Limited*, 60; "Ships, Sea, and Africa," 154; "Slave on the Block," 11, 48; *Simple Speaks His Mind*, 262n16; *Simple Takes a Wife*, 262n16; "Slice Him Down!," 263n38; "Spirituals," 51–52; "The South," 114–15; "That Sad, Happy Music Called Jazz," 196; "To New York," 114, 116; "To the American Troops," 114; "To the Little Fort of San Lazaro on the Ocean Front, Havana," 63–65; "Too Much of Race," 90; *Troubled Island* (opera), 31, 67, 72, 78–79, 81, 83, 103, 257n100; "Trite without Doubt," 113–14; "The Twenties: Harlem and Its Negritude," 113, 228n3; *The Ways of White Folks*, 165; "White Shadows in a Black Land," 78; "Who's Passing for Who?," 50

Hugo, Victor, 125

humanism, 106, 126, 134–35, 137–38, 190, 255–56n77
Hurston, Zora Neale, 22, 209
Huyssen, Andreas, 141
hybridity and syncretism, 29, 55–56, 74, 82, 108, 123, 171, 203–5, 222, 230n33, 231n46, 232nn52–53, 238n38

Ifa, 202
India, 60, 82, 261–62n7
Indigenism, 24, 74–75, 88, 116, 121–22
internationalism, 13, 36, 38, 41, 44, 55, 87, 101, 228n2, 229n16, 240n97, 241n113
Irele, Abiola, 126, 215, 249n1, 252n9
Italy, 84, 154–55, 168

Jack, Belinda, 117, 137, 151
Jackson, Maurice, 73
Jackson, Richard, 228n2
Jahn, Janheinz, 152
Jaji, Tsitsi Ella, 13, 113, 116, 251n49
Jamaica, 24, 36, 38, 43, 51, 56, 61, 67, 93, 110, 162, 172–79, 236n99, 243n33
Jamaica Broadcasting Corporation, 172
James, C. L. R., 68, 73–74, 244n28
Jamestown, 22
Japan, 51, 190–91
Jay, Paul, 57, 188, 230n33, 231n46, 233n59
jazz, 11, 20, 29, 55, 58, 116, 123, 130, 151, 165–66, 191, 193, 195–96, 206, 214–15, 228n9, 240n79. *See also* blues music
Jekyll, Walter, 37, 46
jelly-roll (dance), 51
Jemie, Onwuchekwa, 240n79
Jewish diaspora, 54–55, 64, 94. *See also* diaspora
Jewish Frontier, The, 54
Jews in Egypt, 93
Jim Crow, 20, 192, 201. *See also* segregation
Joan of Arc, 75
Joans, Ted, 19
Johannesburg (South Africa), 3, 49, 62, 154, 164–65, 171, 177, 181, 262n16
Johnson, James Weldon, 23, 39, 54, 116, 123
Jonassaint, Jean, 8, 121, 254n46
Jones, Donna, 239n53, 250n17, 252n6
Jones, Doug, 8
Jones, Eldred Durosimi, 19

Jordan, A. C., 262n22, 264n42
journals, magazines, and little magazines, 2, 8, 19, 23, 27, 63, 75, 107–8, 114, 123–26, 137, 160, 164, 168, 232n51

Kaisary, Philip, 73–74, 82–83, 103, 256n77, 257n101
Kaussen, Valerie, 74–76, 99–100, 102, 248n134
Kelley, William, 211–12
Kennedy, Ellen Conroy, 74, 91, 117, 245–46n86
Kennedy, John F., 112
Kenya, 206
Kenyatta, Jomo, 136, 205, 260n167
Kernan, Ryan, 65, 111, 125, 228n2
Kesteloot, Lilyan, 108, 127, 249n1
Kim, Daniel Wong-Gu, 169, 204, 227–28n2
Kimberley (South Africa), 10, 61
King, Martin Luther, Jr., 200, 206–7
Kingston (Jamaica), 43, 98, 173, 178, 206
Knopf (publisher), 196, 199, 264n42
Knopf, Blanche, 247n121
Krakatoa, 132
Kubayanda, Josaphat Bekunuru, 253–54n33
Kunene, Daniel, 266–67n124
Kutzinski, Vera, 65, 97, 102, 228n2, 243n31

Lafayette, Marquis de, 89–90
Lagos (Nigeria), 33, 89, 156–57, 206, 224, 261n19
La Guma, Alex, 170
Laluah, Aquah, 111
Lamming, George, 68
Langston Hughes Papers. *See* Beinecke Rare Book and Manuscript Library
Largey, Michael, 71, 83
Latin America, 14, 66
Latin American literature, 74, 97, 110, 228n2, 247n121
Latino, Juan, 22
Laveau, Marie, 202–3
Lavé Tête, 216–17. *See also* Vodou
Lawrence, D. H., 45, 239n52
League of American Writers, 54
Légitime défense, 107–8
Lee, Canada, 105
Lee, Christopher, 134–35, 137, 235n34, 256n90

Legba, 80–81, 99, 202, 219. *See also* Vodou
Leiner, Jacqueline, 127, 258n129
Lenin, Vladimir, 75, 106
Lenz, Gunter, 195
Leopold II, 200
Léro, Étienne, 108, 249n7
Lescot, Elie, 90
Lespes, Anthony, 68, 243n37
Lewis, David Levering, 38, 47
Liberator, 36, 47, 53–54
Liberia, 173–74
Lincoln University, 32, 156
Lindsay, Vachel, 195, 268n30
literacy and illiteracy, 22–23, 30, 48, 85, 176
literary triangle trade, 13, 227n2
Locke, Alain, 26, 38, 41, 87, 90, 107, 165, 234–35n80, 249n2. See also *New Negro, The*
London (England), 52, 54, 168, 170, 221, 264n42
Louis, Patrice, 137
Louverture, Toussaint, 72–73, 113, 125, 139, 207
lumpenproletariat, 25–26, 98, 101, 130, 234n78, 235n82

Makhanda, 185
Makiwane, Tennyson, 166
Maimane, Arthur, 156
Mais, Roger, 67
Malan, D. F., 200
Malcolmson, Scott, 160
Mama Water, 143
Manganyi, N. C., 181, 186
Manley, Norman, 175
Maran, René, 59, 107, 242n4, 249n2
Markwei, Matei, 158
Marley, Bob, 160
Maroons, 61, 67–68, 93, 178–79
Marseille (France), 17, 41, 44, 46, 56–58, 98
Marshall, Paule, 3, 5, 11, 17, 30, 33, 131, 150, 210–25, 229n13, 236n99; *Brown Girl, Brownstones*, 211; and Hughes, 3, 30, 33, 211–13, 225, 269n3; *Praisesong for the Widow*, 3, 33, 131, 150, 212–24; "Shaping the World of My Art," 213, 225; *Soul Clap Hands and Sing*, 211; travels of, 3, 211–12; *The Triangular Road*, 33, 211–12, 224
Marson, Una, 67–68, 236n99

Martinican Progressive Party (PPM), 137
Martinique, 2, 31, 51, 122, 128, 130, 133, 137, 151, 208, 218, 228n3, 256n97. *See also* Mount Pelée
Marx, Karl, 74, 234n78
Marxism/Marxists, 10, 25, 49, 91–92, 98–99, 102–3, 109–10, 115–16, 127–28, 179
Masemola, Kgomotso, 173
Masilela, Ntongela, 261n3
Mason, Charlotte Osgood, 36, 47, 70
Matos, Luis Pales, 193
Matshikiza, Todd, 161, 166, 170, 181
Mbari Artists and Writers Club, 27. See also Conference for African Writers of English Expression
Mbembe, Achille, 12, 14, 16, 20, 24, 42, 74, 108, 224, 231nn39–40
Mbom, Clement, 140, 260n169
McBurnie, Beryl, 68
McCarthy, Joseph, 168, 191, 247n119; senate subcommittee chaired by, 63, 111, 168, 191, 212
McClintock, Anne, 76, 84
McDonald, Peter, 186–87
McGill, Lisa, 213
McGrath, Thomas, 194
McKay, Claude, 2, 4, 7, 15, 17–18, 24–25, 29–31, 35–59, 66, 75, 98–99, 101, 107–10, 116–19, 122–23, 125–27, 130, 138, 146, 151, 172, 182, 189–90, 240n95, 242n4, 249n2, 253n27; and Africa, 56, 99, 117; "Africa," 46; *Banana Bottom*, 110; *Banjo*, 17, 31, 39–42, 46, 50, 52, 55–57, 101, 107–8, 110, 119, 127, 130, 249–50n12; and Catholicism, 24, 52; and communism, 24, 36, 38, 49, 52–54, 56; "Enslaved," 46; and Marcus Garvey, 52–53; and Harlem, 17, 42–43, 50; *Harlem*, 42, 53; and Harlem Renaissance, 35, 38, 41; *Harlem Shadows*, 47; "Heritage," 46; *Home to Harlem*, 17, 37–40, 49–50, 110, 130; and Hughes, 2, 7, 15, 30, 35–38, 51, 59, 66, 189; "If We Must Die," 37; "In Bondage," 46; influence on Hughes, 18, 35–36; influence on other writers, 18, 30–32, 107, 118–19, 122–23; and Jamaica, 38, 40, 43, 56; *A Long Way from Home*, 37, 41, 43–44, 50, 52–55, 58; and lumpenproletariat, 25; and Marseille, 17, 41, 44, 46, 56–58; *My Green Hills of Jamaica*, 40, 43, 239n52; and nationalism/national identity,

McKay, Claude (*continued*)
41–42, 45, 55, 172; and Negritude, 31, 36, 107–10, 116; "A Negro Writer to His Critics," 56–57; and pan-African entanglement, 15, 151; *The Passion of Claude McKay*, 38, 49, 51, 53–54, 56–57; presumption of speaking for the black masses, 37, 58; and primitivism, 45–47, 49–50, 58, 239n52; and race, 35, 49–52, 57; *Selected Poems of*, 37; sexuality of, 36; "To the White Fiends," 117; translations of his works, 107

McLaren, Joseph, 245n62

memorialization, 69, 83, 97, 140–41, 144–45, 147–48, 152, 180

memory: ancestral, 2, 11–12, 16, 220 (*see also* Africa); collective/cultural, 6–7, 11–13, 15–16, 22, 26, 33, 51, 60, 65, 73, 80, 93–94, 103–4, 120, 143, 145, 179, 186, 188, 196, 209, 217, 221, 229n13, 231n40 (*see also* Halbwachs, Maurice); multidirectional, 72, 89, 93–95, 203–4 (*see also* Rothberg, Michael); of pan-African entanglement, 4, 6, 12, 16, 22, 26, 31, 59, 65, 84, 89, 103, 120–21, 131, 152, 157, 196, 203, 215; repression of, 94–95, 206; sites of, 64–65, 72, 78–79; traumatic, 92, 94; vernacular/peasant, 4, 144–45

meringue/meringué (dance), 110

Mexico, 91, 98

Middle Passage, 5, 16, 43, 45, 59, 64, 80, 93, 130, 179, 196, 201, 203–4, 217. *See also* slavery

Miller, Baxter, 195, 206

Mississippi River, 10, 29. *See also* rivers and streams

Modisane, Blake, vii, 3, 111, 156, 161, 166–70, 181, 262n22, 263n26, 263n35, 264n42

moon imagery, 12, 47, 80, 130, 151, 154, 202, 244n48

Moore, David Chioni, 7, 161, 167

Morocco, 10, 50

Morris, Mervyn, 239n52

Moses, 53, 75

Mount Pelée, 133, 208. *See also* volcanoes

Mphahlele, Es'kia (Ezekiel), 3, 5, 11, 17, 32, 156, 160–67, 169–70, 180–88, 209, 225, 261n5, 262n22, 264n38; and Peter Abrahams, 162–63, 180–81; "African Identity," 187; *The African Image* (1962), 164–65, 182, 187; *The African Image* (revised edition, 1974), 183–84, 187; *Afrika My Music*, 183–86, 261n5; and Césaire, 187; *Chirundu*, 185; and diaspora, 32, 162, 184–85; and Harlem Renaissance, 182–83, 185, 187; "Homage to Léopold Sédar Senghor," 183; and Hughes, 3, 11, 156, 160–62, 166–67, 169, 181–84, 186, 188, 209; "Langston Hughes," 184; and Negritude, 32, 181–88; "Negritude—a Phase," 181; "Notes Towards the Rationale for the Necessary Inclusion of Africa," 187; and race, 162; return to South Africa, 162, 184, 186, 188, 266–67n124; *Voices in the Whirlwind*, 164, 182, 187; *The Wanderers*, 164. *See also* African Humanism

Mullen, Edward, 75, 243n31

Mussolini, Benito, 154

NAACP, 54

Nakasa, Nat, 262n16

Nañigo, 202

Nanny, 67–68

Nardal sisters, 107

Nardo, 60

National Association for the Advancement of Colored People, 54

national consciousness/culture, 19, 26, 71, 82, 120, 127, 134, 136–38, 150, 169, 232nn52–53, 260n167. *See also* Fanon, Frantz

nationalism: and (anti/post)colonialism, 26, 53, 75, 82–83, 87, 90, 104, 137–38, 172, 192, 197, 204; Césaire and, 137, 150–51; and cosmopolitanism/transnationalism, 14, 16, 41, 55, 63, 170–74, 230nn28–29, 232nn52–53; ethnic, 44, 171; exclusionary or authoritarian tendencies of, 58, 150–51, 170–72; Fanon and, 26, 32, 120, 127, 134, 136–38, 150, 232n52, 256n90, 260n167; fixity of, 45; Hughes and, 14, 26, 45, 63–64, 204; McKay and, 41–42, 45, 55, 172; Roumain and, 24, 87, 90. *See also* African nationalism; black nationalism

navels, 131–33, 223

Nazism, 90, 144. *See also* fascism

Negritude, 32, 86, 88, 91–92, 159, 161–63, 181–88; as concept, philosophy, and aesthetic, 31, 91, 109–10, 113–17, 120, 123, 126–27, 129–36, 138, 140–42, 144, 146, 148–52, 182, 187, 253n30, 256n77; and Harlem Renaissance,

107–10, 113–14, 119, 122, 133, 152; as a literary movement, 2, 4, 16, 18, 30–32, 36, 107–18, 163, 177, 182–83, 206, 222. *See also* Césaire, Aimé; Damas, Léon-Gontran; *Présence africaine*; Senghor, Léopold Sédar
Negritude Poets, The, 246n86
Negro: An Anthology, 245n86
Negro Writers' Guild, 54
networks, 1–3, 6–8, 13–15, 23, 29, 42, 68, 102, 161, 163, 168, 173–76, 180, 185–86, 189–92, 206–9, 224–25
New Masses, 63, 75, 77, 101
New Negro, The, 38, 160, 165–66, 234–35n80. *See also* Locke, Alain
New Negro movement. *See* Harlem Renaissance
New Orleans, 129, 190, 202
New York City: and Harlem Renaissance, 1, 8; as Hughes's home, 67, 190; literary representations of, 62–63, 98, 117, 204; as meeting place for black people, 3, 42, 66, 68, 87, 90, 111, 168, 211–12, 218, 243n33; and publishing, 170, 264n42. *See also* Brooklyn; Harlem
Newport Jazz Festival, 193
Nicol, Davidson, 158
Nicol, Mike, 261n3
Nigeria, 27, 32, 33, 156, 159, 206, 228n7, 261n16, 264n38
Nile River, 10, 29, 147. *See also* rivers and streams
Niles, Blair, 77
Niles, John Jacob, 41
Nixon, Rob, 161, 261n3
Nkosi, Lewis, 156, 183, 193
Nkrumah, Kwame, 32, 156, 163, 192, 204–5, 227n1, 232n51
Nora, Pierre, 64–65, 67, 78–79
Ntantala, Phyllis, 161, 166, 262n22, 264n42
Nuttall, Sarah, 6
Nwankwo, Ifeoma, 231n40, 232n53
Nxumalo, Henry, 161

Obeah, 81, 144, 202
Obee, Ruth, 184
OBIWU, 261n13
Oboe, Annalisa, and Anna Schacchi, 231n46
oceans. *See* seas, oceans, and sea imagery
Ogun, 121, 202. *See also* Vodou
Ojo-Ade, Femi, 260n169

Okara, Gabriel, 156, 158
Okigbo, Christopher, 156
Opportunity, 23
Ormsby, Stephanie, 68
Oya, 215

Padmore, George, 227n1
Page, Patti, 200
Palumbo-Liu, David, 233n59
Pan-African Congress, 25–26, 234n79
Pan-Africanism, 1, 3, 24–26, 39, 54, 73, 81, 107, 137, 151, 162–63, 184, 187, 227n1, 234n79. *See also* Du Bois, W. E. B.
Pankhurst, Sylvia, 52. *See also* *Workers' Dreadnought*
Papiamento, 202
Paris (France), 1, 2, 8, 18, 27, 36, 59, 66, 68, 89–90, 92, 98, 107–8, 111, 168, 196, 198, 242n4, 253n27, 256n97
Parkes, Francis Ernest, 158
Parry, Benita, 126, 135, 137
Parti progressiste martiniquais. *See* Martinican Progressive Party
patois, 38, 40, 66–67, 217–18. *See also* creoles; vernacular languages and cultures
Paton, Alan, 170
Patterson, Anita, 97, 246n90
peasantry and peasant cultures: as global community, 36–37, 40, 91–92, 96–98, 116, 190; as inspiration and material for black art, 24–26, 30, 40, 70–75, 100–101, 105, 122; as keepers of African cultural traditions and values, 4, 85–86, 99, 117, 127–31, 143–47, 154, 178, 203, 213; revolutionary potential of, 26, 33, 82, 86, 91–92, 96, 150–51, 235n81
Pedroso, Regino, 66, 68, 96
Pettis, Joyce Owens, 213, 219, 222, 269n1
PEN Club International (Jamaica), 67
PEN Club International (United States), 112, 251n31
Pétion, Alexandre, 139, 143, 144
Phylon, 23
Picasso, Pablo, 45
Piquion, René, 125, 259n159
Pochmara, Anna, 234–35n80
Pocomania, 202
Poèmes, 111
Poems from Black Africa, 114, 116, 158, 166, 168, 262n22

Poetics of Relation, 13, 41, 190, 219, 230n35. *See also* Glissant, Édouard
Poetry League of Jamaica, 67
Poetry of the Negro, The, 38, 65–68, 111, 113–14, 119, 168, 246n86. *See also* Bontemps, Arna
Pool, Rosey, 264n42
Port-au-Prince (Haiti), 2, 83, 98
Pratt, Mary Louise, 229n25
Présence africaine, 19, 27, 114–15, 135, 137, 183, 232n51, 257n100. *See also* Negritude
Pretoria (South Africa), 186
Price, Leontyne, 196, 199
Price-Mars, Jean, 74–75, 98, 110. *See also* Indigenism
primitivism, 11, 30–33, 45–50, 58, 70–72, 74, 79, 85, 88, 97, 99, 103, 115, 120–21, 123–24, 126–27, 153, 159, 203, 238–39nn51–53, 246n90, 253n33; modern primitivism, 4, 45–48, 118, 176–77. *See also* Guillaume, Paul; Lawrence, D. H.
proletarian art, culture, and aesthetics, 10, 24, 38–41, 87, 91, 97–98, 100–102, 109, 122, 128, 151, 154, 164
Public Opinion, 172
publishers, 2, 7, 19, 27, 164, 170
Puerto Rico, 43

Queen Nanny. *See* Nanny
Quinn, Brian, 250n30

Rabaka, Reiland, 110, 119, 249n1
race, 14, 20, 35, 49–52, 61, 91–92, 103–4, 109, 113, 120, 126–27, 157, 171, 182, 239n53; and blackness, 14, 49–50, 113, 120, 148–49; and communism/Marxism, 49–50, 91–92; and racial mixture/coloured people/mulattoes, 85, 148–49, 171; and racialism, 20, 31, 61, 182; scientific understanding of, 49–50, 52, 99, 126–27, 157
Racine, Jean-Baptiste, 125
radio, 2, 8, 63, 155, 162, 164, 172, 175–76, 264n42, 265n70
Radio Jamaica, 172, 175
Rainey, Ma, 214
Ramazani, Jahan, 230n33, 230n35
Rampersad, Arnold, 36–37, 42, 67–68, 90, 112, 151, 156, 192–95, 244n28, 268n30
Rastafarians, 178
Rastogi, Pallavi, 262n7

Redding, J. Saunders, 193–94
Reid, Junior, 180
Reid, Victor, 67
Relève, La, 75
Rèmy, Tristan, 87, 260
repertoire, 4, 15, 23, 71–72, 78–80, 86, 152, 216, 223, 225. *See also* Taylor, Diana
Research in African Literatures, 161
Revue du monde noir, La, 107–8, 119, 253n27
Revue indigene, 74
Reygnault, Christiane, 114
rhizomes, 2, 190, 206. *See also* Deleuze, Gilles; roots
Rimbaud, Arthur, 126
Rive, Richard, 3, 32, 111, 160–62, 165–71, 182–83, 205, 209, 261n5, 262n16; *African Songs,* 168; and Hughes, vii, 3, 32, 111, 160–62, 165–71, 205, 209, 262n16, 262n22, 264n42; influence of Hughes' work, 32, 165–66, 168; and Negritude, 182–83; and race, 182; *Senghor and Negritude,* 182; "Taos in Harlem," 261n5; *Writing Black,* 166, 168, 261n5
rivers and streams, 10, 12, 28–29, 88, 101–2, 114, 116, 130–31, 143–44, 146–49, 152–53, 197, 203, 212, 220
Robbins, Bruce, 35, 56, 230n28
Roberts, Walter Adolphe, 68
Robeson, Paul, 185
Robinson, Jackie, 61
Robolin, Stéphane, 4, 62, 228–29n10, 236n91
romance, 86, 97, 104–5
Romans, 20, 189–90
roots, 16, 27, 31, 42, 46, 50–52, 108, 157, 162, 172, 175, 178, 189–90, 204, 212–13, 216, 225, 238n38, 250n12. *See also* rhizomes
Roots (Haley), 177
Rosello, Mireille, 126, 133, 258–59n138
Rothberg, Michael, 72, 94
Roumain, Jacques, 2, 4, 11–12, 17–18, 24–25, 30, 44, 65, 68–69, 72, 74–75, 80, 83, 86–106, 110, 116–18, 120–22, 130, 138, 143, 146–48, 182, 190, 194, 225, 235n81, 248n127; and Africa, 11, 88, 99; *Afro-American Poems,* 87; *Le Champ de potier,* 98; and communism, 24, 75, 87, 90–92, 99, 102, 106; "Créole," 87; "Ebony Wood," 91–93;

Index 305

Ebony Wood, 80, 91–98; *Les Fantoches,* 98; "Filthy Negroes," 91, 94, 96; *Gouverneurs de la rosée (Masters of the Dew),* 31, 72, 86, 88, 91, 97–105, 147–48, 194, 218, 235n81, 247n121; "Guinea," 87–88, 246n86; and Harlem Renaissance, 74–75, 87; *L'homme de couleur,* 92; and Hughes, 2, 18, 30, 44, 65, 72, 75, 83, 86–90, 96–97, 101–2, 105–6, 110, 189, 246n98; imprisonment by Haitian authorities, 2, 72, 83, 87, 90, 246n98; and Indigenism, 24, 74–75, 88, 121; "Langston Hughes," 87–89, 102; and lumpenproletariat, 25; *La Montagne ensorcelée,* 98; and nationalism, 24, 87, 90; and Negritude, 18, 30, 86, 88, 92, 116–18; "New Negro Sermon," 95, 101; *On Superstitions,* 100; and peasantry, 30, 98–101, 146; and primitivism, 4; and race, 4, 91–92, 102–4; *Le Sacrifice du tambour-assoto(r),* 246n93; translations of his works by Hughes, 31, 72, 86–88; as translator, 87, 90–91, 97; and Vodou, 88–89, 99–100, 121; "When the Tom-Tom Beats," 87–88, 143, 245–46n86; *When the Tom-Tom Beats,* 88
Roumain, Nicole, 86, 98, 248n128
Roumer, Emile, 68
Roundtree, Martha, 200
rumba (dance), 27
Russia, 38, 52, 60, 190. *See also* Soviet Union
Rutherfoord, Peggy, 169

Saint-Domingue, 73, 100, 139. *See also* Haiti; Hispaniola
Saint-Pierre (Martinique), 133
Salkey, Andrew, 19, 68, 243n33
samba (dance), 110
Sampson, Anthony, 165, 261n3
Samuelson, Meg, 262n7
Sanders, Mark, 182, 233n57
Sandburg, Carl, 1, 38
Santería, 202
Sartre, Jean-Paul, 126
Sauer, Ronald, 88–89
Saul, Scott, 193, 194, 207, 268n24
Saunders, Frances Stonor, 27, 235n89
scale enlargement, 15, 30–31, 59, 107. *See also* Dimock, Wai Chee
Scanlon, Larry, 205
scars, 12, 83–84

Schomburg Collection/Schomburg Center for Research in Black Culture, 21–23, 246n93
Schuyler, George, 237n25
Scottsboro Nine, 60, 242n7
seas, oceans, and sea imagery, 43–45, 56, 59, 88–89, 92, 116, 129, 131, 147–48, 201, 217
Second International Writers Congress, 90
Second World Festival of Black and African Arts (FESTAC'77), 33, 224. *See also* World Festival of Negro Arts
Segal, Ronald, 168, 262n22, 263n38
segregation, 32, 163, 165, 193, 200–201, 207, 210, 212. *See also* apartheid; Jim Crow
Selassie, Haile, 84, 155. *See also* Ethiopia
Semple, Jesse B., 39, 67, 114, 165–66, 229n15, 238n27, 262n16, 263n38; *Simple Speaks His Mind,* 262n16; *Simple Takes a Wife,* 262n16
Senegal, 2, 17, 31, 51, 56, 107, 112, 156, 183, 228n3
Senghor, Léopold Sédar, 2, 11, 31–32, 48, 107–20, 132, 136, 151, 156, 158–59, 182–83, 187, 206, 225, 228n3, 250n12, 250n17, 256n77; and Africa, 115, 117; "The African Road to Socialism," 115–16; "Black Woman," 115, 132; and black women, 115, 159; and communism, 109, 116; "Congo," 114; and Harlem Renaissance, 109, 110, 114, 228n3; and Hughes, viii, 2, 11, 31–32, 107–17, 151, 156–58, 228n3; and Negritude, 2, 108–9, 115, 117, 119, 136, 159, 187, 206, 225, 228, 256n77, 260n167; "Night in Sine," 115; and primitivism, 31, 48; and pan-Africanism, 11, 109, 116; and race, 109, 115, 117; *Shadow Songs,* 115; "To the African Troops," 114; "To the Music of Koras and Balaphon," 115; "To New York," 114, 116–17. *See also Anthologie Africaine et Malgache;* Negritude
separation, ethos of, 20, 102, 160, 171, 179
Seyhan, Azade, 15–16
Seymour, A. J., 68
Shakespeare, William, 142–43, 258n119
Shango, 121, 202, 258n119. *See also* Vodou
Sharpeville Massacre, 159
Shelley, Percy Bysshe, 147

Shepperson, George, 227n1
Shields, John, 239n71
ships, 43–45, 48–49, 80, 86, 131, 148, 153, 171, 183, 196, 214, 217, 221, 224
Shohat, Ella, 146
Shuttlesworth-Davidson, Carolyn, 249n1
Sierra Leone, 10
Simone, Nina, 185
Simple. *See* Semple, Jesse B.
Simpson, Louis, 68
slavery: as a foundation of black identity, 22, 61, 99, 124, 138, 148, 203, 216, 231n40; legacy, heritage, and ancestry of, 15–16, 64, 71–72, 84, 93–94, 97, 130–31, 178–80, 196, 199; revolts and resistance, 12–13, 31, 72, 76–77, 80, 83–84, 93, 97, 99, 102, 131, 140, 144, 176, 203, 220–21; tropes drawn from, 4–5, 12, 22, 32, 43, 162–63, 176–77, 184–85, 203–5, 215, 221, 255n49. *See also* fugitives; Haitian Revolution; Middle Passage; Turner, Nat; Underground Railroad
Smethurst, James, 247n117
Smith, Matthew J., 75, 83
Sophiatown (South Africa), 164, 173
Sophiatown Renaissance, 164, 261n3
South Africa, 3–4, 6, 24, 27, 29, 32, 62, 96, 110–11, 152, 156, 158–59, 160–72, 175–78, 180–87, 189, 193, 200, 205–6, 222, 228n3, 228–29n10, 236n91, 261n3, 261–62n7, 262n16, 262n22, 264n42, 266n124. *See also* apartheid; Cape Town; Johannesburg; Kimberley; Pretoria; Sophiatown; Soweto
South African literature, 110, 152, 159–70, 176–78, 181–82, 184, 189, 205, 222, 261n7
Soviet Union, 10, 18, 36, 52, 60, 63, 95, 106, 129, 190–91, 204
Soweto (South Africa), 173, 185–86
Soyinka, Wole, 152, 156, 158
Spain, 33, 51, 66, 129, 190
Spanish Civil War, 33, 51, 60, 90, 129, 190, 205, 227n2
Spanish Town (Jamaica), 40
Spingarn, Amy, 246n93
Spivak, Gayatri Chakravorty, 52, 120, 240n95. *See also* strategic essentialism
Spoleto Festival of Two Worlds, 168
standing up (literary trope), 122, 129–31, 140–41, 254n46

Stanton, Charles, 89
Stephens, Michelle, 241n113
Still, William Grant, 67, 103
Stowe, Harriet Beecher, 205
St. Peter's Secondary School, 181
strategic essentialism, 52, 118, 120, 163, 240n95. *See also* Spivak, Gayatri Chakravorty
surrealism, 74, 119, 121, 252n9
Sutherland, Efua Theodora, 158

Tarikh al-Soudan. *See* al-Sadi, Abd
Taylor, Diana, 23, 71, 78–79, 216. *See also* archive; repertoire
Taylor, Yuval, 209
Tchicaya U Tam'si, 158
telegraphy, 2, 7–9
telephones, 2, 8
Telemaque, Harold, 68
television, 2, 8, 68, 164
Themba, Can, 161, 166, 169
Thoby-Marcelin, Philippe, 121
Thomas, Dylan, 200
Thornton, Allen, 193
Thurman, Wallace, 27
Titlestad, Michael, 261n3
tom-toms, 11–12, 47–48, 88, 91, 96, 109, 115–17, 123, 143, 154, 161, 171, 178, 182. *See also* drums
Toomer, Jean, 107, 123
Torgovnick, Marianna, 238–39n51
Touré, Sekou, 204–5
tragedy, 31, 80, 85–86
trains and railroads, 93, 197, 201
Transcription Centre, 27, 235n89, 264n42
translation, 2–3, 7, 19, 27, 66, 68, 72, 86–91, 96–98, 101, 105, 107, 111, 113–14, 125, 167, 191, 218, 228n2
transnationalism in literary/cultural studies, 1, 13, 15, 31, 38, 227n2, 230n33
Trinidad and Tobago, 68, 110, 221, 244n28
Tripoli, 10
Tropiques, 123–26, 129, 133, 253n27. *See also* Césaire, Aimé; Césaire, Suzanne
Truth, Sojourner, 22, 61, 209
Tubman, Harriet, 22, 61, 197
Tucker, Sophie, 185
Turner, Nat, 12, 75–76, 93
Tutuola, Amos, 158

Uganda, 113, 152, 156, 158, 173, 175, 230n29

umbilical cords, 131–32
Underground Railroad, 12, 197
UNESCO, 158
Union of Soviet Socialist Republics. *See* Soviet Union
United Asia, 37
universalism, 24, 35, 45–46, 58, 72, 91, 94, 97, 100, 109, 126, 134–35, 138, 171, 180–81, 186, 190, 256n77, 257n101
Universal Negro Improvement Association (UNIA), 53. *See also* Garvey, Marcus
University College of the West Indies, 67
urbanization and urbanism, 4, 10, 30, 36, 39, 45–47, 70, 74, 98, 105, 124, 153, 161, 164–65, 169, 172, 177–78, 182–86

vagabondage, 10, 25, 30, 39, 41, 44, 101–2, 229n16
Vandercook, John W., 77
Van Vechten, Carl, 39
Vassa, Gustavus. *See* Equiano, Olaudah
Vaughan, H. A., 68
Vaval, Duracine, 68
vernacular languages and cultures, 12, 24–26, 38–40, 43, 46, 67, 75, 79, 98, 101, 112–13, 116, 122, 127–30, 143, 151, 176, 194, 205, 207, 218–19, 236–37n1, 254–55n49
Véron, Kora, 150, 256n97
Vichy government of France, 125
Viljoen, Shaun, 261n5
Vincent, Sténio, 83, 90, 260n169. *See also* Haiti
Vinson, Robert, 261n3
Virtue, Vivian, 68
Vodou, 27, 29, 60, 75, 80–82, 84, 88, 99–100, 103, 106, 121–22, 142, 146, 150, 202, 216, 219. *See also* Dambala; Erzulie; Lavé Tête; Legba; Obeah; Ogun; Shango; Wedo; Yemoja
volcanoes, 132–33, 149, 208, 217, 255n63. *See also* Mount Pelée

Walcott, Derek, 68
Walker, Alice, 209
Walrond, Eric, 59, 242n2
Walters, John, 32, 161
Washington, Booker T., 61
Washington, Dinah, 185
Washington, Johnny, 234n80
weaving (trope), 21, 23, 105, 150, 195–96, 213, 223
Wedo, 202. *See also* Vodou
West Indian Economist, 172
West Indies. *See* Caribbean
Weston, Randy, 159
White, Walter, 50, 110, 242n4, 249n2
White House, 112
Whitman, Walt, 1, 38, 124
Williams, Eric, 68
Workers' Dreadnought, 52–54. *See also* Pankhurst, Sylvia
World Festival of Negro Arts (FESMAN), 112–13, 156, 250n30. *See also* Second World Festival of Black and African Arts; Senghor, Léopold Sédar
World War II, 61
Wright, Richard, 18, 90, 136, 166, 183, 198, 232n51, 235n84, 260n167

Yemoja, 215
Yoruba, 106, 202, 215, 258n119
Young, Lester, 214

Zola, Émile, 125

RECENT BOOKS IN THE SERIES
New World Studies

Cultural Entanglements: Langston Hughes and the Rise of African and Caribbean Literature
Shane Graham

Water Graves: The Art of the Unritual in the Greater Caribbean
Valérie Loichot

The Sacred Act of Reading: Spirituality, Performance, and Power in Afro-Diasporic Literature
Anne Margaret Castro

Caribbean Jewish Crossings: Literary History and Creative Practice
Sarah Phillips Casteel and Heidi Kaufman, editors

Mapping Hispaniola: Third Space in Dominican and Haitian Literature
Megan Jeanette Myers

Mourning El Dorado: Literature and Extractivism in the Contemporary American Tropics
Charlotte Rogers

Edwidge Danticat: The Haitian Diasporic Imaginary
Nadège T. Clitandre

Idle Talk, Deadly Talk: The Uses of Gossip in Caribbean Literature
Ana Rodríguez Navas

Crossing the Line: Early Creole Novels and Anglophone Caribbean Culture in the Age of Emancipation
Candace Ward

Staging Creolization: Women's Theater and Performance from the French Caribbean
Emily Sahakian

American Imperialism's Undead: The Occupation of Haiti and the Rise of Caribbean Anticolonialism
Raphael Dalleo

A Cultural History of Underdevelopment: Latin America in the U.S. Imagination
John Patrick Leary

www.ingramcontent.com/pod-product-compliance
Lightning Source LLC
Chambersburg PA
CBHW020110010526
44115CB00008B/768